*The Time
of Our
Lives*

The Time of Our Lives

THE ETHICS OF COMMON SENSE

by

MORTIMER J. ADLER

Introduction by

DEAL W. HUDSON

Fordham University Press
New York
1996

Copyright © 1970 by Mortimer J. Adler
Introduction Copyright © 1996 by FORDHAM UNIVERSITY PRESS
All rights reserved.
Reprinted by arrangement with Henry Holt & Company, Inc.
Fordham University Press edition 1996
LC 96–1629
ISBN 0-8232-1669-1 (*clothbound*)
ISBN 0-8232-1670-5 (*paperback*)

Library of Congress Cataloging-in-Publication Data

Adler, Mortimer Jerome, 1902–
    The time of our lives : the ethics of common sense / by Mortimer
J. Adler
        p.   cm.
    Originally published: New York : Holt, Rinehart and Winston, 1970.
    Includes bibliographical references and index.
    ISBN 0-8232-1669-1 (hard cover).—ISBN 0-8232-1670-5 (pbk.)
    1. Ethics.   2. Common sense.   I. Title.
BJ1012.A3   1996
171'.2—dc20   96-1629
                                                                   CIP

Printed in the United States of America

TO MY SONS

DOUGLAS AND PHILIP

FOR THE TIME OF THEIR LIVES

Contents

Part One

The Common-Sense Approach to the Problem of Making a Good Life for One's Self

Part Two

Defending Common Sense Against the Objections of the Philosophers

Part Three

The Ethics of Common Sense

Part Four

The Present Situation in Which We Find Ourselves

Introduction to the 1996 Edition

THIS book, first published in 1970 but based on lectures from the late '60s, seems like nothing else produced in that chaotic era of American culture. Its author, Mortimer J. Adler, would be not surprised by that observation, but would, in fact, be pleased. The student protests of that generation, the cultural upheaval, the cynicism bred by an unpopular war remain only at the fringes of Adler's reflections. Adler's time frame is far too long to tailor his thinking to the preoccupations of a single generation.

Adler's own preoccupations, it might be said, are transhistorical; he is engrossed by human nature, its genuine needs, and the moral governance of our professed wants. He undoubtedly recognizes the political progress represented by democratic society but measures that progress in terms of human nature as understood over two thousand years ago. For Adler, moral and political freedom are not mere conventions or products of a communitarian consensus; they are the real product of the immaterial intellect belonging only to human beings. Adler's remarkable defense of human nature as differing in kind from other animals is found in *The Difference of Man and the Difference It Makes* (New York: Fordham University Press, 1993).

Adler's reliance on the great books and ideas of the Western tradition in *The Time of Our Lives* was not exactly in vogue with the radicals of the '60s. Matters have hardly improved. The radical that Adler described then, a "self-alienated refugee from reason" (pp. 230–31), has reached maturity a full-grown postmodernist who views human reasoning as nothing more than the expression of political power and class interest. Adler's confidence in the human intellect has withstood all the scientific and philosophical challenges of this century. Darwinianism, Freudianism, positivism, pragmatism, existentialism, phenomenology, deconstruction—all had their heyday and all heralded the end of Aristotelian rationality and human nature. There is no doubt that with each successive wave of determinism a residue of skepticism was left behind. The number of college students who once arrived for the freshman philosophy classes with an implicit trust in their capacity to know has markedly decreased. Students who once came to college as instinctual Aristotelians are now instinctual Nietzscheans. Unfortunately, many professors have neither recognized nor adjusted to that change. Adler's common-sense approach is precisely the antidote that is needed to challenge the nascent postmodernism of the present generation of college students. That Adler continued to build his moral philosophy upon the ideas of Plato, Aristotle, Aquinas, Locke, and Jefferson enables us to profit so greatly from it now and accounts for the ongoing interest in one of the foremost American philosophers of this century.[1]

Perhaps the best way to gauge the enduring value of this book is to begin by reading Part Four, "The Present Situation in Which We Find Ourselves." Adler's analysis of justice and happiness in American society and his prognosis for the future have lost nothing of their relevancy and insight. We need especially to heed his note of caution about the fallibility of human nature in relation to political goals. Public discussions of injustice veer toward utopianism precisely because this point is lost. As Adler wisely points out, political complaints that ignore the "folly and vice" of humanity altogether lose the realism necessary to persuasive argument. For example, when it is said that government should be offering certain benefits to its citizens, it should be kept in mind that human fallibility enables citizens to reject that help.

Political inquiry and analysis, therefore, must focus on the moral character of a society, with the receptivity of the citizenry, for example, to pursue a good life, not just a pleasant one. Such moral weaknesses cannot be completely eliminated, but they can be contravened by the acquisition of virtues and the building of character, a process which takes an entire lifetime—thus the title: *The Time of Our Lives*.

Since Adler's book is about virtue and character, it is appropriate that *The Time of Our Lives* is being made available once again at a moment when virtue has re-entered public discourse about morality and politics. Adler's book is a necessary supplement to all the stories of virtues now being consumed by the general public. Stories about virtue do not necessarily agree; nor do they necessarily measure by the same standard of a happy life. One person can tell a story about courage that contradicts someone else's story about the same virtue. Can one person be right and the other wrong? Are the virtues, as good moral dispositions, determined and measured by an external standard? Adler thinks so, and that standard is our shared human nature and the happiness, or *totum bonum*, proper to that nature.[2]

Adler shows the crucial importance of grounding any understanding of the virtues in a knowledge of what is good for human beings, all human beings, regardless of their ethnicity, gender, or cultural background. His case is made amid a careful, meticulous reflection on what everyone can agree about regarding human nature. Adler's list of basic human activities in relation to basic human goods may seem arid and ordinary, but his method, dating back to Aristotle, holds the key for breaking out of the relativist frame of mind holding our culture captive.

Mortimer J. Adler offers here a way of thinking about the good life built on something that exists within the heart and mind of everyone who reads this book—their humanity. For the past fifty years or more, generation after generation of students has been taught that morality was merely a set of conventions and rules that change from epoch to epoch and from culture to culture. Through all these years, Adler has consistently spoken with a different voice; he has accomplished the task he himself describes as formidable:

> It is extremely difficult for the individual to seek for himself the things that are not honored or valued in a society, or completely to turn his back on the things that are honored there, though wrongly so [p. 210].

Readers of this book will find themselves considering an adversarial position in relation to the culture of ideas in which they live. One hopes they will have the fortitude of its author to swim against the currents of the day, and, thus, profit from his good sense.

Deal W. Hudson

NOTES

1. For a comprehensive account of Mortimer J. Adler's distinctive contribution to philosophy and education, see my Introduction to Adler's *The Difference of Man and the Difference It Makes* (New York: Fordham University Press, 1993), pp. xi–xxxii.

2. Readers interested in a survey of Adler's vast legacy should consult the papers by Charles Van Doren, John Van Doren, Sidney Hyman, Jeffrey D. Wallin, Deal W. Hudson, Russell Hittinger, Otto Bird, and Anthony Quinton published in *The Aspen Quarterly* (Winter, 1995) 7:1.

Preface

THIS book has been developed from the third series of Encyclopaedia Britannica Lectures delivered at the University of Chicago in the Spring of 1969. *The Conditions of Philosophy*, based on the first series of Encyclopaedia Britannica Lectures, projected certain measures to be taken for the revival of traditional philosophical inquiry in the twentieth century. It called, among other things, for the demonstration of the philosopher's ability to handle a difficult mixed question, requiring the assessment of scientific evidence and theory as well as the application of philosophical analysis and reasoning. That task was discharged in *The Difference of Man and the Difference It Makes*, based on the second series of Encyclopaedia Britannica Lectures. The present book is offered as another demonstration of the vitality of traditional philosophical thought—in this case, its ability to answer the basic normative questions, *What ought a man seek in life?* and *How ought he to seek it?*

The distinctive method of philosophical inquiry, as defined in *The Conditions of Philosophy*, involves reliance on the common experience of mankind, and an appeal to it as the test of the validity of philosophical theories, either about what is and happens in the world or about what men ought to seek and do. It also involves an assessment of the validity of common-sense answers to the kind of questions for answering which common experience by itself is adequate, no additional empirical evidence or investigation being needed.

Philosophy thus conceived is a development of the insights already possessed by the man of common sense in the light of common experience; it is a development that adds clarifying analytical distinctions, the precise definition of terms, the reinforcement of systematic reasoning, and the critical exploration of problems to which no satisfactory solution is yet available. The philosophical knowledge achieved by these additions confirms, even as it elaborates, the common-sense wisdom one need not be a philosopher to possess. That is why I have called the moral philosophy expounded in this book "the ethics of common sense."

I have been at work for many years on the questions with which this book is concerned. Many of the conceptions and formulations presented here were broached in a somewhat different form in an earlier book, *A Dialectic of Morals*, published in 1941. That book was a distillation of arguments that I had had with students in courses devoted to the reading of the great works in ethics and politics. It was a response to the challenge of students who questioned the possibility of finding sound and satisfactory answers to questions about the good life and the good society. I should also mention another earlier work, *The Theory of Democracy*, published during the 1940s in an extended series of periodical articles, but not yet in book form. Two articles in that series, one concerned with happiness or the good life, the pursuit of which is man's basic natural right, and the other concerned with the relation to it of the welfare of the political community and the role that the state plays in aiding and abetting the pursuit of happiness, contained analyses and theories that, upon re-examination, have proved useful in the present undertaking.

As in the earlier works mentioned, so, too, in *The Time of Our Lives*, ethics and politics are treated as related branches of moral philosophy; but the present book deals with the shape of the good society only to the extent that it bears on the external conditions required for the pursuit of happiness to give every individual the opportunity he should have to make a really good life for himself. It does not address itself primarily or directly to questions about the nature of the state, the necessity of government, the realization through political means of the fullest possible measures of liberty, equality, and peace, and the progressive development of the constitution that makes democracy the only perfectly just form of government. I plan to devote the next series of Encyclopaedia Britannica Lectures to these basic questions of political philosophy, which I hope subsequently to publish as a book under the title *The Common Sense of Politics*.

The preparation of lectures for delivery to an audience that includes laymen as well as faculty and students, together with the highly instructive experience of answering questions from the floor on the occasion of the lectures, is in my judgment the ideal way to discover the level and style of exposition to be employed in writing a book for the general reader who has active intellectual concerns about the problems that any thinking man must consider. I am, therefore, grateful to the University of Chicago for the auspices it has provided, and to Encyclopaedia Britannica, Inc., for its initiation and support of this lectureship at the University.

Like the two earlier books that were developed from Encyclopaedia Britannica Lectures at the University of Chicago, *The Time of Our Lives* also owes much to the intellectual collaboration afforded by the Institute for Philosophical Research, of which I am Director. It has profited greatly from the critical examination and discussion to which its formulations and arguments have been subjected by my colleagues at the Institute. I am particularly grateful to four of my associates—Charles Van Doren, Otto Bird, George Ducas, and Arthur L. H. Rubin—for the time and effort they put into their reading of the manuscript at successive stages of its development, and for the excellent suggestions they have made for its emendation and improvement. I also wish to thank other members of the Institute staff for bibliographical research, the preparation of the index, and the typing and editing of the manuscript.

Mortimer J. Adler

Chicago
October, 1969

Part One

The Common-Sense Approach to the Problem of Making a Good Life for One's Self

CHAPTER I

Introduction

(1)

THE phrase that serves as the title for this book involves a triple play on words. *First of all,* the phrase refers to the span of time allotted to each of us—the time we use up or consume as we live from day to day, month to month, and year to year. *Second,* there is that colloquial meaning of the phrase we are all familiar with: when we return from a trip, geographical or psychedelic, we often say that we have had the time of our lives —a good time, full of fun, excitement, or pleasure. And *third,* the time of our lives is the century in which we are now alive—our time in history, the twentieth century.

Far from being accidental, this triple play on words quickly focuses attention on two of the main questions this book will consider and attempt to answer.

One is the question of whether a good life consists in having a good time. Is there more to leading a good life than having a good time from day to day? Is there ever a conflict between having a good time and leading a good life, so that we are compelled to choose between them? I hope I will be able to show you that while leading a good life certainly does not exclude having a good time, it often does require us to subordinate the merely pleasant use of our time to other uses of it—to forms of activity no one would describe in terms of having a good time, not at least in the colloquial sense of that phrase.

The other question asks whether this is a good time to be

3

alive. Is it better to be alive in this century than at any earlier period of human life on earth? In addition to asking, *Is this a good time to be alive?*, one can also ask, *Is ours a good society to be alive in?* Is it as good as, if not better than, any other society in the world today? When I respond to these questions in the concluding chapters of this book, I hope I will be able to convince my readers that, while this century is far from perfect, while detrimental influences and even threats of disaster accompany the advantages that have accumulated, nevertheless the time of our lives—this century—is better than any earlier century in human history, and that our society, with all its imperfections, is as good as, if not better than, any other society in the world today.

(2)

These questions call for two brief philosophical comments. Some philosophers, among them the leading philosophers of antiquity, have used the terms *happiness* and *a good life* interchangeably; and when they have done so, they have also distinguished between achieving happiness—or a good life as a whole—and experiencing pleasure, joy, delight, or even contentment from moment to moment, which constitutes having a good time. Hence we see that the possible conflict between a good life and a good time is a possible conflict between happiness and pleasure. To understand how this conflict may arise, it is, of course, necessary to use the word "happiness" as a synonym for "a good life as a whole," and never as a synonym for "pleasure"—a pleasant or pleasing experience.

The words "happy" and "happiness" are generally used by all of us as synonyms for "pleased" or "pleasure." We say that we feel happy at one moment, and not happy at another; we wish our friends happy birthdays or happy new years; we refer to periods or even occasions in our lives when we have experienced the contentment of satisfied desires as times of great happiness, and contrast them with the unhappiness we have felt at times of discontent or frustration; we answer invitations by saying we are happy to accept; we respond to demands made upon us by saying we would be happy to do this or not happy to do that. In all these familiar usages, the words "happy" and "happiness" have a psychological connotation, referring to a relatively short-lived experience, or even to a momentary feeling. In contrast, when we ordinarily speak of a good life as a whole, the connotation is moral rather than psychological, and what is referred to is certainly not a momentary feeling or a short-lived experience. Whatever we may mean by a good life as a whole, we know it involves the whole span of our life's time.

In order to prevent the confusions that might result from the psychological connotations of the words "happy" and "happiness" as used in everyday speech, I am going to forego the use of these words—at least in the early chapters of this book. Later on, I hope it will be possible for me to use *happiness* and *a good life* interchangeably (as terms having exactly the same moral connotation) without any danger of being misunderstood.

Among the philosophers who identify happiness with a good life as a whole, a few also relate the problems of the good life to the problems of the good society. On the one hand, they maintain that it is impossible to solve the problems involved in making a good life for one's self without taking into account the favorable or adverse effects exerted upon one's individual efforts by the society in which one lives—by the political, economic, and social institutions that prevail at the time one is alive. On the other hand, they also maintain that it is impossible to determine whether a particular historic society is good or bad—better or worse than another—without reference to a standard of evaluation based on the meaning of a good human life.

In other words, if we do not know what a good life consists in and what is involved in making a good life for ourselves, we are in no position to judge whether the society or century in which we live is good or bad, better or worse than another. And if we do not know the extent to which the institutions and culture of the society in which we live affect, for good or ill, our efforts to make a good life for ourselves, we will be misguided in our efforts because we will mistakenly suppose that making a good life for ourselves is wholly within our power.

This two-way relationship between the problems of a good life and the problems of a good society was regarded by the ancients as constituting the unity or integration of ethics and politics as the two faces of moral philosophy—one looking toward the life of the individual, the other toward the life of the state or community. Looked at from one point of view, politics is the architectonic or controlling branch of moral philosophy, because it is concerned with matters that affect the good life of all members of the community. Looked at from another point of view, ethics is the dominant branch, because it is concerned with the basic standards or norms that must be employed in order to judge and evaluate the institutions and culture of the community.

The points I have just made should become clearer as we proceed. I have much to say that will explain them and, I hope, make their soundness evident. I have mentioned them here only to stress the double-barreled character of my intentions—aimed at the problems of the good life and also at the problems of the good society.

(3)

I have referred to ethics and politics as traditional branches of moral philosophy. It is necessary to observe that the problems of the good life and of the good society are sometimes also regarded as belonging to moral theology. Great religious teachers have insisted that these problems cannot be adequately solved without reference to God and divine providence, without reference to the life eternal in another world as well as to the temporal life we lead in this world, and without reference to the religious as well as to the secular dimension of our temporal life.

In this book I will not take one side or the other of the extremely difficult and complex issues thus raised. I mention them only to say that I wish to restrict my discussion of the problems of the good life and the good society to the temporal life and to that life on its secular plane. Those among my readers who are religious persons and distinguish between the secular and the religious activities they engage in, as well as between their worldly and their religious aspirations, will be able to affix appropriate qualifications, additions, and even dissents to various things I will say *without regard to religion.* Those who are not religious persons or who make no distinctions between the secular and the religious life will, of course, not be aware of any need for such qualifications, additions, or dissents.

(4)

In the following six chapters of Part One, I will present the common-sense answer to the question of how one can make a good life for one's self, and having done so, I will then turn to the philosophical objections that can be raised against it.

In Part Two, I will state these objections and attempt to defend the soundness of the common-sense answer against them. In doing so, I will necessarily have to go beyond common sense, for the philosophical critics of common sense must be met on their own grounds.

Having begun the transformation of common sense into moral philosophy, I will complete that process in Part Three—expanding and deepening the common-sense answer and explicating the reasons for its soundness. The transformation will also result, I hope, in the presentation of an ethical doctrine that not only makes good sense to the ordinary man, that not only appears to be relevant to his everyday affairs and his practical concerns, but that has the air of truth as well. If this turns out to be the case, it is more than can be said of much that goes by the name of moral philosophy today.

Finally, in Part Four, I will turn to the difficult social, economic, political, and educational problems that must be postponed until we have arrived at a relatively adequate and satisfactory answer to our initial question. If, when we reach Part Four, we know what is involved in making good lives for ourselves, so far as that is within our own power, we will then be ready to consider what measures can and should be taken to deal with the things that are not within our individual control. Here we must face the critics of our century and of our society, critics who think that our time is out of joint and that ours is a sick society. I hope I will be able to show that we can give an affirmative answer to the question, *Is this a good time to be alive, and is ours a good society to be alive in?* I also hope that I can explain why we sorely need a moral and an educational revolution.

CHAPTER 2

How Can I Make a Good Life for Myself?

(1)

THERE is an entry in the *Note Books* of Samuel Butler that reads as follows:

IS LIFE WORTH LIVING?
That is a question for an embryo, not a man!

One might be tempted to say something similar of the question, *How can I make a good life for myself?* It is a question for children, not for adults.

Such a witticism—if it is a witticism—would spring from the consideration that the older one gets, the less of one's life is left open to the choices that are operative in making it either good or bad. However, while it is true that the younger you are, the more time you have before you in which to engage in the effort to make a good life for yourself, it certainly is not true that the question with which we are concerned is only for the young. There are several reasons for this.

In the first place, it is certainly not a question for the very young—those whom the law classifies as infants, and describes in old-fashioned terms as not yet having reached the age of reason or of consent, and not yet knowing the difference between right and wrong. In the second place, such terms as "young" and "old" can be quite misleading if one carelessly identifies mental, moral, or experiential age with chronological age. We all know men of advanced years who are still immature or even childish in character; we also know other men whose maturity greatly exceeds their years. In the third place, the distinction between the mature and the immature can be misleading and irrelevant, if it connotes a difference between persons whose minds are fully developed and whose characters are fully formed, and persons whose minds and characters are still in the process of development and formation.

If the term "mature" is used in that last sense, it is highly doubtful whether there are any mature human beings. I hope there are not, and I certainly hope there are few if any among my readers, for nothing I have to say can be of any practical significance or use to them. The problem of making a good life is a genuine problem only for those who do not regard the job as done; and that includes everyone who is over the age of six or ten and has grown up enough to be able to think about the problem. On the other hand, I must add the observation, made by a wise old Greek, that it is inadvisable to give lectures on moral philosophy to the young. What he had in mind, I think, is that a certain amount of experience in the business of living and a certain seriousness of purpose are required for anyone to understand the problem of making a good life and to judge whether this or that proposal for its solution is practically sound.

With all these considerations in mind, I am going to address this book to persons who, in experience and character, are old enough not only to understand the question but also to judge the answers, and young enough in years to do something about applying what they have learned to their own lives during whatever time remains to them on earth. In other words, I will proceed on the assumption that my readers already have enough common-sense wisdom to become a little wiser through the ways in which philosophy can extend and enlighten common sense. I hope they share with me the further assumption that it is never too late just as (with the one exception of infancy) it is certainly never too early to give thought to the direction one is going in, and to take steps to rectify it if, upon reflection, that direction is seen to be wrong.

(2)

We can put these matters to the test by seeing what is involved in understanding the question—understanding it in the light of common sense and common human experience. When you think about the question, *How can I make a good life for myself?*—

(1) Do you realize that the question concerns the whole of your life, from the moment you begin to direct it for yourself until it is over—or at least until no genuine options remain?

(2) Do you think of the whole of your life, or whatever part of it that remains, as a span of time—of hours, days, months, and years—that is like a vacuum in the sense that it is time you can fill in one way or another, time that, in any case, you are consuming or using up, no matter how you fill it?

(3) Do you recognize that the ways in which this vacuum of time can be filled by you consist of the various activities you engage in, either entirely by free choice or under some form or degree of compulsion?

(4) Do you include among these ways of consuming the time of your life an option that can be called "time-wasting" or "time-killing" because it consists in passing the time by doing nothing or as nearly nothing as possible?

Another and, perhaps, better name for this form of inactivity or relatively slight activity might be "idling." I shall have more to say on the subject of idling and idleness later.

(5) Do you understand that, whereas your choice is not entirely free because you are under some degree of compulsion

to spend time doing this or that, the compulsion is never so complete that your freedom is totally abrogated?

The glaring exception is, of course, the chattel slave, whose life is not his own, whose time belongs to another man to use as *he* sees fit. Slavery is a thing of degrees—from the extreme of complete bondage or chattel slavery, where the human being is owned and used like a piece of inanimate property or a beast of burden, to the milder forms of servitude in which a man's life is not wholly his own, but some portion of his time remains for him to use as he himself sees fit. The question with which we are concerned is clearly not one for chattel slaves; it may not even be a practically significant question for those who are slaves in any degree or form of servitude.

(6) Do you appreciate, in consequence of what has just been said, that freedom in all its forms, especially freedom of choice and freedom from coercion and intimidation, is an indispensable prerequisite for dealing, in any practically significant way, with the question, *How can I make a good life for myself?*

Without the essential freedoms—the two I have just mentioned, and others equally important that I will mention later—the time of our lives is not ours to use and fill. If the distinction between a good life and a bad life, between living well and living poorly, between a life worth living or having lived and a life that is not worth living or having lived, can be made intelligible and can be defended against those who carp against such words as "good" and "bad" applied to a human life or anything else, then freedom is certainly good and slavery or lack of freedom is certainly bad; and the goodness of freedom consists in its being indispensable to our trying to make good lives for ourselves: it is good as a means to this end.

(7) Do you further appreciate that the exercise of your freedom at one time often imposes some limitations upon further use of your freedom at a later time, for the time of your life

consists of stages, and the decisions you make in its earlier stages affect the choices left open to you in later stages?

Hence the decisions any of us make in youth are among the most important decisions we are ever able to make, because they have such far-reaching effects on the range and character of the options that remain open to us. This holds true to some extent of every stage of life. Every choice we make is one that should involve a weighing of its immediate against its remote effects.

(8) To state this last question in another way, do you realize that the use of your time today or this year affects not only the quality of your life in the present, but also its quality in the future? Do the activities with which you now fill your time and which now seem good to you preclude your using your time later in a way that will then seem good to you? Or will they, in addition to seeming good to you now, facilitate your living in a way that will seem good to you later—years later?

(9) If you do realize this, do you also understand the full significance of the statement that, if life were a day-to-day affair, either we would have no moral problems at all or those problems would be so simple as to deserve little or no thought?

If, at the end of each day, we closed the books, if there were no carry-over accounts from one day to the next, if what happened to us in the days of our childhood or what we did when we were young had little or no effect on the rest of our lives, then our choices would all be momentary or passing ones and a jug of wine, a loaf of bread, and thou might well be enough for life on a day-to-day basis. In fact, this is the way that animals do live—on a day-to-day basis, without a thought for the morrow, except in the case of certain hoarding instincts that, being instincts, involve no thought on the animal's part.

(10) Do you, in consequence, understand further that the problem of making a whole human life that is really good—good

in each of its parts, and good in a way that results from each part's contributing what it ought to contribute to the whole— exists for you precisely because, at every stage of your life, in every day of your existence, you are faced with the basic moral alternative of choosing between a good time today and a good life as a whole—a choice between what is only useful, expedient, or pleasant in the short run, and what will contribute, in the long run, to making your whole life good?

Of all the points made so far, this is, perhaps, the one most difficult to understand in the early years of life—the time when, practically, it is most important to understand it. It is in the early years of our lives that we are disinclined to make choices that favor the long as against the short run, probably because the eventualities of the long run then seem so remote. This lies at the root of the generation gap. On one side are those who find the long run unreal or too remote to think about; on the other are those for whom it has become a reality and a dominant consideration. The great misfortune of the human race, in every generation, is that its younger members—at the time of their lives when it is most important to understand this point—find it extremely difficult to understand and often fail to understand it. But if the point is only difficult, not impossible, for the young to understand, then it is of the greatest importance that sound moral instruction and training help them to understand it at the earliest possible moment in their lives. Their elders may finally have come to understand it only too well, and with some measure of remorse that their understanding has come too late for them to make the best use of such wisdom.

(11) In the light of the fact that making a good life as a whole necessarily entails long-range considerations, does it not now seem evident that you cannot make a good life for yourself by choice rather than by chance unless you have some kind of plan for your life as a whole—a plan for the use of its time in the present, in the years immediately ahead, and in the long run?

If everything were left to chance, there would be no point in even asking the question, *How can I make a good life for myself?* Seriously to consider that question is to assume that one can solve it by the choices one can make. But to exercise choice in the earlier stages of life without a plan for the whole is to leave much to chance. Early choices may severely limit our freedom in later stages of life, and so the lack of a plan may result in our having to fill our time in ways we would not have chosen had we foreseen the remote effects of our earlier choices and had we made them with a plan in mind.

(12) Finally, does not this point about the obvious need for a plan suggest the analogy between making a whole life that is good and making a work of art that is good?

In some of the creative arts, such as architecture, the process of building does not begin until a detailed plan or blueprint is ready. In other arts, the plan of the thing to be produced—a painting, a novel, a piece of music—is usually much less detailed than that. It is often only a sketch or an outline of the creative idea. But in any case the work of the artist is always guided by some vision, more or less detailed, of the end result. Without such a guiding plan, the end result would be a thing of chance rather than a work of art. To this extent at least, there is a parallel between the production of a work of art and the making of a good life.

(3)

I have just set forth, in the form of questions, twelve considerations that should be borne in mind—the more explicitly the better—by anyone who seriously confronts the problem with which we are concerned, and even more so by anyone who tries to solve it. These twelve questions provide a measure of anyone's understanding of the problem of making a good life for one's self. They also indicate the steps one must begin to take in order to find a solution that will be sound, adequate, and thoroughly practical.

Before I turn to the solution that I think would be developed by a wise and practical man of common sense, I would like to spend a moment more on the analogy between making a work of art and making a good life. While the analogy may be enlightening, it can also be misleading. Making a good life is, in its fundamentals, radically different from artistic creation. Let me explain why.

The architectural analogy fails not only because the work of building is directed by a plan that is much more detailed in its specifications than any that can be developed for leading a good life, but also because the final product, being a spatial whole, can exist all at one time, whereas a whole life is a temporal whole and exists only as a process of becoming. Even though the plan one can draw up for making a good life may be more comparable to the kind of rough sketch that painters put upon a canvas before they apply pigments, the finished painting has the same kind of existence as a building, and so is not like a human life as a whole.

There is a closer resemblance between the performing arts and making a good life. A good performance, like a human life, is a temporal affair—a process in time. It is good as a whole through being good in its parts, and through their good order to one another. It cannot be called good as a whole until it is finished. During the process, all we can say of it, if we speak precisely, is that it is becoming good. The same is true of a whole human life. Just as the whole performance never exists at any one time, but is a process of becoming, so a human life is also a performance in time and a process of becoming. And just as the goodness that attaches to the performance as a whole does not attach to any of its parts, so the goodness of a human life as a whole belongs to it alone, and not to any of its parts or phases. In neither case can the goodness of the whole be experienced at any moment in the process, as the goodness of the parts is experienced from moment to moment. This has a bearing on the distinction between a good life as a whole and a good time from moment to moment.

However, the analogy between the performing arts and making a good life also fails for a number of reasons, reasons that indicate that making a good life differs radically from artistic making or production of any sort. In the first place, rehearsals in advance are always possible in the case of artistic performances, but never in the case of making a life. In the second place, while a performing artist cannot repeat a single performance he regards as a failure, he can usually try again. But none of us gets a second chance at making a good life for ourselves. When we have finished that job, we are finished—for better or worse. In the third place, the man who has artistic skill does not have to employ that skill to produce a work of art. Whether he does so or not is an option he is free to exercise. But unless we commit suicide, we have no choice about making a life for ourselves. We are engaged in the process of doing so, willy-nilly, like it or not. Our only option is between making our life good as a whole and failing to do so.

This last point, as we shall see, is crucial. It draws a sharp line between the sphere of moral conduct and the sphere of artistic production. Making a good life is not a work of art. The aesthetic approach to life is superficial; it overlooks the underlying difference between life and art. The one point of resemblance that should be retained is the usefulness of some kind of plan. A work of art cannot be well-made without a plan; so too, a life cannot be well-lived without a plan.

Anyone who has read Plato's account of the trial of Socrates will remember his observation that an unexamined life is not worth living. When we understand what he means, I think we will also be led to conclude that an unplanned life cannot be lived well. That conclusion directs the effort of this book to answer the question with which it is concerned, for it tells us in advance what we are looking for—*a sound and practical plan of life that will help us to make our whole life good.*

(4)

A plan of that character consists of a small number of prescriptions about the goods to be sought and the manner and order of seeking them. These prescriptions, formulated with a universality that makes them applicable to all men without regard to their individual differences or the special circumstances of their individual lives, constitute what little wisdom it is possible for the moral philosopher to attain with reasonable certitude, and that little is nothing but a distillation of the wisdom of common sense.

The reader will gradually come to appreciate the significance of what I have just said, as later chapters refine common-sense opinions into philosophical insights—especially the chapters of Part Three, which attempt to set forth the ethics of common sense. By the time he reaches the end of Chapter 15, he should understand the contribution that the wisdom of a common-sense ethics can make to the conduct of his life—not only understand its applicability to his own problems, but also realize both how inadequate and how indispensable it is for their solution. I will repeatedly stress both its inadequacy and its indispensability, for it is of the utmost importance not to overlook either, or to make the mistake of supposing that because moral philosophy cannot by itself solve our individual problems of day-to-day living, it is of no value or use whatsoever. Equally unfortunate is the opposite error of supposing that because moral philosophy has some invaluable wisdom to offer, we need nothing more than it for guidance in dealing with every exigency, moral crisis, or tragic dilemma that life serves up to us. The small core of wisdom that moral philosophy affords may go to the heart of our practical problems, but it does not and cannot cover all the intricacies and complications in which such problems are embedded.

In acknowledging that the reader may not fully understand and appreciate all this until he finishes Chapter 15, and at the same time confessing that I do not know how to bring him more quickly to the state of mind in which I hope to leave him at that point, I am also aware that he may be put off or even turned away by quite excusable misapprehensions of what is being said in the earlier portions of this book. Since I do not want that to happen, I have no other recourse than to caution him here and now about misunderstandings that may occur and that I would like to see him avoid. I do this with some trepidation, not only because I have little faith in the effectiveness of this method of preventing misunderstanding, but also because I fear that the reader will be more impressed by what I have to say about the inadequacy of moral philosophy than by what I have to say about its indispensability. That impression might dissuade him from reading on, which is hardly the result I am aiming at.

Let me start with one misunderstanding that may have occurred already. In this chapter, I have dwelt on the importance of a plan for putting the parts of one's life into some perspective and order, and I have compared such a plan with the kind of rough sketches that an artist makes of the work he is going to produce. The reader may mistakenly suppose that in emphasizing the indispensability of a plan, however sketchy, I am exhorting him to develop one for himself. I am not doing that. If he goes back and reads carefully the last sentence of Section 3, he will see that I am promising him that the effort of this book to solve the problem of making a good life for one's self will be directed toward the exposition of a sound and practical plan that will afford some measure of help and serve as a guide.

But while I am not recommending that the reader undertake at once to develop such a plan for himself if he has not done so before, neither am I recommending that he desist from doing so. If he already has some sort of plan for his life as a whole, my only recommendation to him would be that he be open-minded about it and willing to alter it if the prescriptions for a good life that are developed in this book should appear to contain some points of wisdom he has overlooked or negated. If he has not yet seriously thought about planning his life, then I would hope he might be persuaded and helped to do so by this book.

By emphasizing all the differences between making a good life and making a work of art, I have tried to prevent the reader from mistaking a book on moral philosophy for a how-to book— a book of highly specific rules that can, through practice, be applied, with an acquired perfection of skill, to accomplish unerringly and with some measure of excellence the result aimed at. If there were an art of living, the problem of making a good life could be solved with the same regularity, the same assurance, and the same mastery that the problem of erecting a bridge or of composing music can be solved. But there is no art of living, and no man can ever expect to attain in that domain the skill or mastery possessed by many engineers or musicians in their respective fields of work. The relevant wisdom that moral philosophy has to offer does not consist of specific rules of conduct analogous to rules of art; it goes no further than prescriptions so general that they apply to all human lives, and precisely because the principles of moral philosophy have such universality, they are of use to the individual only if he will make the effort to apply them to the contingent singularities of his own individual life.

Moral philosophy, moreover, cannot provide him with anything more than the most general guidance for particularizing its principles. Unlike a navigating chart, it does not indicate every reef, shoal, or shallow to be skirted, or plainly plot the channels or courses to be followed. It cannot do that because each individual life is an unchartable sea, full of unforeseeable dangers and untoward complications. But that does not mean that such practical wisdom as is available can provide no guidance at all; by defining the problems to be solved and by laying down the principles to be applied by anyone who will exercise intelligence in their solution, it points out the goal to be reached and supplies the only directions that can be formulated for reaching it. Following such directions may sorely tax the individual's intelligence and strain his will-power; nevertheless, the difficulties he encounters in following them should not cause him to make the mistake of thinking he would be better off were he to proceed in life without any destination to aim at and without directions to follow.

In short, moral philosophy, as I have already indicated, does not get down to the nitty-gritty or the nuts and bolts of the vexatious practical problems that each of us has to resolve in the most trying moments of our lives. Frankly to acknowledge this is itself an essential bit of practical wisdom; to pretend the opposite is consummate folly. In setting forth what I have learned from the reflections of common sense on the common experience of mankind, and in expounding it philosophically in the form of the ethics of common sense, I will, in the pages that follow, go no further than such wisdom allows. I will not pretend to be wise about the infinitely varied trials and tribulations that make the business of living—and especially of trying to live well—difficult for every individual. But that does not mean that I am unacquainted with the hard and often harsh realities of the human condition, nor cavalierly oblivious to what many experience as the *angst* and the despair occasioned by the distressing facts of life.

I know that even the best human life, precisely because it is the life of a man and not of a god, may not escape the taint of tragedy. Every human life, even under the most fortunate circumstances, has its share of frustration and discontentment, its burden of remorse for avoidable mistakes committed, its insoluble dilemmas—insoluble in the sense that their only solution requires us to choose between alternatives both of which we desperately wish to avoid. Tragedy thus enters our lives through the evils we must choose to embrace because circumstances present us with alternatives we are compelled to choose between. Even when moral wisdom guides us as well as it can in the task of making a good life, and even when we apply its prescriptions with the most flexible and resourceful intelligence and with a will habitually disciplined to act intelligently, we cannot prevent the intrusion of tragedy because we cannot avoid having to make the tragic decisions that are the price we must pay for being free to make any decisions at all. Much less can we hope to be exempt from some measure of the misfortunes that, in varying degrees, mar every human life. (Nevertheless, I must add, it remains possible—with wisdom and will united in the effort—to lead a good life, one that accumulates, over the years, more goods than evils, and is embellished by joys and satisfactions.)

If the reader supposes that inattention to all these somber facts in the following pages betokens a dismissal of them as matters of no concern, he will mistake the simplicity of moral wisdom for simple-mindedness. Precisely because the few basic truths of moral philosophy are elementary and clear, moral wisdom is truly simple, as it should be; but that should not lead anyone to regard it as a collection of simple-minded homilies or a set of simplistic solutions. It does not get down to the level of life's most perplexing difficulties because that is the level at which no one can be philosophically wise. All that it can do is provide what little guidance wisdom is able to give every human being because of what life is like for all of them.

That minimum guidance, in my judgment, is indispensable for intelligent living. Without it, we move from day to day blindly and aimlessly. The fact that moral philosophy cannot adequately solve life's particular problems certainly does not warrant the conclusion that it makes no contribution at all to their solution. This is an error that many men make. They dismiss a clear definition of justice as of no practical utility because it does not automatically enable them to decide, in a particular difficult case, whether a certain act or policy is just or unjust, forgetting that they would not and could not even be troubled about justice in that particular case if they did not have some definite standard of justice to apply to it. It is equally foolish to dismiss the clarity and simplicity of moral philosophy as of no value—as simple-minded or simplistic—because it does not automatically tell us what to do in this or that trying moment of our lives. Without its wisdom we could not even begin to see our way through those dark moments.

One word more. In what follows, especially in Chapters 4, 5, and 6, I will propose a number of distinctions among the types of human activity, together with a classification of the parts of a human life, in order to discover what common sense can contribute to the solution of the problem of making a human life good—good as a whole. Analytical distinctions and classifications are often misunderstood. Things that can be separated in thought by analysis are usually not separate in actual existence. To convert analytical distinctions into existential or experiential separations is an egregious error, yet one that is frequently made. I therefore hope this advance notice will prevent the reader from making the mistake of supposing that life comes in separate chunks because thinking about it—if we are to do any thinking about it at all—draws lines that divide one kind of activity from another and that isolate the various aspects of life. Such divisions and isolations enable us to see how the things that are divided or isolated in thought combine, overlap, fuse, and flow together in the changing existential mix that is life's actual process.

CHAPTER 3

The Accidents of Fortune and the Need to Earn a Living

(1)

To make a start toward answering the question, *How can I make a good life for myself?* I will set forth what can be said in the light of common human experience and in terms that are familiar and intelligible in our everyday discourse. These are the terms in which a man of common sense thinks about his life. I will postpone until later—until after a common-sense answer to the question has been fully developed—the philosophizing that must be done to see if the common-sense answer stands up against the criticisms it will inevitably elicit. Only after I have been able to defend the common-sense answer against its philosophical critics will I undertake to expand and deepen what we have learned, by trying to transform it into a more systematic philosophical answer that I hope I can show is true.

I pointed out in the preceding chapter that the question we are concerned with is not for infants or very young children. But infancy and childhood—the first ten years, give or take a few—represent a portion of our life's time and, according to the latest and best scientific knowledge we have, a portion that is of the utmost consequence for everything that follows. How, then, can we ignore what happens in infancy and childhood?

How can anyone later plan a good life for himself when the foundations of his life have already been laid through no choice of his own?

While the problem this raises cannot be solved by those who have reached the age of discretion and choice, it is not in itself an insoluble problem. It is a problem to be solved by parents and, with them or in lieu of them, by all other agencies, including the state, that are responsible for the care and rearing of children. Although the problem of making a good life for himself is a problem for each individual human being, it is not a problem he can solve entirely on his own. He needs the assistance of others, starting with his parents and other members of his immediate family and extending to the other smaller and larger communities in which he is born and grows up.

The point I have just made applies not only to the period of infancy and childhood, but to all later stages of our lives as well. There is no time when we can do everything by and for ourselves. Everything is not within our power or control. We are in many respects, some of them crucial, dependent upon others and upon organized society as a whole. This being the case, we shall have to consider how other human beings and organized society as a whole can affect—favorably or adversely— the making of our individual lives. But I am going to postpone this very difficult matter until the concluding part of this book, when we shall be concerned with the problem of leading a good life under the conditions imposed by the twentieth century and in the society we have at present in the United States. Here, for the time being, I will restrict myself to a narrower question, put in such a way that we can answer it quickly and get on to the point where the individual begins to make for himself the choices and decisions that affect the making of his life.

(2)

Instead of asking what elements constitute the optimal or ideal childhood that all of us would wish to have had as a good start in life, let us ask about the minimal conditions of birth, infancy, and childhood, the conditions indispensable to putting the individual in a position to make a good life for himself when he begins to direct his own life.

A life can be adversely affected in its early years by circumstances wholly beyond the control of the individual whose life it is. It can be ruined by crippling disabilities at birth, by deprivations and deficiencies imposed by poverty and neglect, by injuries to the body resulting from misfortune beyond anyone's control, by malformations of the personality engendered by culpable ill-treatment, and so on. Yet we all know of cases in which the individual has overcome disabilities, deprivations, accidental misfortune, and even ill-treatment, often with extraordinary results, because of the extra or special compensatory efforts he has been impelled to make. No one would make these special cases the grounds for saying that adverse circumstances in infancy or childhood are desirable. All of us, I think, would agree that, on the contrary, while it would be too much to ask for the elimination of all such adverse circumstances, it is always to be hoped that they will not be so extreme that the individual cannot surmount them.

From the beginning of man's existence on earth, countless human lives have been ruined by extremely adverse circumstances in their early years. That is still the case in the world today, and in our country. The question, *How can I make a good life for myself?*, is not a question that these unfortunate individuals were ever privileged to answer. One of the problems that we shall deal with later concerns what must be done to increase the number of individuals who enjoy that privilege.

A life can also be adversely affected by native endowments so great that the facility they provide impairs initiative and effort. It can be spoiled by a superabundance of good fortune—by an excess of affluence, comfort, and ease. It can be spoiled by circumstances so propitious they render ineffective the imposition of restraint upon childish propensities for self-indulgence —with an outcome as undesirable as that which results from the imposition of overbearing and harsh restraints. In neither case is the child likely to grow up able to combine the exercise of freedom with the exercise of self-discipline.

Once again it must be pointed out that we all know of cases

in which the individual has been able to triumph over good fortune, to overcome the debilitating influences of superabundance—of an excess of ease, comfort, opportunity, freedom. But here as before, these special cases would not lead us, I think, to regard an excess of good fortune as desirable. Here, however, it is more difficult to state the conditions that must be present in infancy and childhood in order to provide the individual with a fair chance of making a good life for himself. Perhaps the only thing that can be said is that the favorable or propitious circumstances beyond the individual's control should not be so excessive that he is likely to be spoiled by them.

The number of human lives—past and present—that have been adversely affected by affluence and excessive good fortune are, of course, many, many times less than the number that have been ruined by the opposite extreme. But this fact should not lead us to dismiss the problem as of no importance, for every child born into the world should have the conditions prerequisite to trying to make a good life for himself—the fortunate few as well as the unfortunate many.

Thus we see that the problem we shall have to deal with later has two faces. To increase the number of individuals who enjoy the privilege—more than that, the right—of trying to make a good life for themselves, we must consider what is to be done about the extreme of good fortune as well as the extreme of its opposite in the circumstances that surround the individual's early years and are beyond his own control.

(3)

In addition to postponing until Part Four the very serious problem just mentioned, I would like to postpone two other considerations—but just until Chapters 6 and 7 of Part One.

First, let us assume *for the time being* that the same extremes of misfortune or good fortune that would ruin or spoil a life at its beginning will remain absent from your life when the making of it is in your own hands. I realize that this assumption is one that no one can actually make. It is made here as a hypothesis contrary to fact in order to consider how an individual might think about his future *if* he did not have to face the prospect of interference from circumstances beyond his own control.

All of us make this assumption, at least in one very important respect. We plan for our futures on the hypothesis that we are going to be granted the normal span of life—that it will not be cut prematurely short by some disaster. If at any point in our lives except, perhaps, in old age, we knew with certitude that we had only a few days or even a few months to live, we would drastically change our plans, or abandon them entirely. We would probably cease any further effort to make a good life for ourselves, or even to think about it as a meaningful problem, and concentrate on having a good time from day to day. It is true that all of us live with the awareness of the risk that our lives may be cut short, just as all of us live with the prospect that we may suffer serious misfortunes in the course of our lives. But these are only probabilities, not certainties, and one aspect of making a good life for one's self consists in being able to cope with adversity, so far as it is humanly possible to do so. Temporarily, however, let us suppose that we could plan our lives without taking account of the probabilities of misfortune that hang over all of us.

When, in Chapter 7, we remove this provisional assumption and deal with the facts of life as we know them, we shall come to grips with the problem of what resources the individual has in himself for coping with the impact on his life of the things that are entirely beyond his control—fortune, good or bad. But we will still postpone until Part Four the problem of how society as a whole can minimize the extremes of good and bad fortune that can ruin or spoil a life.

Second, let us assume *for the time being* that the individual who begins to think about how to make a good life for himself does not have to include in his considerations the problem of making a living. This second provisional assumption, unlike the first, is not a completely contrafactual hypothesis. There have always been some men—a relatively small number, of course, but nevertheless some—who have had enough property or wealth at their disposal so that working for the means of subsistence, for the comforts and conveniences of life, has not entered into their plans. And some of these—an even smaller number—may have succeeded in making good lives for themselves.

The hypothesis I am suggesting that we adopt is, therefore, not an impossible one, and the reason I am proposing it provisionally is in order to ask what plans any one of us would make *if we did not have to think about earning a living.* Making this assumption eliminates one form of activity from the repertoire of things we can or must do to occupy the time of our lives. In our everyday speech, we call that form of activity "work," "labor," or "toil." I am going to use the word "work" for it, and to be sure that the meaning of that word is always clear, I am going to affix an adjective to it and call it "subsistence-work," to stress one thing that is common to all the diverse modes of this activity, namely, the reason why we engage in it. In Chapter 6, when I remove this provisional assumption, I will examine the various modes of subsistence-work, for though all its modes aim at the same end—the wealth a man needs—they differ in other important respects.

I referred a moment ago to the repertoire of things we *can* or *must* do to occupy the time of our lives. The alternatives suggested by the words "can" or "must" are represented by those activities, on the one hand, that are optional and those, on the other, that are compulsory. Among those that are compulsory, some are compulsory only under certain conditions or circumstances, not absolutely so. Subsistence-work, for example, is compulsory only under certain conditions. Given the circumstances of sufficient wealth, one is not under the compulsion to engage in subsistence-work. Only under the opposite circumstances are we compelled to. Since both sets of circumstances can occur, I am not asking anyone to imagine an impossible situation when I ask him to consider not being compelled to make a living for himself.

My reason for asking my readers to make this assumption provisionally is to get them to consider how they would use the time of their lives if they were not compelled to consume any of it in subsistence-work. Suppose you are fortunate to have enough secure wealth not to have to do another day's work for the rest of your life. Making this supposition, then think seriously

—and with the full exercise of your imagination—about how you would spend all of the time that remained at your disposal. What activities would you engage in? How would you plan the rest of your life? If, on the assumption that I have asked you to make, you can come up with an answer to this question—with a plan of living aimed at making a good life for yourself—you will be prepared to consider how your plan must be altered when this assumption is removed and you are required to include subsistence-work among the activities that consume your time. It will also help you to think about the merits of different kinds of subsistence-work, supposing you are fortunate enough to be able to choose a more rather than a less desirable way of making a living for yourself.

Since my second assumption is intended to eliminate any activity that is circumstantially compulsory but none that is absolutely compulsory, let me extend it to exclude compulsory military service for those who are of an age and condition to be subject to the draft. Extending the assumption in this way still remains within the bounds of possibility, for it could happen that, during an individual's youth, his country would not be engaged in war; and it is even possible that one's country at war might rely entirely upon volunteers. Within that second possibility, the individual might elect, for one reason or another, good or bad, to serve his country or to choose, for a shorter or longer time, a military career. Until war is totally eliminated from human affairs, this will remain one of life's options. When military service is optional, it may be a mode of subsistence-work —a way of earning a living. It may be more than that, of course, but in any case it is not always compulsory, and for the time being my only aim is to eliminate it along with other things that are only circumstantially compulsory.

CHAPTER 4

The Disposition of One's Time

(1)

THE reader may protest at once even when we make the assumption that eliminates subsistence-work as a compulsory form of activity using up a considerable portion of our waking life, the time of our lives is not wholly at our disposal. I have prepared for this objection by distinguishing between these activities, such as subsistence-work, which are compulsory only under certain conditions, and those that are unconditionally or absolutely compulsory. Whatever time is occupied by the latter is clearly not at our disposal.

What features of a human life are absolutely compulsory? A certain amount of time *must* be spent in sleeping, as anyone knows; and still other portions of one's span of time *must* be spent in eating, in cleansing one's body, in preserving one's health and one's vigor. The exact amount is not the same for every individual. The amount varies with individual differences in physique and temperament, with differences in physical environment, and even with differences in the culture of the society one lives in. Nevertheless, no human being can continue to live without some portion of his time being occupied with what I shall call biologically necessary activities. My own rough guess is that such activities consume, on the average, about a third of our life's time. Unusual individuals or individuals living under unusual circumstances will vary from this average in either direction.

Permit me to use the verb "sleep" as the symbol for the whole set of activities that are biologically necessary, even though slumbering is actually only one member of this set. Eating is another, cleansing another, and so on. I hope my use of "sleep" as an omnibus term will not prove a stumbling block to some readers, who may find it difficult to overcome their habitual use of the word for only one of these diverse forms of activity. Sleeping (i.e., slumbering) does, in fact, happen to consume the largest portion of the time we must devote to maintaining our health and vigor, and for that reason, I have chosen to use "Sleep" to name this group of activities instead of a more cumbersome, invented phrase.

I call attention to my use of "sleep" as a verb in order to stress the fact that such things as sleeping, eating, cleansing, and so on are activities. To say these things are biologically necessary activities is also to say that they are useful activities, serving ends or producing results. To name the end that such activities serve, it would be difficult to find better words than "health" and "vigor."

The fact that all the biologically necessary activities I have lumped together under the verb "sleep" are absolutely compulsory does not remove them entirely from the sphere of the voluntary. A certain minimum of these activities must be engaged in if we are to remain alive, but we are free to indulge them beyond the minimum and even to excess—for reasons of pleasure or indolence. We are also free to impair our health and reduce our vigor by the extent or manner in which we engage in these activities. It is only at the level of the bare minimums that we have no choice about such activities as sleeping, eating, and cleansing, and so on—no choice, that is, unless we include suicide as an alternative, or such impairment of our health and vigor that we could not make much use of the time left at our disposal. Above the level of the bare minimums, these activities may still retain their biological utility, but they may also take on another character because of the reasons we engage in them. They retain their biological utility to whatever extent we engage in them for reasons of health and vigor, but when we go beyond that and engage in them for reasons of pleasure or indolence, they pass over into other categories of activity.

(2)

The word "pleasure" gives us the clue to one of these other categories. Just as I used the verb "sleep" as an omnibus term to cover all forms of activity that we engage in *either* because we cannot continue to live without doing so *or* because we wish to preserve or enhance our health and vigor, so I will now use the verb "play" as an omnibus term for all forms of activity that we engage in simply and purely for the pleasure experienced in the activity itself.

Just as I have used "sleep" to cover not only sleeping, but also eating, cleansing, exercising for reasons of health, and the like, so I will use "play" to cover not only playing games but also participating in sports, indulging in amusements of one sort or another, and even engaging in such things as sleeping, eating, and exercising when we engage in them, beyond biological need, for the pleasures that are intrinsic to these activities themselves.

The distinguishing characteristic of all purely playful activities, as contrasted with those that are biologically necessary (at the minimum) or biologically useful (beyond the minimum), lies in the fact that they are neither necessary nor useful. They serve no end and produce no result beyond the pleasure enjoyed in the performance itself. If pleasure be regarded as the objective of these activities, it is something intrinsic to them, not a result that lies beyond them.

When an intrinsically pleasurable activity is engaged in for some reason that goes beyond the pleasure intrinsic to it, the activity is no longer purely and simply play. It is, as many human activities are, a mixture of different types. We can easily think of many examples of activities that combine the features of sleep and play because they are done both for a biological result extrinsic to them and for the pleasure intrinsic to them. We often eat, or shower, or exercise, for both reasons; so, too, we often play games, engage in sports, indulge in amusements, not only for the pleasures involved but also because they help us to relax, to reduce tension, to wash away the fatigue engendered by other activities—in general, to restore or re-create our energies.

In addition to such mixed activities, combining the characteristics of different pure types of activity, we have, of course, the pure types themselves—sleep that is purely sleep because solely for reasons of health or vigor, and play that is purely play because solely for reasons of intrinsic pleasure. And still further, we are also acquainted in our experience with activities that normally belong to one category or type but that, on occasion, take on the character of a different type. Thus, for example, we sometimes eat, drink, or shower purely for the pleasure of doing so; and we sometimes play games, engage in sports, indulge in amusements, purely for recreational purposes, that is, to remove fatigue or tension or to recoup our energies. When, in any of its modes, play is thus transformed into a biologically useful activity, it can be called "therapeutic" or "utilitarian" play. When sleep, in any of its modes, is thus transformed into an intrinsically enjoyable activity, it can be called "unuseful" or "sensuous" or perhaps even "playful" sleep.

One further example may help us to remember this threefold differentiation of activities into the pure, the mixed, and the transformed. Sexual activity is a mixed activity when it is engaged in both for its biological utility (which includes more than reproductive results) and also for the sensuous pleasure it provides. It is purely a form of sleep when it is engaged in for biological reasons alone. And since its primary location is in the category of biologically necessary activities, it is a transformed activity when it is motivated only by the sensuous pleasure to be experienced. As a transformed activity, it may become, just as sleeping or eating when done to excess may become, biologically injurious.

(3)

At the beginning of this chapter I posed a question to be answered on the basis of the two provisional assumptions we have tentatively adopted. Assuming that we did not have to spend any time working for a living and assuming that our lives were unaffected by the extremes of either good or bad fortune, how would we spend the time at our disposal? What would we do with the time of our lives? To help us toward an answer to this question, I began exploring the generic categories of human activity. We temporarily tabled one of them for later consideration—subsistence-work. But before we put it aside, we did note two of its fundamental characteristics. Subsistence-work is, under certain circumstances, compulsory. It is like sleep in being compulsory, but it differs from sleep in that the circumstances of a human life can be such that it is not always compulsory, as sleep always is. Like sleep, it is a useful activity serving an extrinsic end, producing a desired result beyond itself. Just as the result aimed at by sleep can be summed up in the words "health" and "vigor," so the end aimed at by work can be summed up in the word "wealth," standing for all the means of subsistence, the comforts and conveniences of life.

I have also referred to a way of consuming time by doing nothing or as little as possible beyond the involuntary or autonomic actions of the body itself. I used the word "idling" for such minimal activity. I then added sleep and play, generically considered in their pure forms, and observed how each of these could be mixed with the other. We shall subsequently consider whether subsistence-work is ever mixed with play or with idling.

We now have before us four basic types of human activity—sleep, play, subsistence-work, and idling—activities that consume time, activities we can voluntarily engage in or avoid in varying degrees as, from day to day, we use up the time of our lives. Do these four types exhaust the possibilities? Have we overlooked any basic form of human activity that should be mentioned before we take up our guiding question again?

There is at least one other form of activity that must be considered, though it may not be the only one that is left before all possibilities are exhausted. I am going to try to characterize it before I name it. Unlike sleep, it is not absolutely compulsory or biologically useful. It does not contribute to health. Unlike subsistence-work, it is not even circumstantially compulsory. Even when the circumstances are such that subsistence-work is necessary, this type of activity, in its pure form, does not contribute to the production of consumable wealth. Unlike idling and play, and like sleep and subsistence-work, it is a useful activity, serving an end beyond itself, producing an extrinsic result that is desirable.

This last point places it on the side of sleep and subsistence-work and separates it from idling and play, by virtue of one characteristic that it shares in common with sleep and subsistence-work—its usefulness, its having an extrinsic end, its being aimed at a result beyond itself. So in order to distinguish it from sleep and subsistence-work, we need only to identify the extrinsic end or result that is served or produced by this activity in its pure form.

Not health and vigor, nor wealth produced and wealth consumed, but human improvement, individual and social, is the end this activity aims at. Learning in all its forms is the most obvious example of it, since without learning the individual cannot improve himself and with learning he cannot help but do so. In this respect, all learning is useful whether or not it is also useful in serving ends beyond self-improvement or personal growth. Anything that contributes to the growth of the individual as a person, not just as a biological organism, belongs in this category, as does anything the individual does that contributes to the improvement of his society—its component institutions and the elements of its culture, its arts and sciences.

Still one other way of characterizing this type of activity is to call it creative. In a sense, any activity that produces a result can be called creative; thus sleep is creative of health, subsistence-work of wealth. The result produced by a productive activity may be either an extrinsic product, such as wealth, or an immanent condition of the agent, such as health. But it is possible for wealth to be produced by an individual without any improvement resulting in his own person; and it is possible for health to be preserved by an individual without any change in his personality, for better or for worse. In contrast, the type of activity that we are here trying to distinguish from sleep and subsistence-work always produces an immanent result—an improvement in the person who is the agent, over and above any extrinsic product it may result in or any contribution it may make to the improvement of society.

To sum this up, the activity with which we are concerned is

creative in the very special sense of being self-creative, because it always involves personal growth or self-improvement.

The only single English word available to name this type of activity is the equivalent of the word employed by the ancient Greeks for it. Unfortunately, that word—"leisure"—is currently so misused that great effort must be made to overcome the wrong connotations now almost universally attached to it. I am going to ask my readers to make that effort, so that we can use "leisure" to name a type of activity that is clearly distinct from the other four types we have so far considered. Since we are naming an activity, think of "leisure" primarily as a verb, not a noun, and never as an adjective. Like sleeping, working, playing, and idling, leisuring is something we do with our time.

One way to safeguard against falling into the current misuse of the term is never to employ it as an adjective. Let us never say "leisure time" when we mean free time, that is, the time that is left over after compulsory activities have consumed the rest. Another abominable adjectival use occurs in the phrase "leisure class," when that is used to refer to the class of persons who possess sufficient wealth or property to exempt them from the compulsion of having to work for a living. The members of the so-called leisure class often consume their free time in playing and idling rather than in leisuring, though the exceptions are many and significant. Still another egregious misuse of the term derives from the confusion of leisuring with playing, whether it is pure play or therapeutic and recreational play. As a safeguard against this misuse, I am going to add a suffix to "leisure," as I previously added a prefix to "work." I am going to speak of "leisure-work" to indicate that leisuring in its pure form is never to be confused with playing in its pure form, though some activities are mixed, involving aspects of both leisure-work and play.

Finally, to reinforce all these safeguards against being misunderstood when I speak of leisuring or of leisure-work, I must call attention to the etymology of the English word and also to its Greek counterpart. The English word "leisure" comes from the French verb "loisir" and from the Latin "licere"—both of which signify that which is permissible rather than compulsory. Leisuring is something we can do, but are under no biological or economic compulsion to do. Whether or not we are under a moral obligation to engage in leisuring is something we shall consider later, but for the moment it is enough to point out that leisuring is one of the ways of using whatever free time we have —time free from activities we are compelled to engage in. In this respect, leisuring stands on the side of playing and idling, as against sleeping and working. The Greek word that we translate by "leisure" is "scholé," the Latin of which is "schola" and the English of which is "school"—the significance of which is learning. Remembering this should confirm us in the use of the English word "leisure" or "leisure-work" for any mode of useful and productive activity that is not biologically or economically necessary and that, since it always involves learning, is self-creative or self-improving.

To define leisuring by reference to self-improvement as the result it aims to produce appears to carry with it the implication that this type of activity is always good for us; for how could any form of self-improvement harm us or be detrimental to us? The definitions of the other basic types of activity leave open the question of whether we can engage in them to our disadvantage as well as to our advantage. For example, the definition of play by reference to the pleasure intrinsic to that activity allows us to ask whether it may be detrimental to us to indulge excessively in play. The same question can be asked about the forms of sleep, and in the case of subsistence-work, I have already intimated that we might be better off if our circumstances were such that we did not have to do any of it at all.

Let it be granted, then, that the definition of leisuring in terms of self-improvement excludes the possibility of its ever being injurious or detrimental. This provides us with an additional distinction between leisuring and all the other basic types of human activity. But in order to understand this definition of leisuring, must we not first know what self-improvement consists in? May not individuals differ in their conceptions of self-improvement? These questions may appear to be troublesome, but I do not think they really are. I would be quite content with any common-sense answer to them. Accepting anyone's conception of the things that contribute to his personal growth or to his improvement as a human being, I would then add that whatever activity produces such results is leisuring. That cannot be said of sleep, play, subsistence-work, or idling; none of these in its pure form results in self-improvement, *however that is conceived.*

One further consideration remains with regard to leisure-work, and that is its mixture with subsistence-work and with play. I will have much more to say about this in the next chapter when I explore all the modes and grades of work. For the present I need say only that many of our activities involve admixtures of leisure with play, or of leisure with subsistence-work, or of all three together.

In its pure form, leisure-work may be no more intrinsically pleasurable than subsistence-work is. We do both, in their pure forms, for the results they produce. Subsistence-work is often painful and, for that reason, something we try to avoid or cut down. The same is true of leisure-work. We often try to avoid it and turn to playing or idling instead when we have free time at our disposal. Another indication of the same point is that we often resort to recreational or therapeutic play in order to reduce the tensions and fatigues engendered by leisure-work, just as we resort to play to get over the effects of subsistence-work. On the other hand, there is no intrinsic reason why leisure-work cannot become as pleasurable as play, and the more one enjoys leisuring, the better.

Is leisuring ever admixed with idling? I do not think so. With sleeping in any of its many modes? Not for the most part. The one possible exception is sexual activity. When sexual activity is engaged in as an aspect of human love or friendship, conjugal or otherwise, the aspect of leisuring may be added to its biological utility and to its pleasurable aspect as play. Quite apart from sex, acts of love and friendship are eminent among the modes of leisure activity. While it may be jarring at first to consider love and friendship as forms of leisure-work, it should be remembered that one seldom succeeds in the sphere of love or friendship unless one seriously works at it and unless one learns in the process.

CHAPTER 5

The Five Parts of Life

(1)

I AM now ready to sketch an answer to the question, *How can I make a good life for myself?* If I think of my future as blessed with good fortune and containing ample free time—all of it, except for the hours used up by sleep—I think I can say the following as a matter of common sense.

First, I cannot make a good life for myself if I spend the rest of my time in play and idling and omit leisuring in all its forms.

Second, I cannot make a good life for myself if I devote myself entirely to the pursuits of leisure and eliminate all forms of play and idling.

Third, I cannot make a good life for myself if I idle away too many hours or over-indulge in play, so that little time is left for leisuring—much less than is spent in play or idling.

Fourth, while each of the three types of activity we have been considering must be limited to allow some time for the other two, it remains the case that, within such limitation, one should leisure as much as possible.

Only the fourth point requires a word of further explanation. Play and idling do not contribute to one's personal growth, as leisuring does; if we expanded the amount of time devoted to play and idling and contracted the amount of time devoted to leisuring, we would tend to stunt or stultify ourselves. We would come to the end of our lives not much better men than we are now. Let us imagine, furthermore, that day after day, and month after month, we spent most of our non-sleeping hours in play and idling. In contrast, let us imagine those hours occupied in large part with leisuring, without excluding some play and idling. Which of the two imagined states of affairs would strike any of us as the more repetitious, the more likely to give rise to boredom and *ennui?* Certainly the former.

The foregoing is only the bare beginning of a common-sense answer to the question, *How can I make a good life for myself?* The whole picture will become clearer in the next two chapters, when, removing our provisional assumptions, we consider the role of economically necessary work in human life, its various forms, its relation to leisuring and play, and deal with the problem of what to do about the elements of chance or fortune we must somehow cope with if we are to prevent misfortune from ruining our lives or excessive good fortune from spoiling them. With the five parts of life—the five basic forms of human activity —fully described and seen in relation to one another, we should be able to put them in some order. We should be able to construct a scale of values governing the use of our time which would be a rough plan of life. That will bring us closer to the full answer to our question.

The words I have used to name these five types of activity are employed, as has been pointed out, in a generic or omnibus sense to cover all the diverse modes of each type. The five basic categories or types of activity I have named in this way are idling, sleeping, working, playing, and leisuring. I have now said enough about each to identify it as distinct from all the rest, but I postponed a more complete discussion of subsistence-work until this chapter. In treating it more fully here I shall have more to say about leisure-work and play as well. The only one of these five basic activities that is more like a passivity than an activity is the one I have called idling. I have included it simply because we do elect to spend or kill time that way; all of us have voluntarily idled away many hours of our life. Why? To what purpose? Is it right to kill time? Can we avoid doing it? These are all questions

I will return to later. For the present I will only repeat that idling probably cannot be omitted from the things one does with the time of one's life if one is to make a good life for one's self.

(2)

When we attempt to distinguish the remaining four types of activity from one another, we find that they differ in three significant respects. I touched on these in the preceding chapter, but I think I can make the three points of difference much clearer now.

First, activities differ accordingly as they are compulsory or optional. Among those that are compulsory we must distinguish between generic sleep, on the one hand, a certain minimum of which is absolutely compulsory, and subsistence-work, on the other hand, which is compulsory only under certain circumstances (that is, if we do not have enough wealth to exempt us from working for a living). Even in the case of an absolutely compulsory activity, such as sleep, we can exercise an option with regard to the degree to which we indulge in it, going above or even below the requisite minimum. The distinction between the compulsory and the optional divides sleep and subsistence-work from play and leisure-work. The latter two are entirely optional. With or without wealth, we do not need to engage in them to any degree in order to live—in order to subsist. But if there is more to living than just subsisting, if there is a significant difference between just *living* and *living well,* then even though playing and leisuring are not biologically or economically necessary, they may be necessary in some other sense—as activities we have to engage in in order to live well, or make a good life for ourselves.

I intimated as much at the beginning of this chapter when I said, as a matter of common sense, that playing and leisuring— the latter to a considerable degree—cannot be omitted from the plan for a good life. To omit play in all its forms would be to lead a life devoid of pleasurable experiences, and that can hardly be recommended. To omit leisuring in all its forms would be to lead a life devoid of learning, of self-betterment or self-improvement, of growth in the stature of one's person. Would not the individual leading such a life be a stunted human being at its end, just as much as he would be physically stunted if he stopped growing at the age of six?

Second, activities, compulsory or optional, differ in regard to whether they are done for some extrinsic result to be achieved or done entirely for their own sake. In both cases they aim at some good, but in one case that good lies outside the activity, and in the other it resides in the activity itself. When activities are differentiated in this way, we must add one over-riding qualification. Everything we do can be done for the sake of leading a good life as a whole. In this sense, no activity may be engaged in entirely for its own sake. With this qualification borne in mind, play, in all its pure forms, is the only one of the four major types of activity that we indulge in for its own sake—for the pleasure it gives us during the time we are at play and for no good beyond that except the goodness of a good life.

The other three—sleep, subsistence-work, and leisure-work—always aim at a result that endures beyond the actual time spent in the activity itself. For example, sleep in all its forms aims at health and vigor, to be enjoyed by us not just during the time we are engaged in sleeping, whereas, in contrast, the pleasures we experience in play cease when we stop playing. So, too, subsistence-work aims at wealth, and although its main purpose is to obtain consumable wealth—the means of subsistence—the fact that we consume it does not alter the point being made. The result exists and endures for some time after the activity has been completed. This should be most obvious in the case of leisuring; the change for the better that results from learning or personal growth in any of its myriad forms is a result that endures beyond the time of the activity itself. Even when, as a form of leisuring, we engage in learning solely for the sake of acquiring knowledge and without reference to the further use of that knowledge, the leisuring is for the sake of a result that lies beyond the activity itself—the possession of the knowledge that has been acquired.

When we examine more closely the three activities that, unlike play, we do not engage in for their own sake but rather for an extrinsic result (that is, a result that lies outside the activity itself), we can see that the extrinsic result aimed at may be either immanent or transitive or both. It is an *immanent* result if, like the health we preserve or the knowledge and skill we acquire, it is something that remains *in us*, as a state or property of *our own being*. (In this sense, the pleasure we experience in play is an immanent result, though it is intrinsic to the activity itself rather than extrinsic to it.) In contrast, the result is *transitive* if, like the goods we produce or the services we perform when we engage in subsistence-work, it consists of things or changes that *exist apart from us* or at least *not* as a state or property of our own being.

Sleep, in all its pure forms, always aims at an immanent result. In contrast, subsistence-work, in its pure forms, aims only at a transitive result. Unfortunately, it also produces an immanent result, but one at which we certainly do not aim. While aiming at a good—consumable wealth—subsistence-work usually results in some degree or measure of self-deterioration, and thus is the very opposite of leisure-work, which aims at the good result that it produces—self-improvement. Self-deterioration is one of the most significant characteristics of pure subsistence-work—subsistence-work that is unmixed with leisure or has no aspect of leisure.

Unlike subsistence-work, leisuring sometimes produces only immanent results—studying or thinking when the only result is something known, or when we come to understand what was not understood before. But in many of its forms leisuring produces transitive results as well—a book written, a picture painted, a scientific discovery published, a garden cultivated, a friendship made, a change in the laws, an alteration in a social institution, a candidate for public office elected, and so on.

While sleep in its pure form aims at and produces only immanent results (the goods of health and vigor), and while subsistence-work in its pure form aims only at transitive results that are good (consumable wealth), though it usually produces an immanent result that is not good (self-deterioration), the pure forms of leisuring often aim at and produce both types of result, both of them good (the immanent result of self-improvement and the transitive result of social or cultural goods). But it is not leisuring if it produces *only* transitive results, even if it looks as if it belonged in that category. Teaching certainly looks like a form of leisure, but if in the course of teaching the teacher

FOUR MAIN TYPES OF ACTIVITY AND THEIR RESULTS

	IMMANENT RESULT	INTRINSIC TO ACTIVITY	IMMANENT RESULT	EXTRINSIC TO ACTIVITY	TRANSITIVE RESULT	EXTRINSIC TO ACTIVITY
COMPULSORY						
Absolutely			Health and Vigor	Sleep		
Conditionally					Wealth	Subsistence-work
OPTIONAL	Pleasure	Play	Self-improvement	Leisure-work ↑	(which may or may not also have a transitive result extrinsic to the activity)	

learns nothing and the only result is the transitive result of some change in the students, then that instance of teaching is in no sense leisure. If the teacher is teaching only for the compensation involved, the activity is pure subsistence-work. Other examples come readily to mind in the case of the arts. The artist who uses his skills to produce something he can sell and who, in using those skills, in no way improves himself as an artist is engaged in subsistence-work, not in leisure-work.

Third, activities can be divided into those that aim at results which are *both* immanent and extrinsic to the activity itself, and those that aim at results which are either immanent or extrinsic, but *not* both. By this criterion, sleep and leisure-work in their pure forms differ from both play and subsistence-work in their pure forms. Of the two activities that aim at an extrinsic result that is immanent, sleep produces a better rather than worse condition of the body, and leisure-work produces a better rather than worse state of the human person. Subsistence-work in its pure form aims at an extrinsic result that is always transitive; at the opposite extreme, play in its pure form never aims at a result that is extrinsic to itself. The pleasure it produces is always an immanent result, as well as intrinsic to the activity itself. See the diagram on page 43 for a summary of this.

(3)

I have already called attention to the fact that, in addition to the pure forms of each of the four basic types of activity, we often engage in mixed activities—activities that combine aspects of two or more of the basic types—and also in activities that, while belonging to one category in their pure form, become transformed by wholly assuming the character of a different type of activity. Thus, play may become mixed with sleep when we engage in it not only for the pleasure it provides but also for therapeutic or recreational reasons—the contribution it can make to health and vigor. Similarly, we can eat or drink, bathe or exercise, to a degree that exceeds any real biological need because we seek the pleasure intrinsic to the activity itself, and then activities that retain some aspect of sleep also take on the aspect of play. Sexual activity engaged in *solely* for the pleasure intrinsic to it is an activity that, belonging primarily in the category of sleep, is thus transformed into play. The same is true of excesses in eating and drinking that are of no biological utility, may even be injurious, and yet are found intrinsically pleasant in the process.

The picture becomes more complicated when, in addition to sleep and play, we consider leisure-work and subsistence-work. The period of infancy and childhood provides us with striking examples of mixtures involving leisure-work and subsistence-work. The play of children, unlike that of adults, is often admixed with the aspects of leisure. In fact, insofar as children's toys and games are "educational," the leisure aspect may predominate. The child is learning under the guise of playing. On the other hand, the formal learning in which children engage when they begin school has, unfortunately, the unpleasant aspect of subsistence-work because it is compulsory. Hence the phrase "school work." As a result, we see that the leisure-work of childhood, insofar as it is optional as leisure-work should be, is usually admixed with play, and insofar as it is compulsory, it often feels to the child as subsistence-work feels to the adult—something he would rather not do or do as little as possible.

In adult life, activities that belong primarily in some other category often get transformed into subsistence-work. We have already considered the example of the teacher who learns nothing in the course of teaching and engages in teaching only to earn a living. Here we have an activity, by nature belonging to the category of leisure, transformed entirely into subsistence-work. The same holds for all the so-called learned professions and for the so-called creative arts. The practice of law, medicine, engineering, and perhaps even the ministry, can be transformed in this way. So, too, can the production of literature, music, and paintings, and so can the performing arts. In the same way, activities that by their very nature belong in the category of sleep or play can be transformed into subsistence-work. The professional athlete often performs without pleasure and does not need to perform for the sake of his health. A baseball player may have lost interest in the game, but he will employ his skill as a means of earning a living. A wrestler may no longer take any pleasure in his sport, nor derive from it any benefit to his health.

(4)

I said in Chapter 3 that subsistence-work has many modes. Let us now consider them. In its pure form, subsistence-work consists of any activity we would not engage in at all—not for a moment of our life's time—if we did not have to make a living for ourselves and if the activity in question were not a way of earning the means of subsistence. At this extreme in the spectrum of the modes of subsistence-work, we have what can only be called pure unadulterated drudgery or chores, usually accompanied by feelings of pain and boredom and almost always by the wish to finish as quickly as possible. The only good result of drudgery is the wealth produced for society and the means of subsistence obtained by the individual, whether in the form of money or consumable commodities. But pure subsistence-work, or unadulterated drudgery, as we have seen, also has an immanent result that is not good and is not aimed at—the self-deterioration of the individual doing it. In addition, it may be injurious to his health or seriously deplete his vigor, and it seldom provides him with any pleasure. That is why no one, except under the compulsion of need, would engage in such work, and why those who are forced to engage in it want to do as little of it as possible.

At the opposite extreme, we have that mode of subsistence-work that may not only be intrinsically pleasurable, as play is, but that also produces extrinsic results that are immanent as well as transitive. This is the type of subsistence-work anyone might engage in even if he had enough assured wealth not to have to make a living. At this extreme in the spectrum of the modes of subsistence-work, we have what might be called compensated leisuring, and usually it is leisuring with an aspect of play. The only feature of such work that entitles it to be called subsistence-work is that it involves extrinsic compensation, in the form of money-payments or otherwise. Except for this, it is not subsistence-work at all, but pure leisure or leisure admixed with play, because the individual would do it even if he had all the wealth he needed for himself and his family.

There are many teachers, artists, scientists, professional men of every variety, and officers of government who, under circumstances that relieved them of the necessity of making a living, would go on spending a considerable portion of their time in the exercise of their skills because they enjoy doing so and because, as a result, they achieve some measure of self-improvement and contribute to the improvement of society. Although it is seldom recognized and although there are some who refuse to recognize it, the same is true of business—of commerce and industry. In the hierarchy of tasks that exist in the complex business establishment of an advanced industrial society, some—and, of course, only some—call for activities that contain the aspect of leisure and even of play to so high a degree that individuals who now earn a living by discharging them might continue to discharge them if the need to earn a living were removed.

In between these two extremes, with unmitigated drudgery at one end and extrinsically compensated leisuring at the other, lies the whole spectrum of the modes of subsistence-work, varying according to the proportions in which they mix the aspects of drudgery, leisure, and play. Anyone who holds a job by which he earns compensation, small or large, can place that job at one point or another in the scale of this spectrum by asking himself what aspects of it he would be willing to undertake if he did not need to earn a living. If a job—the job that an individual has or one that he contemplates taking—is more attractive than other jobs, it must be either because of the amount of compensation involved as compared with other jobs or because, given relatively equal amounts of compensation, the subsistence-work is sufficiently admixed with leisure-work and sufficiently exempt from chores or drudgery to make it the kind of job that would be, to some extent, worth undertaking even if one did not have to earn a living.

One further comment is called for. The unqualified benefit that technological advances and automatic machinery of all sorts have conferred upon human life is the elimination of a great deal of drudgery—not only the back-breaking physical tasks that are now taken over by machines more powerful than men, but also the dull, repetitive tasks, such as calculating, book-keeping, and household chores, that machines can do much more quickly and efficiently than human beings. I mention this here not to praise technology, though it certainly deserves our gratitude in this respect. I mention it because it will help us to sharpen the line between subsistence-work in its pure form and leisure-work in its pure form.

Pure subsistence-work is essentially mechanical and, therefore, the kind of work that can be done much better—more quickly and more efficiently—by machines than by men. Its repetitive and non-creative character is precisely what makes it possible for us to build machines to do it. When men do such mechanical work—repetitive and non-creative—day after day, the time they spend in doing it stultifies them and stunts their growth.

In the class-divided societies of the past, the difference between mechanical and creative work divided the pursuits appropriate to the so-called leisure class—the free men and men of property —from the tasks assigned to slaves and artisans. The latter did the sub-human kinds of work we have now been able to build machines to do. It would almost seem to be axiomatic that whatever can be done by machines, or done better by them, should not be done by men, and a corollary would be that the kind of work that machines can do is sub-human and not appropriate for men.

As against pure subsistence-work, pure leisure-work is non-mechanical or creative—the kind of work that machines cannot yet do, even though they sometimes *appear* to do it. In consequence, its effect upon the individual is the very opposite of stultifying. It is not only the kind of work that is most appropriate for men to do, precisely because they are men and not machines, but it is also the kind of work that is its own reward—in the sense that the good immanent result it produces is the improvement or betterment of the individual doing it.

That is why the man who, lacking wealth, is compelled to make a living for himself and is fortunate enough to be able to do so by engaging in pure leisure-work would—or certainly should—continue to carry on the same activity even if he were suddenly to come into a fortune adequate for all his needs. The more a man derives pleasure from doing leisure-work—the more it gives him the immediate satisfactions of play—the better. But whatever those immediate satisfactions, it would still remain leisure-work for him and not become play as long as it produced the lasting result of self-improvement.

CHAPTER 6

What Should One Do About Earning a Living?

(1)

INSTEAD of imagining a life free from the necessity of earning a living, let us deal with the reality that confronts most of us. During some period of our lives, and probably throughout a large part of our years, we have to work for a living. How does this fact affect the general outlines of anyone's plan for making a good life for himself—not *just* a living, even a good living?

In considering a life exempt from the need to work, we have seen that sleep and play should be kept to reasonable minimums. In the case of sleep, only a little more than is necessary, but no more than is useful. More than is useful becomes converted into play—because beyond need and utility, such things as sleeping, eating, and bathing are done only for the pleasure the doing affords. In the case of play, only a modicum over and above what is recreational or therapeutic; although pleasures enrich or enhance a life, the pursuit of them consumes time, and too much time consumed in play leaves too little time for what, upon closer examination, may prove to be more important pursuits.

When the man of common sense says that in the overall economy of our life's time, sleep and play should be kept to reasonable minimums, his common sense leads him to acknowledge that the standard of a reasonable minimum varies with differences in individual make-up, with differences in external circumstances, and above all with differences in age. There can be no hard and fixed rules about the proportion of one's time to be devoted to sleep and play. To say this is not to say that anything goes—that any and every use of one's time is equally reasonable. It is only to say that the standard of a reasonable minimum must be applied by individual judgment in the individual case. When we use the term "playboy" or "wastrel" derogatorily—as most of us do—we are calling attention to the violation of this standard, for no peculiarity of individual temperament or circumstance can condone the excess of consuming all of one's time in sleep, play, and idling. Differences in age do call for different applications of the standard. The amount of time devoted to sleep and play should diminish as one passes from infancy and childhood to youth, and from youth to middle age and full maturity. In the case of sleep, the decrease is owing to a diminution of need (until old age, when one needs more). In the case of play, the reasons are a little more difficult to state, but I can indicate them by saying that the variety of pleasures is not infinite and after we have explored them in our earlier years, and have repeated again and again the experience of those we have enjoyed most, the lure of novelty diminishes and the luster of the repeated pleasure wears off.

(2)

The standard of a reasonable minimum, particularly as applied to play, should be more stringently applied in a life that involves working for a living than in a life that does not. When biologically necessary activities consume about a third of one's time and economically necessary activities consume another third, the remaining third must be more carefully husbanded in order to assure that over-indulgence in play does not reduce leisuring to a negligible quantity or exclude it entirely. Yet, paradoxically, the individual who must earn a living and does so by a mode of subsistence-work that is full of drudgery would seem to have good reasons for resorting to what would otherwise be excesses of sleep and play.

Drudgery is fatiguing and painful. Under such circumstances, the individual has a greater need for sleep and for therapeutic play and his over-riding pursuit of pleasure can be justified as an anodyne for his hours of painful toil. The paradox of this situation lies in the fact that it is the very character of the subsistence-work this individual does—work that involves little or no aspect of leisure—that would appear to justify his using what free time he has left from sleep and work for play rather than for leisure.

As a result, a life that involves a low grade of subsistence-work (work near the drudgery end of the spectrum) tends to become a three-part life, the whole time of which is consumed in sleep, work, and play. If a good life is at least a four-part life, and one that involves as much leisure-work as possible, then the full answer to the question, *How can I make a good life for myself?*, includes the proposition that low grades of subsistence-work should either be avoided entirely or reduced to the minimum, in terms of the number of hours and years that must be spent in it.

Before we look into the implications of this proposition, one point may need to be cleared up. In dealing with the apportionment of one's time to sleep, play, idling, and subsistence-work of a low-grade variety, I have stressed minimums, whereas I have advocated a maximum use of one's free time for leisure-work. This confronts us with a striking contrast between one of the five major activities or parts of life and the other four. Why should four be kept to the minimum that is necessary, useful, or reasonable, while we are urged to devote as much time as possible to the fifth? Why cannot leisuring, like play, idling, drudgery, or sleep, be indulged in to excess?

The answer should be as obvious as it is simple. The only limitation that must be placed upon leisuring is one we have already observed; namely, that it should not occupy the whole of our free time—that reasonable minimums be left for other activities. With such allowances made, one cannot over-indulge in leisuring. No one can ever learn too much. No one can ever know or understand all that he is capable of knowing and understanding. No one can ever attain the full development of his personality. No one can ever reach by personal growth the full stature of which he is capable. No one can ever exhaust his creative resources, no matter how fortunate he is in health and length of life, no matter how much free time he has at his disposal, no matter how prudent he is in limiting the amount of free time he spends in play.

With this point clarified (and it is a point of critical importance in the common-sense answer to our question), let us return to the consideration of what should be done about subsistence-work in a life in which a certain amount of it is, for economic reasons, unavoidable. First, if one has a choice, what kind of subsistence-work should one choose to do in order to make a living for one's self? In view of what has already been said, the ideal is easy to state. Choose an occupation that not only pays a living wage but consists entirely in leisure-work, or else has that character predominantly and so involves little painful drudgery. By a living wage, I mean one that provides more than bare subsistence—more than the bare necessities of life. In addition to providing the necessities, it should enable one to enjoy the amenities—the comforts and conveniences of life. In other words, a decent living. To say this is to say that wealth should serve not only as a means to health and vigor but also as a means to pleasure.

If you are able to choose an occupation that consists entirely in leisure-work, then there is no reason to limit the amount of time you devote to it. It is the kind of work you would do even if you did not need the compensation attached to it. Whatever time is left free by such economically compensated employment can be spent in play as well as in other forms of leisure-work.

If, however, you have to make a second-best choice—taking a job that involves an admixture of drudgery with leisure-work—then there is some point in being concerned about the time the job consumes. There is, in addition, some point in seeking a higher compensation for doing it, in order to speed and prepare for the day when one can retire from it. And to the extent that the job is not pure compensated leisure-work, one should apportion more of one's free time to leisuring rather than to play.

In short, if one has a choice of jobs, one should certainly avoid pure subsistence-work—unmitigated drudgery—and try to take a job that involves as much leisure-work as possible.

With regard to compensation, I have so far said only two things: first, that the compensation should provide a decent living—the amenities of life as well as the necessities; and second, that one should, perhaps, seek more extrinsic compensation (higher pay) in proportion as the job involves less that has the intrinsically rewarding aspect of leisure. This second point involves economic difficulties, for the market value of the work done probably does not justify higher pay, even though it would appear to be reasonable to seek it as compensation for the drudgery involved. This is glaringly true of the jobs at the lower end of the spectrum of subsistence-work. For economic reasons that cannot be lightly dismissed, work that is almost entirely drudgery is usually also at the lower end of the compensation scale.

In other words, assuming for the moment that no one is paid less than a living wage as that has been defined, it would appear to be the case that the market value of the work done is not inversely related to its value for the individual doing it. To say that the highest extrinsic compensation should be allotted to the jobs that involve pure drudgery because the work has no intrinsic value for the individual, or to say that the pay should be lower in proportion as the job has more and more the character of leisure-work, would be to posit a dream-economy that has never existed and may not be possible. Since the economic problem we have just encountered is not one that the individual can solve by himself, let us postpone it until we return later to the complex question of how organized society as a whole should operate—both economically and politically—to facilitate the individual's efforts to make a good life for himself.

(3)

There remains one thing to consider that is a matter of individual choice. Let us suppose that, of two jobs, the one that carries a much higher compensation is humanly less attractive on the grounds that it involves less leisure-work and more drudgery. Which should one choose?

The common-sense answer, I submit, is as follows. Other things being equal (the number of years you would have to devote to both jobs being equal, the provisions for economic security after retirement being equal, and so on), one should choose the job that carries less pay but has greater human value, that is, the one that does more for the worker as a human being.

The reason for this is clearest in the extreme cases and may be very much less clear when the alternatives are less disparate in the incomes and in the human values that attach to the jobs being compared. To perceive the reason, let us consider the following extreme alternatives: on the one hand, a job that has little or no intrinsic value for the individual but yields an income that can buy unlimited luxuries; on the other hand, a job that is self-rewarding to a high degree but yields an income that can buy no luxuries at all—nothing beyond the necessities of life and a moderate amount of its amenities.

If wealth is for the sake of health and a moderate amount of pleasure, if luxuries consist in more than is needed to live and live well, then only a man who does not understand the difference between living and living well, or who does not know what is involved in living well, would choose drudgery for the sake of a very large income. If making a lot of money involves a lot of time and effort devoted to an activity that involves no intrinsic rewards, the better choice would be a job that pays less but is more self-rewarding.

What about the individuals (and there are, unfortunately, many in this position) who have little or no choice with respect to the jobs open to them and who must take jobs that often pay less than a living wage as we have here defined it, jobs that carry little or no intrinsic reward for those who do them? This, once again, raises a problem for society as a whole. If society permits any of its members to be in the situation just described, it may have prevented them from making a good life for themselves; certainly, it has greatly impeded their efforts to do so. Nevertheless, even in a society that has not yet solved this problem, the individual may be left with certain options. He should make whatever efforts he can to obtain higher pay and shorter hours. Even more important is the use such an individual makes of his free time during whatever period, long or short, that he cannot find another type of job. As a result of the pain and tedium of the work he has to do to earn a bare living, he may be sorely tempted to fill the rest of his hours with diverse forms of sleep and play, but he should resist that temptation and counteract the stultifying drudgery of his subsistence-work by a heroic effort to increase his stature as a human being through one or more forms of leisure-work.

This may seem like a hard line to take, but it is necessary to remember that making a good life for one's self is, under normal circumstances, a hard thing to do, and it is an even harder thing to do for the individual who is impeded by abnormal circumstances beyond his own control.

CHAPTER 7

Why Strength of Character Is Needed to Lead a Good Life

(1)

WE must now consider the problem the individual faces when the circumstances of his life are such that he must take into account the effects of both good and bad fortune. Before I suggest how this problem is to be solved, let me clarify its terms.

By fortune, I mean any aspect of our lives that is beyond our own control—the things that happen to us, the accidents that befall us, for good or ill. By bad fortune or misfortune, I mean the accidents or circumstances that are adverse or unfavorable to making a good life for one's self. And by good fortune, I mean the opposite—the accidents or circumstances that are facilitating or favorable.

In an earlier chapter, we saw that a life can be ruined at birth or in infancy or childhood by extreme misfortunes of one kind or another. What is true of these early years is also true of the middle and later years of life. Extreme misfortune can be ruinous. We also saw that an individual can be adversely affected—we sometimes say "spoiled"—in his early years by an excess of good fortune. While this extreme is not likely to be as ruinous if it occurs later, it is still possible for excessive good fortune to be a serious impediment, for it involves highly seductive temptations. The individual who earns a bare subsistence by work that is drudgery is sorely tempted to fill the rest of his hours with diverse forms of sleep and play. At the other extreme, the individual who is surrounded by luxuries or who has the means of obtaining them is also subject to strong temptations that may have as adverse an effect on his life as deprivation has on the life of the unfortunate.

By normal circumstances, then, I mean circumstances that lie in the middle range between the extremes of good and bad fortune. By abnormal circumstances, I mean circumstances that tend toward either of the two extremes, yet fall short of the limiting cases that are so extreme that no individual could be expected to surmount the obstacles they present.

Here, then, is the problem. If it is hard to make a good life for one's self under normal circumstances, and harder still when the circumstances are abnormal, what resources do we have within ourselves to cope with the extremes of good and bad fortune, as long as they are not so extreme as to be beyond anyone's power to cope with them?

I do not claim that common sense can offer a satisfactory solution to this problem. What it does have to say will certainly be relevant, and may be satisfactory as far as it goes. If it does not go far enough, that will be because what it recommends is easier to understand than to accomplish.

(2)

Let me deal with bad fortune first—the things that can happen to us which are adverse or unfavorable to our effort to make a good life for ourselves. These include such things as protracted ill-health or disability; the inability to make or get a decent living through no fault of one's own; serious personal injuries suffered at the hands of other men or imposed by organized society as a whole; the loss of one's friends or loved ones and, for that reason or any other, loneliness; the effects upon one's own life of war, or of civil disorder and violence; and, last but not least, the effects upon one's self of a culture that, by its scale of values—the things it esteems and dis-esteems—is inimical to one's making and carrying out a plan of life that so orders its component activities or parts that a good life will result.

I have omitted from this list the misfortunes of birth, infancy, and childhood because they occur before the individual begins to cope with the problems they create for him—such things as deficient schooling, a deficient home environment, inferior native endowments, and other deprivations. However, they, too, can and should be considered, but only with the proviso that they, like the unfortunate circumstances that may occur in later years, are not so extreme as to be unsurmountable.

How can the individual cope with bad fortune? The common-sense answer is, in a word, by strength of character. The Latin word for this is "fortitudo"—in English, "fortitude." It simply means having the moral strength or will-power to overcome adversities of all sorts. There are two reasons for calling fortitude or strength of character "moral" rather than "physical." One's physical strength is, for the most part, a natural endowment, and although the individual can, perhaps, enhance it a little, it is not something he can attain entirely by choice or effort on his part. In contrast, moral strength belongs in the sphere of things that can be acquired by individual initiative and effort. The second and deeper reason for calling fortitude "moral strength" lies in the use to which it is put. It has the moral connotation carried by the word "virtue" only when the individual exercises his will-power to overcome obstacles that stand in the way of his making a good life for himself.

It is conceivable—more than conceivable, it is unfortunately only too familiar to us—that a man may have the strength to overcome obstacles that stand in the way of his success, where what he is aiming at is not a good life, but a bad one—a life of crime, a life of ease and idleness, the life of a playboy, a life filled with luxuries to the exclusion of other goods, and so on. He would appear to have the same kind of will-power or strength of character that is possessed by the man who, aiming at a good life for himself, is not deflected from that goal by adversities. If, as a matter of common sense, we would not consider such a man virtuous or a man of good moral character, that is because of the end at which he aims and the use to which he puts his inner resources when confronted with obstacles in his way. The will-power he manifests may *look like* the strength of character exercised by the man who is striving to make a good life for himself, but because it is not directed to the same end, it does not have the same moral quality. It is a counterfeit of the fortitude that is an element of good moral character or an aspect of virtue.

Whether or not fortitude is indispensable to making a good life for one's self depends on whether any human life is ever, during its course, totally exempt from serious adversities. If not, as common sense and common experience would testify, then some degree of fortitude would seem to be a necessary ingredient in the process, for it to succeed.

This answer is satisfactory as far as it goes, but it does not go far enough. Common sense does not tell us how to develop the degree of fortitude required for the adversities we may encounter. No one knows enough about how a good moral character is formed to be of much help to anyone needing guidance in this respect—parents, preceptors, or the individual himself who, having understood why fortitude is desirable, seeks to develop it. The result, of course, is a profoundly unsatisfactory state of affairs, but no one, to my knowledge, has found a remedy for it.

(3)

Let us turn now to the other side of the picture, in which we see the individual beset by an excess of good fortune, an excess that is bad because of the solicitations and seductions it engenders—temptations to make it easy to waste time, to over-indulge in the pleasures of the passing moment, to luxuriate in extravagances of all sorts, in short, to have a good time from day to day rather than make the effort, often difficult and sometimes painful, to lead a good life. How can the individual who understands the difference between a good time and a good life and who makes the latter, not the former, the goal of his efforts —how can such an individual cope with the excess of goods that fortune sometimes bestows?

The answer common sense offers is the same as before— strength of character or will-power. Only now the relevant aspect of a good moral character has, in everyday parlance, a different name—not fortitude, but temperance or self-control. In everyday speech, we call a man temperate when he is able to restrain himself from over-indulgence in pleasures of one sort or another, or when he can avoid excess in the acquisition of things that, while genuinely good, are good only in moderation. (Thus, it would take a temperate man to turn down the job that offered a very large income but involved little or no leisure in the work to be done.)

Temperance is not asceticism, not in the least. It does not eschew the pleasures of life; it does not despise the gratifications of play; it does seek to pare life down to its bare necessities, so that all the time left free from obtaining them can be sedulously devoted to personal betterment. Based on the common-sense truism that you can often have too much of a good thing, temperance consists in the will-power to resist the kind of good fortune that makes an excess of such goods available. Like fortitude, it is strength of character, and like fortitude it is an element of good moral character or an aspect of virtue only when it is developed and exercised for the sake of leading a good life, and for no other reason. As two related aspects of virtue, both of them giving a man the moral strength he needs to lead a good life, fortitude and temperance differ in that the one is a settled disposition or attitude toward adversities, difficulties, or pains, and the other is a settled disposition or attitude toward excesses of the opposite kind—toward blessings, facilities, or pleasures.

The same reason that makes fortitude indispensable applies in the case of temperance, though perhaps less obviously because the excesses of good fortune do not seem to afflict every human life, as serious adversities do. Yet no human life is free from the seductions of pleasure or from the temptation to substitute having a good time for what is much harder—leading a good life. As the Roman emperor and Stoic philosopher Marcus Aurelius observed, it is difficult but not impossible "to live well even in a palace."

To this, first of all, must be added the observation that even apart from the extremes of good or bad fortune, we need strength of character—we need fortitude and temperance—to carry out a plan for our whole life, precisely because that plan requires us always to weigh the interests of the moment against the interests of our life as a whole. The temptations of a good time, of pleasure in the passing moment, are great. It is so easy to want more wealth than we need. It is so easy to shirk or wish to avoid the pain and effort involved in doing leisure-work. What is required to make the moral choices we ought to make in order to work for the end we ought to seek—a whole life that is really good because it involves all the things that are really good for a man, all of them in the right order and proportion—is *moral virtue*, which is nothing but a habitual disposition to prefer a good life to a good time, to choose what is really good in the long run over what is apparently good here and now.

Insofar as all pleasures are things of the moment, they have an immediacy and vividness of appeal that give them great force in competition *against* the wish to make our whole life good—a goal not only remote, but one we can never actually experience or enjoy as we can the pleasures of the moment. Even if the circumstances of the individual's life are normal rather than abnormal, he still needs the strength of character that is temperance to forego or limit immediate pleasures for the sake of a greater though remote and ineluctable good—the good of his whole life. On the other hand, sleep, play, and idling are easy, while serious leisure-work is hard, and often painful and fatiguing. Since the plan for a good life calls for the employment of one's free time in as much leisure-work as is consonant with having a reasonable minimum of idling, play, and sleep, the strength of character that is fortitude is needed to endure the pains or difficulties that may be attendant on making a good life instead of just having a good time from day to day.

A second additional consideration concerns the bearing of the pathological weaknesses of mind or character that we call mental illness. Irremediable organic infirmity or disease can be so disabling as to constitute an insuperable obstacle to making a good life; the same is true of incurable mental illness—the types of insanity that require hospitalization and usually receive forms of treatment that fall short of restoring the patient to normal life. But those of us who are not so unfortunate may, nevertheless, be subject to neurotic disorders that tend to incapacitate us from making the choices a virtuous man would make. We may not be able to acquire or exercise the will-power or self-control that is requisite for choosing one course of action rather than another in order to make a good life for ourselves. The remedy is medical, not moral. What is called for is the recommendation of some form of psychotherapy, not hortatory remarks about virtue or a good moral character. Some of us need help to overcome neurotic tendencies that may prevent us from being or, at least, make it more difficult for us to become, masters of our own lives.

But when the medical problem is solved, the moral problem remains. The removal by therapy of an incapacitation for making the right choices does not automatically confer the power of making them. The person who has been cured of a disabling neurotic disorder is in exactly the same boat as the rarely fortunate individual who grows up without being subject to such disabilities. Each must somehow acquire and exercise virtue—will-power, self-control, strength of character—to choose what is really good for himself in the long run as against what is only apparently good from day to day.

In the third place, it must be added that the inner resources required by the individual for making a good life for himself include more than strength of character—more than temperance and fortitude. Common sense recognizes the indispensability of another power or disposition—usually called "sound judgment" and sometimes "prudence." This is a disposition of mind rather than of character. Action always takes place under particular circumstances, and insofar as it is voluntary and involves choice, the relative merits of particular alternatives must be judged—judged not only for their immediate value but also for their value in the long run of a whole life. Sound judgment is required for weighing the merits of competing alternatives not only in terms of what they offer in the way of gratification here and now but also in terms of long-range consequence as against present gratifications.

Finally, let it be said, as emphatically as possible, that these dispositions of character and of mind, which are virtuous insofar as they are employed in making a good life, cannot be formulated in rules or guidelines for action. If the exercise of virtue consisted in putting a set of rules into practice, then virtue could be taught and learned, as any art can be taught and learned by putting its rules into practice. But that, as we have seen, is not the case. In this most fundamental respect, making a good life for one's self is radically unlike all the arts, in which rules can be formulated to guide the practitioner. Not so in the business of living. A plan is needed, yes, and that is the point of resemblance between making a good life and turning out a good work of art; but there the resemblance ends, for in the arts there are rules of technique and procedure for carrying out the plan, whereas in making a good life, the virtue requisite for carrying out one's plan takes the place of rules. I will have much more to say on this point in Chapter 18.

Part Two

Defending Common Sense Against the Objections of the Philosophers

CHAPTER 8

The Philosophical Objections Stated

(1)

Anyone who is at all acquainted with the prevailing currents of philosophical thought, at least in England and the United States, will already have anticipated the critical response of professional philosophers to the common-sense answer that has been developed in Part One. He will also probably be aware that the reasons for their adverse reaction are manifold.

The common-sense answer has employed words that everyone uses in everyday speech, without much thought or reflection but, nevertheless, without any serious misgivings about their intelligibility and validity. In the exposition of the common-sense answer, it has been said (1) that a *good* life is possible, that there is a difference between just living and living *well*, and that the latter is *preferable* or better; (2) that the *improvement* or *betterment* of the individual person is an essential ingredient in his making a *good* life for himself; (3) that making a *good* life for one's self is *better than* or *to be preferred to* having a *good* time from day to day; (4) that affecting an individual's life but beyond his own control are *good* fortune and *bad* fortune, or *misfortune;* (5) that freedom is *good* and slavery *bad*, because the one is an indispensable means, and the other is an insuperable obstacle, to making a good life; (6) that each of the basic activities in which the individual can engage aims at some *good:* sleep, at *health;* subsistence-work, at *wealth;* play, at *pleasure;* leisure-work, at *personal growth*, including the acquisition of *knowledge* and *friendship;* and that health is *better* than illness; wealth, *better* than poverty; having pleasure, *better* than its deprivation; personal growth, *better* than stultification; knowledge, *better* than ignorance; friendship, *better* than loneliness; (7) that among the basic activities, there is an *order* or *scale* of values, with leisure-work of *paramount worth*, with moderation required in sleep, play, and idling, because, while good, they are *not good* when indulged in beyond reasonable minimums; with the recommendation to spend as little time as possible in the drudgery of *low-grade* subsistence-work, and as much time as possible in the diverse forms of leisure-work; and also with the recommendation that it is *better* to earn less money by work that is intrinsically rewarding than more money by work that is less rewarding or not rewarding at all; (8) that making a good life for one's self requires inner resources, such as the strength of a *good* moral character, consisting mainly in two aspects of moral *virtue*, fortitude and temperance; and (9) that making a good life also requires a virtue or *good* disposition of the mind—*sound* judgment or prudence.

All the words or phrases I have italicized and stressed in this summary of the common-sense answer are red flags to the contemporary philosophers who have become experts in challenging common-sense discourse, experts in suspecting that common sense does not understand what it is saying or know what it is talking about. All these words or phrases are terms of value, not of fact. This immediately raises a problem of which common sense appears to be blithely innocent—the problem of what verifiable meaning can be attached to such terms. In addition, these words or phrases have been used by common sense to express judgments—judgments that some things are good, and some bad; some better than others and to be preferred; some so bad that they are to be avoided at all costs.

These are all value-judgments or statements of value, not statements of fact that attempt to describe things as they are. Such judgments raise many thorny problems for the philosopher, none of which common sense seems to have in mind when it expresses its evaluation of the things or factors that must be considered in making a good life. Do value judgments have any objective validity at all? Can they all be reduced to statements of fact? What is the relation between fact and value? Can values be defined in terms of facts, and can value judgments be based on matters of fact?

(2)

From the critical philosopher's point of view, common sense compounded the difficulties into which it unwittingly stumbled by explicitly using such words as "should" and "ought" or by implying their use in assertions to the effect that one thing *is to be preferred* to another.

Common sense cannot defend itself from this charge by pointing out that it asked only, *How can one make a good life for one's self?* True, it began with that question, and if it had resolutely stuck to it, the question might have remained hypothetical, in the form: "*If* anyone wants to make a good life for himself, how should he go about it?" In that form, the "should" raises no greater difficulties than the "should" in the question, "*If* anyone wants to bake an angel-food cake, how should he go about it?" Such questions are asked and answered all the time without provoking any special concern on the philosopher's part. They are really questions of fact about what means are effective to achieve a certain result, a result that, as a matter of fact, you *may* or *may not* wish to achieve.

But common sense was not content to leave its original question in this hypothetical form. In the course of trying to answer that original question, it soon became evident that common sense was implying or declaring that everyone *should* or *ought* to try to make a good life for himself, because leading a good life is better than having a good time, and so on. And having said categorically, not hypothetically, that a good life *ought* to be everyone's ultimate objective, common sense then proceeded to answer its original question (in the form of "How can one . . . ?") by laying down a whole series of judgments about what one ought to do or ought not to do in order to achieve the objective that one ought to aim at.

These, the philosopher is quick to point out, are normative

judgments, prescriptive of how men should behave, not descriptive of how in fact they do behave. Furthermore, they are made categorically, not in the hypothetical form in which they are manageable. Can common sense explain the relation between its value judgments and its normative judgments? Can common sense defend its normative judgments? Can it set forth the grounds on which they are made categorically? Can it establish their validity?

<h1 style="text-align:center">(3)</h1>

Even though he has used all these value terms, even though he has made so many value judgments, and even though he has categorically declared that an individual ought to try to make a good life for himself, and that he ought or ought not to do this or that to accomplish it, the man of common sense might still side-step or avoid all these barbs and arrows of philosophical criticism, if he were willing to concede that he was voicing only his own opinions, opinions that may, perhaps, be shared by other fellows like himself—other men of common sense untutored in contemporary philosophy.

Unfortunately, the man of common sense often makes contrary claims, especially if he has not had a college education and has not been intimidated by courses in sociology and anthropology, which teach the relativity of values and the mores, or by courses in moral philosophy that concentrate almost exclusively on what are called "meta-ethical" considerations, concerned with an examination of the language and logic of moral discourse, seldom with the problems that concern those who engage in such discourse, and almost never with the problem of using one's time to make a good life for one's self. In any case, I am quite willing to make certain claims for the common-sense answer, because as a philosopher as well as, I hope, a man of common sense, I have not been intimidated by the meta-ethics of the last sixty or seventy years, nor am I deterred by the moral relativism and skepticism of the social sciences.

I think the following claims, that even an educated man of common sense would have unhesitatingly made a century ago, can all be defended—and defended with every philosophical objection in mind: (1) that the common-sense answer is knowledge, not opinion, knowledge as objective as the knowledge we have in the empirical sciences, and with a validity as open to inspection; (2) that being objective knowledge, rather than private or personal opinion, the common-sense answer applies to all men at all times and places, not just to men living under the influence of a certain set of cultural circumstances; (3) that the knowledge includes knowledge of values as well as knowledge of facts, and is expressed in *true* normative judgments as well as *true* statements of fact; (4) that the value judgments and the normative prescriptions involved, though related to statements of fact and descriptive statements, cannot be reduced to the latter, nor wholly derived from the latter; and (5) that these judgments of value and normative prescriptions have a truth of their own, a truth that is not the same kind of truth that is to be found and tested in statements of fact or descriptive statements, yet nevertheless is a kind of truth that can be tested by reference to appropriate criteria. [1]

(4)

Against such claims, contemporary philosophers, especially those devoted to meta-ethics, but others as well, such as the existentialists and the empiricists in ethics, raise a number of objections—objections that, with two exceptions, have already been indicated. These objections—again with the exceptions noted —come from schools of thought that go by such names as "ethical naturalism," "ethical intuitionism," "utilitarianism," "hedonism," and all the varieties of "non-cognitive" doctrines—ethical skepticism, relativism, subjectivism, emotivism, prescriptivism, and existentialism. [2]

Since these schools of thought do not agree with one another, the criticisms leveled against the claims I have made for the common-sense answer do not form a coherent and consistent set of objections. Nevertheless, my defense of common sense will attempt to answer all of these objections. In doing so, I will necessarily find myself in partial agreement with one contemporary school of thought as against others with which it disagrees, but never wholly in agreement with any of them. In other words, each speaks some truth that can be saved when it is disentangled from the errors or mistakes that surround it, and all these partial truths, when put together and supplemented by some truths that are not to be found anywhere in contemporary thought, will constitute the truth of the ethical doctrine I hope will emerge from my defense of the common-sense answer.

The three disparate objections already indicated are as follows. (1) All value judgments and normative prescriptions can be reduced to statements of fact and descriptive statements, and as such their truth is nothing but the truth of the latter. (2) It is impossible to derive basic values or norms from observable facts. They in no way depend on facts, nor are they grounded in human experience, but must be intuitively known, and as so known, their truth can be known with certitude. (3) Statements of value or normative judgments do not constitute knowledge in any sense of that term, nor can they have any kind of truth, since the only kinds of truth are those to be found in the analytic, non-empirical statements of mathematics and logic, and in the synthetic or empirical statements of science, which are descriptive, not evaluative, prescriptive, or normative. Of these three objections, the first and the second are diametrically opposed. The third is also opposed to the second and, in different interpretations, may or may not be compatible with the first.

Finally, we come to two objections not yet mentioned. The first, and most important, of these is one that would come from the school of philosophers who are sometimes called "intuitionists" (because they claim an absolute autonomy for moral philosophy, based on its complete independence of empirical knowledge) and sometimes "deontologists" (because they hold that moral philosophy should concern itself exclusively with categorical obligations or duties). It is not the common-sense answer that this school of philosophers would reject, but the common-sense question itself. These philosophers maintain that we should not be concerned with making good lives for ourselves, but with doing our duty toward other men and toward society. If we have any duty toward ourselves, it consists in an obligation to achieve self-perfection through conforming our will to the moral law, not in an obligation to try to make a good life for ourselves. Even if the common-sense solution to the problem of making a good life were sound and defensible against other philosophical objections, it would leave all the central questions of moral philosophy untouched. In concentrating on what is good and bad for the individual, that is, what is desirable and undesirable from his point of view, in the light of what we know about the consequences of pursuing one or another course of action, common sense ignores what is right and wrong as a matter of strict duty—right and wrong without regard to human desires and without reference to the foreseeable consequences of action.

Along with this objection goes one other that has not been mentioned. It comes from the opposite corner of the philosophical lot—from the act-utilitarians and the rule-utilitarians. While these philosophers reject the notion of duty and moral obligation as proposed by deontologists, they make much of the criteria by which one can judge the goodness or badness, the rightness, or wrongness, either of particular human acts or of rules that can be formulated for guiding human conduct.

What they would find wanting in the common-sense answer are such criteria for making moral judgments. They would also object to the fact that the common-sense answer offers only a general plan of action, but no specific rules of conduct. Deficient in these respects, it can hardly be adequate as an ethical doctrine or moral philosophy. Furthermore, the utilitarians are concerned with an individual's conduct in relation to the good of other men and the good of the community in which he lives, not just in relation to his achieving a good life for himself. In their view, the greatest good for the greatest number takes precedence over the good of the individual, and while they would not reject the problem of the good life for the individual, as the deontologists do, they, like the deontologists, would criticize the common-sense answer, as given so far, for apparently ignoring the relation of the individual to his fellow-men and to society.

(5)

I will try to deal with these objections, and with others that may emerge, in the remaining chapters of Part Two. [3] It will be helpful to observe that these objections or criticisms are of two kinds.

On the one hand, there are what I will call the *formal* objections, as distinct from the *substantive* ones. I have elsewhere distinguished between first-order considerations in moral philosophy, concerning what ought to be sought or ought to be done, and second-order considerations concerning the logical or linguistic aspects of moral discourse about what ought to be sought or ought to be done. [4] It is the latter to which the name "meta-ethics" is now applied. Criticism of the common-sense view that challenges the meaning of its value-terms or the validity and basis of its normative judgments—its ought-statements—constitute formal objections.

On the other hand, there are what I call the *substantive* objections or criticisms. These all arise from first-order considerations and are raised by moral philosophers who find the common-sense view wrong or inadequate in one respect or another. They are, as we have seen, mainly concerned with the apparent omission from the common-sense view of any consideration of the individual's duties or moral obligations toward others. Attention seems to have been paid exclusively to what is good or bad for the individual; what is right and wrong for him to do with respect to others seems to have been neglected.

With regard to both the formal and the substantive criticisms, I would like to make one preliminary observation that may come as a surprise to some readers or may appear to be an extravagant claim on my part. It is that all the formal objections we shall consider—whether applied to the common-sense view or to traditional moral philosophy—were answered long before they were made. When I say they were "answered," I mean that the errors or mistakes charged were not in fact made or that the points in question had been handled in such a way as to make the objections untenable. Had these things been known, the objections need not have been raised.

Why, then, were they raised? The only possible answer, I submit, is that the philosophers of this century who have filled their journals and their books with "meta-ethics" proceeded in what can only be called an amazing ignorance of insights and analyses that existed in earlier centuries of Western thought, especially second-order considerations of what, logically and linguistically, is involved in thinking about moral problems, or for that matter in thinking about anything. I leave it to the reader to judge for himself whether "meta-ethics," like so many of the other things that twentieth-century thinkers claim to have invented, is not merely a new name for something quite old—the reflexive self-examination of their own language and logic, in which philosophers have engaged from the beginning. [5]

Because of the point just made, I regard the substantive objections we shall consider to be more serious and penetrating than the formal ones. In dealing with the formal criticisms, I will be giving philosophical precision to the common-sense answer. But in replying to the substantive objections, I will be doing more than that; I will be developing it philosophically and, I hope, deepening it.

CHAPTER 9

The End We Seek Can Be Ultimate
Without Being Terminal

(1)

THE two formal or meta-ethical criticisms I shall deal with in this chapter and the next are both concerned with the relation of fact and value.

Although there are many terms in which human beings express their evaluation of things, "good" and "bad" are the archetypical value terms. All other evaluative adjectives are variations on or derivatives from these two. For brevity and simplicity, I will confine our attention to the meaning of these two basic value terms as they relate to matters of fact.

What I have just said does not apply to the words "ought" or "should." These are not adjectives; they are the operative verbs in prescriptions or what are called "normative" as opposed to "descriptive" judgments—"ought-statements" as opposed to "is-statements." "Ought" and "ought not" are the other two fundamental or archetypical terms we shall have to deal with. But it will be easier to deal with them after we have clarified the meanings of "good" and "bad," for then we shall see that *ought* and *ought not* are strictly correlative with only one of the two basic meanings of *good* and *bad* and totally irrelevant to the other. [1]

Of the two formal theses that have a critical impact on the common-sense view, the first is associated with the naturalistic or empiricist approach to moral philosophy and the second with the repudiation of naturalism and empiricism. The first thesis is that all evaluations are reducible to describable facts—that, for example, whenever we call something good or bad, these words serve as short-hand for a state of facts that can be reported or described. Although this is the position of the philosophical school that goes by the name of "ethical naturalism" or "ethical empiricism," it might be more appropriately called "ethical reductionism," since it holds that whatever can be *validly* said in discourse that uses terms of value or makes moral judgments can be *reductively* equated to what we know about the *nature* of things through our *empirical* sciences or through other *empirical* knowledge. It denies that moral philosophy is even a relatively autonomous discipline that has principles of its own.

The second formal thesis is expressed in the proposition that the good is indefinable. This not only (1) excludes the possibility of defining good and bad by reference to the describable properties of observable natural things or processes; it also (2) excludes the possibility of defining good and bad by reference to unobservable or trans-empirical entities. Of the two foregoing points, only the first involves the repudiation of naturalism and empiricism in ethics; neglect of the second point has resulted in the adoption of a misleading name for the logical mistake made by those who attempt to define an indefinable predicate, such as good, whether they attempt to do so in naturalistic or in non-naturalistic terms. Although G. E. Moore, who called this logical mistake the "naturalistic fallacy," explicitly noted the inaccuracy of that name for the error he is often credited with discovering, the name has, unfortunately, stuck and has been the source of misunderstandings and embarrassments in the controversy he provoked. [2]

If statements of value and normative judgments can all be reduced to statements of fact and descriptive judgments, as the naturalists and empiricists in ethics claim, then it follows, as we have seen, that moral philosophy has no principles of its own and so has no autonomy whatsoever as a discipline. The opposite view—that ethics does have independence as a discipline, either an autonomy that is relative or one that is absolute—is advanced by those who maintain, as Moore does, that the good is indefinable, and also by those who go beyond Moore in maintaining that the fundamental principles of ethics (concerning right and wrong conduct and our unconditional duties or obligations) are known to be true not only without any dependence on empirical evidence, but also without rational demonstration. It is for this reason that they are often grouped together as "intuitionists," though it must be noted, in fairness to Moore, that this grouping overlooks the fact that such writers as Carritt, Ross, and Pritchard take the more extreme view that ethics is absolutely autonomous, whereas Moore thinks it has only a relative autonomy—not all its propositions are independent of empirical evidence or unsusceptible to proof, but just those that involve the indefinable predicate *good*. [3]

In this chapter, we shall be concerned only with the reductionism of the naturalists or empiricists in ethics; in the next chapter, we will deal with the indefinability of the good and with the mis-named naturalistic fallacy. Being incompatible with one another, the position of the naturalists and that of the anti-naturalists cannot both be true; but since they are not contradictory and do not exhaust the alternatives, they can both be false. I am going to try to show that both are wrong, each for a different reason, because each goes to an opposite extreme, extremes that can be avoided and were avoided in earlier centuries. No moral philosopher of note prior to the eighteenth century claimed absolute autonomy for ethics; none prior to the nineteenth century attempted to reduce all statements of value to statements of fact, or normative judgments to descriptive propositions.

(2)

Can we defend the distinction between statements of fact and statements of value, and are the latter irreducible to the former?

Waiving for the moment the point at issue (whether statements of value are completely reducible to statements of fact), let me first explain how these two kinds of statements *appear* to differ. On the one hand, a statement of fact is one that asserts that something *is* or *is not*, or asserts that it has certain observable properties, that it behaves in certain observable ways, that it stands in certain observable relations to other things; and it may even take the form of an explanation of the facts described by positing the existence and operation of non-observable entities. On the other hand, a statement of value is one that asserts that something that exists, or some property that it has, or something that it does, or something that has happened or will happen, is good or bad. And the *apparent* difference of such statements from statements of fact is that the words "good" and "bad" do not designate *observable* properties or attributes of existent things or processes. Goodness and badness are not matters of observable fact. When we say that something looks or sounds good to us, we do not mean that we see or hear its goodness with our eyes or ears, but rather that what we do see or hear is something we appraise as good.

What has just been said about statements of fact and statements of value can be expanded to include descriptive and normative statements—is-statements and ought-statements. These certainly *appear* to be formally different: To describe the way things are is one thing; to prescribe how they ought to be is quite another. Applied to human conduct, it appears to make all the difference in the world whether one says how men do in fact behave or how they *should* or *ought* to behave. This *apparent* difference is made much of by those who deny that normative judgments or ought-statements can have objective truth; such truth, in their opinion, can be found only in descriptive propositions or is-statements. I will return to this point in Chapter 13. I mention it here only to clarify the *apparent* difference between fact and value, between descriptive statements and normative statements.

The naturalist in ethics unhesitatingly concedes the *apparent* differences that have just been pointed out, including the one concerning the attribution of objective truth or falsity exclusively to statements of fact or descriptive statements; but he contends —and this is his central contention—that the differences are *only* apparent and without significance, for upon examination it can be shown that every statement of value or normative judgment can be reduced to a statement of fact or descriptive judgment. What truth there is in statements of value or normative judgments is ultimately descriptive truth—truth about matters of fact.

How is this reduction accomplished? I submit that it can be accomplished only in the following two ways.

(1) The first consists in equating the good with the useful, and the better with the more useful. A thing is called good if it serves as a means to some desired end; one thing is better than another if it is a more efficient means. The relation of one thing to another as a means to an end is reducible to a cause-and-effect relationship, or at least to an observable sequence in which the first is seen as leading to the second or resulting in it. When we say that X is good, we are saying something that is subject to empirical observation and testing; namely, that in fact X serves as a means to or results in Y—a state of affairs that we think is good. One further step must be taken by those who claim all values can be reduced to matters of fact. They must argue that everything that is called "good" is so called because it is a means to something else or useful in reaching some result beyond itself. Nothing can ever be called good in itself, good simply as an end and not as a means to anything else, good without being in any way useful. [4] Thus, when we say that X is good because it results in Y and then describe Y as a state of affairs that we also think is good, we must be calling Y good in the same way that we called X good, because it in turn is a means to Z, as X was a means to Y. And if any question is asked about the goodness of Z, we must answer it in the same way that we previously answered the question about the goodness of Y and of X, and so on *ad infinitum*, for there is nothing that can be called good in itself or good simply as an end.

(2) What we have just seen is how the naturalist reduces statements of value to statements of fact. We must now see how he reduces normative judgments or ought-statements to descriptive judgments or is-statements. The principle of reduction is very much the same. The first mode of reduction equated the good with the useful and asserted that nothing can be called good except as a means. The second mode of reduction converts all ought-statements into hypothetical statements. Just as the first mode of reduction rested on the denial that anything can validly be called good simply as an end, so the second mode of reduction rests on the denial that there are any valid categorical ought-statements.

A hypothetical ought-statement always takes the following generic form: "*If* you want Y, *then* you ought to do X." There are many species of this generic form: the hypothetical *penal* ought: if you want to avoid the sanctions imposed by the law, then you ought to behave in conformity with it; the hypothetical *approbative* ought: if you want the approval of your fellow-men or of your community, then you ought not to behave in a certain fashion; the hypothetical *technological* or *artistic* ought: if you want to produce a certain result, then you ought to take the following measures; the hypothetical *pragmatic* ought: if you want to make a good life for yourself, then you ought to do this or that in order to achieve it.

I have mentioned these sub-forms of the hypothetical ought-statement to indicate that unlike is-statements which express the kind of knowledge that can be called "know-that," these hypothetical ought-statements express a kind of knowledge that can be called "know-how." We can see at once that know-how is purely factual knowledge, as much as descriptive know-that is. Know-how consists in knowing what steps to take, what means to employ, in order to achieve or avoid a particular result. [5] Thus we see that the second mode of reduction also turns all ought-statements into statements of fact by making all of them hypothetical. If the condition precedent that constitutes the hypothetical part of the statement is questioned, the reduction is simply carried one step further. You may in fact want Y, but *should* you? *Ought* you to want Y, which is the condition given for asserting that you ought to want X as a way of getting it? The only answer admitted by the naturalists is that, *if* in fact you do want Z, and if in fact Y is a way of getting Z, then and only then ought you to want Y.

(3)

If the foregoing contentions were tenable, the ethical naturalist would be right in maintaining that all statements of value can be reduced to statements of fact and all normative or ought-judgments to descriptive or is-statements. But that is not the case, for two reasons.

First, because there is at least one end that is not a means to anything beyond itself. That is the end posited in the question that common sense has tried to answer, *How can we make a good life for ourselves?* Whether or not the common-sense answer is true or adequate, the question remains a thoroughly intelligible question, and it asks about something that is good as an end, not as a means. When we say of a whole life that it is good, we cannot be saying that it is good as a means to anything else. Unless the naturalist dismisses the question about a good life as meaningless—which in fact he does not and which, without begging the question, he cannot—the meaning of "good" in the phrase "good life as a whole" cannot be reduced to a matter of fact because a whole life cannot be called "good" as a means to be used for anything beyond itself. But the naturalist may still say: "*If* you want to make a good life for yourself, *then* everything you do in the course of it can be regarded as useful to that end and, therefore, good only as a means." Whether it really is or not is always a question of fact.

This brings us to the second reason for saying that the reductionism of the naturalist is untenable. It would be tenable only if it could *not* be said, *categorically*, that I ought to make a good life for myself. Were that the case, then either an individual does or does not in fact *want* to make a good life for himself, and only if *in fact* he does, do hypothetical oughts follow. The only residual difficulty the naturalist might then have to slough off is the inexplicable meaning of "good" when it is said of a whole life. That residual difficulty would, in my judgment, be a serious stumbling block for him. In addition, I think I shall be able to show that it can be said *categorically* that one ought to seek that which is really good for himself. We will see that this is self-evidently true when, in Chapter 10, we understand the distinction between the real and the apparent good. With that clear, I hope to show, in Chapter 11, that the meaning of "good" when said of a whole life is not inexplicable, as it must always remain for the naturalists.

(4)

Before I leave ethical naturalism, let me explain the misunderstanding that lies at its root, a misunderstanding that need not have occurred if the work of earlier philosophers had been more carefully studied.

This misunderstanding is most explicit in the writings of John Dewey, in the chapter on moral conceptions in *Reconstruction in Philosophy* and in his major work, *Human Nature and Conduct*, the very title of which bespeaks the essence of naturalism. That book, by the way, is concerned with the problem of leading a good life, and its attempt to solve the problem by reference to the facts about human nature is quite sound in general and in many of its details. But throughout that book, as well as in his earlier writings, Dewey wages an unremitting attack on the notion of what he calls "fixed ends" or "ultimate ends"—ends that are not themselves means to further ends. [6]

If, by an end, one must always mean a *terminal end*, an end that can be fully attained at a given moment in time, and an end in which the person seeking it can come fully to rest and say of that moment, as Mephistopheles promised Faust he would be able to say, "Stay, thou art so fair!"—if this were the case, then Dewey would be completely right, because there are no terminal ends in this life. This life's only termination is in death.

However, long before Dewey struggled with this matter, philosophers had distinguished between two senses in which an end can be called "ultimate"—*terminally*, in the sense just described, and *normatively*. An end is a final or ultimate end in a purely normative sense of ultimate *if* (a) it is a *whole* good toward the achievement of which all other partial goods serve only as means, and *if* (b) that whole good is *never attained at any moment in time*. The only good that satisfies these two conditions is a good life as a whole. It is the only good that is not a means to anything else and so is always an end; and as an ultimate end, it is purely normative and in no sense terminal. [7] Not understanding this is Dewey's fatal error.

Just as Dewey and other naturalists are right in thinking that, with one exception, all goods are good as means (that one exception being a good life as a whole), so they are also right in thinking that, with one exception, ought-statements are all hypothetical (that one exception being, once again, in discourse about the good life as an end to be sought and about the means to be employed in achieving it). This last point will, I hope, become clearer in the next chapter.

CHAPTER 10

The Significance of the Distinction Between Real and Apparent Goods

(1)

THE refutation of naturalism in ethics rests on the truth of two propositions: (1) that there is at least one good to be sought entirely for its own sake and not as a means to anything beyond itself; and (2) that there is at least one categorical ought that is self-evident. If these two propositions are true, then it is impossible to reduce all judgments of value or all ought-statements to statements of fact.

Among the philosophers who assert the truth of these two propositions and who, in so doing, also assert the relative or absolute autonomy of ethics, some charge the naturalists or empiricists in ethics with committing an error that has been misnamed "the naturalistic fallacy." This has beclouded the issue by introducing irrelevant considerations; for the root error of the naturalists does not consist in committing the so-called naturalistic fallacy. Rather, as I have pointed out in the preceding chapter, it consists in failing to recognize that an end can be ultimate without being terminal—a failure that leads the naturalists to deny that there can be any end that is not also a means. [1]

It may be useful, nevertheless, to examine the so-called "naturalistic fallacy"; by correcting the mistake implicit in the formulation of it, we can clarify the meaning of "good" without attempting to define it. But, first, it is necessary to distinguish two forms of the "naturalistic fallacy," the one pointed out by David Hume in the eighteenth century, the other by G. E. Moore at the beginning of this century.

The logical fallacy to which Hume called attention is formally similar to the violation of the rule governing considerations of modality in reasoning. It is logically invalid in reasoning to infer a necessary conclusion from premises that are contingent in their modality, or to assign contingency to a conclusion that is inferred from premises that are necessary in their modality. It is similarly and just as obviously fallacious to draw an ought-conclusion from premises that consist entirely of is-statements; for the difference in logical type between descriptive and normative propositions is as great as, if not greater than, the difference in modality between two descriptive propositions. That is why I regard the logical mistake pointed out by Hume—the violation of the rule that an ought-statement cannot be validly inferred from premises that are is-statements—as an analogue or special form of the modal fallacy. I will have more to say later about this special fallacy but, in passing, it is worth remembering that Hume did not discover it. It was explicitly recognized in antiquity, and to my knowledge, no moral philosopher of note—certainly none prior to the eighteenth century—ever committed this error. None is in fact named by Hume.

I wish to deal now with the other form of the so-called "naturalistic fallacy"—the form to which attention has been called by Moore and which has been made the subject of so much discussion in the last sixty-five years. [2] Let me say, first of all, that it has no logical connection with the modal fallacy discussed by Hume, which is truly a logical fallacy, and that, in addition to not being a logical fallacy, it also has no special relevance to naturalism. If there is any error revealed in Moore's discussion of attempts to define the good, it is the mistake that Moore himself makes in supposing that definitions are statements of identities.

No exception can be taken to Moore's endorsement of Bishop Butler's observation that "everything is what it is, and not another thing." A is A; it is not non-A. But definitions, properly conceived, never violate this law of identity. To say, for example, that gold is a fusible metal is not to say that gold is non-gold, but merely to offer the defining properties of that which is gold.

If to define anything at all—the good or anything else—one had to violate the law of identity, then no definitions at all would be logically valid, and every term would be indefinable.

The question of the correctness in fact of a particular definition is, of course, another matter. While defining gold as a fusible metal does not violate the law of identity, that by itself does not assure us that fusibility is in fact a defining property of the metal gold. On the other hand, when that definition of gold is empirically arrived at and accepted in the light of the available evidence as factually correct, then it is no longer an open question whether or not gold is fusible. That question has been settled *pro tem* by the establishment of the definition. [3]

I have gone this far into the logic of definitions in order to point out that Moore's much vaunted "open-question argument," far from calling attention to a logical fallacy or anything that has a bearing on the relation of facts to values, was merely his cryptic and contorted way of trying to explain why he thought that the good is indefinable. [4] Moore was correct in this contention, but this was hardly an original discovery on his part, as it is sometimes mistakenly supposed. Only massive ignorance of the theory of the good in the first twenty or twenty-two centuries of Western thought could have fostered that illusion. [5] In addition, the argument by which Moore tried to show that the good is indefinable is itself based on a misunderstanding both of definitions and of indefinable terms.

(2)

It is necessary to correct this misunderstanding in order to avoid the erroneous conclusions that Moore draws from the fact that the good is indefinable—conclusions that have a critical bearing on the relation of values to facts, and of ought-statements to is-statements. The indefinability of the good does not support the view that our knowledge of what is intrinsically good—good as an end to be sought for its own sake—has no basis in the facts of nature. To get this clear, let us begin by examining Moore's "open-question argument" in its own terms. The argument proceeds as follows.

Let anyone attempt to define the meaning of "good" by using the term "X" as the defining property, and let "X" stand either for something observable or something merely thinkable. It makes no difference to the argument which it is. The definition of good would then take the form "whatever is good is X." In Moore's view, it would also be true that whatever is X is good, because in his view of definition, the good and X are identical. The words "good" and "X" are strictly synonymous. [6]

Now, says Moore, if "good" is defined by "X," then the proposition "Whatever has the property X is good" should be an analytical proposition and as such it should be true beyond question. But when we consider the proposition, "Whatever has the property X is good," we find we are still able to ask, "Is this particular instance of X *really* good?" Since the possibility of asking a question of this form always remains open, no matter what property is used in place of X to state a definition of "good," we see that a definition of "good" cannot be constructed, for if it could be, it would produce an analytical proposition that would be self-evidently true and no further questions could be asked. Thus, according to Moore, the open-question argument shows that the good is indefinable.

Earlier philosophers, as I have already remarked, knew on other and better grounds that the good is indefinable; they did not need this argument to discover it. They knew that not all terms can be defined, and that certain primitive terms transcend the categories which make definition possible. Terms of this sort are indefinable. Among them are such basic philosophical terms as being and non-being, one and many, same and other. These terms are predicable of any subject, and as predicable of any subject, they are predicated in an analogical, not a univocal, sense; any term that is thus predicable must be indefinable. [7]

Earlier philosophers, however, did not let the matter rest there. They recognized that a term that was indefinable was not, therefore, unintelligible or less intelligible than terms that can be defined. On the contrary, the indefinables are, of all terms, the most intelligible, even though we cannot state their meanings in definitions. How, then, can we state their meanings? The ancient answer to this question is: *in axioms or self-evident propositions*—propositions that were called "common notions" because they do not belong to any particular discipline, propositions that Aristotle spoke of as correlating "commensurate universals" because their constituent terms are of equal scope as universal predicates. Such equi-valence makes these propositions convertible. [8]

One example of this very special type of proposition is Euclid's common notion that a whole is greater than any of its parts, or the converse proposition that any part is less than the whole to which it belongs. Since the meaning of "whole" cannot be stated without reference to parts, and the meaning of "parts" cannot be stated without reference to whole, neither term can be defined. But the statement that the whole is greater than any of its parts, or the converse statement that any part is less than the whole, explicates the meaning of both of these indefinable terms, which are commensurate universals, by stating their relation to one another. When we call these statements axiomatic or self-evident, we are saying it is impossible to understand what a whole is and what a part is without knowing these statements to be true. They are known to be true as soon as we understand the meaning of their constituent terms. That is why they were once called propositions *per se nota*—propositions known to be true through the understanding of their terms.

My reason for this little excursion into ancient and medieval logic is to call attention to the fact that when a twentieth-century philosopher like Moore refers to analytic propositions, he does not have in mind what the philosophers prior to the seventeenth or eighteenth century would have called axioms or propositions *per se nota*, but only that conception of analytical or tautological propositions which he inherits from Locke and Kant.

In Book IV of his *Essay Concerning Human Understanding*, Locke discusses "trifling" or "uninstructive" propositions, and mentions two main types: (i) simple identities, such as "a law is a law," or "right is right and wrong is wrong"; and (ii) propositions in which the predicate is contained in the meaning of the subject as that is defined; for example, "Lead is a metal" or "Gold is fusible." It is the second type of trifling proposition that Kant calls "analytic" and contrasts with synthetic propositions in which the predicate lies entirely outside the meaning of the subject as defined. Later writers return to Locke's broader formulation and include statements of identity in the class of analytic propositions. [9]

It is this sense of "analytic" that most twentieth-century philosophers employ when they regard self-evident or necessary
truths as nothing but tautologies. That is clearly what Moore
has in mind when he thinks that if there were a definition of good,
it would produce an analytic proposition (in his view, a statement of simple identity) that should preclude any further question. But the proposition about wholes and parts is neither
analytic in this sense nor synthetic. Yet it is clearly a self-evident
and necessary truth, and it is instructive, not trifling or tautological. When we understand its truth, no open questions of fact remain. We cannot ask, "Is it really true that this part is less than
the whole to which it belongs?" or "Is this whole greater than
any one of its parts?"

(3)

Now let us apply this elementary logic to the problem of the
meaning of "good" as an indefinable term. Its commensurate
universal is expressed by the term "desire"—or any of the synonyms for this word, such as "appetite," "yearning," "seeking,"
"aiming at," "tending toward," and so on. The correlation of
these commensurate universals is stated by such terms as "satisfies" and "aims at"; thus we can say, "The good is that which
satisfies desire," and "Desire is that which aims at the good."
Here the correlating terms "satisfies" and "aims at" function exactly as the correlating terms "greater than" or "less than" in
the case of whole and part.

The self-evident propositions or axioms which correlate the
good and desire not only show that good and desire, like whole
and part, are primitive and indefinable terms; the axioms also
explicate the meaning of these terms. We understand the meaning of "good" and "desire" in the same way that we understand
"whole" and "part." Hence, when we say of any particular
whatsoever that it is good, we cannot then ask, "Is it in fact an
object of desire," any more than we can ask of any particular
that we say is a part, "Is it in fact less than the whole to which
it belongs?" When the meaning of "good" is thus understood
without the term being defined, Moore's open-question argument
no longer applies. But it now becomes necessary to correct an-

other mistake of Moore's, together with an opposite mistake that is made by others.

The correlation of the good with desire can be summed up in the statement that the good is the desirable and the desirable is the good. These statements are merely short forms of saying that desire aims at that which is good, and the good is that which satisfies desire. Remembering this will safeguard against the error of supposing that the correlation of the good with desire is a statement of their identity. They are no more identical in meaning than whole and part are. But even with this error removed, the statement that the good is the desirable and the desirable is the good has been subject to two misinterpretations. One is Moore's mistake in thinking that the word "desirable," like the word "detestable" or "admirable," can only mean "*ought* to be desired" (or detested, or admired). [10] The other is the opposite mistake made by the naturalists and also by the non-cognitivists in ethics, who think that "desirable" can mean only "can be desired," as evidenced by the fact that it *is* desired by someone.

Each of these mistaken interpretations of the statement that the good is the desirable turns it into a half-truth. The whole truth consists in putting both together, and this, as we shall see presently, can be done only by distinguishing, on the one hand, between the real and the apparent good and, on the other, between two quite distinct modes of desire. Unaware of these distinctions, neither the naturalists nor the anti-naturalists can understand the partial truth that resides in their opponent's position.

The anti-naturalist, it would seem, can say that if the good is the desirable (in his restricted sense of "desirable"), then no empirically discoverable facts about human nature or human behavior can be relevant to determining what is intrinsically good and is to be sought for its own sake. The naturalist or empiricist, it would seem, can say that, if the good is the desirable, then all evaluations of things as good are reducible to the observable facts of desire—to our empirical knowledge of what men do in fact desire. And the non-cognitivist in ethics (whether an emotivist such as Professor C. L. Stevenson of the University of Michigan, or a prescriptivist such as R. M. Hare of Oxford) can say that when men call things good or bad, they are doing no more than expressing their approval or disapproval, their likes or dislikes, their wish to persuade others to take attitudes similar to their own, or their interest in prescribing what other men should react to favorably or unfavorably. [11]

All of these interpretations seem to fit—it might be said, seem to follow from—the fact that the meaning of the good is the desirable. Furthermore, since individuals do in fact desire different things—since what is desirable to one may be an object of aversion to another—the non-cognitivist, it would seem, can claim that his relativism or subjectivism in moral matters is thoroughly warranted.

(4)

While still holding to the truth that the good is the desirable, how can we avoid these consequences? Here, as everywhere else in this meta-ethical discussion, the answer was available long before the question was raised.

At the beginning of Western philosophy, in the early dialogues of Plato, Socrates repeatedly observes that no man seeks that which in fact he *deems* injurious, harmful, or disadvantageous to himself and, conversely, that everyone seeks that which in fact he *deems* beneficial, advantageous, or good for himself. In making such remarks, Socrates always lays great stress on the word "deems." He does so in order immediately to add that the deeming or *opining* of what is beneficial or harmful, advantageous or disadvantageous, may, of course, be mistaken. In other words, that which *appears* good to the individual (that which he deems advantageous to himself) may in fact be bad for him (disadvantageous, injurious, or harmful). If this were not the case, if that which the individual deems good could not in fact be bad for him, then he could never be mistaken in his estimates—his *deeming* or *opining* of what is good or bad. Here, in its seminal form, is the basic distinction between what later came to be called the real and the apparent good. [12]

In the seventeenth century, Spinoza asked a pivotal question that, by implication, adverted to this distinction. He asked: "Do

I call this good because I do in fact desire it, or do I desire it because it is in fact good?" In the context in which he raised that question, he gave the answer that Hobbes had given before him; namely, that good and evil are nothing but terms of approbation and disapprobation, expressions of what in fact we like or dislike, seek or avoid; in short, the fact of desire is primary and from it flows our calling the object of our desire "good." "Good" is simply the name for that which we do in fact desire. [13]

This is also the sense of Montaigne's famous remark, echoed by Shakespeare, that there is nothing good or evil but thinking makes it so. Montaigne's essays are replete with the moral relativism—a relativism with regard to all values, stemming both from individual differences and from cultural differences—that follows from taking his famous remark as the whole truth about questions of value. And if Hobbes, Spinoza, and Montaigne were right, then the non-cognitivists, and especially the emotivists, of our own day are also right, but not very original. [14]

But were they right? Or was Socrates right, and with him all the philosophers prior to the seventeenth century who thought they could make a valid distinction between the real and the apparent good?

Before I answer that question, let me say a word more about the meaning of the distinction itself. By the apparent good, we mean that which is *called* "good" by an individual because, and only because, it is in fact desired by him. It is not an apparent good for some other individual who does not in fact desire it. By the real good, we mean that which is good for an individual whether or not he is aware of desiring it; if he feels a desire for it, then the real good is also an apparent good for him; but if he does not, it still remains a real good for him.

However, this fuller explication of the distinction between the real and the apparent good *seems* to violate the axiom that the good is the desirable, for if something can be really good for an individual even if in fact he does not feel a desire for it, must we not having a meaning for good other than the one that derives from the correlation of the good with desire? The solution of this problem lies in a distinction between two modes of desire, each correlative with a different mode of the good.

In our own day, a distinction between two modes of desire is clearly recognized—not by the moral philosophers, but by such critical writers in the fields of technology and economics as Lewis Mumford, R. H. Tawney, John Maynard Keynes, and John Kenneth Galbraith. Their language for it varies. Sometimes they speak of "real" and "artificial" needs; sometimes they refer to "natural wants" and "stimulated" or "induced" wants—wants that are cultivated in consumers by the producers and advertisers of goods the consumers do not really need. Whatever language they use, the central point they are all trying to make is quite clear; namely, that certain desires are elements in the make-up of man, whether or not the individual consciously acknowledges them, whereas other desires come into existence only as a result of factors that operate on the individual. The desires that are thus elicited in him, the individual is always conscious of, as he is not always conscious of the desires that are elements in his nature or make-up. [15]

It is an obvious corollary of the above distinction that desires of the first type, inherent in the specific nature or make-up of men, are the same for all men by virtue of their all being members of the same species. In contrast, desires of the second type, the conscious desires elicited by or induced by circumstances, will differ from individual to individual, or from culture to culture, varying with the circumstances.

The philosophers prior to the seventeenth century who recognized this distinction between two modes of desire called desires of the first type "natural desires," and desires of the second type "conscious desires." For brevity of speech, and also for mnemonic reasons, I am going to substitute the two short words "need" and "want"—using "needs" for all the desires inherent in the nature of man and common to all men, and "wants" for all the desires elicited by circumstances and thus as various as the circumstances of individual experience. [16]

(5)

We have now reached an understanding of the good in relation to desire, which repudiates the reductionism of ethical naturalism, on the one hand, and will enable us to reject the various forms of non-cognitive ethics, on the other. Let me summarize it briefly in the terms that have become available to us.

The axiom that the good is the desirable and the desirable is the good covers both modes of desire and both modes of the good, but *not in the same way*. The good and desire are still correlative, but the real good is the good that is correlative with needs, and the apparent good is the good that is correlative with wants. Thus, that which I *need* is that which is really good for me, whether I consciously deem it to be so or not (whether I consciously want it or not). That which I *want* is that which appears good to me; it is that which I deem good for me and about which I may be mistaken (it may or may not be that which I need).

There are still other ways of formulating the two distinct relationships covered by the correlation of the good with the desirable. Each contributes some additional illumination and, for that reason, is worth mentioning.

Real goods satisfy natural desires or needs; needs aim at real goods. Here it is the natural desire or need that makes the thing that is good really good for a man, not just apparently so. In contrast, conscious desires or wants lead us to call "good" the things they aim at and that satisfy them. Here it is the want that makes the thing appear to be good, whether it really is so or not. The correlation of apparent goods with wants means that apparent goods are things we do in fact consciously desire. In contrast, the correlation of real goods with needs means that real goods are things we *should* or *ought to* desire, whether in fact, at this moment, we consciously do or not. This takes care of the half-truth that lies in Moore's restricted sense of the desirable as that which ought to be desired. [17]

This last point is of the greatest importance for carrying the argument forward to new ground. It adds to the intuitive truth that the good is the desirable, another intuitive truth that takes the form of a normative judgment; namely, that the *real* good *ought* to be desired, and nothing but that which is really **good** *ought* to be desired. These two intuitive truths, by the way, are the only self-evident principles required in order to establish ethics or moral philosophy as a relatively autonomous discipline.

I think I will be able to show, in Chapters 11 and 14, that all the other propositions that the intuitionists in ethics regard as self-evident are not only capable of being derived from these two fundamental intuitions but also must rely on empirical evidence for their truth. [18]

I hope I have succeeded in showing that Moore's view of the indefinability of "good" and his open-question argument contribute little or nothing to the discussion, or at least that they do not involve the meta-ethical bugaboos or stumbling blocks that many contemporary philosophers have found in his version of the "naturalistic fallacy." But what about the other mis-named version of the "naturalistic fallacy"—actually, the modal fallacy—that David Hume is credited with discovering? I promised earlier that I would return to it, and will do so now.

(6)

This matter can be handled briefly. I will first indicate why it might appear that, in the preceding pages, I have committed the modal fallacy mentioned by Hume in his *Treatise on Human Nature*. [19] I will then show that that is really not the case.

I have said that real goods are those which satisfy needs (that is, desires inherent in human nature). I have also said that one ought to desire that which is really good. But when we know the needs or natural desires of men, as a result of knowing the elements of human nature and the universal features of human behavior, and when, knowing what is really good for men, we let that lead us to normative conclusions about what all men *ought* to desire, are we not inferring normative or ought-judgments in conclusion from premises that are entirely descriptive or factual, that is, is-statements? If so, are we not committing the modal fallacy Hume had in mind when he referred to unnamed authors in whose books he found an ought-conclusion issuing from a series of is-statements about matters of fact?

It is of historical, but of no logical, importance that Aristotle had spotted the possibility of such fallacious inference twenty-two centuries earlier, in his formulation of the canons of practical reasoning. Aristotle had laid down the rule that in order validly to conclude that something ought to be done, the premises must involve at least one ought-statement. Valid practical or normative reasoning always takes the form: "Murderers ought to be punished; John Doe is a murderer; therefore, John Doe ought to be punished." This paradigm of the practical or normative syllogism makes clear that a normative or ought-conclusion cannot be validly inferred from premises that consist entirely of non-normative propositions, that is, statements of fact, is-statements, descriptive propositions. [20]

Are my conclusions about what all men *ought* to desire (conclusions that appear to be drawn from the facts of human nature) products of invalid inference—reasoning that violates Aristotle's rule, which is equivalent to saying reasoning that commits the modal fallacy pointed out by Hume? The answer is No. While the conclusion is drawn from the facts of human nature and behavior, it is *not* drawn *exclusively* from matters of fact. Matters of fact—the facts about human nature and behavior, however many and complicated they are—constitute that which functions as the minor premise in the reasoning under consideration. The major premise is the normative principle that we *ought* to seek that which is *really* good for us. This self-evident or indemonstrable principle—an ought-judgment—is intuitively known; it is known to be true when we understand the meaning of the good and the distinction between the real and the apparent good. As such, it is not only a normative proposition, but also one that is independent of all matters of fact; that is, of any empirical knowledge we may have or may be able to attain about human nature, and especially about human needs or natural desires. [21] Being independent of all matters of fact, it can be validly combined with such matters of fact as we may know, to produce by valid inference a whole series of conclusions taking the following form: (since X as a matter of fact is something that we need) X *ought to be desired;* (since Y as a matter of fact is something that we need) Y *ought to be desired;* and so on. [22]

In Chapter 13, I will have much more to say about the kind of truth possessed by such validly inferred normative conclusions—a kind of truth quite distinct from the kind to be found in descriptive propositions. I will also try to indicate how such normative conclusions tell us what each of us *ought* to do in order to make a good life for himself—a normative end or goal that each of us *ought* to aim at.

There is only one further observation I would like to add here. Since the basic normative principle (that one ought to seek what is really good for one's self), is an intuitively known, axiomatic, or self-evident proposition, it is something we know with certitude, just as we know with certitude that a whole is greater than its parts. But normative conclusions which state that this X or that Y, being really good, ought to be desired, do not have such certitude. The reason is, first, that these conclusions depend for their validity on factual minor premises about human nature and its needs, as well as upon the basic normative principle that is the major premise. And, secondly, while the basic normative principle can be known with certitude, none of the factual premises, being matters of empirical knowledge, can be so known. They are all capable of being falsified by empirical tests, as the basic normative premise is not. Consequently, our knowledge of what is asserted in normative conclusions is as contingent, and as subject to falsification, as the factual premises on which they rest. [23]

CHAPTER 11

The Obligation to Make a Good Life for One's Self

(1)

THE defense of common sense against the philosophical objections considered in the two preceding chapters has given the common-sense view a degree of philosophical development that will serve in dealing with still further objections. Before going on to them, it may be useful, therefore, to make that philosophical development as explicit as possible.

The common-sense view of what is involved in making a good life for one's self can appeal to the truth of two basic propositions —both self-evidently true, both intuitively known. The first is that the good is the desirable. The second is that one ought to desire or seek that which is really good for one's self and only that which is really good. In the light of these two propositions, common sense can see that one ought to make a good life for one's self, but only if a good life is conceived as consisting of things that are really good—the things that a man needs, not just those that he may want whether he needs them or not. In the sphere of the desirable, the distinction between things needed and things wanted (between objects of natural desire and objects of conscious desire), together with its correlative distinction between the real and the merely apparent good, enables common sense to understand that although everyone may in fact seek or wish to make a good life for himself, the individual may or may not have a correct conception of the things that ought to enter into making a good life if his whole life is to be one that is really good, not just one that appears good to him.

That men can make mistakes about what is good for them—that they can desire things which, after obtaining them, they regret having sought—is so pervasive a fact of human experience that it is unhesitatingly acknowledged by the man of common sense. He does not need instruction from the philosopher on this point. On the contrary, it is the common-sense opinion, maintained with a reasonable measure of certitude, that it is possible to make mistakes with regard to the things we desire, which gives the philosopher the insight he needs in order to pass from the proposition that the good is the desirable to the proposition that one ought to desire or seek that which is really good for one's self and only that which is really good. Since the second of these two propositions is as self-evident as the first, the transition from one to the other cannot be accomplished by steps of reasoning or demonstration. Nevertheless, it can be explicated in the following manner, employing, as has just been suggested, the basic insight afforded by common sense.

Starting with the proposition that the good is the desirable, our first step consists in seeing that men regard as good the things they consciously desire. That which we consciously desire appears good to us. Now add to this the common-sense insight that men can be mistaken in their conscious desires; that is, they can desire things they subsequently recognize were not really good for them, but only appeared to be good. Men can also make the opposite mistake of failing to desire that which is really good for them. Putting these two mistakes together, we arrive at the distinction between the merely apparent good and the real good.

At first blush, this distinction creates a problem for us. If there can be objects that appear to be good but are not really good for us, or objects that are really good but do not appear good to us, then it would seem to follow that the self-evident truth with which we started is not true at all. How can the good be the desirable, how can the good be correlative with desire, if some things that are really good for us are things we do not desire, and if some of the things we do desire are not really good for us?

The problem can be solved only if, in addition to conscious desire, there is another kind of desire, with which the real but not apparent good can be correlated. It is at this point that philosophy enlarges the common-sense view by introducing the concept of natural desire, understood as a potentiality to be realized, a capacity or emptiness to be filled, a privation to be overcome. While natural needs and conscious wants are not desires in exactly the same sense, they are nevertheless both genuine instances of desire in analogous senses of that term. [1] In both cases, the thing desired is something not possessed; if it were possessed, it would be neither needed nor wanted. [2]

We have thus amplified our understanding of the truth that the good is the desirable, by seeing that it covers the correlation of the real good with natural desire as well as the correlation of the apparent good with conscious desire. This, in turn, leads us to the recognition of three possibilities: (1) a given object is really good for us (it is naturally desired), but it does not appear good to us (it is not consciously desired); (2) it appears good to us (it is consciously desired or wanted), but it may or may not be really good for us (it may or may not be naturally desired or needed); and (3) it is both consciously wanted and naturally needed by us, and so it is an object that both appears good to us and is also really good for us. By considering each of these possibilities, we will discover how the notion of *ought* enters into the picture.

In the first case, in which we do not consciously want the real good that we naturally need, we can see at once that we ought to desire it. In what mode of desire? Obviously, in the mode of conscious, not natural, desire, for we already do in fact naturally desire it. The second case, in which we consciously want that which we may or may not naturally need, envisages two alternatives, one in which the object that we consciously want is something we do not naturally need, and one in which it is something we do need. On the first alternative, we cannot say that we ought consciously to want that which we do already in fact want, but which we do not in fact need. [3] The second alternative is identical with the third possibility mentioned above; for that is the case in which we consciously want that which we naturally need, and so the object that appears good to us is something we not only do in fact consciously want, but is also something we ought consciously to want, because it is really good for us in addition to appearing to be good.

We now see the connection between the truth that the good is the desirable (covering, as it does, two modes of the good as correlative with two modes of desire) and the truth that we ought to desire that which is really good for us and only that which is really good for us. What we have learned by making this explicit throws light on the application of *ought* in the sphere of desire.

If we could not make any mistakes about the objects of our conscious desires, there could be no meaningful application of *ought* or *ought not* in that sphere. That is why *ought* and *ought not* have no meaning in the sphere of natural desires. Natural desires belong wholly to the world of fact; *ought* and *ought not* do not apply there. But conscious desires belong both to the realm of fact and also to the realm of the normative—the realm in which *ought* and *ought not* apply. They apply there because our conscious desires can be right or wrong, correct or mistaken; that is, they can either conform to our natural needs or run counter to them.

It has been repeatedly said by modern philosophers that *ought* implies *can:* it is meaningless to say we ought to do something if it is impossible to do it. It should be added that *ought* presupposes *will* and *will not:* it is equally meaningless to say we ought to do something if we are not free to respond by saying we will or will not do it; and it is only in the sphere of conscious desire that we are free to desire or not to desire a particular object. It is only here, not in the sphere of natural desire, that we can obey or disobey the prescriptions expressed by *ought* and *ought not;* only here that our desires can be right or wrong, according to whether we want that which we *ought* to want or refrain from wanting that which we *ought not* to want.

(2)

We are now prepared to consider an objection that comes from the group of philosophers who are called deontologists and also sometimes intuitionists—deontologists, because their central contention is that the fundamental principles of moral philosophy must be expressed in the form of categorical *oughts* (unconditional obligations or duties); and intuitionists, because they think that the truth of these categorical *oughts* can be known without reference to experience and without any dependence on our empirical knowledge of matters of fact. In consequence, moral philosophy has for them absolute, not relative, autonomy.

The primary name in this group is, of course, the great German philosopher Immanuel Kant, and it behooves us to pay closest attention to his views. In the twentieth-century controversy about moral philosophy, similar views have been advanced by two English philosophers, H. A. Pritchard and Sir David Ross. We need not be concerned with the ways in which these thinkers differ from Kant or from each other, for our concern is only with the critical attack that they direct against those whom they regard as guilty of making fundamental errors in moral philosophy. Is their criticism sound? And does it apply to the common-sense view concerning the good life that is being developed here? In order to answer these two questions, it is necessary, first, to state their critical objection in its own terms.

I begin with an essay by Pritchard—"Does Moral Philosophy Rest on a Mistake?"—which was published toward the beginning of this century and which was directed against the ethics of G. E. Moore, on the one hand, and against all forms of naturalism in ethics, on the other, especially that of J. S. Mill and other exponents of utilitarianism. [4] G. E. Moore, it will be remembered, was himself an arch-opponent of naturalism and especially that form of it which he found in Mill's *Utilitarianism*. One is, therefore, impelled to ask how the same criticism can apply to both Moore and Mill. The answer lies in the fact that both Moore and Mill gave primacy in ethics to the notion of the good and attempted to derive the notions of right and wrong from it, as well as to determine man's duties and obligations in terms of it. Pritchard's contention that the primary notion is the right, not the good, and that our attachment or devotion to the good does not impose any categorical obligations or duties upon us, would seem, therefore, *if correct*, to undermine Moore as well as Mill.

Is Pritchard's contention correct? If the good covers whatever it is that men do in fact consciously desire, and if, in saying this, the term "good" is used without reference to the distinction between real and apparent goods and the term "desire" is used without reference to the distinction between conscious and natural desires, then Pritchard's contention cannot be gainsaid. He is quite correct in arguing that an individual's consideration of the good as the desirable imposes no categorical obligations or duties upon him. The things he actually desires are the things he regards as good, and there is no *ought* or *ought not* about it, at least not in a categorical sense of *ought*. The individual may recognize, of course, that if he wishes to achieve a certain end that he desires and regards as good, he ought to do this or that as the means to it, but this is a hypothetical, not a categorical *ought;* and as we observed earlier, such hypothetical *oughts*, as the naturalist maintains, can all be reduced to statements of fact about the causal relation of means to ends, and so they are not truly normative statements, as categorical *oughts* are. [5]

The force of Pritchard's criticism applies to reductive naturalism in ethics and to Mill's *Utilitarianism*, but not with the same effect. The reductive naturalist is, in his own terms, unembarrassed by it, since it is his own central contention that there are no categorical *oughts*, no normative propositions that cannot be reduced to statements of fact. While the common-sense view being developed here rejects such reductionism and would, therefore, appear to be on Pritchard's side of the issue, it does not accept Pritchard's basic contention about the primacy of the right. On the contrary, it affirms the primacy of the good as the basic term in ethics, and its argument against the reductive naturalist, as we have seen, consists in pointing out that there is an ultimate good—a good life as a whole—which is never a means to anything beyond itself, and so resists the naturalist's effort to reduce all values to facts. [6]

As far as Mill's *Utilitarianism* is concerned, Pritchard's criticism cannot be brushed aside. It reveals the speciousness of Mill's efforts to introduce the notions of right and wrong, and of duty or obligation, into a theory that identifies the good with whatever men in fact consciously desire. As we have seen, *ought* and *ought not* can be introduced into the sphere of our conscious desires and the actions that follow from them *only* when we distinguish between real goods, which ought to be consciously desired whether they are or not, and apparent goods, which are consciously desired whether they ought to be or not; and it is this same primary distinction between the real and the apparent good that underlies the distinction between right and wrong as applied to our desires and actions. Since Mill is totally unaware of this basic distinction in the sphere of the good as the desirable, his theory and that of his followers cannot be defended against Pritchard's criticism. Once again, the common-sense view being developed here appears to be on Pritchard's side of the issue, but here as before it does so without accepting Pritchard's central contention concerning the good, the right, and moral obligation.

G. E. Moore escapes from Pritchard's attack, or at least side-steps it, but only insofar as he interprets "desirable," as having exclusively the meaning "ought to be desired." This, as we have seen, is an error on Moore's part; he also fails to recognize the distinction between the real and the apparent good and the two modes of desire with which they are correlative. [7] Had he made use of that distinction, Moore might have adopted, as his basic, intuitively known normative principle in ethics, the proposition that one ought to desire that which is really good for one's self and only that which is really good. In that case, Pritchard's criticism would not have applied to his position, as it does not apply to the common-sense view here being developed.

What all this comes to can be summarized by giving an answer to Pritchard's question that is radically different from the one he himself gives. Does moral philosophy rest on a mistake? Yes, certain types of moral philosophy do, but it is not the mistake of regarding the good—or even the good for one's self—as the primary term in ethics; it is rather the mistake of not recognizing the distinction between that which is really good for one's self and that which only appears to be good. And this mistake is made by Pritchard as well as by the moral philosophers whom he criticizes—the naturalists, the utilitarians, and even certain anti-naturalists and anti-utilitarians, such as G. E. Moore.

(3)

The same mistake is made by Kant in his criticism of any moral philosophy that regards happiness as the *summum bonum*—the highest or supreme good—and proceeds by prescribing the means to be employed or the courses of action to be followed in order to achieve happiness as the ultimate end or goal of human activity. Such prescriptions, according to Kant, take the form of hypothetical, not categorical, oughts. Even though, as a matter of fact, all men may want happiness, the recommendations for achieving it are purely pragmatic or utilitarian, and lack the quality of moral rules, because they are concerned exclusively with means to an end that *is* desired, not one that *ought* to be desired. In Kant's view, the only end or good the individual ought to desire for himself is his own moral perfection—the perfection of his will—and this means that he ought to desire, not happiness, but being morally worthy of happiness. The *summum bonum*, in the sense of the highest good, is the moral perfection of a good will, but if the *summum bonum* is interpreted to mean not the *highest* good, but the *complete* good, then it consists in the combination of being happy with the state of being worthy of happiness through the attainment of moral perfection. [8]

Before I point out how Kant's failure to recognize the distinction between the real and the apparent good vitiates his argument, I would like to show why Kant's argument appears to challenge the soundness of the common-sense view that one ought to make a good life for one's self. His analysis of duties or obligations leads him from the consideration of legal duties that can be enforced by external sanctions to the consideration of ethical duties that cannot be so enforced. Kant describes these duties as "Ends which are also Duties"; that is, they are goods that impose moral obligations upon us: we *ought* to seek or promote them. They divide into one's duty to one's self and one's duty to others. The former consists exclusively in one's obligation to seek one's own moral perfection by willing and acting in conformity with the moral law. The latter consists, also exclusively, in one's obligation to promote the happiness of others. In expounding these two basic ethical duties, Kant explicitly denies, on the one hand, the existence or even the possibility of an obligation on the individual's part to seek his own happiness; as, on the other hand, he just as explicitly denies the existence of even the possibility of the individual's having a duty to act for or promote the moral perfection of others. [9]

To give the foregoing analysis the appearance of relevance to the common-sense view being developed, let us for the moment suppose that what Kant means by happiness is identical with the conception of a good life. If that were the case, then Kant would have to be interpreted as maintaining that the individual is under no obligation to make a good life for himself, though he is under an obligation to do what he can to promote a good life for others. The common-sense view that each of us ought to make a good life for himself would have to be rejected. [10]

Can the common-sense view be defended against this objection to the validity of its basic principle—its fundamental categorical ought? The appropriate answer to this question is not that it can be defended, but rather that it needs no defense because the Kantian objection simply does not apply. The trouble is with the supposition I suggested a moment ago; namely, that what Kant means by happiness is identical with the conception of a good life I am expounding. Only if that supposition were true, would the Kantian objection be relevant—and seriously damaging. But that supposition is not true; happiness as discussed by Kant differs in essential and crucial respects from the good life as we have been considering it. Although Kant is quite right in thinking that the individual has no categorical obligation to seek his own happiness, *in his sense of that term*, and although the critical force of his argument applies to any ethical doctrine, such as utilitarianism, which conceives happiness in the same way, it does not apply at all to the common-sense view of what is involved in making a good life for one's self.

The conception of happiness that runs through the whole of modern philosophy, from John Locke to Kant and Mill and into the twentieth-century discussion of these matters, is primarily a psychological conception mixed with quasi-moral overtones. For Kant, as for Locke before him and for Mill after him, happiness consists, ideally, in the complete satisfaction of all one's desires; and since the ideal of complete contentment may be unattainable, happiness is enjoyed in varying degrees according as the ideal is more or less approximated. [11] This psychological state of contentment that is enjoyed when an individual's desires are completely or almost completely satisfied derives its quasi-moral overtones from the fact that it is assigned the role of the *summum bonum*—the supreme good which is the goal of human striving, the end which is not a means to anything beyond itself, the end which somehow embraces all other goods either as aspects of itself or as a means to itself.

This mixed psychological and ethical conception of happiness raises many difficult questions, such as whether the satisfaction of all our desires can itself be an object of desire over and above the objects of the desires being satisfied; whether some measure of happiness, or even complete happiness, can be attained and enjoyed at some moment or period of one's life and lost at another; whether happiness as thus conceived does not appear to be equally attainable by good men and bad, by virtuous and vicious men, by men who in the common opinion of mankind deserve to be happy and by those who do not. [12] Such questions need not concern us, for they apply only to happiness as a mixed concept, not to the good life, which is a purely ethical concept—one that has no reference to a psychological state that can be experienced and enjoyed, or that can be attained at one time and lost at another. The only critical observation needed here is one that I have already made—that Kant's failure to recognize the distinction between the real and the apparent good vitiates his argument. It does so in two ways: first, it undermines basic propositions in Kant's own moral philosophy; second, it renders Kant's argument totally irrelevant and inapplicable to the common-sense view of a good life.

Since the conception of an individual's happiness as the psychological state in which all or most of his desires are satisfied involves only his actual conscious desires without reference to their relation to the natural desires that are common to all men, what constitutes happiness may vary from individual to individual in as many ways as individual desires vary. Furthermore, since in the absence of any distinction between natural and conscious desires, there can be no tenable distinction between real and apparent goods, each man's happiness consists in the possession of the things that appear good to him according to his actual individual desires. The set of apparent goods that satisfies one man's desires may be quite different from the set that satisfies another man's; one man may place his happiness in the possession of things not wanted by the other, and that other may, in turn, exclude from his version of happiness things that the first man would not be happy without. But no matter how many different versions of happiness there are—even if there are as many as there are individuals—none is the one and only right version, for none can be wrong. The mixed psychological and ethical concept of happiness employed by Locke, Kant, and Mill provides no standard for judging desires as right and wrong, and no basis for prescribing what ought to be desired by all men, precisely because it is developed entirely in terms of conscious desires, and lacking the notion of natural desires, it also lacks the notion of real goods as distinguished from merely apparent goods.

Operating with this defective conception of happiness, Kant is sound on only one point; namely, that the individual does not and cannot have a categorical moral obligation to seek his own happiness. But that same defective conception of happiness renders untenable Kant's views on two other points that are central in his moral philosophy. If it is impossible to say that the individual ought to seek his own happiness, as thus conceived, without reference to real and apparent goods, or right and wrong desires, then, for the same reason, (1) it is equally impossible to say, as Kant does, that the individual ought to do what he can to promote the happiness of other men according to the version of happiness that each of them cherishes; and (2) it is impossible to combine, as Kant attempts to do, the attainment of happiness with the worthiness to be happy that is based on the moral perfection of a virtuous or good will. A virtuous or good will can be related to the attainment of happiness only if happiness were to be conceived as consisting in the possession, throughout the course of a whole lifetime, of all those real goods that a virtuous man ought to seek for himself.

If happiness were so conceived, it would then be identical in meaning with a good life—a whole life made good by the possession of all the real goods that, corresponding to the needs inherent in human nature, ought to be desired by each and every human being. Happiness, like the good life, would then be the same for all men insofar as it was correctly conceived as constituted by the possession of real goods; and since men can be mistaken in such matters, it would be possible for men to entertain a wide variety of wrong notions about their own happiness by holding it to consist in the possession of things that might appear good to them but are not really good. [13]

Whether or not happiness is so conceived—whether or not modern philosophers adopt a meaning for "happiness" that identifies it with "a good life," or persist in using the word in the sense which not only makes Kant's rejection of an ethics of happiness irrefutable, but also undermines the role that he assigns to happiness in his own moral philosophy—the essential point with which we are here concerned remains clear. It is that the Kantian objection to an ethics of happiness, *in his sense of the term*, does not apply to the common-sense view of a good life, *as we have come to understand what is involved in that view*. The proposition which it has been the effort of this chapter to defend— that each of us has a categorical obligation to make a good life for himself, a whole life made good by possession of all the things that are really good for a man—stands untouched by objections and criticisms that apply with destructive force to other ethical doctrines, but not at all to the morality of common sense. The truth of that categorical obligation is nothing but an expansion of the self-evident truth that one ought to desire that which is really good for one's self and only that which is really good. [14]

CHAPTER 12

Relativity to Individual and Cultural Differences

(1)

T HE distinction between the real and the apparent good, which has been so important in the defense of the common-sense view against its philosophical critics, contributes as well to our fuller understanding of the good life as a goal to be sought. I have in mind particularly the point that emerged in the discussion (toward the end of the preceding chapter) of the notion of happiness, as that term is used by modern philosophers from Locke and Kant to Mill and the present day.

Happiness, for them, consists in the satisfaction of whatever desires the individual may have, without regard to their being right or wrong desires. This means that happiness for each man consists in getting the things he wants, whether he ought to want them or not, and so the components or elements of happiness may be as various as the variety of individual wants. In sharp contrast, the shape of a good life is the same for all men. Its component parts, the elements that make it up and are the constitutive means of achieving it, consist of things that are really good for a man—things that he needs, not just things that are apparently good because he wants them whether he needs them or not. Since the needs to which all real goods correspond are needs inherent in the specific nature of man, they are common to all men, and so whatever is really good for one man is really good for everyone else.

In the sphere of wants and apparent goods, individual differences tend toward an infinite variety. The diversity of human wants, like the diversity of individual tastes, predilections, interests, and opinions, is an essential feature of the human world, and one that can never be denied or overlooked. But underlying this diversity of individual differences lies the common or specific human nature that is individually differentiated in this man and that. Each of us is not only this unique human being, individually differing from all the rest; each of us is also an individual instance of the human nature we share with all the rest. This fact is as obvious and undeniable as the fact of individual differences, though it is often ignored and even explicitly denied —by philosophers and social scientists, if not by men of common sense.

The human good, the good for man as man, is a whole life made good by the possession of all the real goods toward which the common human nature of each individual tends for the satisfaction of its inherent needs. Since real goods are goods we ought to seek, the ideal of a good life as constituted by the sum total of real goods functions normatively as the complete or ultimate goal toward which we ought to strive. It is, as I shall explain presently, not the *summum bonum*, not the *highest* good in an order of goods, but the *totum bonum*, the whole of goods. And the moral obligation that each man has to make a good life for himself—to achieve this *totum bonum* in his individual life—is not only a categorical ought; it is also one that is universally binding on all men in the same way. [1]

Much more remains to be said in order to show, not only more clearly but also more concretely, how a good life as a whole is constituted by the possession of the totality of real goods, goods that correspond to natural needs. Our understanding of the good life as the *totum bonum* which leaves no needs unsatisfied must be such that it does not obscure or negate any essential feature of the *totum bonum* as the ultimate goal of our efforts to live well. Although the *totum bonum* is an end that is never a means to anything beyond itself and although, in this sense, it is the only ultimate end of human activity, it is not and cannot be a terminal end, one that the individual is able to arrive at and come to rest in at any moment in his life. Rather, as I pointed out earlier, it is purely a normative end, one that imposes categorical obligations upon us and sets the standards by which the particular choices we make in life and the courses of action we embark upon can be judged as right or wrong—as directed toward the achievement of a really good life as a whole or as directed toward the attainment of merely apparent goods that the individual may mistakenly suppose would make his life good.

All this must be understood with sufficient concreteness to make it meaningful to the individual who is often more intensely aware of his own special predilections, interests, and wants—the expressions of his individual temperament—than he is of the deeper or underlying needs inherent in the human nature he shares with all other men. This requires us to deal with all the incontrovertible facts of individual and cultural differences as they bear on and affect the meaning of the proposition that every human being is aiming at the same thing when he obeys the injunction to make a really good life for himself. But before I attempt to enlarge on these matters, I would like to return briefly to the subject of happiness in relation to the good life. For reasons that will become evident, I am unwilling to relinquish the use of that term, in spite of its misuse in modern philosophical discourse as well as in everyday speech.

(2)

In the opening pages of this book, I pointed out that the terms *happiness* and *a good life* had been used interchangeably by certain philosophers in antiquity. But in view of the fact that the ethical meaning of happiness has been overlaid and mixed with psychological connotations in modern thought and in current usage, I told the reader that I was going to refrain from using the word in the early chapters of this book, expressing the hope that it might later become possible for me to use *happiness* and *a good life* as terms having exactly the same moral connotation, without any danger of being misunderstood. [2]

One contemporary philosopher for whose book, *The Varieties of Goodness*, I have great respect, was led to the opposite decision by his understandable repugnance for the word "happiness." Professor Georg Henrik von Wright felt that "happiness" could not be shorn of its misleading psychological and hedonic connotations to be serviceable as the name for the ultimate good of man. He decided to use instead the term *human welfare*. While the significance he attaches to that term does not correspond in all essentials with the significance of *a really good life* as we have come to understand it, it comes much closer than the term *happiness* as that is used by Locke, Kant, Mill, and other modern philosophers. [3]

My chief reason among others for not wishing to relinquish the term *happiness* is the political significance of Thomas Jefferson's famous phrase "the pursuit of happiness." I hope to be able to show that Jefferson's use of this phrase to signify one of man's basic, unalienable natural rights—the primary natural right which, as we shall see, underlies all the others, such as the rights to life and to liberty—is unintelligible and indefensible unless "the pursuit of happiness" and "the effort of the individual to make a really good life for himself" are identical in meaning. For this to be so, the terms *happiness* and *a really good life* must be interchangeable or synonymous.

In order to make them interchangeable or synonymous, we must denude the term *happiness* of its psychological connotations and retain only the ethical or moral connotations that it has as well. When these are exclusively stressed, the term *happiness*, as we shall see, becomes identical in meaning with *a really good life*.

The following rules of usage indicate the psychological connotations of "happiness" that must be exorcised. (1) "Happiness" must not be used to name an experienceable or enjoyable state of mind or feeling, such as the experience of feeling pleased or satisfied when one's immediate desires are realized by getting the things one wants. (2) It must not be used to name an enjoyable state of contentment of any temporal duration which, whatever its length, occupies only a portion of the time of one's life. (3) It must not be used to name an experience that can be enjoyed at one time and not at another, something that can be gained at one time and lost at another.

With these psychological connotations of the word removed, the term *happiness* can then be given the following ethical connotations, so that its meaning coincides with the meaning of *a good life* as we have come to understand it in the development of the common-sense view.

(1) What is meant or understood in both cases is something—a goal or objective—that everyone desires. No one desires to be unhappy or miserable. No one desires a bad life, one that is utterly ruined or spoiled.

(2) In both cases, the objective or goal is never desired as a means or stepping stone to anything that lies beyond itself. So understood, happiness or a good life is an ultimate end, an/ end that is not in turn a means to anything else; and it is the only ultimate end, the only end that is not a means to or a part of something else that is sought. No one can meaningfully finish the sentence "I want to be happy because . . . ," just as no one can meaningfully finish the sentence "I want a good life for myself because . . ." This is true of nothing else. Let X stand for anything other than happiness or a good life, and it is always meaningful to say "I want X because I want to be happy" or "I want X because I want a good life for myself."

(3) Finally, in both cases, the achievement of the goal—the attainment of happiness or a good life—omits nothing that ought to be desired. Nothing could have been added to it that would have increased its goodness. In other words, both *happiness* and *the good life* signify the *totum bonum*—the whole or sum total of goods.

I should not need to remind the reader that these elements of meaning common to *happiness* and *the good life* do not make either a term of purely ethical significance, divested of all psychological connotations, *unless the goods involved in the* totum bonum (whether it is called "happiness" or "a good life") *are all real goods, goods that every man ought consciously to want because they satisfy his natural needs.* If the distinction between real and apparent goods, or between the things one ought to desire and the things one merely wants, does not govern our interpretation of the three points made above, the word "happiness" retains its psychological connotations; and even if some quasi-ethical connotations also remain in virtue of its standing for an ultimate end that men in fact desire, "happiness" would still signify an end that each individual could envisage in his own individual way, and no one could be mistaken about the things that constituted his happiness. The same would be true of "a good life" if that phrase were not understood as meaning *a really good life*, for then each man could make a good life for himself in his own way as he saw fit, and two individuals who were utterly opposed in the things they wanted for themselves could be equally successful in making good lives.

One test of whether we are using *happiness* as a purely ethical notion, identical in meaning with the notion of a really good life, is our affirmation and understanding of the proposition that happiness is the same for all men, for that is precisely what we are able to affirm and understand when we speak of a really good human life. Another test is our recognition of the fact that moral virtue—the habitual disposition to make the choices we ought to make in order to achieve the *totum bonum*—is an indispensable means to happiness, as it is an indispensable means to a really good life. A morally bad or vicious person cannot attain happiness any more than he can succeed in making a good life for himself. [4]

Still another test by which to tell whether we have separated the ethical from the psychological connotations of "happiness" is our ability to relate the psychological to the ethical connotations in the following way. We should be able to understand that *happiness* (in the ethical sense of the term in which it is identical with *a really good life*) may include moments that can be described by the words "happy" and "unhappy" when these words are used in their purely psychological sense. In other words, we must see that it is possible to make a good life for one's self or to attain happiness, even though in the course of doing so, there will be only certain times when we *feel* happy or contented, as there will be other times when we *feel* unhappy or discontented. [5]

The pursuit of happiness or the making of a good life does not exclude the frequent enjoyment of happiness (in its psychological connotation), but it might almost be laid down as a rule that the person who seeks to be happy (in this sense) *all* the time is one who will fail to make a really good life for himself and be defeated in his pursuit of happiness. He has committed the cardinal error of wanting a good time—from day to day—above all else, and in preference to making for himself a whole life that is really good. His mistake, stated in other terms, is the error of the hedonist who makes pleasure—whether as an object of desire or as the satisfaction of his wants, whatever they may be—either the highest good or the sole good; for the hedonist, who uses "happiness" with a mixture of psychological and quasi-ethical connotations, it is the hedonic character of happiness—pleasure experienced and pleasure sought—which makes it appear to be the *summum bonum* or highest good. [6]

Mention of the *summum bonum* leads me to one further observation that bears on the meaning of happiness and a really good life. It would be a serious mistake to call a good life the *summum bonum*. The use of that epithet presupposes an order or scale of goods, in which some are lower, some are higher, and one at least is the highest or supreme among all the things that are really good. It should be clear at once that a good life, as constituted by the possession of all real goods, cannot be called the "*summum bonum*." It is the whole or sum total of all real goods, not one good among others, even though that is the best of all. [7]

The same thing is true of happiness—a point that has not been recognized by those who have used that term with a mixture of psychological and quasi-ethical connotations. They have repeatedly referred to happiness as the *summum bonum*, understanding thereby the highest good, the good to be preferred to all others. But if happiness were the *summum bonum*, then it would be possible to attain and enjoy happiness while still lacking other and inferior goods, in which case one's happiness would be increased if, in addition to having the supreme good, one also had one or more of the inferior goods. This is manifestly a self-contradiction in terms, if happiness is conceived, psychologically, as a state in which all desires are satisfied and, ethically, as an ultimate end to be sought. We are thus brought to the conclusion that happiness, like a whole life that is really good, must be the *totum bonum*, not the *summum bonum*, for only as *totum bonum* can it function, normatively, as the ultimate end to be sought; and "happiness" can have this meaning only when it is used, in a purely ethical sense, as a synonym for a whole life that is really good. [8]

(3)

Henceforth, we should be able to use the word "happiness," when convenience recommends it, as short for the more cumbersome phrase "a whole life that is really good," which, if its meaning were fully spelled out, would read: "A whole life made good by the possession of all the things that are really good for a man, and by the possession of them to the fullest extent that they are really good, neither more nor less, together with the possession of such other goods as the individual may want, on the condition that obtaining these goods does not interfere with his getting real goods that he needs." Thus understood, "happiness" and "a good life" are simply different names for the *totum bonum*, the totality of real goods among which the goods of leisure constitute the highest in the order of goods—the *summum bonum*.

Each type of real good that is a constituent element in the *totum bonum* corresponds to a different natural need. They are such things as health, pleasure, wealth, friends or loved ones, and knowledge (where this term "knowledge" stands for all the things that develop or perfect man's ability to inquire, understand, and know). As the common-sense view recognizes, these real goods are either the intrinsic accompaniments of or the extrinsic results aimed at by four basic human activities—sleep, play, subsistence-work, and leisure-work. [9] As we have seen, the needs or natural desires that these real goods satisfy consist in human capacities that call for realization or fulfillment. Let me repeat what was said earlier on this last point. A native capacity is both something positive and something negative. It is a disposition or tendency to act in a certain way, but it is also a lack or privation that calls for a remedy—an emptiness that calls for filling—and it is in this sense that every capacity is a need, every native ability a natural desire. Thus, by nature social animals, we have a capacity for social life, and this is the root not only of our tendency to associate with other men, but also of our need for friendships of one sort or another. So, too, by nature cognitive animals, we have a capacity for knowledge of all sorts, and this is the root not only of our tendency to inquire and to learn, but also of our need for more and more knowledge and understanding. The biological need we call "hunger" is the plainest paradigm of need as a tendency or impulse to action and also as a lack or emptiness to be filled. [10]

When the common-sense view speaks of the result aimed at by all forms of leisure-work as personal self-improvement or betterment, it has in mind the acquisition of all those real goods that fulfill distinctively human capacities, such as man's capacities for acquiring arts and sciences or for making friendships. But what about certain things that common sense calls good, such as freedom from coercion or impediment, favorable circumstances bestowed by fortune, a good moral character, and sound judgment? Are these real goods? And if so, what need or natural capacity do they fulfill? The problem raised by these questions is a difficult and complicated one, but a brief answer for the moment consists in admitting, first, that these things do not correspond to natural needs in the sense in which food satisfies hunger, or knowledge our natural desire to know. We must go on to say, second, that these things are, nevertheless, all real goods, at least in the sense that they are goods that men do need and ought to seek. The apparent inconsistency of these two statements will be removed later when, in Chapter 15, we come to see that some real goods are needed only in the sense that they are recognized by human reason to be necessary as means for achieving a good life—man being by nature the kind of animal he is, and the circumstances of a human life being what they are. [11]

Before going on, it may be useful to reiterate three points that have been made about a whole life that is really good, or about happiness when that is identical in meaning with a really good life. The first is that, being the *totum bonum*, it omits nothing that is really good and so leaves no need unfulfilled, no natural desire unsatisfied. [12]

The second is that happiness or a whole good life can never

be experienced at any moment or period during the course of living, though the exercise of memory and imagination does enable us to consider our life as a whole. We can never say, during a man's life, that he is happy, any more than we can say, before his life is over, that he has succeeded in making a good life for himself, since while he is still alive, his whole life is still in the process of becoming. In view of this, we can say of a man who is succeeding in the task of making a good life for himself only that he is *becoming* happy or, in other words, that he is on his way to doing the job, but he has not yet finished doing it. [13] This is the profound insight that lies concealed in the phrase "pursuit of happiness" and, as we shall see, this also explains why the basic natural right that a just society or government should try to secure—and aid or abet—for every individual is not, and cannot be, the right to happiness, but is rather the right to its pursuit. One way of remembering this point is to remember the qualification that must be added to the famous definition of happiness given by Boethius. He said: Happiness consists in the possession in aggregate of all good things—all the things that are really good for a man. [14] The qualification that must be added is that life being a temporal whole and a good life something that can be made only in the course of using up the time of our lives, the possession of all good things can be achieved only successively and cumulatively —from day to day, and from year to year; it cannot be achieved in this life by the simultaneous presence of all good things at a single moment in time.

The third point is that a good life can include apparent goods of all sorts—things that men want even if they have no natural need for them and even if they cannot be rationally justified as necessary for achieving a good life. But this is true only with the stringent qualification or restriction that the apparent goods a man goes after, or the way he goes after them to satisfy his wants, do not in any way conflict with his getting all the real goods he needs, or with getting them to the fullest extent to which they are really good for him. In other words, the moral obligation to make a really good life for one's self does not preclude satisfying one's wants and seeking things that are apparent but not real goods, but only if they are *innocuous—only if* the pursuit of them *does not interfere* with the pursuit of happiness. [15]

(4)

The foregoing clarifications and developments of the common-sense view cannot help but elicit from psychologists, sociologists, and cultural anthropologists an objection that was not mentioned earlier when I enumerated the various criticisms that philosophers would level against it. The objection is to the proposition that the *totum bonum*—happiness or a really good life—is the same for all men at all times and all places, and under all circumstances; in consequence of which, all men are under the same moral obligation when it is said that each ought to make a good life for himself. The empirical psychologist objects to this on the grounds that it ignores the whole range of individual differences in physique, temperament, and talent—intelligence and native endowments or aptitudes. The sociologist or cultural anthropologist objects to this on the similar grounds that it ignores the whole range of societal and cultural differences—differences in all the man-made circumstances that surround an individual life, and perhaps differences in the physical environment as well that often occasion or help to form particular social or cultural institutions.

The reply to both objections is the same. It consists, first, in acknowledging the relevance of all the facts about individual and cultural differences that we either know as a matter of ordinary experience or have learned from investigations conducted by the behavioral scientists. But these are not the only facts to be taken into account. There is also the pre-eminent fact that all men belong to the same biological species and, as such, are the same in nature, that is, have the same biological properties, the same basic native capacities—dispositions and needs. [16] When this fact is put together with the facts of individual differences, we see that while the general outlines of a good life are the same for all men because they all have the same specific nature, the details that fill that outline in differ from man to man because men all differ individually from one another.

That is one reason why it was said earlier that the plan for making a good life—one that would be a common plan for all men to follow—can only be sketched in its general outlines and cannot be worked out in all its concrete details. The latter can be done only by each individual and only from moment to moment in the course of a whole life. A few examples may help to make this point clearer. Being the animals they are, all men must devote a portion of their time to the biologically necessary activities we have grouped together under the term *sleep*. But differing from one another in temperament and physique, as well as in external circumstances, they will not all engage in these activities in the *same* way or to the *same* degree. Similarly, though all men ought to devote as much of their time as possible to *leisure-work*, because they cannot do too much of this for their own good, their individual differences in temperament and talent, as well as in the external circumstances of their lives, will lead them to engage in different types of leisure-work and to engage in them in different ways. The same holds for *playful activities*, which will differ both in degree and in manner from man to man, because of their individual differences and the differences in the circumstances that affect their lives. And it also holds for *subsistence-work* in the case of those men who, for want of enough wealth or property, are under compulsion to make a living for themselves.

Hence it is possible to say that happiness or a good life, conceived in its general outlines as the same for all, is attainable by all men, except those who are prevented by abnormal individual disabilities or incapacities or those who are prevented by the extremes of good or bad fortune. With the exceptions noted, all men have an equal opportunity to attain happiness or to make a good life, but this equality is one of proportionality. Differing individually in their capacities, each can fulfill his capacities to the utmost, and although the degree of happiness attained may not be identical for all, it will be proportionally equal for all who make an equally successful effort. This does not mean that all men will in fact make the degree of effort they ought to make or that, given differences in circumstances, the same degree of effort will be equally successful. As a result, all men may not achieve happiness or a good life to the fullest degree of which they are individually capable. In addition, quite apart from considerations of degree, the manner in which men engage in the pursuit of happiness will differ from individual to individual.

(5)

I said earlier that the same answer applied not only to individual differences, differences in native endowment, but also to societal and cultural differences, all of them environmental and circumstantial. But when we consider differences of the latter sort—the circumstantial differences—one qualification must be added that is not called for in the case of differences in native endowment.

Plato long ago observed that what is honored in a society is cultivated there. It would also seem to be true that what is not honored in a society—or, more emphatically, what is socially or culturally regarded as having little or no worth—cannot be cultivated there. It may be too much to expect any individual—or any but the rarest exception—to be so extreme a non-conformist that he will earnestly and steadfastly seek for himself things that, while really good for him because he is a man, are not honored by the society in which he lives or, worse, are strongly disapproved of. The converse of this may also be true; namely, that the individual, conforming to the *mores* and value-system of the society in which he lives, will indulge in activities, or indulge in them to a degree, that lead to results that are not *really* good for him or any other human being, yet are generally *deemed* good by his society or culture. Consequently, it is highly probable that under certain societal or cultural conditions, it may be extremely difficult, if not impossible, for an individual to satisfy all his natural needs or to attain, to the requisite degree, all the things that are really good for him as a human being.

This being the case, we can judge human societies or cultures as good and bad, better or worse, in spite of all the injunctions against doing so delivered by the sociologists and cultural anthropologists. The sociologists and cultural anthropologists tell us that we cannot transcend what they call the "ethnocentric predicament" in which we find ourselves. Any judgment we make about a culture other than our own will assume the soundness or validity of the *mores* and value-system of our own society or culture. This would, of course, be true if *all* value-systems were relative and had validity—or acceptance—only for the culture in which they were inherent. However, the value-system involved in the scale of real goods that constitute a good human life is relative only to human nature, and not to societies or cultures. As such, it provides a standard that transcends the mores and the diverse value-systems that are inherent in diverse cultures. It is a universally applicable standard because it is based on what is universally present in all societies—human beings, the same in their specific nature. [17]

Hence, by applying this standard, it is possible to judge any society or culture as good or bad, better or worse, including our own, and we can do so without falling into the ethnocentric predicament that is the bugaboo of the sociologists and anthropologists. A society or culture is good if it does not prevent its members from making a really good life for themselves, and one is better than another if, to a greater degree than that other, it facilitates the pursuit of happiness for all or for more of its members. A society or culture is bad if it prevents some or all of its members from achieving the *totum bonum* that constitutes a really good human life, and one is worse than another if, to a greater degree than that other, it interferes with the pursuit of happiness for all or for more of its members.

It is by this standard—*there is and can be no other to serve the purpose*—that we shall judge the society and culture of the United States in the twentieth century when we come, in Part Four of this book, to consider the question whether this is a good time to be alive and whether ours is a good society to be alive in. Now, however, we must turn to the one remaining formal objection to the common-sense answer as that has been philosophically developed—an objection that would, if it were sound, support the relativism of the ethnocentric predicament because it denies that any value-system can have objective validity, that is, the kind of objective truth found in the empirical sciences. [18]

CHAPTER 13

Oughts Can Be True

(1)

IN preceding chapters, I have defended the common-sense view against criticisms and objections that I associated with the names of John Dewey, G. E. Moore, H. A. Pritchard, and Immanuel Kant. In each case, my defense consisted in pointing out a basic defect or deficiency in the thought of the philosopher from whom the criticism stems, either a positive mistake or a negative one—a failure to take into account relevant distinctions that would have prevented the objection from having been raised. The three basic defects—mistakes or failures—to which I called attention are as follows.

The first is Dewey's mistake in denying that there are any final or ultimate ends, a mistake he made because he was unaware of the distinction between a final end that is purely *normative* and one that is *terminal*. With this mistake corrected, reductive naturalism in ethics becomes an untenable position. There are value judgments that are not reducible to observable matters of fact, and there are oughts that cannot be construed as hypothetical and, therefore, cannot be converted into statements of fact.

The second is Moore's mistake in thinking that the meaning of the good cannot be stated—stated, not defined—by correlating it with an element of observable nature, such as desire. In his case, the mistake stems from uncritical reliance upon the inadequate modern distinction between analytic and synthetic propositions. Moore, like most other modern logicians and analysts, does not recognize the difference between (a) an analytic proposition in which the subject and predicate are identical or one in which the predicate is contained in the definition of the subject, and (b) a self-evident proposition or axiom that correlates universal predicates, both of which are primitive terms or indefinables. The former is a verbal tautology. The latter is neither a synthetic proposition, subject to empirical verification and falsification, nor is it a verbal tautology or an analytic proposition in the sense that modern logicians adopt from Locke and Kant. With this mistake on Moore's part corrected, his thesis that the good is indefinable remains in force, but his openquestion argument loses all force and does not apply to the axiom or self-evident truth that the good is the desirable.

The third mistake is Kant's ambiguous use of the term "happiness," but underlying it is a more serious defect—one that lies at the core of almost every approach to moral problems in modern times. It is ignorance of the distinction between real and apparent goods, together with ignorance of the correlative distinction between natural and conscious desires. It is the source of the fundamental error made by Kant and Pritchard with regard to the primacy of the right over the good; it is equally the source of the error in the opposite—the utilitarian—approach, which affirms the primacy of the desirable or the good, but is unable to derive from man's desire for the good a single categorical ought, universally binding on all men in the same way. Only with this mistake corrected, can happiness be identified with a really good life, the same for all men because it fulfills the needs inherent in human nature, and as such the object of a categorical moral obligation binding on all men in the same way. If Kant and Mill, who can be regarded as the principal opponents in moral philosophy since 1800, had conceived human happiness as identical in its constitution with a whole life that is really good, it is difficult to see how they could have differed from each other or from the common-sense view. [1]

(2)

We are not yet done with meeting important and relevant objections to the common-sense view. We must now turn to one based on the dictum that no satisfactory answer can be given to the question, *How can an ought-statement be true?*

This attack on the common-sense view or, for that matter, on any form of moral philosophy which claims to be a body of knowledge and to have some measure of autonomy, can be associated with the name of A. J. Ayer. His early book, *Language, Truth and Logic*, set forth the tenets of logical positivism, some of which were later adopted by the analytical and linguistic philosophers. Among these, a tenet generally accepted by the analysts and linguists was Ayer's exclusion of value-statements or ought-judgments from the realm of propositions that can be true or false. He pointed out that his criticism applied only to value-statements that could not be reduced to or converted into statements of fact, and only to those normative propositions that, being categorical ought-judgments, cannot be converted into descriptive propositions.

Ayer's early position with respect to value statements rested on this simple argument. There are only two kinds of truth: (a) the formal truth of analytical statements, such as those to be found in logic and mathematics; and (b) the empirical truth of descriptive—and synthetic—statements, such as those to be found in the sciences that deal with matters of observable fact. The former are sometimes called *a priori* truths, for they are not subject to empirical testing—to falsification or confirmation by observable facts. The latter are *a posteriori* truths, dependent on empirical evidence and subject to empirical falsification. Descriptive statements about what is or is not the case are true when they conform to the ascertainable facts of the matter, by reference to which they can also be either falsified or confirmed. Now, since a statement of value or an ought-judgment that is not convertible into a statement of fact is neither an analytical proposition nor a descriptive proposition, it can be neither true nor false. Insofar as such statements are not descriptive of matters of observable fact, Ayer maintains that "they are not in a literal sense significant, but are simply expressions of emotion, which can be neither true nor false." And in another place, Ayer writes: "Exhortations to moral virtue are not propositions at all, but ejaculations or commands which are designed to provoke the reader to action of a certain sort." [2]

If Ayer's argument is sound, if there is no answer to it and no way out of it, then two things follow that cannot be gainsaid. *First*, as I have already pointed out, there can be no moral philosophy if by that one means a discipline that makes value-statements and ought-judgments for which truth is claimed—or for which it is even claimed that they are capable of being true or false. Even though I seem, so far, to have been able to answer all other objections to or criticisms of the common-sense view, both in itself and as it has been philosophically developed, my failure to answer Ayer's argument would be fatal. The conclusions we have reached would cease to be significant—at least they would not be significant in the sense in which they were intended—if they could be neither true nor false. *Second*, if the statements made in first-order moral discourse cannot be either true or false, then they are non-cognitive. They are in no sense expressions of knowledge. [3]

This opens the way to all the varieties of what is called "non-cognitivist ethics"—interpretations of moral discourse that, beginning with the negative declaration that value-statements or ought-judgments are *not* cognitive, undertake to offer some positive explanation of them. Pre-eminent among these interpretations are Stevenson's emotivist theory of value-judgments and Hare's prescriptivist theory of ought-judgments. There are others, but all of them are essentially and ultimately relativistic, for any non-cognitive theory of moral discourse must somehow relate moral judgments to the character of the individual who makes them or the circumstances under which they are made. The gist of all non-cognitivist theories is aptly summed up in Bertrand Russell's witty remark that ethics is the art of recommending to others what they should do in order to get along with one's self. The diverse non-cognitive interpretations of moral discourse conflict with one another, but these internecine quarrels are of interest only if the fundamental premise common to all the non-cognitive theories is correct. [4]

Since I am going to try to show that it is not correct—that Ayer's argument does not hold up—we need not be further concerned with the differences between the interpretations advanced by Stevenson and Hare or others. However, it may be useful to point out that while the existentialist ethics of Sartre and others in his group is both non-cognitivistic and relativistic, it rests on a principle that is peculiarly its own. That principle is the familiar existentialist proposition that "existence precedes essence," which translated into ordinary language and made relevant to our present concerns means that there is no such thing as human nature. When, at birth, an individual man begins to exist, he begins with *nothing determinately given*. If this proposition were true, it would follow that what each individual does with his life and makes of himself is a project all his own, susceptible to no trans-subjective standards and involving no categorical oughts. Why anyone should accept the basic principle of existentialism, I have never been able to understand, for it is simply asserted without a single cogent argument or a single shred of inspectable evidence to support it. [5]

Even if one were to grant the existentialist's credo that existence is absurd—that there is no reason for being rather than for non-being—nevertheless, given the fact that one does exist and is not impelled to commit suicide, the basic and unavoidable choice for any one who continues to remain in existence and alive is the choice between trying or not trying to make one's life as good as it can be made.

(3)

As in my handling of other objections to the common-sense view, I will, first, try to indicate why Ayer's argument appears to be correct, and then I will try to show that it does not hold up. I will confine myself to the question of whether categorical ought-statements can be true or false. I do so for two reasons. First, because any value-statement that declares that something is really good leads to the judgment that it ought to be desired; second, because the injunction that one ought to desire that which is really good is always categorical, not hypothetical. It does not take the form "If you want X, you ought to do Y"; but rather the form "You ought to desire X," or "You ought to do Y."

Let us now consider such statements as "You ought to desire X" or "You ought to do Y" where "X" or "Y" stands for some determinately specified object or activity, such as knowledge or leisure-work. Clearly, such statements are not axiomatic. They are not self-evidently true as are the statements "The good is the desirable" and "That which is *really* good is that which *ought* to be desired." Statements of the latter sort, even though they include a value term such as "good" or a normative verb such as "ought," have the same kind of truth that is to be found in non-evaluative and non-normative axioms, such as "The whole is greater than any of its parts."

Let us call the kind of truth that such propositions have "truth of understanding"—a truth that is perceived as soon as the terms of the proposition are understood. Earlier I distinguished such propositions, involving the correlation of universal predicates that are primitive or indefinable terms, from the propositions that modern philosophers call "analytic," which are either statements of identities or propositions in which the predicate is contained in the definition of the subject. [6] Propositions of the latter type are said to have "formal truth," as distinguished from the empirically falsifiable truth of synthetic propositions. The formal truth of analytic or tautological propositions is purely verbal, and is not a special case of what I have called "truth of understanding." [7]

The only point that does concern us is that in contradistinction from the axiom "one ought to seek that which is really good and that alone" (a self-evident proposition which has the mode of truth that I have called "truth of understanding"), normative propositions of the type "X ought to be sought" or "Y ought to be done" are clearly not self-evident, for we do not immediately know them to be true when we understand the meaning of the terms "X" and "Y" and the meaning of "ought to be sought" or "ought to be done." The question is not primarily, "How can the latter type of statement *be known* to be true or false?" but rather "How can such statements *be* true or false?" Only after we can see how they can be either true or false will we be concerned with how we know which they are. Since such statements are not descriptive statements, since they contain the verb "ought" rather than the verb "is," they cannot be true or false by reference to a state of facts, to which they either correspond or fail to correspond. To say that X ought to be sought or that Y ought to be done does not assert that anything is or is not the case, or that it has or has not been the case, or that it will or will not be the case. [8]

At the very beginning of the development of formal logic, Aristotle, in his analysis of propositions, restricted them to declarative or assertive statements, capable of being true or false, and said that sentences expressing prayers (or entreaties and exhortations) were not propositions because they were not capable of being either true or false. [9] If only declarative sentences, sentences that assert something, express propositions capable of being true or false, it would certainly appear to follow that interrogative sentences (or questions), imperative sentences (or commands), and subjunctive sentences (or wishes) do not express true or false propositions. Since a categorical ought-statement is convertible into an imperative sentence or command—for to say "You ought to do X" is to say, imperatively, "Do X"—Aristotle's position with regard to the types of sentences that do not express true or false propositions would seem to agree perfectly with Ayer's position that value-statements or categorical ought-judgments can be neither true nor false.

(4)

Strange as it may seem, it is Aristotle who also provides us with the refutation of Ayer's argument, by answering the question, "How can an ought-statement be true or false?" Stranger still is the fact that no modern philosopher appears to be aware that the answer to this question is to be found in Aristotle's writings, especially none who *has been* or *should be* concerned with the question.

Before I report the answer, let me say that it is given in a single sentence that Aristotle nowhere expands. Aristotle also failed to connect what is said in this sentence with what he said in another place about declarative sentences being the only ones that express propositions capable of being true or false; yet, upon closer examination, we will find there is no inconsistency. [10] The sentence occurs in a passage in which Aristotle explains the difference between the kind of truth that he calls practical (the kind that is attributable to ought-statements) and the kind of truth he calls speculative or theoretical (the kind that is attributable to is-statements). The point he is making can be summarized as follows.

The truth of is-statements, which Aristotle calls speculative or theoretical truth, consists in an agreement or correspondence between what the statement asserts and the ways things in fact are. [11] The truth of ought-statements, which Aristotle calls practical truth, consists in an agreement of the statement "with right desire." Thus, an ought-judgment of the type "You ought to seek X" or "You ought to do Y" is true if it agrees with right desire, and false if it does not. In other words, in relation to ought-statements, conformity with right desire plays the same role that conformity with the facts, with the way things are, plays in relation to is-statements. [12]

We already have some understanding of the term "right desire," but that now needs to be refined and made more precise. Up to this point we have understood it simply as desiring what ought to be desired. But what ought to be desired may either be the ultimate end, the *totum bonum*, a whole life constituted by the possession of all real goods, or it may be any one or more of the constitutive means to a good life—the various real goods that are parts of the *totum bonum*, each of which is indispensable to the making of a good life, but none of which is sufficient in itself.

The standard of right desire is set by the one basic categorical ought that states our obligation to seek the complete good, the *totum bonum* that leaves no need unsatisfied. Formulated with maximum explicitness, that categorical *ought* with respect to the end can be expressed as follows: one ought to make a really good life for one's self by desiring each and every real good that is part of the *totum bonum*, and by seeking each in such order and proportion with respect to the others that all can be possessed to the fullest extent that each is really good; and one ought not to seek anything the possession of which would interfere with achieving a good life for one's self.

I will henceforth refer to this basic categorical ought concerning the ultimate end as the normative principle that governs the making of a good life and also sets the standard of right desire by reference to which all other normative propositions—all of them conclusions about the means to a good life—are to be judged true or false. Now let us examine the logic of employing the standard of right desire as a basis for judging the normative truth of conclusions about the means to a good life. It cannot be understood without careful attention to the following points.

In the first place, it must be observed that the truth of the normative principle is not itself an instance of normative truth, but is rather the kind of truth I have called truth of understanding. It has the kind of truth that is possessed by any self-evident proposition, whether it be an is-statement such as "The whole is greater than any of its parts," or an ought-statement such as "One ought to make a really good life for one's self by seeking the *totum bonum*." [13] Were this not the case, were the truth of the normative principle normative truth rather than truth of understanding, we would be involved in a vicious circle; for the principle that sets the standard of right desire would then have to be judged by reference to the standard that it itself sets. [14]

In the second place, it must be observed that all normative propositions other than the one basic normative principle must have the twofold character of being (a) conclusions, and as such not self-evident, and (b) statements concerning the means to a good life—the means that ought to be desired and employed in order to achieve the end that ought to be sought, the *totum bonum*. Let X stand for any one of the partial real goods that enter into the making of a good life, such as health, wealth, pleasure, or knowledge. As parts of the *totum bonum*, each is a constitutive means to a good life. Let M stand for any course of action or any set of circumstances that operates to bring about the possession of one or another of the real goods that we ought to seek as a part of the *totum bonum*—as taking a vacation serves us with respect to the goods of health and pleasure, or having the opportunity for schooling serves us with respect to the good of knowledge. Such operative factors are the instrumental means to a good life, by virtue of their functioning as the means of getting the real goods we need. Other than the one normative principle, all normative propositions are either

of the form "One ought to desire X," which is a normative conclusion about a constitutive means to the good life, or they are
of the form "One ought to do or have M," which is a normative
conclusion about an instrumental means to the good life.

In the third place, it must be observed that such propositions
depend upon knowledge of matters of fact. Thus, to know that
one ought to desire X as a real good and constitutive means, one
must know, as a matter of fact, that there is a natural need
which X satisfies. To know that one ought to do or have M as an
instrumental means, one must know, as a matter of fact, that Y
is causally connected with X in such a way that doing or having M functions as a means of getting X. When we have such
knowledge, we can conclude that we ought to desire X or we
ought to do or have M. But although descriptive, empirical
knowledge of matters of fact has entered into our reaching
these conclusions, the conclusions themselves are normative
propositions, and their truth is not descriptive, but normative
truth. The conclusions are normatively true by virtue of conforming to the standard of right desire—desire for the end, the
totum bonum, that ought to be sought.

In the fourth place, it must be observed that the modal fallacy
is not committed in the reaching of such conclusions. When, for
example, we conclude that we ought to desire X, the major
premise is the normative proposition that we ought to desire
anything that is really good as a part of the *totum bonum*. Only
the minor premise is a descriptive proposition about a matter of
fact, one drawn from our knowledge of human nature and human behavior, in the light of which we can say that there is
a definite natural need that X satisfies. We have not drawn an
ought-conclusion from premises that are entirely is-statements.
Normative conclusions are always drawn from mixed premises—
partly factual and partly normative. That is the only way they
can be validly established. Though a normative conclusion would
not be true if its factual premise were not true, it still remains
the case that it has normative truth by virtue of conforming to
the standard of right desire, not by virtue of the factual truth
that underlies it.

In the fifth place, and finally, it must be observed that our
knowledge of such matters of fact as are involved in reaching

normative conclusions is empirical knowledge, subject to the same empirical tests by which any statement of fact can either be falsified or have its degree of relative truth confirmed. Hence, although the one basic normative principle, being a self-evident truth of understanding, can have certitude, all other normative propositions, being normative conclusions that rest, in part, on empirical knowledge of matters of fact, lack it. To make this point clear, we must distinguish between two aspects of the truth of normative conclusions. Since they are derived, as we have just seen, from mixed premises, their truth is also mixed—in part factual, in part normative. It is the factual aspect that deprives them of certitude, for what the conclusion normatively asserts about this or that means to the ultimate end conforms to right desire for that end only *on the condition* that the thing regarded as a means is, as a matter of fact, the means it is thought to be.

(5)

Let me now summarize the way in which Ayer's objection has been answered. Ayer rests his case on an inadequate twofold division of the kinds of truth. While truth can be divided, first, into two major kinds—(I) the *a priori* and (II) the *a posteriori*—each of these kinds must be further subdivided into two subordinate modes of truth that can be clearly distinguished from each other.

By (I) *a priori* truth, we understand truth that is not dependent on empirical evidence and is not subject to empirical falsification. Two different types of proposition can have *a priori* truth: on the one hand, (Ia) analytic propositions, in which the subject and predicate are identical or in which the predicate is contained in the definition of the subject; on the other hand, (Ib) axioms or self-evident propositions, the truth of which is seen as soon as their constituent terms are understood. I have called truth of type (Ia) *verbal truth*, or tautological truth, and I have called truth of type (Ib) *truth of understanding*. Truth of understanding, as we observed earlier, is attributable to ought-propositions as well as to is-propositions, when these propositions are axiomatic or self-evident. The truth of the basic normative principle, that one ought to seek the *totum bonum* or a really good life for one's self, is truth of understanding, not normative truth: it is a self-evident expression of right desire, not a normative conclusion that is true by conformity to the standard of right desire.

By (II) *a posteriori* truth, we understand truth that is dependent on empirical evidence and is subject to empirical falsification. Once again, two different types of proposition can have *a posteriori* truth: on the one hand, (IIa) factual propositions, or is-statements, the truth of which consists in conforming to the way things are; on the other hand, (IIb) normative propositions, or ought-statements, the truth of which consists in conforming to the standard of right desire. I have called truth of type (IIa) *descriptive truth;* and truth of type (IIb) *normative truth.* In both types—(IIb) as well as (IIa)—the propositions are synthetic, which is to say that they are not self-evident; they are conclusions, and as such both need grounds of one sort or another for their establishment as true: purely factual grounds, in the case of descriptively true propositions; mixed factual and normative grounds, in the case of normatively true propositions.

Ayer and his followers can, of course, stipulate that by "truth" or "objective truth," they mean only the *verbal truth* of analytic propositions and the *descriptive truth* that is attributable to synthetic propositions when what they assert to be the case conforms to the way things are. Such a stipulation on their part would lead necessarily to the conclusion that normative statements, such as "One ought to desire X" or "One ought to do or have M," cannot be objectively true. But if Ayer's argument rests merely upon such a stipulation, then it can be rejected by showing that the stipulation is arbitrary and unwarranted. It is warranted only if Ayer can *show* that there are but two kinds of truth—(Ia) the verbal truth that is attributable to analytic propositions, and (IIa) the descriptive truth that is attributable to synthetic statements of fact.

I submit that that cannot be done. It should now be abundantly clear that the twofold division of the modes of truth, which has reigned in modern philosophy since the days of Hume and Kant, must be replaced by the fourfold division that subdivides

(I) *a priori* truth into (Ia) *verbal truth* and (Ib) *truth of under-standing;* and (II) *a posteriori* truth into (IIa) *descriptive truth* and (IIb) *normative truth.*

By calling attention to the distinct mode of truth that is at-tributable to normative conclusions when what they enjoin us to seek or do conforms to right desire, Aristotle removed the grounds of Ayer's objection to the validity of moral philosophy long before the objection was raised. It should, perhaps, be added that the discernment of the difference between the truth of understanding that is attributable to axioms and the merely verbal or tautological truth of analytic propositions is of almost equal importance in undermining Ayer's objection, because the one basic principle of moral philosophy—that one ought to make a really good life for one's self by seeking the *totum bonum*—is an axiomatic or self-evident proposition that has the kind of truth that I have called "truth of understanding."

One point already touched on deserves reiteration. The truth of normative conclusions depends, in the first place, on the truth of understanding that belongs to the basic normative principle about the ultimate end to be sought, and, in the second place, it depends on the empirical truth of a large number of de-scriptive propositions which relate to whether, as a matter of fact, something in question is or is not a means to the end. Hence the truth of normative conclusions is at best a relative degree of truth, lacking certitude. It is always the truth of *doxa,* never the truth of *episteme.* [15]

CHAPTER 14

Real Goods Make Natural Rights

(1)

ONE further objection remains to be considered, but this time it does not come from any particular school of moral philosophy. Reviewing the course of the argument so far, it is an objection that common sense itself would raise against the philosophical development of its views on the good life for man.

In the course of that development, we have learned that the individual has a moral obligation to make a good life for himself and that a good life is the *totum bonum*, constituted by all the real goods that satisfy man's natural needs. We have also learned that categorical oughts can be true, and have seen the two ways in which they can be true. We have thus arrived at the point where we can understand how it can be truly concluded that a man ought to seek this or that real good for himself, or ought to employ this or that instrumental means to achieve his end, *if* and *when* he knows, as a matter of fact, what his specifically human needs are and how they can be satisfied. Knowing this, he knows what he ought to seek and do in order to obey the injunction to make a good life for himself.

So much for the individual by himself. So much for his own good life. But what about other men and their happiness? What about the individual's duties or moral obligations toward them? If the common-sense view cannot be philosophically developed to cover the individual's moral obligations to other men, it is seriously defective. The man of common sense knows this without the benefit of philosophical instruction; he recognizes, in the normal transactions of his everyday life, that he has duties to others and he expects others to discharge their obligations toward him.

Yet in obeying the injunction to make a good life for himself, it would appear that the individual does not have to take the good of other men into account. The plan for making a good life does not seem to involve any rules or even recommendations concerning the behavior of the individual in relation to other men or to the organized society in which he lives. It may be wondered why the discussion so far has exclusively focused on what is good for the individual, and has totally disregarded his obligation toward others.

This apparent self-centeredness in the development so far of the common-sense view has not been accidental. It springs, in the first place, from the fact that our point of departure was a question with which common sense is concerned and to which common-sense wisdom provides the outlines of an answer— *How can I make a good life for myself?* But that is not the only reason why we have concentrated on what is good for the individual.

The second, and much more important, reason is the common-sense conviction that only by the individual's knowing what is really good for himself can he know what is really good for other men, too, and only through knowing this can he determine what an individual's rights are—rights that ought to be secured by society and respected by other men. Stated in philosophical terms, this common-sense conviction asserts the primacy of the good and the derivative character of the notions of right and wrong. The determination of what is right and wrong in the private or social conduct of the individual is based on what is really good for each individual, and on the *totum bonum* or ultimate end that he ought to seek for himself. [1]

The common-sense view would be seriously defective in its philosophical development if it remained entirely self-centered, but it is not defective by virtue of having made the concern of the individual with his own happiness or good life the point of departure. Quite the contrary. Beginning with self-concern is the only sound approach to the solution of moral problems that involve other men and organized society as well as one's own life. [2]

On the one hand, ethical doctrines, such as the various forms of utilitarianism, which make the greatest good of the greatest number or the general happiness of mankind the ultimate objective to be accomplished, cannot satisfactorily explain how that objective is the ultimate desideratum of the individual, and yet they are logically under the necessity to explain it since they maintain that the good is the desirable and that the good is the primary notion from which the notions of right and wrong can be derived. On the other hand, ethical doctrines, such as those of Kant and later deontologists who insist upon the primacy of right and wrong, cannot satisfactorily deal with what is right and wrong for the individual to do in the pursuit of his own ultimate good; nor can they find a single *raison d'être* for all his moral obligations, those he has toward himself as well as those he has toward others. They present us with a catalog of unrelated duties, each of which they mistakenly claim is self-evident, as Pritchard does, or all of which they mistakenly claim can be derived from the logical principle of universalization, as Kant does.

In Chapter 12, we were concerned to defend the commonsense view against those who deny that the individual has a categorical obligation to seek his own happiness or to make a really good life for himself. Here we are going to take the offensive, and criticize the views of those who fail to see that this one categorical obligation is the source of all others, not only determining what is right and wrong in the individual's conduct of his own life, but also what his duties are to others on the basis of the rights they have that he is morally obliged to respect.

The title of this chapter may be cryptic in its brevity. Its meaning spelled out amounts to this: from the obligation that each individual has to make a really good life for himself come all the natural rights he has *vis-à-vis* other individuals and the organized society in which he lives; and those natural rights are, in turn, the basis of an individual's duties to other men, and of organized society's duties to *all* the human beings who are its members. [3]

In the immediately following sections of this chapter, I will expand the philosophical development of the common-sense view to cover the individual's moral obligations to others, postponing until Chapter 16 the obligations of organized society to its members. In both cases, as we shall see, the controlling principle is the same; namely, the primary obligation that the individual has to make a really good life for himself, from which he derives his basic natural right to the pursuit of happiness. Having shown how the moral obligations of one individual to another stem from the basic moral obligation that each individual has to make a good life for himself, I will, in the concluding section of this chapter, try to show what is unsatisfactory about the opposite approach to this problem—the one taken by Mill and the utilitarians and the one taken by Kant and the deontologists. These are negatively alike in that they both fail to see that the individual's own ultimate good is not only the object of his primary moral obligation, but also the source of all his subsidiary obligations, governing either the conduct of his own life or his conduct toward others.

(2)

Resting on the distinction between the real and the apparent good, a basic tenet of the common-sense view is that what is really good for any single individual is good in exactly the same sense for every other human being, precisely because that which is really good is that which satisfies desires or needs inherent in human nature—the make-up that is common to all men because they are members of the same biological species. The *totum bonum*—happiness or the good life—is the same for all men, and each man is under the same basic moral obligation as every other—to make a good life for himself.

Two things follow from this controlling insight. Every real good is a common good, not an individual good, not one that corresponds to the idiosyncratic desires or inclinations of this or that individual. The same, of course, holds true of the *totum bonum* as the sum total of all real goods. The pursuit of happiness by individuals of every shade of individual difference and under every variety of outward circumstance is the pursuit of the same objective.

In addition, when I know the things that are really good for me and what my happiness consists in, and when I understand that each real good and the *totum bonum* as the sum of all of them are common goods, the same for all men, I can then discern the natural rights each individual has—rights that others have which impose moral obligations upon me, and rights that I have which impose moral obligations upon others. By an individual's rights, we understand the things he has a right to demand of other men or of organized society as a whole. His rights are legal rights when they are granted to him by organized society through the institutions of positive law, including the constitution of the state in which he lives. Conferred upon him by society, they can also be revoked, but while they are in force, each man's legal rights impose legal obligations upon his fellowmen. Where there is no legal right, there is no legal obligation, and conversely, where there is no legal obligation, there is no legal right. The same co-implicative connection exists between moral rights and moral obligations. I can have moral obligations toward another man, and he can have moral obligations toward me, only if each of us has moral rights one against the other.

But what is a moral right as contradistinguished from a legal right? It is obvious at once that it must be a right that exists without being created by positive law or social custom. What is not the product of legal or social conventions must be a creation of nature, or to state the matter more precisely, it must have its being in the nature of men. Moral rights are natural rights, rights inherent in man's common or specific nature, just as his natural desires or needs are. Such rights, being antecedent to society and government, may be recognized and enforced by society or they may be transgressed and violated, but they are inalienable in the sense that, not being the gift of legal enactment, they cannot be taken away or annulled by acts of government.

The critical point to observe is that natural rights are correlative with natural needs. I said a moment ago that where one individual has an obligation—legal or moral—to another, it must be in virtue of some right—legal or moral—possessed by that other. There is a deeper and more significant connection between rights and obligations, but one that obtains only in the case of moral rights and moral obligations. I do not have any moral rights *vis-à-vis* others unless I also have, for each moral right that I claim, a moral obligation to discharge in the sphere of my own private life. Every moral right of mine that imposes a moral duty upon others is inseparable from a moral duty imposed upon me.

For example, if I have a moral—or natural—right to a decent livelihood, that can be the case only because wealth, to a degree that includes amenities as well as bare necessities, is a real good, part of the *totum bonum*, and thus indispensable to a good life. The fact that it is a real good, together with the fact that I am morally obliged to seek it as part of my moral obligation to make a good life for myself, is inseparable from the fact that I have a natural right to a decent livelihood. If I did not need a modicum of wealth to live well or achieve happiness, it would not be a real good, I would not have a moral obligation to seek it, and *ipso facto* I would also have no natural right to a decent livelihood. That which I do not need for my own good life or that which is not an essential ingredient in my pursuit of happiness does not impose a duty on me, as far as my own private conduct is concerned, nor does it impose a duty on others with regard to their conduct toward me because such matters give me no natural or moral rights that others must respect.

Let me summarize this by calling attention to the set of basic notions that are inseparably connected with one another: (a) natural needs, (b) real goods, (c) the duties or moral obligations I have in the conduct of my own life, (d) moral or natural rights, and (e) the duties or moral obligations I have in my conduct toward others. Natural needs make certain things really good for me; the things that are really good for me impose moral obligations on me in the conduct of my private life; these, in turn, give me certain moral or natural rights, and my having such rights imposes moral obligations on others with respect to me. The order of enumeration can be reversed, but it cannot be scrambled, and no link in the chain can be omitted. And just as natural needs and the real goods correlative to them are the same for all men because they have the same specific nature, so too, and for the same reason, the remaining items on the list are the same for all men. We all have the same moral obligations in the conduct of our private lives; we all have the same natural rights; and we all have the same duties toward others.

As our primary moral obligation is to make a really good life for ourselves, so our primary natural right is our right to the pursuit of happiness. To respect this right that I have, others are under the obligation not to do anything that prevents me or seriously impedes me from discharging my basic obligation to myself. If I did not know in some detail the things I ought to do in order to discharge the obligation I am under to make a good life for myself, I could not know what behavior on the part of others interfered with my pursuit of happiness and so was wrong—a violation of my natural rights. In other words, all my subsidiary natural rights—rights to life, security of life and limb, a decent livelihood, freedom from coercion, political liberty, educational opportunities, medical care, sufficient free time for the pursuits of leisure, and so on—stem from my right to the pursuit of happiness and from my obligation to make a good life for myself. They are rights to the things I need to achieve that end and to discharge that obligation.

I will subsequently discuss these subsidiary natural rights at greater length. [4] The only point I wish to reiterate here, because it is of such prime importance, is that the individual would not have a natural right to the pursuit of happiness if he did not have a moral obligation to make a good life for himself; and if he did not have that one basic natural right, he would not have any subsidiary natural rights, because all other natural rights relate to the elements of individual happiness or to the parts of a good life—the diverse real goods that, taken together, constitute the whole that is the sum of all these parts.

(3)

The foregoing discussion of natural rights and moral duties not only throws light on the primacy of the good over the right, but also enables us to connect the good and the right with the notion of justice and injustice. Let me briefly expand both of these points.

If we did not know or could not know what is really good

or bad for the individual, we would not and could not know what is right and wrong in the conduct of one individual toward others; nor could we know what is right and wrong in the individual's conduct of his own life. If, without reference to others, we speak of an individual as acting rightly or wrongly, we are saying no more than that he is or is not discharging his moral obligation to make a really good life for himself. So when, with reference to others, we say that an individual acts rightly or wrongly, we are similarly saying that he is or is not discharging his moral obligations toward them, based on their natural rights—rights that are grounded in each man's moral obligation to make a good life for himself.

Ordinarily we use the terms *just* and *unjust* when we are considering the right and wrong acts of one individual in relation to others, but seldom or never do we use them when concerned with the individual's moral obligation to himself. What I have described as a matter of ordinary usage can, for good reasons, be made a matter of stipulation. There is some point in preserving the distinction between an individual's moral obligations to himself and his moral obligations to others. He does not claim any rights against himself, as he claims rights against others. His moral obligations toward others are grounded in their rights, and determine the rightness or wrongness of his conduct toward them. To preserve this distinction, the words "just" and "unjust" should be applied only to an individual's conduct toward others —to say, in other words, that the individual is just only when he acts rightly toward others, and unjust only when he acts wrongly toward them. [5]

Two further points emerge with regard to justice. One concerns the ancient observation that justice consists in virtuous action toward others. We have seen that fortitude and temperance, which are aspects of moral virtue or strength of character, and prudence or soundness of judgment, operate instrumentally as necessary means toward the end of making a good life for one's self. A good moral character and sound judgment would also seem to be involved in making the effort that we are under a moral obligation to make in our conduct toward others —to act rightly toward them and to avoid wronging them, which is another way of saying that we ought not to injure them by preventing them from making good lives for themselves. Thus we can see what is meant by saying that justice in general consists in having the moral character that the individual needs in the effort to make a good life, for when his moral character or virtue is directed toward the good life that others are under an obligation to make for themselves, it has the aspect we refer to as justice rather than as temperance or fortitude.

The second point concerns the obligations of organized society as a whole toward its individual members, and leads us to the consideration of justice and injustice in our social institutions, our economic arrangements, our laws, our constitution, and our government. Our basic natural right to the pursuit of happiness, and all the subsidiary rights that it encompasses, impose moral obligations on organized society and its institutions as well as upon other individuals. If another individual is unjust when he does not respect our rights, and so injures us by interfering with or impeding our pursuit of happiness, the institutions of organized society, its laws, and its government, are similarly unjust when they deprive individuals of their natural rights. Just governments, it has been correctly declared, are instituted to secure these rights. I interpret that statement as going further than the negative injunction not to violate the natural rights of the individual, or deprive him of the things he needs to make a good life for himself. It imposes upon organized society and its government the positive obligation to secure the natural rights of its individuals by doing everything it can to aid and abet them in their efforts to make good lives for themselves—especially helping them to get things they need that are not within their power to get for themselves.

This, as we shall see, is the meaning of "promote the general welfare." [6] That organized society and its government have a positive obligation to promote the pursuit of happiness by its members, as well as the negative obligation not to deprive them of the things they need, to which they have natural rights, is an important point of distinction between the duties of one individual to another and the moral obligation of organized society to its members. The individual's duties are all negative; justice does not require him to promote, or aid and abet, the pursuit of happiness by his fellow-men, it requires him only *not* to injure them by preventing or impeding them from making good lives for themselves.

This, too, will be more fully explained later. [7] For the present, suffice it to remark that the point I have just made directly contravenes Kant's thesis that each of us has an ethical duty to promote the happiness of our fellow-men, as well as Mill's "general happiness principle," that calls upon each of us to work for the greatest good of the greatest number. Neither Kant nor Mill, as we have seen, conceived happiness as a common good, the same *totum bonum* for all men. That failure on their part, by itself, would make it impossible to conceive how the individual could promote the happiness of other men or work for the general happiness of all. But even when happiness is correctly conceived as a common good, which makes it possible for organized society to promote the happiness of its members, the individual's only positive obligations are those involved in making a good life for himself. His obligations in justice to others are all negative—all based on the rights involved in their making good lives for themselves, all duties not to prevent them from doing so. [8]

The foregoing criticism of Kant and Mill applies, in a somewhat different way, to many others outside the circle of professional philosophy—to social scientists, to college or university students, and to "reformers" or "rebels" generally, old as well as young, who cry out against the injustice of our society and its institutions but who, at the same time, do not know the elements of the *totum bonum* as a common good or who, if they did, would reject the view that happiness or the good life is the same for all men. Lacking such understanding or rejecting it, they have no grounds whatsoever for charging injustice, and they can have no sound ideas about what ought to be done to remedy it, if it exists.

The man who does not correctly understand what is involved in his making a good life for himself, or who would deny that he is under a moral obligation in this regard, which is binding on all other men in the same way, is one who is in no position to talk about the rights of men and the obligations of society. Justice and injustice are purely emotional words in his mouth, empty of any objective meaning, expressions merely of what he likes or dislikes, what he wants or does not want. Yet those who are most vocal and vociferous in their outcries against injustice, and usually utter their condemnations with unqualified and unembarrassed certitude, are those for whom the word "injustice" can have no objective meaning because it is unconnected in their minds with an understanding and affirmation of the real goods which create the natural rights that injustice transgresses or violates.

They also tend to be individuals who either fail to understand or refuse to acknowledge the instrumental role of moral virtue in their lives, as an indispensable means to their achieving really good lives for themselves; yet they seldom hesitate to denounce, again with certitude, the lack of virtue in other groups of men whom they diabolize and make out to be knaves or villains in their conduct toward their fellow-men and misguided fools or hypocrites in the conduct of their own lives. They are full of the specious morality of "do-gooding" toward others, but devoid of the sound morality that consists, first of all, in knowing and seeking the things that are really good for one's self, and then considering and respecting the rights of others that are grounded in the same real goods.

Without knowing what is really good for a man and what is involved in his achieving a good life for himself and, therefore, without being able to know what aspects of society facilitate or militate against the achievement of the *totum bonum*, they do not hesitate to pass moral judgments on the evils of technology, to censure the oppressiveness of corporately organized big business, to decry the multiplication of commodities that is a feature of the affluent society, or to complain about the mismanagement of the universities and the subservience of the educational system to the wrong purposes or goals. I am far from saying that such criticisms are not, in many respects, objectively well-founded; I am only saying that even when they are well-founded, they are too often made without the knowledge and understanding—and, above all, the moral commitment to a good life correctly conceived—which provides the foundation that makes them objectively sound.

(4)

At the beginning of this chapter, I promised I would return at the end to alternative solutions of the problems with which we have been concerned, especially those offered by Kant and the deontologists and by Mill and the utilitarians. By this time the reader should be able to surmise the main tenor of my criticism of these alternative solutions. In the case of Kant and the deontologists, it is mainly directed against all the consequences of giving primacy to the notions of right and wrong rather than to the good as the desirable; in the case of Mill and the utilitarians, it is mainly directed against the substitution of the general happiness principle or the greatest good of the greatest number for the common good—the *totum bonum* that is the same for all men—as the ultimate end to be sought and the object of every man's primary moral obligation. I will, therefore, comment only briefly on certain points that have not yet been mentioned or indicated.

First of all, I would like to dwell for a moment on an insight that has been stressed by modern writers on moral matters, from Kant to the present day. It is an insight that certain twentieth-century utilitarians, especially those who call themselves "rule utilitarians," have adopted from Kant, often without acknowledging the lineage of the idea. The insight is sometimes called the "generalization principle," and sometimes the "universalizability thesis." [9] It consists in the observation that moral truths must be capable of unrestricted universalization. This is the case whether the moral truth is expressed in the form of an obligation to be discharged, in the form of an end to be sought or served, or in the form of a rule of conduct to be obeyed. In Kant's version of the insight, the generalization principle is stated in one of his many formulations of the categorical imperative: so act that the maxim of your action can become a universal law or rule. Another way of saying the same thing is as follows: whatever you regard as really good for you to seek or morally right for you to do should be really good for everyone else to seek or morally right for everyone else to do. Still another way is M. G. Singer's formula: "What is right (or wrong) for one person must be right (or wrong) for every relevantly similar person in relevantly similar circumstances." [10] In short, a normative proposition of any sort, whether it is a normative principle or a normative conclusion, fails to comply with the generalization principle and so cannot be regarded as morally valid, if it applies only to some men, and not to all, in respects in which they are all essentially alike.

The generalization principle is thought by many to be a novel discovery of modern thought. Some of the formulations of it, such as Kant's, may be novel in their phrasing and in their systematic connotations, and some of the arguments in support of the principle and some of the qualifications attached to it may be novel in detail, but the principle itself has always been implicit in the common-sense view. It is most succinctly conveyed by the insight that the real good is the common good, which is expanded in the proposition that whatever is really good for any one human being is really good for all other human beings and, hence, that whatever moral obligations the individual has are universally binding on all other men in the same way. It is also expressed in the proposition that natural rights, being grounded in the needs inherent in human nature and in the real goods that satisfy them, are the same for all men.

The only important novelty in the contemporary discussion of the generalization principle lies in its futile effort to establish the soundness of the principle while at the same time denying or refusing to employ the only matter of fact that can make it valid—the sameness of specific human nature, in which all men participate equally as men, regardless of all their differences as individual men. If men are not the same in kind and if, in addition, they do not differ from other animals in kind, then the generalization principle cannot be validated, nor can the rule that calls for the treatment of all men as equal in respect of their humanity be sustained. The fundamental equality of men as men is, as we have seen, their equality with respect to the natural rights that every man has because he is a man—because he has the same specific nature that is to be found in every other man, with the consequence that he has the same natural needs, that the same things are really good for him and everyone else, and that the good life which each man is morally obliged to make for himself consists in a *totum bonum* that is the same for all who engage in the pursuit of happiness. The rule that calls for equality of treatment cannot be deduced from or based on the generalization principle, nor can the generalization principle be derived from the rule with regard to equality; they are co-implicative, however, because both rest on one and the same common premise, namely, the sameness of all human beings in their specific nature. It is, therefore, impossible to affirm that all men should be treated equally and to deny in the next moment that happiness is the same for all, or conversely, to affirm that the *totum bonum* is the same for all and all men are under the same obligation to make good lives for themselves, while denying that all men should be treated equally. The basic premise which validates the affirmation of one of these propositions makes the denial of the other invalid. [11]

As formulated by Singer, the generalization principle has the appearance of being self-evident by virtue of the reference to "every relevantly similar person in relevantly similar circumstances." As thus stated, it is a purely formal, almost tautological, truth. Whether it has any substantive significance for moral philosophy depends on whether men are relevantly similar—or, more precisely, the same in all essential respects. This becomes clear when we formulate the principle by declaring that every moral truth must be capable of unrestricted universalization. That proposition is certainly not self-evident; yet we know it to be true once we know that all men have the same specific nature and, consequently, the same natural needs, the same real goods, the same ultimate end, the same moral obligations, and the same natural rights.

Not only does the generalization principle pervade the whole framework of the common-sense view as that has been developed, but it must also be added that only the common-sense view, by affirming the specific nature of man, can establish the truth of the generalization principle, interpreted in a way that gives it substantive significance for moral philosophy. That cannot be done by Kant and his followers in the vacuum of pure reason by any contrivance of logic; nor can it be done by Mill and his followers, by arguments in favor of the reasonableness of the principle, at least not so long as they are accompanied by an approach to the good wholly in terms of individual wants, and without reference to the common needs of man.

Kant's solution of the problems with which we have been concerned in this chapter is unsatisfactory for other reasons. We saw earlier the indefensibility of Kant's position with respect to what he calls "ethical duties"—duties attached to ends. [12] It is also indefensible with respect to what he calls "legal duties" —the duties that are discharged by obedience to the moral law. These duties, such as the duty to keep promises, the duty to pay debts, the duty to tell the truth, are neither self-evident in themselves, as later deontologists incorrectly suppose, nor can they be logically derived from the categorical imperative, as Kant's sharpest critics have pointed out again and again. [13] Since they are not self-evident, some reason must be given for regarding them as obligations that govern our conduct toward our fellow-men. The only reason that can be given must involve a reference, first, to the possibility that my telling another man a lie, my refusing to pay him back what I owe him, or my failing to keep my promise to him, may injure him, that is, may prevent or impede his making a good life for himself, and second, it must also involve some assessment of the probability that such is the case. The question of probability is one of fact; the possibility under consideration can be established only by thinking, first, in terms of what is really good and bad for the other man in order to decide, second, what may be right or wrong for me to do in relation to him. On both counts—the primacy of the good over the right and the appeal to empirical facts—we have had to depart radically from Kant's scheme of things in order to give any defense, however weak, of the moral obligations he regards as legal duties. [14]

The harshness of Kant's moral philosophy has made it generally repugnant to men who do not confuse being reasonable with being rationalistic. It demands of us, in the sphere of legal obligations, that we do our duty simply and purely for duty's sake and without any regard for our natural inclinations or needs, or concern for our own happiness. It calls upon us, in the sphere of ethical obligations, to act for the happiness of others but not our own. And in both spheres, it proceeds without any reference to the facts of human nature and human behavior, and rules out any consideration of such facts—or, for that matter, of particular circumstances—as irrelevant to the determination of what is good and bad, right and wrong. Nevertheless, one might be reluctantly driven to accept Kant's harsh and arid ethics if the only alternative to it were what he calls "the serpentine windings of utilitarianism"; then our only choice would be between a moral philosophy that has autonomy, on the one hand, and a purely pragmatic doctrine on the other. Fortunately, we are not confronted with the choice; the ethics of common sense involves the cautionary consideration of circumstances, the pragmatic calculation of the utility of means, and the regard for individual differences which are to be found in utilitarianism, while at the same time it is a moral philosophy that has autonomous principles and normative truths capable of unrestricted universalization.

The main trouble with utilitarianism is not the principle of utility itself, for that must govern any moral thinking that is done in terms of end and means. Any teleological ethics, such as that of common sense, is utilitarian or pragmatic in its employment of the principle of utility in appraising the goodness of means. The trouble with utilitarianism is that it is a teleological ethics with not one but two ultimate ends, and the two cannot be reconciled to each other or fused into a single overarching goal that can be the object of one primary moral obligation.

By consulting the actual desires of men, Mill concludes that everyone seeks his own happiness. Let us waive for the moment the error of identifying the happiness made up of the things an individual happens to want with the happiness constituted by the real and common goods every man ought to seek. Still using happiness to signify the sum total of satisfactions experienced by the individual who gets whatever he wants for himself, Mill then tries to substitute the general happiness or the greatest good of the greatest number for individual happiness as the ultimate goal.

Having first said, as a matter of fact, that each man desires his own happiness, conceived by him in terms of his own wants, Mill then shifts to saying that the ultimate standard or objective, in accordance with which the principle of utility should be applied, is "not the agent's own greatest happiness, but the greatest amount of happiness altogether." With regard to the individual's own happiness, Mill sees no need to argue for it as the ultimate end, since in fact all men do desire it. But when he comes to the "general happiness," Mill finds it impossible to say that, as a matter of fact, everyone desires this as his ultimate end. He considers the man who says to himself, "I feel that I am bound not to rob or murder, betray or steal, but why am I bound to promote the general happiness? If my own happiness lies in something else, why may I not give that the preference?" [15] Does Mill have an answer to this question, a question that would be asked by anyone who regarded his own individual happiness as his ultimate end? Answer it Mill must try to do, since he has employed the fact that all men do desire their individual happiness for its own sake and for nothing beyond itself, in order to establish happiness as the ultimate end that men do seek. He cannot dismiss this question lightly.

Coming from one of the world's most eminent logicians, the answer Mill gives is a model of sophistry. It runs as follows: "No reason can be given why the general happiness is desirable [Note: "desirable," not "desired"] except that each person, so far as he believes it to be attainable, desires his own happiness [Note: "his own happiness" is what each person desires, not the "general happiness"]. This, however, being a fact, we have not only all the proof which the case admits of, but all which it is possible to require, that happiness is a good [granted]; that each person's happiness is a good to that person [granted, and more, it is his ultimate good]; and the general happiness, therefore [does "therefore" signify a valid logical *sequitur*?] a good to the aggregate of persons." [16]

Not only is this plainly a non-sequitur, as a matter of logic; it is also meaningless as a matter of fact, for even though an aggregate of persons may, as collectively organized, have a collective goal, it is not the object of their individual desires, nor can it be distributively identified with the diverse individual goals each seeks for himself.

In addition to suffering from the serious defect of its failure to distinguish between natural needs and conscious desires, and between real and apparent goods, utilitarianism is fatally hung up by positing two ultimate ends. The teleological and utilitarian ethics of common sense has only one basic normative principle, only one ultimate end, and only one primary moral obligation; and precisely because that one end, the *totum bonum* which is the same for all men, is a common good, and not the greatest good for the greatest number, common sense is able to pass from the obligations an individual has in the conduct of his own life, aiming at happiness, to the obligations he has in his conduct toward others, who are also aiming at the same happiness he seeks for himself. [17]

Although I think I have made clear why the common-sense solution of the problems of social conduct is much more satisfactory than either of the two main alternative solutions—that of Kant and his followers and that of Mill and his—I have not yet shown the common-sense answer to be completely satisfactory. The discussion so far has left a number of extremely difficult questions unanswered.

One is the question why the individual should be just to others. We have seen that the individual is under a moral obligation to be just in his actions toward others—to respect their rights and not to injure them. But what has not been explained is how his being just toward others is, like his being temperate or prudent, an instrumental means toward making a good life for himself. We must try to discover how justice to others serves the individual in relation to his own end—in the pursuit of his own happiness. That is the point of the question which Mill signally failed to answer.

Another unanswered question concerns the possibility of a conflict between the individual's pursuit of his own happiness and his moral obligation to others in regard to their efforts to make good lives for themselves.

A third and final question is about the good of the community as such—the welfare of the state. Does the individual have a moral obligation to serve the welfare of the state, to *act for* the good of the community as such (the *bonum communitatis*), as well as a moral obligation not to act against the good of other individual men (the *totum bonum commune*)? And can his obligations to the state, if they exist, come into conflict with his primary obligation to make a good life for himself?

I will try to answer these questions, and deal with related considerations, in Chapter 16.

Part Three

The Ethics of Common Sense

CHAPTER 15

The Common-sense View Philosophically Developed: A Teleological Ethics

(1)

IT may be helpful to review the course we have taken so far in order to set the stage for the problems that remain to be considered.

We began, in Part One, with the question, *How can I make a good life for myself?* After clarifying the question in terms of what a whole life means as a use of the time allowed us on earth, I dealt with certain considerations that an intelligent man of common sense would face in trying to answer the question. I then expanded the common-sense answer by distinguishing the five basic types of activity in which men can engage to occupy the time of their lives, and I named, relative to each, the types of goods that are achieved respectively by these activities. Of the five basic types of activities, one—leisure-work—makes a greater contribution to leading a good life than all the others, for it is the one by which an individual improves himself as a person and promotes the good of his society and its culture.

In the opening chapter of Part Two, I stated a number of objections that modern philosophers, especially those writing and teaching today in England and the United States, would raise against the common-sense answer. I attempted to answer all these objections in the rest of Part Two by pointing out the error, misunderstanding, or ignorance that was involved in the

philosophical criticisms of the common-sense answer: (1) ignorance of the distinction between an end that is normative and an
end that is terminal, which leads to the erroneous denial of an
end that is ultimate; (2) misunderstanding of the indefinability
of the good as the object of desire; (3) ignorance of the distinction between conscious and natural desires (wants and needs)
and, with it, the distinction between apparent and real goods;
(4) failure to understand that the only self-evidently true normative principle or ought-statement is the proposition that we ought
to seek that which is really good for ourselves; (5) the erroneous
supposition that normative, unlike descriptive, statements cannot
be true or false, an error resulting from ignorance of the special
kind of truth that is the property of normative conclusions when,
in addition to being based on truths of fact, they conform to the
standard of right desire; (6) the misconception of happiness in
psychological and quasi-moral terms, displacing the conception of
it in purely ethical terms, as identical with a whole life that is
really good; and (7) the misconception of the good that is the
ultimate end as the *summum bonum* instead of as the *totum
bonum*.

Not only were the philosophical objections to the common-
sense answer thus removed, but the process of doing so had the
positive effect of giving philosophical development to the common-sense answer itself. The most important feature of this development was the transformation of the question with which
these lectures began, with a consequent transformation of the
answer that had so far been developed. The original question,
How can I make a good life for myself?, became *What ought I
to do in order to make a really good life for myself?* This transformation came about through recognizing the fundamental normative truth that I ought to make a really good life for myself
or, in other words, that a whole life that is really good is the
ultimate normative end, the *totum bonum*, that I am categorically
obliged to pursue. All other normative truths—all other true
ought-statements—are propositions about the goods that ought
to be sought as constitutive parts of a whole good life or as
means to the *totum bonum* which is the ultimate end.

The philosophical development of the common-sense answer
resulted in two other insights of great importance—first, that all

real goods are common goods, the same for all men because their specific needs are the same and, second, that whatever is really good for me constitutes a right in everyone else, a natural right that I ought to respect as I would have my own natural rights respected.

(2)

The foregoing review of the course we have followed explains why I call the ethics of common sense a teleological ethics. It is an ethical theory or moral philosophy in which the first principle is the end—the ultimate normative end, the *totum bonum* to which all other goods are ordered as means.

When the common-sense man thinks practically, that is, when he thinks about how to act or what choices to make, he thinks in terms of end and means. As a matter of simple fact, there is no other way to think practically. One can act aimlessly and without reflection or deliberation, but if one acts purposefully and thoughtfully, one must do so, first, by having some goal or objective in view, and then by considering the steps that must be taken to achieve it. When, in any sphere of action or production, men set a goal or objective for themselves, the practical problem to be solved is one of discovering the best—the most effective—means for accomplishing it. And when the practical problem is solved, its solution is expressed in a set of normative judgments, such as "To reach the objective, A, that we have set for ourselves, we should do X, Y, and Z" where X, Y, and Z represent the most effective means for attaining the end.

Such normative judgments are hypothetical rather than categorical, because the practical problem arose as a result of a goal that an individual or a group of individuals set for himself or themselves. They did not have to set this goal for themselves; they elected to do so. The normative judgments involved, made more explicit, take the form, "If we wish to achieve A, we ought to do X, Y, and Z."

The man of common sense may think about the practical problem of making a good life for himself in the same way that he thinks about other practical problems: if one wants to make a good life for one's self, one ought to do this or that, so-and-so or such-and-such. It is at this point that the philosopher steps in to make one correction in common-sense thinking, a correction that converts the problem of making a good life from a practical problem like any other practical problem into a practical problem that is *also* a moral problem.

It becomes a moral problem as soon as it is seen that the end in view is set for us, rather than one that we do or do not set for ourselves, as we wish. The end is set for us by the recognition of the self-evident truth of the categorical normative judgment that we ought to seek what is really good for us, and nothing less than everything that is really good for us. With this recognition that the *totum bonum commune*, a whole life that is really good, is the ultimate end that we ought to seek, the solution of the practical problem that is also a moral problem takes the form of categorical ought-judgments concerning the means we ought to employ in order to achieve the one and only end we ought to seek.

By this one correction, common-sense thinking about the practical problem of achieving a good life is thus made philosophically sound, and as thus philosophically developed, it becomes a teleological ethics; but—and this is a point of the greatest importance—it does not cease to be a practical or pragmatic moral philosophy because it attaches categorical oughts to the end and to the means.

It is generally supposed by modern philosophers that if an ethical doctrine is deontological (one that is set forth in terms of categorical oughts), it is diametrically opposed to an ethical doctrine that is pragmatic and teleological (one that is set forth in terms of end and means). It is further supposed by the exponents of a deontological ethics that teleological thinking about a good life or happiness must be purely pragmatic or practical, and cannot be moral or ethical because the only ought-judgments it can make are hypothetical, not categorical. Both of these widespread suppositions are erroneous.

Moral philosophy not only *can* be both teleological and deontological at the same time; it also *must* be both if it is to be a sound ethical doctrine that is at once moral and practical. If it is teleological without being deontological, it is purely pragmatic or practical, as some forms of utilitarianism are, and so it is not moral philosophy. If it is deontological without being teleological, it is purely rationalistic and out of touch with the facts of life, and so, by ceasing to be practical or pragmatic, it becomes basically unsound. Although the moral philosophy based on common sense is both teleological and deontological, I shall refer to it simply as a teleological ethics because its first principle is an ultimate end that is the whole of real goods and because, given that first principle, all its conclusions are about means that ought to be employed because they are necessary for achieving the end. [1]

Only one controlling insight is needed to construct an ethics that is both teleological and deontological. It is that nothing can be either an end or a means for action unless it is also a good—an object of desire. When the end and the means are seen to be real, not apparent, goods, then these real goods, related as end and means, become objects of categorical moral obligation as well as objects of desire.

(3)

The philosophical development of the ethics of common sense adds a number of other fundamental insights that express the moral wisdom of a teleological ethics. They are as follows.

First, the most egregious moral error that anyone can make is to convert a means into the end. All misconceptions of the good life are examples of this error. They substitute a part for the whole—identifying happiness or a whole life that is really good with one of the partial goods that is an element in the good life. To identify happiness with the possession of wealth without limit, or with the maximization of pleasure, is to misconceive happiness in this way. Wealth and pleasure are real goods, but only parts of happiness, not the whole of it. It is equally an error to identify the good life as a whole with being virtuous, with acting justly toward others, or even with acquiring as much knowledge as possible, for even though these are goods of which one cannot have enough, they are still only partial goods. None is the *totum bonum;* none is the end, but only a means. This error is, of course, compounded when happiness is identified with an apparent rather than a real good, such as power or domination over other men, for this is not even a means to the end of a good life.

Second, the means are the end in the process of becoming. As we have seen, when the end is a temporal whole, such as a good life, it is always a becoming, never a complete being. Strictly, we should not speak of human happiness as the "well-being" of a man, but rather as his "well-becoming." Nevertheless, since this process of well-becoming is a series of stages of development, the end exists to some extent at each stage of development, in the form of the means already acquired, the means now being acquired, and the means about to be acquired.

Third, a correct understanding of the end we ought to seek and of the means we ought to employ is not enough, practically, for achieving the end through the means. It is also necessary to desire the end we ought to seek, and to choose the means we ought to employ; and these represent non-cognitive acts on our part. This is just another way of saying that knowledge, even in the form of moral wisdom, is not the same as moral virtue, which consists in desiring and choosing as we ought.

Moral virtue consists in a habitual disposition of appetite, desire, or will, which inclines a man in the direction of the end he ought to seek, and consequently also controls his choice of means in the same direction. Since it is frequently the case that several alternative means are available, all of them good because they serve the end, the man of moral virtue or good character also needs prudence or sound judgment to choose the better or the best—the more or most effective—of these means.

When it is said that as a man's moral character is, so does he conceive the end that he ought to seek, the point to be stressed is that a correct conception of the end is implicit in the disposition that constitutes a good moral character. Correspondingly, a mistaken view of the end is implicitly present in a man of bad moral character. In this sense, moral virtue by itself involves a form of knowledge—an implicit, non-intellectual acknowledgment of the end that ought to be sought. But the converse is not true: intellectual knowledge by itself does not involve moral virtue. A man can explicitly know the end he ought to seek, and not in fact desire it or choose the means for attaining it.

Fourth, when we understand that happiness or a whole life that is really good consists in the possession of all the things that are really good for a man to have, we can also see that this *totum bonum* or ultimate end cannot be achieved unless the partial goods that constitute it and are means to it are chosen in the right order and proportion. Some of the partial goods that enter into the constitution of a good life as a whole, such as health, wealth, and pleasure, can be sought to an extent that prevents or impedes the acquirement of other real goods that are indispensable elements of a good life as a whole. Furthermore, since partial goods are not all equally good, and since some of them are means to others, the pursuit of happiness can be frustrated or defeated by choices that do not conform to a right ordering of the partial goods.

Once again we see the role that moral virtue plays in the pursuit of happiness, for since the means are the end in the process of becoming, moral virtue, in disposing a man to seek the end that he ought to seek, also disposes him to seek it by choosing the means to it in the right order and the right proportion of the partial goods that constitute a good life as a whole. This is another way of saying what was said earlier: the moral problem we face from day to day is always one of choosing between what is really good in the long run of our life as a whole and what is really or only apparently good in the short run—here and now.

Fifth, in addition to distinguishing among partial real goods by seeing that some may serve as means to others, we must also make a more fundamental distinction between (i) the partial goods that are *constitutive* means to the end of a good life as a whole and (ii) partial goods that are *operative* or *instrumental* means to this end. The constitutive means are those partial goods that answer to natural needs, as health does, or wealth, pleasure, friendships, the peace of the civil community, or knowledge in any of its many forms. The operative or instrumental means are the actions we perform to obtain the real goods we need; or even more basically, they are the means whereby we are disposed to choose real goods in the right order and proportion, and to choose the better or the best among available goods.

Moral virtue or a good moral character and prudence or sound judgment are thus seen to be the principal operative or instrumental means to happiness. Although the primary real goods are those that satisfy natural needs, and although moral virtue and prudence are good only because they are indispensable or necessary factors in the process of satisfying all of our natural needs, it is nevertheless the case that the operative or instrumental means are of primary importance in the pursuit of happiness. A human life is good through the possession of all the real goods that constitute the *totum bonum*, but it becomes good through the choices that are made from moment to moment, and so in the process of becoming happy, the goods that are the instrumental means to happiness are the primary factors. [2]

I just said that moral virtue and prudence are the principal operative or instrumental means to happiness. There is at least one other, and that is freedom.

One form of freedom, sometimes called internal freedom and sometimes moral freedom, is identical with moral virtue. It is the freedom possessed by the virtuous man who is able, by habitual disposition, to will as he ought, or, stated negatively, it is a freedom from the contrary pressure of immediate wants, which enables a man to seek what he needs in the long run.

Another form of freedom—the freedom to act as one desires or chooses, a freedom from coercion, duress, or the lack of enabling means—is not a freedom that is acquired with moral virtue, but is rather one that men possess only when the external circumstances of their lives confer it on them. Such freedom of action is clearly an operative or instrumental means to leading a good life, but it is also a real good that answers to a natural need, and as such it is a constitutive as well as an instrumental means.

The same holds true for still another form of freedom—political liberty, the freedom that men possess when they are governed with their own consent and with a voice in government. Like freedom of action, this, too, is a circumstantial freedom, and one that, answering to a natural need, is a constitutive as well as an instrumental means to happiness. That both freedom of action and political liberty are real goods that answer to natural needs is implied in the recognition of them as natural rights, which a just government should secure for all its people. [3]

Sixth and last, among the constitutive means of a good life, we must distinguish between the goods of choice and the goods of chance or fortune—on the one hand, the means that are wholly within our own power to employ or not employ according to our own choices, and on the other hand, the means that are made available or unavailable to us by the favorable or unfavorable circumstances that surround our lives. Some of the constitutive means to happiness are wholly goods of choice; some are wholly goods of chance, conferred or withheld by favorable or un-favorable circumstances; and some are mixed in character—partly gifts of fortune and partly within our own power of choice. With this distinction in mind, we can understand the meaning of the compact statement that the pursuit of happiness consists in choosing and acting in a manner that manifests a virtuous disposition, under favorable circumstances that confer a requisite minimum of the goods of fortune. [4]

(4)

The six points just stated outline the framework of a teleological ethics but do not exhaust its substance. Of the substantive points that remain, we need consider only two. The first concerns the enumeration of the real goods that are constitutive means to happiness, and the types of activity by which they are obtained —activities that use up the time of our lives and that are thus the temporal parts of life.

The real goods that have so far been mentioned can be grouped under four heads. In naming them, I will also name the type of activity by which they are obtained, insofar as they are within our power of choice.

(1) *Bodily health and vigor:* all biologically necessary activities, such as sleeping, eating, cleansing, and sometimes playing when playing is therapeutic or recreational; for which I have used SLEEP as an omnibus term.

(2) *Wealth* (the means of subsistence and the comforts or conveniences of life): economically necessary activities such as working for a living or managing one's estate; which I have called SUBSISTENCE-WORK.

(3) *Pleasure* (in all its experienceable forms, sensual, aesthetic, and intellectual): all forms of activity engaged in wholly for their own sake, with no result beyond themselves; for which I have used PLAY as an omnibus term.

(4) *The goods of self- or social-improvement:* all forms of activity by which the individual improves himself and contributes to the improvement of his society and its culture; for which I have used the term LEISURE or LEISURE-WORK. Among these goods are: (a) friendships; and (b) knowledge in all its forms—skills or arts, sciences, understanding and wisdom.

In addition to these goods that are wholly or partly within our power of choice, there are all the goods that are conferred upon us by favorable external circumstances and that are nonetheless constitutive means to the end of a good life. Among these goods are: (a) the good of communal life, which is peace; and (b) a good society and a just government, one that promotes the general welfare and treats all men equally by securing the natural rights of each, including his right to life and his right to a decent livelihood, his right to freedom of action, and his right to political liberty.

Is this enumeration exhaustive? I think it is exhaustive of the real goods that are constitutive means to a good life as a whole. But on the side of the activities that can occupy the times of our lives, the foregoing enumeration fails to mention two.

One of these has been referred to in earlier chapters. It is *idling.* I have not included it here because it does not appear to aim at the acquirement of any type of real good that answers to a natural need. Yet it should not be lightly dismissed as of no importance, in view of the fact that many men, perhaps all of us, consume many hours in idling. Let me appeal to a machine metaphor in order to explain idling. We say that an automobile engine idles when it runs while the auto remains in place, going nowhere. The engine turns over, but the usual appropriate result —locomotion—is not achieved. So, when men idle, they are not asleep, or at work, or at play, or engaged in leisure. They are awake but doing nothing productive of a desired result. Nevertheless, idling may produce results not consciously or intentionally planned, as when, in the course of idling, thoughts or decisions spring unpremeditated from the unconscious.

Another form of activity not yet mentioned goes by the name of rest, in that connotation of the term expressed in the meaning of the Sabbath as a day of rest, or when it is said that after performing the work of creation in six days, on the seventh day God rested. Clearly, in this meaning of the term, rest is not to be confused with sleep, or recreational play, or even with leisuring. Also clearly, the term as thus used has a religious and theological connotation, which signifies a form of activity that is apart from or transcends our secular and worldly lives. Since I have restricted our discussion of the good life to one that is lived in this world, on the natural plane and in a secular fashion, the activity of rest cannot enter into our considerations. But, in passing, I would like to suggest that on the secular plane, some forms of *idling*, which involve moments of quiet contemplation, reverie, or fantasy, may perform a function that is the secular equivalent of the function performed by *rest* in the religious life.

(5)

The second substantive point to be made concerns the order of goods, or what is sometimes called the scale of values. Among the constitutive means to happiness, some are limited and some are unlimited goods, and the latter are superior to and take precedence over the former. By an *unlimited good*, I mean one of which we cannot have enough, such as knowledge in any of its forms, or friendship and love. By a *limited good*, I mean one that is good only in some quantity, the kind of good about which it is true to say you can have too much of a good thing. [5]

Consider wealth, in the form of consumable goods. The quantity of wealth that is good, that is not excessive or superfluous, is obviously relative to our needs for the necessities and amenities of life. The same holds for the pleasures of play in all its forms. Although the principle of limitation is not as obvious here as it is in the case of consumable wealth, it is nevertheless clear that since play does not result in self-improvement, the devotion of all of one's free time to play would be stultifying. In itself, health would appear to be an unlimited good, but on the side of the activities productive of health, it is certainly possible to devote more time than is necessary to the care of the body and to the development of its physical vigor.

Of the five basic types of human activity, only one—the one that is productive of unlimited goods—calls for the maximum investment of our time, and that one is leisure-work. The limitation to be imposed on the amount of time devoted to the other types of activity is solely for the sake of allowing as much time as possible for the pursuits of leisure. The goods of leisure are thus seen to be the highest goods among those that constitute a good life.

Biologically necessary activities are common to men and all other animals. While the effort we make to maintain health is characteristically a human undertaking, bodily health and vigor are not characteristically human goods. Health and wealth are functionally interdependent as goods. On the one hand, a sufficient degree of bodily health and vigor is needed as a means to the performance of subsistence-work, and on the other hand, some degree of consumable wealth beyond the minimum necessities serves as a means to the maintenance of bodily health and vigor. Nevertheless, of these two, there is a sense in which health is the higher good. If we were compelled by circumstances to subordinate one to the other, we should give health priority or precedence in our scale of values. It contributes more, in the long run, to making a good life for ourselves.

Purely playful activities are good in themselves in that they provide us with immediately enjoyable pleasures; they do not serve as means to any other partial good, as wealth serves health, and as both of these serve as means to engagement in leisure and to the goods that leisure-work produces. The immediately enjoyable pleasure of play satisfies a natural need and so is a part of or a constitutive means to a good life as a whole, but since the pleasures of play do not increase our human stature one cubit, play should be subordinated to the activities of leisure, which do.

Only leisure activities—activities that are creative in the primary sense of being self-creative, not productive of other things—contribute, first of all, to the growth of a human being as specifically human and, second, to the improvement of human society and the advancement of human culture. It is for this reason that the goods of leisure are the highest goods in the scale of partial goods, and that among the parts of life—the activities that use up our time—the activities of leisure make the greatest contribution to a good life as a whole. [6]

Hence, in the choices that we make from day to day in the use of our time, we ought to subordinate all other activities to leisure-work. We ought to engage in the others only to an extent that is based on our natural needs, or in a way that is limited by the consideration that nothing we do should unnecessarily consume the time left for the pursuits of leisure.

CHAPTER 16

Obligations to Self and to Others:
Individual and Common Goods

(1)

AT the conclusion of Chapter 14, three questions were posed but not answered. All three concerned the good of others —either the good of other individuals or the good of the organized community. Let me recall and elucidate the three questions.

First, why should I be just in my conduct toward other individuals? Let it be granted at once that I have a moral obligation to respect the rights of others. Let it be granted, furthermore, that the rights of others, like my own rights, are founded in the primary moral obligation of each of us to make a really good life for himself. It is this that creates the problem to be solved. Precisely because the one and only primary moral obligation of each man, from which alone all other moral obligations are derived, is the obligation to make a good life for himself, it becomes necessary for us to understand how being just toward others is involved in the individual's effort to make a good life for himself. We must be able to see how our being unjust toward others can interfere with the pursuit of our own happiness. Or, conversely, we must be able to see how a well-planned effort to make a good life requires the individual to act justly toward others.

Second, can there be a conflict between my obligation to make a good life for myself and my obligations toward others? Is the pursuit of happiness cooperative or competitive? Are there conditions under which one individual's success in making a good life for himself is achieved at the cost of misery to others—the defeat of their efforts to make good lives for themselves?

Third, does the individual have an obligation to act for the good of the organized community as well as justly toward other individual men? How does this obligation derive from his primary obligation to make a good life for himself? And here, once again, we must ask whether his duties to the community can interfere with his making a good life for himself.

As we consider these three questions, we can see that they are intimately related, and related in such a way that the attempt to answer any one of them will appeal to considerations involved in answering the other two.

In the first place, it is clear that if man were not a social animal, dependent not only for his very life, but also for the leading of a good life, on association with his fellow-men, none of these problems would arise. We have seen earlier that man has a natural need for association. This natural need makes having friends one of the real goods that enter into making a good life. It also makes participation in the life of an organized community —whether it is that of the family or of the state—a real good.

Seeing this, we can see that the relation of the individual to the community or to other individuals, either as friends or as members of that community, cannot be thought of as something adventitious to his effort to make a good life for himself. On the contrary, it is an integral part of that effort. If the individual could live and live well in complete isolation from his fellow-men, he would have no duties to them or to the organized community that could be derived from his obligation to make a good life for himself.

If it could be shown, as I think it cannot be shown, that the individual's obligations to others and to the community are independent of his obligation to make a good life for himself, then the discharge of such obligations would impose a burden on him that might interfere with or even frustrate the pursuit of his own happiness. I would like to add, in passing, that those who regard their duties to others or to the community as independent of their obligation to make a good life for themselves are either sentimentalists or thoughtless do-gooders who often do more harm than good—not only harm to themselves, but also to others and to the community itself.

In the second place, it should be clear that the primacy of the individual's moral obligation to make a good life for himself, taken together with the fact of his social nature, is the pivotal point in the solution of all three problems. The point is that all the other obligations that are derived from this one primary obligation concern means that are indispensable to the end—a whole good life—that each of us ought to seek.

Just as my obligation to engage in leisure activities flows from this one primary obligation because the goods achieved by such activities are indispensable to my making a really good life for myself, so my obligation to be just toward others or to act for the good of the community flows from the same primary obligation because the good of the community and the good of others are real goods for me and, as such, means to or integral parts of the *totum bonum* that is my good life as a whole. Whatever means are indispensable to the ultimate end we ought to seek are means we are obliged to employ; our obligations with regard to such means, being derived from our obligation with regard to the end, cannot come into conflict with the latter or with each other.

(2)

Let us now apply these insights to the solution of each of the three related problems that concern the rights of others and the good of the community. Let us begin with the good of the organized community.

An organized community consists of men associated in a common life, cooperating in the achievement of things that are really good for each of them but which no one of them alone can achieve for himself. The goods achieved by the organized community are thus goods in which its members participate or share. But what about the good of the community itself? What, by its very nature as an association of men engaged in a common life, does the community itself need in order to endure and function? The answer is peace—first of all, civil peace, and second, peaceful relations with other communities.

Let us for the moment consider only civil peace. The maintenance of civil peace depends not only on the enforcement of laws, but on the justice of those laws. When the laws or other institutions of a community are unjust and, hence, violate the natural rights of its members, or of some part of its population, civil peace may be disrupted by the violence of justified rebellion on the part of those who have suffered a long train of abuses or an oppression that has grown intolerable.

But it is not only the justice of the laws or of the institutions of a community that is indispensable to civil peace, which is the essential good of the community itself. Just conduct on the part of each individual toward others is also a factor in the preservation and promotion of civil peace. Every criminal act—an act that injures other men or the community itself—is a breach of the peace. It is not difficult to see that the community would not long endure if most of its members were criminals, or if they for the most part acted criminally. It would soon disintegrate into a state of war—the war of each against all the rest.

The civil peace that is the good of the community itself is a good that each of us needs as a means toward the end of making a good life for himself. Hence when I act unjustly toward others or act in any way that is contrary to the good of the community, I am injuring myself. It may not appear to be so in the short run; I may gain apparent goods by my injustice toward others or by criminal activities that injure the community itself. But in the long run, I may have gained these apparent goods only at the loss of a real good that I need—the civil peace of the community in which I live. It is only in the short run that injustice can appear to be expedient. In the long run, which is the run of my whole life, the just tends to be the expedient.

This leaves one further question to be answered. Can my obligation to serve the good of the community ever adversely affect the pursuit of my own happiness? Under *ideal conditions*, the answer is no. I will presently explain what I mean by ideal conditions. For the moment, let it suffice to say that since the good of the community serves as a means to my making a good life for myself, I can never be asked to subordinate that end to one of its means. When the conditions are *not* ideal, I may be asked to take certain risks that adversely affect my pursuit of happiness, but even under such conditions the risks do not constitute the subordination of my pursuit of happiness to the good of the community. [1]

(3)

I turn next to the question about the possibility of a conflict between my making a good life for myself and your making one for yourself. Once again I must refer to ideal conditions in order to say that, under such conditions, no possibility of conflict exists.

I injure other men when what I seek for myself deprives them of what they need. Thus, for example, I may seek to exercise power over them in a way that deprives them of the freedom they need to make good lives for themselves. But power or domination over other men is only an apparent good—something I may want, but not something that answers to a natural need. Not being a real good, it is not a means toward making my own life good.

This one example leads us to the insight that when an individual seeks only those things that are really good for him, he does not infringe on or interfere with the pursuit of happiness on the part of others through their seeking the same real goods for themselves. This insight is confirmed by the consideration of the real goods achieved by leisure-work. Nothing that an individual does when engaged in leisure can injure another man; on the contrary, through his engagement in leisure, the individual not only benefits himself but usually benefits others.

Wealth and pleasure are also real goods, but only in limited quantities and only as subordinated to the goods of self-improvement—the goods achieved by leisure. Hence it is possible for an individual to seek wealth or pleasure to an extent or in a manner that is injurious to others. But this can happen only when what he seeks or the way he seeks it is, like power or domination over other men, not really good for him—something he may want, and so something that is an apparent good, but not something that answers to a natural need, and so not something that is really good.

If what I have just said were not so, two things would follow. My seeking the things that are really good for me would lead me to infringe on the rights of others—their rights to the things that are really good for them. It would then be impossible to say that the pursuit of happiness is the basic natural right a government must attempt to secure for every individual, if it is to be a just government, for if some men's pursuit of happiness required them to impede or frustrate others in the exercise of the same right, no government could discharge its obligation to be just to all its subjects. [2]

I have not forgotten the qualification that it is only under ideal conditions that the pursuit of happiness is cooperative rather than competitive. Under less than ideal conditions, it may be impossible for some men to achieve good lives for themselves except at the expense of misery for others, and equally impossible for a government to secure basic human rights for all. This raises the question of whether a government is morally condemnable as unjust for not doing, under certain conditions, what it is impossible to do under those conditions, and the related question of whether an individual is morally reprehensible for doing, under certain conditions, what it is impossible to avoid doing under those conditions. [3]

(4)

I come, finally, to the problem of how my being just toward others, under ideal conditions that make such conduct on my part possible, promotes my own pursuit of happiness—in short, how justice toward others is an integral part of my making a good life for myself. The solution of this problem is contained to some extent in the solutions to the other two related problems we have just considered. On the one hand, there is the positive point that justice toward others is a means to the civil peace of the community, and that—the essential good of the community—is in turn a means that serves me in making a good life for myself. On the other hand, there is the negative point that under ideal conditions, my seeking the things that are really good for me does not require me to injure anyone else. It is only when I seek goods that I may want but do not need, that I may be led, even under ideal conditions, to deprive others of the things they need; and so I may be led to violate their natural rights.

The negative point just made can be given a positive rendering and one that enhances its significance. We have seen that moral virtue, in the aspect of fortitude or of temperance, disposes a man to choose between alternatives in such a way that his choice of this rather than that is for the sake of making a good life for himself. The virtuous man, in short, is not only one who has this end in view, but also one who is disposed to choose, from day to day, what is really good for himself in the long run, as against what is only apparently good here and now. But it is only when a man is disposed to prefer apparent goods to real goods that he is also inclined to gratify wants or to gratify them in such a way that he injures others by depriving them of what they need for a good life. Hence the man who, in the conduct of his private affairs, lacks fortitude and temperance is also one who will be unjust in his conduct toward others, and for the very reason that he is not well-disposed in the conduct of his own life.

The other face of the same truth is that the man who is inclined to be unjust toward others can be so only through lack of virtue in the conduct of his own life, whereby he is disposed to prefer apparent to real goods for himself. This amounts to saying that the good moral character a man must have in order to make a good life for himself is identical with the good moral character he must have in order to act justly toward others. When a man's moral virtue operates in the sphere of his private affairs, temperance and fortitude are the appropriate names for the aspects of his good character. When his virtue operates in relation to the rights of others or the good of the community, justice is the appropriate name for the aspect of good character involved. But since, in any of its aspects, virtue consists in being disposed to choose real as against apparent goods, justice toward others is existentially inseparable from fortitude and temperance. It is analytically distinct from them only in its relational aspect—its relation to the good of others. [4]

Since a good moral character is a necessary means toward making a good life for one's self, it follows that justice toward others is also a means to the same end, for justice is nothing but a good moral character operating in relation to the rights of others and the good of the community.

(5)

I think it is now clear how the individual's pursuit of happiness, how his effort to make a good life for himself, is related to the rights of others and to the good of the organized community. But in making this clear, I have repeatedly qualified what I have said by referring to *ideal conditions*. The significance of that qualification must now be explained.

By "ideal" I do not mean a state of affairs that is perfect in every way. That is utopian and unattainable. I mean no more than normal or healthy. Thus, if the purpose of men in associating is to enjoy the good of communal life, which is peace, then war in any form represents a pathological social condition, one that defeats the very purpose for which men associate. A society rent by civil strife or one that is engaged in external war is malfunctioning, and in the medical sense of the term, it is pathological or abnormal. If I speak of war as an instance of social pathology or abnormality in this sense, I am obviously not using the word "abnormal" to mean *unusual in a statistical sense*, since either through civil strife or external conflicts, almost all societies from the beginning of history have been abnormal or pathological.

Another example may help to reinforce what I have just said. The purpose of men in associating in families or in states is not only to enjoy the blessings of peace, but also to achieve other goods that the isolated individual could not achieve for himself. Among these are wealth, a decent supply of the means of subsistence, and sufficient free time for the goods that can be achieved through play and leisure. So when the technological conditions of a society are such that widespread poverty or destitution cannot be eliminated, and the lives of most men are consumed in back-breaking toil from dawn to dusk, working in a state of chattel slavery or abject servitude, the society is pathological or abnormal in the sense indicated. It is not functioning as a society should; that is, it is not serving the purpose for which men form associations. Once again it must be said that from the beginning of history to the present time, most, if not all, societies have been pathological or abnormal.

When I use the word "ideal" to signify the opposite of pathological or abnormal, I am expressing the conviction that the pathological conditions so far mentioned are remediable or curable. We have reached that point in the historical development of man's life on earth where we can at last begin to see how war, poverty, and slavery or servitude can be eliminated. Therefore, by "ideal conditions" I mean no more than a state of society in which all eliminable evils have been eliminated. The amount of crime can be reduced, but it is highly doubtful that crime can ever be totally eliminated. I would not include the elimination of crime as an element in what I mean by ideal conditions.

How does social pathology, or the absence of ideal conditions, affect the problems with which we are concerned?

In the first place, the conditions of social life may be such that no man can succeed in making a good life for himself; or, when the pathology is less extreme, the opportunity of making a good life may be open only to the few. In the latter case, the fewer still who make use of that opportunity and do succeed in making good lives for themselves will necessarily have done so at the expense of misery for the many who are deprived. I say "necessarily" to indicate that it may have been impossible at the time, the state of technology being what it was, to provide sufficient free time or a decent supply of the means of subsistence for more than the few. [5]

Earlier in this chapter, I suggested that neither individuals nor governments are guilty of injustice when the conditions are such that it is impossible to secure for all their natural rights. It is only under ideal conditions, conditions which make doing justice possible, that an individual or a government is morally condemnable for failing to act justly. That is why I said earlier that it is only under ideal conditions that an individual can make a good life for himself without injuring anyone else in the course of doing so; more than that, under such conditions, he will not succeed in making a good life for himself if his character is such that he is disposed to injure others in the course of seeking what he wants in preference to what he needs.

The social pathology that is war, especially war between states, has a different effect. We have seen that the good of the community is a means to the ultimate end of each of its individual members; namely, the good life or happiness of each. To subordinate the individual's ultimate good to the good of the state is to pervert this order of goods by converting what is only a means into an ultimate end. Yet when the state is at war with other states, individuals are called upon to take risks or to use their time in such a way that their success in making good lives for themselves is seriously jeopardized or at least impeded to an extent.

What is true of the pathological condition that is external war is also true when civil strife breaks out, and when natural disasters, such as earthquakes and floods, famines and pestilences, occur. In all these cases, individuals are called upon to act for the good of the community, sometimes even for its survival, in a way that either jeopardizes their success in the pursuit of happiness or at least seriously impedes their efforts. Nevertheless, none of these instances of social pathology, not even the most extreme, should lead us to the false conclusion that the good of the community is the ultimate good in which resides the primary moral obligation of men.

Even under the most extreme pathological conditions, the state cannot rightly ask the individual totally to sacrifice his life, or his pursuit of happiness, for its own good, or its survival. It can rightly ask the individual to do no more than take risks or suffer temporary inconveniences. To understand this is to understand that, under ideal conditions, the individual who acts for the good of the community is acting wholly and in every way for his own ultimate good. Under such conditions, nothing he does for the good of the community either jeopardizes or impedes his efforts to make a good life for himself. [6]

(6)

I will return, in Part Four, to the points I have just made about the effects of pathological and ideal social conditions on the good life for the individual man. They are all highly relevant to our estimation of the time in which we are now alive, and to our evaluation of the society we live in. Here I would like to summarize what we have learned from the solution of the problem we have been considering. To accomplish this summary with maximum brevity, let me propose the following distinctions among goods in order to formulate the way in which these goods should be ordered or related.

I have already referred to all real goods as common goods, common in the sense that they are the same for all men because they answer to natural needs, needs inherent in the common or specific nature of man. A good life as a whole is the ultimate common good. The partial goods that constitute this whole or are in some other way means to it are elements or parts of the common good as a whole.

The good of the community is one of these partial goods, and as such it is a means to and element in the ultimate common good. Unlike other real goods that are elements in the ultimate common good, such as health, wealth, pleasure, or knowledge, the good of the community is one that is also common in the special sense of being participated in or shared by the members of a community. Such real goods as health, wealth, pleasure, or knowledge can be possessed and enjoyed by the individual in isolation. They are goods that have their being in the fulfillment of his own natural needs. In contrast, the good of the community is a good that exists not in the individual as such, but in an organized association of individuals. Nevertheless, it is a good that individual members of the community come to possess and enjoy through their association, and in this sense it is a participated or shared common good. But it must never be thought of as the whole or ultimate common good, for it is only a part or element in the ultimate common good—only a means to the good life for the individual.

I would now like to introduce the phrase "individual goods" to signify the things that an individual wants, whether or not he stands in natural need of them. Individuals differ from one another with respect to their wants or conscious desires, as they do not differ with respect to their needs or natural desires, and it is this fact of individual difference that is being stressed when certain goods are called individual rather than common. What I have just called individual goods are all apparent goods—the things that appear good to the individual or that he calls "good" because he consciously wants them. In a particular instance, the thing that appears good to the individual may also be really good for him because it answers to a natural need. In other words, some of the things men call "good" because they want them are also real goods because they answer to natural needs, but not all apparent goods are also real goods. In many instances, men want things that are not really good for them, or they want things that are really good, but they want them in a quantity or in a manner that is not really good for them, because the extent or manner in which they want them interferes with their obtaining other real goods that they need. With these considerations in mind, I shall restrict the meaning of the phrase "individual goods," using it to signify only these apparent goods that are *not* really good for the individual, and so are *not* elements in his ultimate common good.

Once these distinctions are understood, the proper order or relation of these various goods becomes immediately evident. It is evident that only the common good that is the whole of all real goods (the *totum bonum commune*) can be the ultimate normative end that is the source of the one primary moral obligation of each individual man—his obligation to make a really good life for himself. It is evident that all other real goods, being partial goods and elements of the *totum bonum*, must be regarded as means to the one ultimate, normative end that is a good life as a whole. It is evident that the good of the community (*bonum commune communitatis*) is ordered to the ultimate common good of man (*totum bonum commune hominis*) as part to whole, or as means to end. Finally, it is evident that individual goods (*bonum individuale*)—goods that are not elements in the total common good of the individual, nor indispensable means to his making a good life for himself—can be either detrimental or innocuous. They are innocuous when the individual's effort to obtain these merely apparent goods that he wants does not in any way interfere with or impede his getting the real goods that he needs. They are detrimental when the pursuit of them results in the loss of real goods.

Since the good of the community (*bonum communitatis*) is a real good, an element in the total common good of the individual (*totum bonum commune*), no disorder results when the state requires the individual to sacrifice or to give up individual goods (*bonum individuale*) for the good of the community. On the contrary, the state is then only requiring the individual to give up individual goods that are detrimental to his own ultimate good, since the good of the community is a means to that end. The same principle of order applies to the individual's private life; his pursuit of individual goods, according to his individual wants, is thoroughly permissible as long as they remain innocuous. However, when they become detrimental, he is morally obligated to desist from their pursuit, for they then become obstacles to, instead of means to, the ultimate end, his good life as a whole, that he is morally obligated to pursue. [7]

(7)

To the summary just given, I would like to add two further points concerning the obligations of justice. The first of these concerns the obligation of the individual man to his fellow-men; the second concerns the obligation of the organized community and government to its people.

The obligation of the individual to act justly toward his fellow-men requires him, *as far as that is possible*, to do nothing that inflicts injury on them by depriving them of the things they need in order to make good lives for themselves. This is negative rather than positive. The positive side consists of actions that facilitate or enhance the pursuit of happiness by others, through helping them to obtain goods that they need, but that they cannot obtain wholly by their own efforts.

Does justice obligate us positively as well as negatively? Do we have a duty to take steps to benefit our fellow-men as well as to avoid injuring them? My understanding of the difference between love and justice leads me to say *No* to this question. It is love, not justice, that impels us to act benevolently toward those whom we regard as our friends. The duties of justice relate only to the rights of others that we are obliged to respect, and this is but another way of saying that justice requires us not to injure them by depriving them of the things they need. In contrast, love, unlike justice, does not consist in rendering to others what is their due—what they have a natural right to. It consists in giving them generously more than is their due—in helping them, beyond respecting their rights, to achieve what they cannot achieve for themselves.

When one understands the friend or loved one as an *alter ego,* as another self, one acts positively for that other's ultimate good as one acts for one's own happiness. Just as one who is virtuously disposed to make a good life for himself would do nothing to injure himself, so he would do nothing to injure his friend, and beyond this, he would take positive steps to advance his friend's pursuit of happiness, even as he takes such steps to advance his own. This is the meaning of the profoundly wise observation that if all men were friends, justice would not be necessary. But even when they are members of the same community, all men are not friends, and so the restraints of justice are necessary to prevent one man from injuring another. [8]

The obligation of the organized community, or of its government, to act justly toward its members or subjects, is both positive and negative. A just government is one that secures, as far as that is possible, the natural rights of all who are subject to it. In other words, it is under the obligation to injure no one. Beyond this, however, a just government is under the positive obligation, as a matter of justice, not of benevolence, to promote the general welfare. What does this mean?

It means, first, that it ought to preserve and enhance the common good of the community itself—the *bonum commune communitatis*—in which its subjects participate or share, a good that is essential to their making good lives for themselves. In addition, it means that a just government ought to help its subjects obtain the real goods that they cannot obtain wholly by their own individual efforts. As Lincoln observed, a government should do for its people what they, individually, cannot do for themselves.

This merely repeats what was said earlier about the purposes of human association, especially of the political community. The purpose of the state is to help men not only to live, but also to live well; it is, by its very nature, a means to these ends, and it serves these ends only when it promotes the general welfare by preserving peace and helping its people to obtain the things they need that they cannot obtain by their individual efforts. I shall have much more to say on this score in Chapter 19. Here I would like to add only one further comment.

Since the individual is, as a matter of justice, obligated to work for the good of the community in which he lives, and since that good involves not only the peace of the community but also other aspects of the general welfare, the individual in discharging this obligation acts positively for the ultimate good of others as well as for his own ultimate good. What I said earlier about the individual's not having an obligation, as a matter of justice, to act positively for the good of others is thus qualified.

In other words, the positive steps that he takes to help his friends or those whom he loves, he takes directly on their behalf and out of benevolence. But the positive steps he takes to help those members of the community who are not within the circle of his benevolence, he takes indirectly through discharging his obligation, in justice, to act for the good of the community, in which all its members share. Once again I must repeat that all the foregoing statements carry the qualification *under ideal conditions*. No one can be expected to do what, at the time, is impossible; failure to do the impossible is not morally culpable. This, of course, raises a crucial question of fact about what is possible or impossible—a question we shall have to consider in Chapter 20, when we concern ourselves with this century as the time of our lives. [9]

CHAPTER 17

Presuppositions About Human Nature

I have now outlined the framework of the teleological ethics that is the moral philosophy of common sense, and I have expounded some of its substance. On what factual presuppositions about the nature of man does a teleological ethics depend for the truth of its normative conclusions? There are, it seems to me, only four.

First, that man, like any other animal, has a certain, limited number of natural needs, and that the natural needs that are specifically human will differ from those of other animals, as man differs specifically from them. I have dealt with the question of how man differs from other animals in an earlier book, *The Difference of Man and the Difference It Makes*. I think that book decisively establishes the proposition that man differs in kind from other animals by virtue of his having the related powers of propositional speech and conceptual thought, powers totally lacking in all other animals. Future scientific discoveries may falsify this proposition, but at the moment there is not a shred of empirical evidence to the contrary. [1]

Second, that man, because he has the power of conceptual thought, is uniquely a time-binding animal—the only animal whose consciousness embraces an extensive past and a far-reaching future. Human memory and imagination, augmented and transformed by the power of conceptual thought, emancipate man from imprisonment in the immediate present. This proposition about man, like the preceding one, is supported by all the scientific evidence now available. The importance of its truth for the truth of a teleological ethics should be evident on a moment's reflection. Man could not engage in the pursuit of happiness—he could not seek the ultimate end of a whole good life—if that temporal whole, encompassing his past and his future along with any present moment, were not an object he could hold before his mind at all times in his life, except perhaps the period of his infancy. [2]

Third, that man does not have any genetically pre-formed patterns of species-specific behavior, that is, he does not have definite instincts, as other animals, such as the insects, do. While he does have instinctual drives or needs, these are subject in man's case to inhibition and sublimation by his power of conceptual thought, with the result that each man determines for himself the manner in which he responds to or satisfies his instinctual drives or needs. Although this proposition is challenged by some behavioral scientists, and especially by popularizers of ethology, it has the support of overwhelming empirical evidence. Its significance for a teleological ethics should be evident: that each man ought to make a really good life for himself presupposes that he can determine for himself how he shall respond to his natural needs, including those that are called "instinctual," such as the sexual drive. This would not be so if his instinctual needs were fulfilled by genetically determined patterns of behavior, the same for all men because they are species-specific. [3]

Fourth and last, that man, having the power of conceptual thought, also has freedom of choice—a freedom that enables him, at any moment of his life, to choose one partial good rather than another, without being determined to do so by his past experience, the habits he has formed, or the character he has developed up to that moment. In other words, he has, through freedom of choice, the power of self-determination, the power of creating or forming himself and his life according to his own decisions. Freedom of choice is presupposed by any form of moral philosophy that involves categorical oughts, for a categorical ought is meaningless unless the individual it obligates is free to obey or disobey it. Unless he had freedom of choice, the individual subject to categorical oughts could not be held morally responsible for his acts. This presupposition is even more important for a deontological ethics that is also teleological, for without freedom of choice at every critical moment in a man's life, he could not be responsible for making or failing to make a whole good life for himself. Is this presupposition factually true? All I need say on this score is that there is no scientific evidence against it. I have dealt elsewhere with the philosophical dispute about free will and determinism [4] and with the possibility that freedom of choice will be falsified or confirmed by scientific evidence in the future. [5]

To sum up: in the present state of the empirical evidence, none of the factual presuppositions of a teleological ethics can be dismissed as false. On the contrary, the scientific evidence now available and the evidence of common experience overwhelmingly favor the first three presuppositions, and while the fourth is still philosophically disputed, there is as yet no decisive evidence to the contrary.

CHAPTER 18

The Only Moral Philosophy That Is Sound, Practical, and Undogmatic

(1)

THE teleological ethics of common sense is the only moral philosophy that is *sound* in the way in which it develops its principles, *practical* in the manner in which it applies them, and *undogmatic* in the claims it makes for them.

Why or in what way is it the only sound moral philosophy? I mean by "sound" both adequate and true. So when I say that the teleological ethics of common sense is the only sound moral philosophy, I am saying that it is the only ethical doctrine that answers all the questions that moral philosophy *should* and *can* attempt to answer, neither more nor less, and that its answers are true by the standard of truth that is appropriate and applicable to normative judgments. In contrast, other theories or doctrines try to answer more questions than they can or fewer than they should, and their answers are mixtures of truth and error.

Thus, teleological ethics includes the truth of naturalism in that it fully recognizes the moral relevance of empirical facts, especially the facts of human nature and human behavior, but without committing the error of naturalism—the error of denying the distinction between fact and value, the error of attempting to reduce normative judgments to statements of empirical fact. Avoiding this error, it also avoids the fallacy of attempting to draw normative conclusions from premises that are entirely factual.

Its understanding of the indefinability of the good corrects the error of those intuitionists who suppose that the indefinability of the good excludes any relation between the good and a natural phenomenon, such as desire. While agreeing with the intuitionists that ethics must have some principles that are intuitively known (that is, self-evident), teleological ethics maintains that there need be and can be only one such normative principle, and that all other normative judgments can be derived as conclusions from it. It thus avoids the error of regarding as intuitively known (and known without any relation to empirical fact) a whole series of propositions about moral duties or obligations that are not self-evident and depend for their truth upon matters of fact.

Precisely because it is teleological—because its first principle is the end, the whole good to be sought, and because all its conclusions are about the partial goods that are either constitutive or instrumental means to this end—the ethics of common sense includes the truth of utilitarianism, which also proceeds in terms of end and means. But it avoids the mistakes of utilitarianism that lie in a wrong conception of the ultimate end and in an erroneous treatment of the relation between the individual's pursuit of his own ultimate good and his obligations to the rights of others and the good of the community. By correcting the most serious failure of utilitarianism, one that it shares with naturalism—the failure to distinguish between needs and wants, or between real and apparent goods—it is able to combine a practical or pragmatic approach to the problems of human action in terms of means and ends with a moral approach to them in terms of categorical oughts. Whereas, in the absence of categorical oughts, utilitarianism and naturalism are merely pragmatic, the ethics of common sense, at once teleological and deontological, is a moral philosophy that is also practical. [1]

By virtue of its distinction between real and apparent goods, this pragmatic moral philosophy retains what truth there is in the various forms of "non-cognitive ethics," such as the "emotive theory of values"; it concedes that all judgments concerning values that are merely apparent goods are nothing but expressions of emotional inclinations or attitudes on the part of the individual who is making the evaluation. While conceding this, it avoids the error of supposing that *all* value judgments or normative statements must be emotional or attitudinal expressions of this sort, incapable of having any objective or ascertainable truth, comparable to that of descriptive statements of fact. It avoids this error by correcting the failure to recognize that the truth of descriptive or factual statements is not the only mode of objective truth, and that there is a standard of truth appropriate to normative judgments quite distinct from that appropriate to descriptive statements.

The foregoing explanation of the soundness of teleological ethics—by virtue of its encompassing whatever is sound in other approaches, divorced from the errors with which it is mixed in these other approaches—also helps to explain why teleological ethics is the *most* practical form of moral philosophy, or the *only* practical form of it.

On the one hand, it accepts as thoroughly correct Kant's criticism of all the merely empirical, pragmatic, or utilitarian substitutes for moral philosophy, which proceed solely in terms of means and ends and wholly by reference to matters of fact, without acknowledging a single categorical ought. In the absence of categorical oughts, thinking about the problems of action may be practical or pragmatic, but its conclusions lack the character of moral judgments. On the other hand, by thinking in terms of categorical oughts, as well as in terms of end and means (the latter on the basis of factual knowledge), teleological ethics is a moral philosophy that is also empirical and pragmatic—the only form of moral philosophy that is.

In contrast, the deontological ethics of Kant or of his followers is, by the self-limitations it insists on—the exclusion of all reference to matters of fact as bearing on means and ends—a moral philosophy that is neither empirical nor practical. It is rationalistic or *a priori* and purely formal to an absurd extreme. It is offered as a product of *pure practical reason* which, precisely because it tries to be *pure*, ceases to be *practical*. Confronted with the prescriptions of a purely deontological ethics, out of all touch with the facts of life, any man of common sense would know at once that it is of little or no practical guidance to him in solving the problems of life or action, especially the central and controlling problem of a good life for himself and right action toward others. [2]

(2)

I come finally to my claim that the moral philosophy of common sense, at once teleological and deontological, is less dogmatic than any other doctrine or theory that offers itself as a guide to living well or acting rightly. It is less dogmatic because it avoids what, in my judgment, is the worst error that is committed not only by a purely deontological ethics but also by most current forms of utilitarianism.

First, let me state what I mean by "dogmatism" in this connection. I call "dogmatic" any judgment that, employing the terms *good* and *bad*, or *right* and *wrong*, claims for itself a degree of certitude and universality that it cannot possess. I also call "dogmatic" the supposition that there are moral laws or rules of conduct which can be applied to particular cases without regard to the contingent circumstances that surround and condition every instance of human action.

The moral philosophy of Kant, or any other form of purely deontological ethics, is dogmatic in this sense of the term, and dogmatic to an extreme that deserves the ridicule it has elicited from certain of its critics. While neo-utilitarianism, whether in the form now called "rule utilitarianism" or in the form now called "act utilitarianism," does not go to this extreme, nevertheless it tends to be dogmatic in its effort to apply criteria for declaring that this or that rule of conduct is universally good or bad, or that one or another particular action is clearly right or wrong. Reacting against the dogmatism of universal rules of conduct applied with unembarrassed certitude and without regard for the circumstances of the particular situation in which action must take place, there are those who go to the opposite extreme of holding that the problems of action in particular cases must be solved without the guidance of moral principles or rules of any sort.

Confronted with this opposition between two untenable extremes—the extreme of dogmatism, on the one hand, and the extreme of completely unprincipled relativism, on the other—something that is now called "situation ethics" has arisen to offer a middle-of-the-road resolution of the conflict between these extremes. [3] Unfortunately, the exponents of "situation ethics" in all its varieties, together with its critics, seem to be totally unaware that the ethics of common sense avoids both extremes—on the one hand, by recognizing the remoteness from action of the universal principles that can be asserted with certitude and, on the other hand, by filling the gap between such principles and the exigencies of action by practical policies and prudent decisions that do not have universality and are not expressions of moral certitude.

The solution offered by "situation ethics" is itself unsound, for it appeals to love and love alone, and worse, to a mode of love that transcends the bounds of human nature, in order to find some form of guidance for the individual in the particular case in which he must act one way or another. [4] Not only is the solution offered by "situation ethics" totally unrealistic; it is, in addition, the solution of a problem that is factitious rather than genuine. It assumes that it is making a genuine contribution by finding a middle ground between the extremes of dogmatism and relativism in dealing with the problems of human life and action. It is totally ignorant of the fact that that middle ground already exists in the teleological ethics of common sense. The problem that is its point of departure is one that has been solved, and solved in a much sounder and more adequate way than by the one untenable proposal it advances.

Let us now look at the way in which teleological ethics avoids the extremes of unwarranted dogmatism and unprincipled relativism.

The man of common sense does not need much, if any, philosophical enlightenment to know that in the particular situation in which he must act, he must take account of contingent circumstances that could not have been foreseen or acknowledged by the soundest and most adequate set of moral principles or rules that the wisdom of man can devise. On the other hand, he also knows how unwise it would be to decide on a course of action in the particular case without a plan of life that relates his decision here and now to the problem of making a whole good life for himself, and without policies for applying that plan in a way that takes account of his individual constitution, his idiosyncratic capacities and temperament. Philosophical analysis merely makes explicit these points already recognized by the man of common sense. It does so by distinguishing three levels of practical thinking, and by formulating the exactitude and scope appropriate to each.

The highest level and also the one that is most remote from action in the particular case is the level of those normative judgments or categorical oughts that concern the ultimate end to be sought and the means that should be employed in attaining it. If I refer to this as the level of universal principles, I do not mean thereby to restrict it to the one self-evident principle that concerns the ultimate end. I mean to include as well all the conclusions concerning means that can be established on the basis of the specific human nature that is common to all men. The universality of these principles consists in their applicability to all men simply because they are men and without regard to their individual differences and the conditions of their individual lives—the circumstances of their time and place in human history.

The certitude with which these universal principles can be affirmed is, first of all, the absolute certitude appropriate to the one self-evident truth that each man ought to make a really good life for himself and, after that, the somewhat diminished certitude that is appropriate to propositions about the means that any man must employ to discharge this obligation—propositions about the real goods that answer to his natural needs and so are constitutive parts of his good life as a whole, and propositions about the instrumental means that are indispensable to his effort to achieve a good life for himself. I say "somewhat diminished certitude" in the latter case because the truth of propositions about the means depends upon propositions of fact, which are never more than relatively true, being always subject to falsification by evidence that may yet be discovered.

Four further points must be made about this level of universal principles, which have a certitude that is appropriate to their character as self-evident truth or as factually established conclusions. One is that such moral wisdom as men can attain exists at this level, and only at this level. In other words, it is on this level of practical thinking that moral philosophy is developed, never going beyond the formulation of the universal principles applicable to human life and conduct. A second follows from the first; the plan of life that moral philosophy outlines must always remain a sketchy outline and can never become a detailed blueprint, precisely because it cannot go further than a statement of the ultimate end to be sought and the necessary means to be employed. A third point follows from the first and second, namely, that the wisdom attainable by moral philosophy—the plan of life that it can propose with appropriate certitude as having universal applicability—is by itself inadequate for individual action in particular cases. It is inadequate precisely because of its universal applicability; it does not take account of all the contingent circumstances of the individual life and of action in particular cases. Having said this, it is necessary to add, as a fourth point, that its inadequacy in no way diminishes its importance as a guide to individual life and action. To say that moral wisdom or moral philosophy is by itself insufficient should hardly lead to the conclusion that a plan of life provides no guidance at all. [5]

The second or intermediate level of practical thinking is the one on which general policies must be formulated by each individual for applying the plan of life, or the universal principles that outline it, to his own individual nature and to the circumstances of his individual life. These policies are only general, not universal in scope. They are not universal because they do not apply to all men at all times and places; they apply only to this individual man and other men of the same general type, and they apply only to some set of historic circumstances that are general in the sense that they surround the lives of a number of individuals living in a certain society or culture.

Precisely because they are general rather than universal in scope, precisely because they must take into account innumerable and complex sets of conditions or circumstances, the statements of policy by which the individual applies to his own life a plan of life that moral philosophy formulates for all men must remain relatively inexact and uncertain. To expect greater exactitude or certainty than is appropriate at this level is folly, and to claim it where it is unwarranted and impossible is dogmatism. [6] For all its inexactitude and uncertainty, the thinking that men must do at this level is nonetheless indispensable, for it bridges the gap—it mediates—between the universal principles of moral philosophy and the unique singularity of the particular case in which the individual must choose between alternatives and carry out his choice in action.

Because it is more proximate to action than the level of universal principles, this intermediate level of general policies is more fully practical. [7] When I said earlier that a purely deontological ethics is a moral philosophy that is not practical, I had in mind the fact that it denies the indispensability of practical thinking on this level, as well as on the even more practical level below it. Such moral wisdom as deontological ethics may contain is, therefore, practically useless.

The third and lowest level of practical thinking is the one immediately proximate to choice and action in the particular case. This is the level of prudent decisions, the scope of which is neither universal nor general, but absolutely singular, applicable to this one case and this alone. The difference between the prudent man or the man of sound judgment and one who lacks the virtue of prudence or sound judgment lies not in the correctness of the decision that he reaches in the particular case, but rather in the correctness of the way in which he reaches it—by taking counsel, by considering the relevant circumstances, by weighing the merits of competing alternatives, and by thus deliberating before deciding rather than by deciding rashly or impetuously, and without due thought or deliberation.

The process of coming to a decision *prudently* gives no assurance that the decision reached will always be the correct one in the particular case, yet it has more chance of being correct than one not so reached. The degree of chance will vary with the complexity of the circumstances in the particular case, and with the difficulty of choosing between the competing alternatives; the degree of uncertainty that attaches to a prudent decision will vary accordingly, but in any case, the uncertainty of particular decisions tends to be greater than that of general policies, especially in difficult cases, just as the uncertainty of general policies is, for the most part, greater than that of universal principles.

Nevertheless, it is at this lowest level of practical thinking, with all its uncertainty or inexactitude, that prudent decisions must be made if a wise plan of action is to be applied by the individual in the choices he makes from moment to moment in his effort to make a good life for himself. [8]

(3)

With this analysis of the levels of practical thinking before us, we can see, first, that moral philosophy becomes dogmatic when it goes beyond its limits to lay down with certitude general policies for action or general rules of conduct. And, second, we can also see the limitations it must impose upon itself with respect to passing moral judgments on particular acts, as good or bad, or as right and wrong.

Consider, first, those particular actions that affect only the individual's success or failure in making a good life for himself and do not in any way impinge on the rights of others or the good of the community. In the sphere of private life or purely self-regarding conduct, no particular act can be judged absolutely right or wrong, absolutely good or bad. The moral quality of a particular act lies wholly in its tendency; it is right or good insofar as it tends toward the achievement of the ultimate end of a good life as a whole, it is wrong or bad insofar as it has the opposite tendency. Since habits or dispositions are formed by particular acts, the goodness or badness of particular acts lies in the habits or dispositions that are thereby formed, and these habits are, in turn, good according as they incline or dispose a man in the direction of his ultimate end—a really good life as a whole—or bad according as they incline or dispose him to seek a good time, merely apparent goods, or things that are good only in the short run rather than in the long run of his life as a whole. Hence if men are to be morally praised or blamed, in the sphere of their private lives and self-regarding conduct, such approbation or disapprobation should not be directed to their particular acts but to their moral character in general, which consists in their settled tendencies or dispositions to act either for their own ultimate good or against it.

Thus, it is possible to condemn the miser (or the over-acquisitive man) who, contented though he may be with the hoard (or the excessive accumulation) that is the main thing he consciously wants, manifests a settled disposition to get it by depriving himself of the health, the friends, and the knowledge that every man needs to make a good life for himself. The moral character that his pattern of life reveals indicates his misconception of his own ultimate good—his substitution of a means for the end, of a partial good for the whole good. The same holds true of the *bon vivant* whose pattern of life reveals his exaggeration of the importance of sensual pleasures, or of the power-hungry man who, seeking domination over other men more than anything else, mistakes an apparent for a real good.

In each of these cases, we are justified in censuring the individual for the badness of character that his pattern of life reveals, a badness of character that indicates his settled disposition to act against his own ultimate real good; but our censure must always be hedged by an acknowledgment that manifest signs of character are never crystal clear and that we may have misinterpreted the evidence available to us.

When we pass from the sphere of private to that of social life, from purely self-regarding action to action that affects other individuals or the organized community, the standards of approval or disapproval are somewhat different. Here it is possible for a single act to be absolutely wrong, if it infringes on the rights of another man in such a way that it irremediably deprives him of something he needs in order to make a good life for himself. Murdering another man is, perhaps, the clearest case of an absolutely wrong action, though owning and using another man as a chattel slave, thus depriving him of his freedom, would seem to be equally clear. [9]

When one leaves these clear cases, and there are very few such, one moves into the realm of acts that, while infringing on the rights of others, may not do them irreparable injury. Such, for example, are actions by one individual that deprive another of property that he can replace, of a good reputation that he can re-establish, or of bodily health and vigor that he can regain. In all these cases, and there are many more like them, injustice has been done, but in a way that may impede but does not absolutely prevent the injured party from making a good life for himself. The degree of the wrong done must be assessed by reference to the degree of the impediment suffered, and this may be extremely difficult to do with any accuracy or certainty in particular cases.

Beyond these cases in which the degree of wrong-doing must be measured in terms of the long-range effect of the injury done another, there are the even more difficult cases in which it may not even be possible to tell whether an injury has been actually done. The act by which I intend to deceive another or tell him a lie may not actually mislead him in any way that injures him; if it does mislead him, the injury may be readily remedied, or in the rare case, it may cause him irreparable harm. We may never be able to assess the wrong done by such acts, as far as the good of another man is concerned. So if we condemn such acts with any degree of assurance, it must be on the basis of the bad effects on the individual himself of his having the moral character of a habitual liar. [10]

The foregoing analysis applies also to actions that affect the good of the community. In this case, as in the case of actions that affect the individual's achievement of his own good or actions that affect the good of other individual men, the particular act must be judged by reference to its tendency to impair the peace and security of the community. It is not difficult to condemn as unjust or injurious certain crimes against the state, certain types of anti-social behavior, and certain forms of civil violence. But in many cases in which the individual's conduct appears to place his own private interests ahead of the public good and the general welfare, it is extremely difficult to assess the degree to which the individual's behavior militates against the good of the community or impedes a government's efforts to promote the general welfare. Only if it can be known with fair assurance that the individual's conduct definitely runs counter to the public good or definitely frustrates the promotion of the general welfare can it be judged morally reprehensible because it is unjust. In difficult and complex cases, we seldom have such knowledge, with the requisite degree of assurance that we are in possession of all the relevant facts and have an accurate measure of their probable consequences.

(4)

To sum up the foregoing discussion, let me briefly make three points.

First, although the teleological ethics of common sense does involve categorical oughts that will always appear repugnant to those who mistakenly think that their freedom is thereby infringed, it is nevertheless relatively undogmatic—an ethics without hard and fixed rules of conduct and one that tends to restrain us from passing moral judgments on the rightness and wrongness of particular acts, or on the goodness and badness of particular men. It limits the instances in which such judgments can be made with any degree of assurance to very, very few. [11]

Second, by recognizing that moral wisdom goes no further than the universal principles that outline a sound plan of life for all men at all times and places, it allows for the contingencies that must be considered at the lower levels of non-philosophical practical thinking that attempt to apply such wisdom to the particular case in which a choice must be made and action taken. This gives to such practical thinking on the part of the individual, and especially to his virtue of prudence, the creative opportunity to make a good life for himself that is his very own and unlike that of any other man, even though it conforms to a plan of life that he must share with all other men who see the wisdom of that plan.

Third, we can now reiterate with increased emphasis and understanding what was said in the opening chapters of this book about the essential prerequisites of success in making a good life for one's self. They are as follows: (a) a sound plan of life that embodies true principles, the substance of moral wisdom; (b) a good moral character that consists in a habitual disposition to act in accordance with such a plan; (c) the prudence that safeguards the process by which the individual reaches decisions in particular cases; and, finally, (d) the good fortune of not being injured or hindered by others and of being helped by the society and the culture in which one lives, helped to obtain the real goods that one needs but which are either wholly or partly beyond one's own power to attain for one's self.

Part Four

The Present Situation in Which We Find Ourselves

CHAPTER 19

Are There Criteria by Which We Can Judge Our Century and Our Society?

(1)

W E can have objective criteria for judging our century and our society only if value judgments have validity —only if we know what is really good for man as man. The objective truth of moral philosophy thus enables us to transcend what the anthropologists and social scientists like to call the "ethnocentric predicament." We could not extricate ourselves from that predicament if there were no way of judging the value-system of another culture or the institutions of another society without assuming the validity of our own. But if that were the case, we could not even assess our society or culture without begging the question. (Let me again say in passing that some of the professors in our universities who appeal to the ethnocentric predicament seldom hesitate to pass harsh moral judgments—often in a tone of high certitude—about our own society and culture.) However, since there are real goods that correspond to natural needs, things that are good for every human being because he is human, without regard to the social or cultural circumstances under which he lives, we are in a position to judge the value-systems and institutions of particular cultures and societies—our own as well as others— by using the scale of values that our teleological ethics sets up as a measure of their goodness or badness.

We have already done precisely that when, at an earlier point, we considered the external factors or circumstances that affect the individual's pursuit of happiness in its relation to the good of others and the good of the community. In this connection, I distinguished between ideal or pathological conditions of society. I explained that I meant by pathological conditions the social or economic circumstances of civil strife or external war, of poverty and destitution, of chattel slavery or back-breaking toil. I pointed out that the conditions of social life may be so poor and so primitive that no man can make a good life for himself and that when the social conditions are still far from ideal but the pathology is less extreme, the opportunity of making a good life may be open only to the few. To recognize, as we must, that in the whole of human history the social conditions of human life have been, in varying degrees, defective from the point of view of human happiness is to judge all historic societies by reference to the real goods that constitute a good human life as a whole. To do this is to transcend the ethnocentric predicament by reference to a scale of values relative only to the nature of man, and not to any historic culture.

One other earlier point is relevant here. Man's basic natural right is his right to the pursuit of happiness; all subsidiary natural rights are rights to the partial goods that are means to the end of a good life. We have in these natural rights the objective and trans-cultural standard for measuring the justice of governments, and the justice of economic and social institutions as well. A just government is one that secures to every man his natural rights and protects him from injury by other men. In addition, in order to be fully just, a government, by shaping the economic and social arrangements of society to this end, must promote the general welfare in which all men participate equally, thus helping each and every one of them to attain real goods that they need but that are not wholly within their power to get for themselves.

We are now in a position to formulate in summary fashion the standard by which we can judge the relative merits of different societies and cultures. One society and culture is better than another in proportion as its technological conditions, its political, economic, and social institutions, and its actual value-system promotes or facilitates a really good life for a *larger percentage* of its human beings. One society and culture is worse than another in proportion as its various components (those just mentioned) work in the opposite way—to deprive a *larger percentage* of its members of the external conditions they need in order to make good lives for themselves, or to impede, interfere with, or even discourage their efforts in this direction. The ideal, of course, is a society and culture that provides *all* its members—all *without exception*—with the external conditions they need, and at the same time encourages them in their pursuit of the good life.

In these summary statements, I have not separated political, economic, and social conditions, on the one hand, from cultural conditions, on the other. Since these two sets of conditions do not operate in the same fashion—since, in fact, there may be a large gap between the promise held out by the one and the degree of performance promoted by the other—it is necessary to deal more fully with each set of conditions by itself.

(2)

What should government do, in shaping the political, economic, and social institutions of a society, to safeguard, facilitate, and advance the pursuit of happiness by all its people?

On the conceptual plane, there can hardly be a better statement of the objectives of government than the one made in the Preamble to the Constitution of the United States. These objectives are:

> To establish justice, insure domestic tranquility, provide for the common defense, promote the general welfare, and secure the blessings of liberty.

Taken together with the proposition in the Declaration of Independence, that all men, being by nature equal, are equal in all their natural rights, rights that a just government must attempt to secure equally for all, the objectives set forth in the Preamble provide a standard for measuring the goodness of any government, including our own at various stages in its history from the beginning to the present day.

Let us now consider these objectives in relation to the parts of a good life—the constitutive and instrumental means that the individual must employ in his effort to make a whole good life for himself. For the present purpose, I am going to set forth these elements or factors in a fashion somewhat different from earlier enumerations of them. There are, in this enumeration, seven classes of goods.

(1) *Goods of the body*, such as health, vigor, and the pleasures of sense.

(2) *Goods of the mind*, such as knowledge, understanding, prudence, and even a modicum of wisdom, together with such goods of the mind's activity as skills of inquiry and of critical judgment, and the arts of creative production.

(3) *Goods of character*, such aspects of moral virtue as temperance and fortitude, together with justice in relation to the rights of others and the goods of the community.

(4) *Goods of personal association*, such as family relationships, friendships, and loves.

(5) *Political goods*, such as domestic tranquillity—both civil and external peace—and political liberty under constitutional government, together with the protection of individual freedom by the prevention of violence, aggression, coercion, or intimidation.

(6) *Economic goods*, such as a decent supply of the means of subsistence; living and working conditions conducive to health; medical care; opportunities for access to the pleasures of sense, as well as to the pleasures of play and aesthetic pleasures; opportunities for access to the goods of the mind through educational facilities in youth and in adult life; and enough free time from subsistence-work, both in youth and in adult life, to take full advantage of these opportunities.

(7) *Social goods*, such as equality of status, of opportunity, and of treatment in all matters affecting the dignity of the human person.

Of these seven classes or categories of goods, the first four belong to the inner or private life of the individual. They are acquired and preserved by him as a result of the way in which he conducts himself, employs his faculties, and husbands his personal resources. Whether or not he acquires and accumulates these goods in the course of his life depends mainly on him. This is particularly true of the goods of character and of personal association; these are the least dependent on the good fortune of beneficent external circumstances. With regard to his acquirement of the goods of the body and the goods of the mind, the individual is more dependent on favorable external conditions—on conditions conducive to health and provisions for medical care, in the case of bodily goods; on opportunities for schooling, learning, and creative work, and on having enough free time to take advantage of these opportunities, in the case of the goods of the mind. So with regard to all the goods subsumed under the first four categories, the actions of government can do no more than abet the pursuit of happiness *indirectly* by the action it takes in the sphere of political, economic, and social goods.

The last three classes of goods are environmental or external in the sense that the individual's possession of them is mainly dependent on the outer or public conditions of his life. Thus, unless he is fortunate enough to live in a republic—under constitutional government or a government of laws—and unless he is among those who are enfranchised as citizens with suffrage under that constitution, he will be deprived of political liberty. Unless he has either income-producing property or what I am going to call the "economic equivalents of property," he will not have, through forms of wealth and the things wealth can provide, the economic goods he needs for the pursuit of happiness—things that are good not only because they maintain his life and health, but because they facilitate his acquirement of other goods, especially the goods of the mind or the goods of leisure. [1] Unless he enjoys equality of status, opportunity, and treatment, he will, in varying degrees, be deprived of access to the goods he needs for his personal development and for the enhancement of his dignity as a person.

Therefore, insofar as government can shape and control the political, economic, and social institutions of the community, it secures the individual's right to make a good life for himself largely through measures that directly affect his possession of political, economic, and social goods and, indirectly, through them, other goods that are not wholly within the power of the individual. It cannot do anything about the acquirement and possession of the goods that are wholly within the individual's own power, such as the goods of character. And with respect to the goods of the body, the goods of the mind, and even the goods of personal relationships, it can contribute only indirectly through the external or environmental goods that minister to them. [2]

Thus, it may be practicable now, though it was not always practicable in the past, for a government to see that no individual starves or is under-nourished; but no government, now or ever, can see to it that he is temperate and does not ruin his health by gluttony. Similarly, it may be practicable now for a government to provide adequate educational facilities for every child and even for every adult; but no government can prevent an individual from neglecting these opportunities, or compel him to acquire and use the goods of the mind. A government can give every man suffrage and, therewith, political liberty, but it cannot give him the civic virtue whereby he uses that freedom well, just as it cannot make him just in his use of other forms of freedom that it grants him and safeguards.

In the light of the foregoing, let us look once more at the objectives of government, set forth in the Preamble, in relation to the individual's right to the pursuit of happiness, and his right to the life and liberty he needs to pursue it.

We can now see that security of life and limb, political liberty, and freedom from coercion and intimidation are themselves among the environmental goods that contribute to the individual's making a good life for himself. We can see, furthermore, that with respect to these political goods, the individual's pursuit of happiness can be directly promoted by government. This also applies to the political good that is peace, both domestic and foreign. All these goods are covered by the clauses in the Preamble that mention domestic tranquillity, the common defense, and the blessings of liberty as fundamental objectives of government. But security of life and limb does not exhaust the meaning of the right to life, for that involves economic as well as political conditions. Nor do political liberty and free-dom from coercion or intimidation exhaust the meaning of the right to liberty. That also involves economic factors, conditions that provide the freedom of a man's time from subsistence-work and a certain degree of independence from other men with re-gard to his hold on the means of subsistence. These economic aspects of the right to life and liberty, together with all the other economic goods that are elements of human happiness and are involved in its pursuit, are covered in the Preamble in the clause concerning the promotion of the general welfare—both economic and social welfare.

Add to this the clause calling for the establishment of justice, and the picture is completed. Justice is concerned with the distribution of economic and social as well as political goods. If justice requires a government to treat equals (that is, all human beings, equal in their specific nature) equally, and to render to each what is due him by natural right, then to es-tablish justice a government must establish social and economic as well as political democracy. It establishes political democracy by the institution of universal suffrage, whereby it grants to every man the equal status of enfranchised citizenship and, with that, the political liberty and a share in the sovereignty to which all are equally entitled. It establishes economic democracy by whatever measures or institutions promote the general economic welfare in such a way that every man has at least the indis-pensable minimum of economic goods he needs for a good life. [3] It establishes social democracy by its efforts to remove all forms of ethnic and racial discrimination, and by eliminat-ing whatever residual class distinctions may remain after the division of society into political and economic classes has been overcome. By all these institutions, measures, and efforts, a just government moves toward the ideal of the classless society, in which alone an equality of conditions is fully achieved for all men. [4]

(3)

So much for the obligations of government to safeguard and promote the attainment of human happiness. In what ways does the culture of a society—especially the value-system that underlies its *mores*—encourage the individual's efforts to make a good life for himself, or impede and frustrate those efforts?

Earlier I quoted Plato's remark that what is honored in a society is likely to be cultivated there. Few individuals can be expected to have the heroic virtue to be such complete non-conformists that they will seek what they ought to seek in their own lives, against the over-bearing pressure of social disapproval or even social disinterest. It is extremely difficult for the individual to seek for himself the things that are not honored or valued in a society, or completely to turn his back on the things that are honored there, though wrongly so.

Another quotation relevant here is the passage from Pericles' *Funeral Oration,* in which he praises the culture of Athens as one that honors the things that should be cultivated in a society whose scale of values accords with the order of the real goods. Let us ignore his rhetorical purpose to bolster the morale of the Athenians at a dark moment of the Peloponnesian war, when they had suffered defeats in the field. What he tells his fellow-citizens may not have been true of Athenian society in his day; it none-theless depicts what should be true of a society if its culture is to promote the pursuit of human happiness.

Pericles says first:

> Our constitution . . . favors the many instead of the few; this is why it is called a democracy. If we look to the laws, they afford equal justice to all in their private differences . . . class considerations not being allowed to interfere with merit; nor again does poverty bar the way. . . . The free-dom which we enjoy in our government extends to our ordinary life. . . . But all this ease in our private relations does not make us lawless as citizens.

Then he goes on to make the following observations about Athenian culture:

> We provide plenty of means for the mind to refresh itself from business. We celebrate games . . . all the year around, and the elegance of our private establishments forms a source of daily pleasure. . . .

We cultivate refinement without extravagance and knowledge without effeminacy; wealth we employ more for use than for show, and place the real disgrace of poverty not in owning to the fact, but in declining to struggle against it. . . .

In short, I say that as a city we are the school of Hellas. [5]

Partly by paraphrasing the words of Pericles and partly by extending his remarks, let me now briefly summarize the criteria for judging one culture as better than another by reference to its favorable or adverse effects on the pursuit of happiness. One culture is better than another (1) if it regards wealth always as a means to an end, and so does not look upon the continual expansion of the economy, beyond the production of useful wealth, as an end in itself, to which everything else should be sacrificed or subordinated; (2) if it subordinates business to the pursuits of leisure, the production and consumption of wealth to the goods of the mind; (3) if it provides ample means for the mind to refresh itself from business, through the pleasures of play, through the enjoyment of the arts, through the advancement of the sciences, and through all forms of learning and of creative work; (4) if it subordinates the goods of the body to the goods of the mind, and places its disapproval upon unlimited indulgence in sensual pleasures or even upon excessive preoccupation with amusements and recreations that do not contribute to the growth of the mind or the improvement of the individual as a person; (5) if it cultivates the refinements of life and even a modest degree of elegance, but at the same time censures extravagance and the lust for luxuries, or even creature comforts and conveniences beyond all reasonable needs; (6) if it honors the man of private and civic virtue above the man who succeeds, by foul means or fair, in the rat-race for power, fame, or wealth; (7) if, in short, it esteems intrinsic human excellence above any and every form of merely external or worldly success.

How does a society honor the things that should be cultivated if its members are to be aided and abetted in their pursuit of happiness? One part of the answer lies in the cultural institutions that it creates, maintains, and develops at the public expense—its libraries, its museums of art and of science, its theaters, its public parks, and so on. But the heart of the answer lies in that one of its cultural institutions that most directly affects every individual—its educational system, not only its schools, colleges, and universities, but also the educational facilities it provides for continued learning in adult life.

I am not concerned here with equality of educational opportunity, but rather with the quality of the schooling and other educational opportunities afforded both young and old. If, for example, all children were given an equal number of years of schooling from kindergarten through college or university and if, in addition, they enjoyed equal educational facilities during those years, but the schooling they received was directed mainly toward technological and economic advances rather than to the pursuits of leisure and the development of human excellence, the educational system would operate against rather than for the individual's making a good life for himself.

To know whether the culture of a society is favorable to the pursuit of happiness, one need look no further than the scale of values embodied in its educational system—the objectives it is designed to serve. Only if an educational system subordinates every mode of specialized, technical, professional, or vocational training to discipline in the liberal arts and to all forms of humanistic learning for their own sake—only if it places truly liberal education first, and relegates all merely utilitarian programs of education to second place—does it reflect a scale of values that accords with the order of real goods in the pursuit of happiness. Then and only then do we have a persuasive sign that the culture of a society is beneficent because it honors the things that should be cultivated there for the sake of a good human life.

CHAPTER 20

Is This a Good Time to Be Alive?

(1)

To this question, the only answer that makes sense is a qualified affirmative. While it is, perhaps, not the best of times, it is better than any earlier period of human life—better in that it provides the external conditions of a good human life to a greater extent and for more human beings than ever before on earth.

For the first million years of human life on earth, members of the hominid family led bestial, not characteristically human, lives —that is, they lived mainly, if not exclusively, on the bare subsistence level, two-part lives of sleep and toil. Beginning about 35,000 years ago, technological progress slowly began to be made, which in the course of thirty millennia, brought man to the verge of civilization. But not until 6,000 years ago, with the emergence of civilized societies, with the domestication of animals, with the transition from stone to bronze and iron implements, with the establishment of permanent settlements, with superior agricultural technology, with political or quasi-political institutions, with an increased division of labor, and almost always with human slave labor—not until then were the external conditions of a good human life provided for a fortunate and privileged few.

In short, from the beginning until 6,000 years ago, the external conditions for leading a good human life were available *to no one*. Beginning 6,000 years ago, with the rise of cities and civilized societies (which are one and the same), and from then until now—or rather, until the end of the nineteenth century—we have had all over the world what I am going to call the parochial civilizations of privilege, based on an inequality of conditions for their human members.

In all these historic, parochial civilizations of privilege, the external conditions of a good human life were provided only for the few, at the expense of misery for all the rest. And it seems fair to say that under the circumstances of the time, especially the poor technology of the time, these inequalities of condition could not have been rectified—except, perhaps, by going backward to a state of affairs in which no one could lead a good human life.

The second great revolution in human affairs began yesterday —with the opening of this century. The twentieth-century revolution, which began first in the United States and Western Europe, is now sweeping the world. Please note that I said "began," for the twentieth-century revolution has only just begun, even in the countries where it originated. It may take anywhere from 100 to 500 years, maybe even 1,000, before this revolution yields its full results on a world-wide basis, with the emergence, for the first time, of a world civilization based on universal conditions of equality for every human being on earth—for *all* men with *no* exceptions.

(2)

What is the twentieth-century revolution? It involves, first of all, extraordinary advances in science and technology, resulting in vastly increased power to produce wealth, in the elimination of inhuman forms of subsistence-work at the level of sheer drudgery, the reduction in the amount of time that must be spent in producing wealth, and so on. All these changes indicate that it may at last be possible to eliminate slavery, poverty, unequal educational opportunities, unequal conditions of health and so on. [1]

I am well aware that it seems to be a historical fact that the very forces that bring marked improvements in the conditions of human life also add increments of evil. This is particularly true of advances in technology which, along with the great benefits they confer upon human life, carry threatening evils in their train. The uncontrolled applications of technology for the sake of industrial production, military efficiency, or even human convenience threaten us with water and air pollution, serious imbalances in the economy of nature, unlivable urban concentrations, thermonuclear holocaust. Nevertheless, it remains the case that all these threatening evils can be overcome by controlling technology or by using it to solve some of the problems it creates.

On balance, one is compelled to say that the advances in technology already made and to be made promise that mankind's future, with effective population control, can be much brighter than its past. If technology makes highly destructive world wars possible for the first time in this century, it is also true that, for the first time in this century, the technological conditions are such that world government has become a practicable project. [2] If technology results in uncontrolled industrial expansion and sometimes wasteful affluence, it is also true that our power to produce consumable wealth has reached the point that, for the first time in this century, the elimination of poverty is even conceivable; more than that, this is the first century in which any steps have been taken to reduce its extent.

Second, the twentieth-century revolution involves a commitment, in varying degrees, to the democratic and socialistic principles that all men, being by nature equal, are entitled to an equality of social, economic, and political conditions. It calls for the elimination of all class-divisions, especially the division between the economic *haves* and *have-nots*. It calls for political equality of citizenship, with political rights, liberties, and privileges for all. It is not only democratic but socialistic in that it accepts the ruling principle of the welfare state—that the state should make every effort to promote the general economic welfare, in which all citizens shall participate up to at least the minimum level of a decent and secure standard of living.

Therefore, this is not only the first century in which men can project the elimination of war by the constitution of a world federal government; it is also the first century in which men can project the advent of a truly classless society, pervaded by a universal equality of conditions. [3] For the first time in history, it seems practicable to eliminate the twin evils of class and war that, as Toynbee points out, have beset civilized life from its beginning. [4] Even though these great advances in the condition of mankind may take centuries more to bring to their full fruition, even now, in this century, many more men than ever before on earth *can* think about their lives as a whole because external conditions are now such that it has at last become possible for them to make *good* lives for themselves.

(3)

This twentieth-century revolution was foreshadowed first in the Preamble to the Constitution of the United States and in the Declaration of Independence, especially in the paragraph that starts with the proposition that all men are born equal, and then conceives the just society as one that will secure to every man his natural rights, among which the primary one is his right to the pursuit of happiness, from which all his other rights flow. But these truths, however self-evident, could not have been realized under the technological conditions of the eighteenth century. That is why Lincoln wisely described the Declaration not as a statement of fact, but as a pledge to the future. And it is in these same terms that Tocqueville presented his vision of that future, in which the revolution that had just begun in America, would, under God's providence, ultimately sweep the whole world. [5]

That future has now in part been realized. One need only compare the best country in the world in the middle of the nineteenth century—any one you wish to choose—with a dozen or more present-day states in which the twentieth-century revolution has begun and taken hold, to see that in the latter the external conditions of a good human life are provided for more human beings than ever before on earth. [6]

CHAPTER 21

Is Ours a Good Society to Be Alive In?

(1)

L ET us now compare the states or countries in which the
twentieth-century revolution has begun and taken hold,
limiting our attention for the moment to political, economic, and social conditions. We will examine their cultural
characteristics presently.

In varying degrees, all these states are characterized by political
democracy, economic welfare programs, the broadening of public
education, public health programs, reduction in the hours of
human labor, improvement in the types and conditions of subsistence-work, increase in recreational facilities, participation in
the enjoyment of the arts, increases in longevity, advances in
communication and public information, and so on. Let me designate this type of state as the technologically advanced, democratic, welfare state, moving toward—approximating, but not yet
fully achieving—the ideal of the classless society, with a universal
equality of conditions and with ample free time for all.

In the world as it is today, we find this type of state realized
in varying degrees:

(1) In the highest degree, by the United States, Sweden,
Japan, and a few states of the British Commonwealth.
(2) In the next rank, by Great Britain, the states of Western
Europe (with the exception of Spain and Portugal), by
the Soviet Union, and to a lower degree by the smaller

socialist republics, such as Yugoslavia, Czechoslovakia, and perhaps Poland and Romania.

(3) Far below this are most if not all of the states of Central and South America.

(4) The twentieth-century revolution may have begun, but it has not yet taken hold to any appreciable degree in the Middle East, in Africa, in China, and in Southeast Asia. The two possible exceptions in Asia are North Vietnam and South Korea.

All of the states in which the twentieth-century revolution is now underway, and especially those in which it has made substantial progress, are vastly superior to any societies that ever before existed on earth, as far as their political, economic, and social conditions are concerned. They are vastly superior to the best of ancient societies—to the Athens of Plato, which unfortunately did not live up to the encomiums heaped upon it by Pericles fifty years earlier, to the Rome of Cicero and the China of Confucius, in all of which the conditions of a good life were accessible only to the *very few*, and then at the cost of misery to the great mass of men whose lives were either ruined by slavery or consumed by stultifying toil. [1]

(2)

How does the United States compare with other leading states of the same type—states that are technologically advanced and that have begun to approximate an equality of conditions, political, economic, and social?

The comparison is difficult to make, because it is multi-dimensional. Thus, the United States is much less class-structured than England, has a higher median income than Sweden, has achieved a greater equality of educational opportunity than most European countries, though not more than Australia or Canada, and so on. It also has more political equality and liberty than the U.S.S.R. and its satellites. On the other hand, economic equality may be more fully achieved in Sweden and in New Zealand; public health may be better cared for in any number of European countries; political democracy may work more responsibly in England; and so on.

With all such considerations in mind, I still think it is fair to say that from the point of view of *providing* the external conditions of a good human life for a larger percentage of its citizens, the United States, is, *on balance*, as good as, if not better than, any other country in the world today, and vastly better than any state that ever existed in the past. [2]

How, then, can we explain the adverse criticisms of the United States that are current—the complaints and dissatisfactions that are so widely and emotionally voiced, often in a tone of high moral indignation and almost always with incredibly dogmatic certitude, by dissident or disaffected professors, by rebellious minorities, young and old, by the anarchists or nihilists whose only aim is to destroy what they call "the establishment," and by the New Left in all its varieties?

In the first place, let me point out that some of these criticisms are directed against the cultural atmosphere and the prevalent value-system or *mores* of the community. They are, in my judgment, much more justified than the attacks on our political, economic, and social institutions. I will deal with these criticisms presently.

In the second place, let me add that I have repeatedly stressed the fact that the twentieth-century revolution has just begun, even in the United States, and that it still has a long way to go before it reaches its full fruition—the full realization of the sound principles that have motivated it, the reaping of all the advantages that advanced technology has the power to confer while at the same time overcoming the serious threats that are the avoidable, not inevitable, consequences of these advances. The war on poverty has just begun; so has the struggle against racism in all its forms. These efforts must be carried forward, and it will take many years to see them through to complete success.

No country is free from the evils of war or the chicanery of foreign policy, and none can be, as long as the jungle or anarchy of sovereign states exist. Foreign affairs is the domain of power politics, and will remain so until we have advanced to world peace secured in the only way it can be secured—*by world government*. That, by the way, is the next revolution that lies ahead, the step forward from our parochial societies, always in a state of war with one another, and with an irremediable inequality of conditions existing between the *have* and the *have-not* nations, to a world society, under world government, with an equality of conditions for all men everywhere. [3] Until that happens, all sovereign states, *vis-à-vis* one another, are about equally bad, and the United States is no better but also no worse than the rest. And until that happens the evils of poverty and racism cannot be eradicated on a world-wide basis—and, perhaps, not completely even at home.

(3)

With all its past and present imperfections, the United States has shown itself more susceptible to social improvement than any other country. Its history has been the history of a continuing revolution prosecuted mainly by due process of law. [4] More radical institutional changes have been made in a relatively short time in American history and, for the most part, with less violence, than in the history of most other countries—with the possible exception of England. [5] This holds out great promise for further positive developments by peaceful means.

The revolution must go on. The twentieth-century revolution must be carried forward until it has accomplished all its goals. We cannot dismiss criticisms of our institutions in their present stage of development if those criticisms call, as they should, for carrying the American revolution forward. But we can dismiss the purely negative and nihilistic type of criticism that, failing to acknowledge the revolutionary accomplishments so far, does not propose carrying the revolution forward, but instead calls for the complete demolition of our institutions, the present state of which holds out so much promise for the future. [6]

Ideal conditions have never existed in the past, and do not yet exist anywhere on earth. All existing countries, including the United States, are socially defective or *pathological*. If the word "pathological" means "sick," it also raises the question of whether the pathology is remediable, whether the sickness is curable. It seems to me perfectly clear that the existing social pathologies are all remediable. If that were not the case, the twentieth-century revolution could go no further, as it must and will. Hence those who call the United States a sick society, and mean by that one that is mortally or incurably ill, are willfully shutting their eyes to all the available facts and refusing to acknowledge obvious trends of change that support reasonably optimistic predictions.

There is a middle ground between the perfection of blooming health and mortal or incurable disease. And that is where we are —a relatively healthy society with some spots of pathology, some curable defects or deficiencies. The importance of recognizing the soundness of the middle ground in criticizing the United States can be illustrated by the difference between two questions one can ask about a house one is thinking of buying because one wants to live on its site. One can ask, "Is it so bad a house that the only thing to do is to tear it down or gut it, and start from the ground up?" Or one can ask, "With all its defects, is it nevertheless good enough to remodel, improve, and redecorate?" The present state of the U.S.A. should inspire us to ask the second of these questions. And we should answer it by saying that the United States, with all its defects, is good enough to deserve our trying to improve it by carrying forward the peaceful revolution, reform by due process of law, that has been the course—more than that, the genius—of our development from the beginning. Recourse to violence is justified only when civil or legal measures are not available.

While saying this we should also recognize the justifiable impatience of all those who are still oppressed by injustices that are not yet rectified and may not even be rectifiable with sufficient speed to satisfy them. The deep unrest that exists among those who are still oppressed, even the revolutionary violence that the wrongs they have long suffered now impel them to incite, is itself a sign that the time is at last ripe for the needed reforms. The politically, economically, and socially oppressed have always spearheaded the revolutionary changes needed to right the wrongs they have suffered and can no longer tolerate. Sometimes the time is not ripe for the changes demanded in justice, and revolution is then bloody and abortive. But today we are confronted with oppressed groups, all over the world as well as in our own country, whose revolutionary impulses are fired by rising expectations—by the great progress that has already been made and that promises the possibility of further progress, and by the possibility, now as never before, of institutional reforms that will make the twentieth-century revolution, when completed, the first revolution in the history of mankind that will have really meant "all"—all without exceptions —as it moves toward its ultimate goal of an equality of political, economic, and social conditions for every human being on earth.

When that revolutionary goal is reached, there will exist for the first time in human history external conditions that provide for every man the opportunity to make a good life for himself. Unfortunately, opportunity is one thing, and making good use of it is another. Not all who have the opportunity now—and that is a large majority of the American people—succeed in making good lives for themselves. [7] A distressingly large number do not understand the problem, do not know how to solve it, and are not even emotionally disposed to learn. Most of them lead unexamined lives, and lives that represent their unwitting adoption of the perverse system of values embodied in American culture and expressed in the prevalent *mores* of our people.

This brings us to the final question we must face, the question about the culture of the United States—its *mores*, its scale of values. From this point of view, we must once more ask, *Is ours a good society to be alive in?*

CHAPTER 22

The Moral and Educational Revolution That Is Needed

(1)

D OES the scale of values implicit in the prevalent *mores* of the United States—and in most other countries of the same type—encourge or discourage, facilitate or inhibit, the making of a good life by all those who are given the opportunity to do so by favorable political, economic, and social conditions? In attempting to answer this question, I will confine myself to two observations, one concerning the moral atmosphere set up by the goals most Americans prize and honor, the other concerning the effects of that moral atmosphere upon our educational system.

The things most prized and honored in America are the expanding production of wealth, whether or not the wealth produced satisfies real needs or artificially induced wants; technological advances either for their own sake or for the sake of creature comforts and conveniences in excess of genuine need; external or worldly success as measured by the acquisition of money, fame, or power rather than development of the inner man and the growth of the human being as a person; the expansion of the sensate life rather than the intensification of the life of the mind. The high value set upon these things represents a fundamental disorder of goods, a perverse scale of values, placing lower over higher goods, mistaking merely apparent for real goods, and even transforming goods that are only means into ends to be sought for their own sake, as if they constituted the good life as a whole. Whereas the favorable political, economic, and social conditions that have been achieved in our type of soicety make it possible for a large proportion of our population to make good lives for themselves, this unfavorable moral atmosphere or climate militates against the possibility of their succeeding; it disinclines them to make the effort; it turns their lives in one or another wrong direction.

This adverse criticism of American culture applies to the quite similar cultural characteristics of all the other technologically advanced and technologically oriented industrial societies that Professor Herbert Marcuse attacks as repressive and that Professor Kenneth Galbraith, with marked ambivalence, describes as the New Industrial State. [1] If the criticism applies with any special force to the United States, that is only because the United States is in the forefront of the twentieth-century revolution. It is technologically the most advanced, the most powerful and affluent, and so the best exemplar of the New Industrial State, having to a higher degree than any other country the vices as well as the virtues that evoke Galbraith's ambivalence.

Unfortunately, Marcuse and Galbraith sometimes appear to think that a political and economic or even a social revolution is called for to remove the repressiveness or to correct the overproduction and maldistribution of goods that they deplore. It is true that the goal of an ever-expanding economy, which strives for a greater production and consumption of commodities than is necessary, involves a grievous misuse of the time of human lives—time that is freed by technological advances, all of which are labor-saving devices. Instead of the free time being used for the pursuits of leisure, through which a human being develops as a person and grows mentally, morally, and spiritually, it is used in the consumption, as well as in the production, of commodities of questionable value, and for over-indulgence in frivolous activities that make little or no contribution to the good life. To change this pattern of life calls for a moral revolution, not an economic revolution. Similarly, it is not a political or social, but a moral revolution that is needed to free the individual from the *mores* that now, according to Marcuse, inhibit and maim his personal development.

Also, unfortunately, neither Marcuse nor Galbraith manifests much, if any, understanding of the order of goods that constitute a good life, and both, as extreme libertarians and individualists, would recoil from a teleological ethics that not only conceives the ultimate human good as essentially the same for all men, but also imposes on each the categorical obligation to seek a really good life and to seek it by making right choices with regard to the means of attaining it. While leaving each individual free to decide what is a good life for himself, according to his wants, Professor Marcuse recommends an expansion of the sensate life that, if followed, would cripple personal development almost as much as the misuse of his time in the overproduction and over-consumption of commodities. [2] Professor Galbraith carries his argument to the point where it is clearly evident that all the advantages conferred by the New Industrial State must be subordinated to the pursuit of happiness, and controlled as means to the end of a good life for all human beings. But on the subject of what human happiness is, he then bows out, citing Bertrand Russell, of all persons, as authority for the view that "the notion of happiness lacks philosophical exactitude; there is agreement neither on its substance nor its source." Therefore, he leaves it up to each individual to decide what makes his own life good—*apparently* good according to his own individual wants. [3] Revolutionaries like Marcuse and libertarians like Galbraith have their hearts negatively in the right place, but they are inhibited by their prejudices, or prevented by their philosophical ignorance, from putting their minds positively there as well.

Let me repeat once more that the unfavorable moral atmosphere or cultural influences under criticism here exist, in varying degrees, in all technologically advanced industrial societies. The perverse scale of values that sets up cultural obstacles to leading a good life in the United States today prevails in the *mores* of every other country of the same general type. "Materialism"— a preference for external goods over the goods of the human spirit—is as prevalent in Europe as in the United States, and in Eastern as well as Western Europe. The cult of sensuality, addiction to a life of play and frivolity, the existentialist cop-out which consists in living from day to day with no accounts carried forward and with no thought of a good life as a whole—

these things flourish everywhere, not just in America, and unfortunately it is to these things that too many of the young tend to turn when they are disaffected with the materialism of their elders, not only in the United States but in Europe as well. The conflict between the younger and the older generation with regard to values is a case of pot and kettle each calling the other black. The moral obtuseness of the young on certain points is as inimical to leading a good life as the moral crassness that the young deplore in their elders. The fact that the young appear to be more sensitive to injustices that cry out for remedies may give them a moral edge on their elders, but it does not alter or condone the moral misdirection of their own lives.

What all this calls for is a moral revolution, but a moral revolution that can begin only after the moral problem is itself understood and the solution of that problem is envisaged in all its details. That, in turn, calls for an educational revolution, but these two revolutions would seem to be so interdependent that, in fact, neither may be possible unless both come into being simultaneously.

(2)

I would like to say a few words about the educational revolution that is needed in the United States—one that will reverse the so-called "academic revolution" that Professors Jencks and Reisman have so accurately described in their recent book. [4] I confine my attention to the United States not because the educational revolution is most needed here, but because it is here that all the externals of equal educational opportunity have been more fully achieved than anywhere else. This makes the misdirection of our educational system to the wrong ends so great a travesty on our success in the externals.

The rebellion of the students in our colleges and universities is thoroughly justified by wrongs they are suffering at the hands of their institutions, but wrongs of which most of them are only dimly and, at best, inchoately aware. They are being cheated and defrauded by an educational system that has displaced genuinely liberal and humanistic training by forms of specialized, technical, and vocational training intended to fit the young for their places in the industrial machine rather than to fit them for a good life by preparing them to make good use of their free time in the pursuits of leisure.

As I pointed out earlier, the reform of abuses is usually spear-headed by those who suffer under them. Today the young feel abused, but many of them project their complaints against the wrong objects—the political, economic, and social institutions of our society. The root cause of their malaise is rather the cultural disorder of a society devoted mainly to technological advances and industrial development, a disorder reflected in the misdirection of the educational system to the wrong ends.

The young complain again and again of the inadequacy and irrelevance of the education they are receiving. They are right. They have suffered, and the generations to come will suffer even more, unless the university system is radically reformed, unless colleges are emancipated from the heavy and deadening hand of graduate and professional schools, and unless the universities themselves become once more communities of scholars and cease to be service stations for the industrial state, Research and Development agencies for government and private industry, or even havens for professors to pursue their special interests without regard to the best interests of the students they should be serving. [5]

It is particularly in the classrooms of our colleges that the young are suffering the worst abuses. To correct these abuses, not only must curriculums be revised, but faculties must once again consist of teachers rather than professors, of men interested in liberal and humanistic learning, for themselves as well as for others, more than in research or in the advancement of knowledge in some specialized or technical field. Unfortunately, most of the young, precisely because they are so poorly educated, do not and cannot know the kind of education they so sorely need —the kind that would have maximum relevance not to business or worldly success, but to the business of making good lives for themselves and to success in that effort. [6]

Applying here the critical distinction between natural needs and conscious wants, what must be said is that all our young need genuinely liberal and humanistic learning as a means to the good life, the dullest among them as well as the brightest. But the brightest among them do not now want the kind of education they most need, as indicated by the types of courses they themselves arrange for when they set up their own Free Universities. They do not want the kind of education that they need because they have not been taught the basic moral lessons about the shape of a good human life, about its constituent parts and the means they must employ to achieve it. Miseducated and, therefore, misguided, they thrash about in a variety of wrong directions, hitting out against political, economic, and social conditions that have favored them, instead of against the deficiencies and deformities of an educational system that has mistreated them so badly. [7]

(3)

We saw earlier that the time of our lives—our century—was better than any earlier period of human life. That judgment must now be qualified in one significant respect. The statement is true for all the external conditions of a human life on earth, conditions provided by technological advances and by a greater approximation to the ideals of democracy and socialism—the ideals of the classless society and the welfare state—brought about by the beginning of the twentieth-century revolution. Included among these external conditions is, of course, equality of educational opportunity in all its external aspects. But it is precisely in the sphere of education that the twentieth century is inferior to the oligarchical, class-divided, slave-holding, poverty-ridden societies of the past, in which the possibility of making a good life was open only to the very few.

When schooling was given only to the privileged few, it was directed to the right ends. It was essentially liberal and humanistic and, therefore, prepared the few whose time was free from toil to use that free time in all the forms of learning and creative work that constitute the activities of leisure. In this way it helped them to make good lives for themselves. The irony of our present situation is that now, when a large proportion of our population is provided with external conditions that help them to make good lives for themselves, the educational facilities do not fulfill that promise by affording them the kind of education they need. Instead of being the kind of education appropriate to free men, and men with ample free time for the pursuits of leisure, it is the kind of education appropriate to slaves or workers, men whose time will be mainly consumed by economic activities rather than devoted to the activities of leisure. [8]

CHAPTER 23

A Concluding Word About the Critics of Our Century and Our Society

(1)

M ANY of the critics, old as well as young, direct their complaints at the wrong objects. One of the most regrettable features of our century and our society is not that it has a large number of highly vocal critics who complain about it, but rather that the complaints are voiced in ways that are so often mistaken, unreasonable, and off-the-beam.

On the one hand, the dissident young, frequently under the influence of their professors, together with the leaders of the New Left and others full of complaints about our century and our society, do not hesitate to make moral pronouncements about social evils they think must be immediately eliminated. [1] It is perfectly clear that they do not know or understand the moral principles that would give support to their charges, and that they have not engaged in the moral reasoning that could make their criticisms tenable. Exactly the same principles that might support criticism of the war in Vietnam, racism, and poverty should lead them to criticize a society that exaggerates the importance of sensual pleasures, that engages in the over-production of superflous commodities, and that does not draw a line between the frivolous and the serious use of free time. Exactly the same principles and reasoning would also help them to understand what is wrong with being a beatnik, a hippie, a self-alienated refugee from reason, or an existentialist cop-out—wrong in a way that can ruin a human life—or what is wrong with over-indulgence in sex, what is wrong with psychedelic escapism, with attempts to expand the sensate life but not the life of the mind, or what is wrong with pure emotionalism and the rejection of reason, and so on. [2]

Whether it results from alcohol, pot, LSD, or stronger narcotics, drunkenness is drunkenness—a state of aggravated passions, disordered imagination, and uncontrolled impulses, ending in torpor, all of which is incompatible with the exercise of prudence and moral virtue in the choice of goods. Show me a person who condones drunkenness by any means, and I will show you one who does not understand what a good life is or how to achieve it. That same person will be one who, when he speaks out against this or that social injustice, will not be doing so with a commitment to the good life, correctly conceived, and so will be lacking a rational basis for his social complaints.

If this estimate of the character of the most vocal and emotional critics of our century and our society, both old and young, appears to be harsh, I can mitigate its severity only by saying that the fault is not theirs. It lies in the dismal failure of our educational system, under which most of them have been defrauded of a schooling they had a right to expect. Their minds have not been opened to any wisdom or trained to seek it; their minds have not been disciplined in the ways of reason, and so they have not learned to respect it.

On the other hand, the self-appointed guardians of the morals and patriotism of our society are no less dogmatic in their pronouncements, or in their suggested cures for the evils they profess to see. They propose, for example, the re-injection of morality into the schools in the form of simple homilies that are as irrelevant today as they were in the past, when they abounded; and they propose, too, that patriotism be taught by distortions of history to emphasize the contributions of persons they think were "patriots," while ignoring those of persons they disapprove of. But morality cannot be taught by homilies, nor patriotism by the example of men who were often foolhardy and sometimes not patriots at all.

It is true of these critics, too, that they do not know or understand the principles that would give moral support to their charges. Exactly the same principles that might support their criticisms of the educational system, or of the young, or of corruptions in government, should also lead them to criticize a society that exaggerates the importance of wealth and wealth-getting, and an economy that depends too much on defense contracts. Exactly the same principles would help them to understand what is wrong with being a businessman (when business is considered an end in itself)—wrong in a way that can ruin a human life—what is wrong with over-indulgence in alcohol or sports or television, what is wrong with intellectual escapism, combined with ignorance of and contempt for the life of the mind, what is wrong with cruelty and the excessive use of force, with the rejection of compromise, and so forth.

(2)

Most important of all, these critics—all of them, left and right—fail to recognize that many of their criticisms, leveled against America and Americans, apply to all societies and to the human race generally.

The greatest satire on the human race ever written—*Gulliver's Travels* by Jonathan Swift—would be egregiously misread if it were interpreted as an attack only on eighteenth-century England or Englishmen. It is the great diatribe against mankind that it is because the follies and vices it satirizes are all human—to be found in every country at all times, because every country is populated by men, not by angels or by Swift's gentle, rational horses, the Houyhnhnms.

In the course of the centuries, human institutions have been greatly improved, and they might be further improved without limit, as William Graham Sumner once remarked, *were it not for folly and vice*. [3] Folly and vice are human defects, not American defects. Twentieth-century America has no monopoly on folly and vice, nor do the critics of the twentieth century have a monopoly on conscience-stricken reactions to human folly and vice. Plato charged the Athenians who condemned Socrates with folly and vice. The dialogues of Plato are a more penetrating critique of the false values of Athens, at the time when it was the glory of antiquity, than anything said about America now, because Plato had a true scale of values on which to base his criticisms. That is clearly not the case with the most vociferous and emotional critics of American society today.

Let me suggest three considerations that must be borne in mind when one examines the current attacks on our society and our century. First, one should ask whether or not the objects of attack are simply human folly and vice. Second, to put these attacks or criticisms into historical perspective, it is necessary to consider the facts in terms of which the twentieth century must be compared with all earlier centuries, and the United States with all other countries in the world today. Many of the critics of our country seem to be totally oblivious of these facts or emotionally unwilling to acknowledge their obvious significance when they are presented. Third, one should ask whether those who criticize their country and their fellow-countrymen have the moral wisdom—a correct understanding of the good life and an adequate formulation of the plan for achieving it—that would commit them to a really good life for themselves and direct them in its pursuit. One should also ask whether their own scale of values, the end they aim at and the means they employ, manifests their possession of moral virtue and of prudence.

The evidence—too often, I regret to say—suggests that they do not. They are as much subject to folly and vice as are the objects of their criticism. And the only salvation for them, as for all the rest of us, is the moral wisdom that must be learned to correct the folly, and the moral discipline that must be cultivated to correct the vice. [4]

(3)

To this end we need a moral revolution and an educational revolution together, for each would appear to be impossible without the other.

Although it is reasonable in other areas of human life to expect revolutionary changes to be called for and engineered by the oppressed, we cannot expect a moral and educational revolution to come from those who are deeply dissatisfied with the moral climate in which they live, but who also lack the moral training and the liberal education needed to reform the *mores* of our society and its educational system. We appear to be in a *cul-de-sac*. It may be too much to expect the moral and educational revolution we need to come from anyone now alive. The discontented have not learned enough and are not likely to, because most of them do not trust reason as a way of learning what must be learned. Perhaps if, in some way, the generations to come could learn what a good life is and how to achieve it, and could be given the discipline, not only of mind but of character, that would make them willingly responsive to the categorical oughts of a teleological ethics, perhaps, then, the moral and educational revolution might begin and take hold.

To hope for this is to hope for no more than that the restoration of a sound and practical moral philosophy will enable enlightened common sense to prevail in human affairs.

Postscript

(1)

W HEN I first thought of writing this book, I conceived it as little more than a re-writing of the *Nichomachean Ethics* of Aristotle, expounding the moral insights I had learned over many years of reading and teaching it. The contribution I hoped to make I thought of mainly as a communication of its fundamental insights in language, imagery, and examples that have currency today, thus making them more accessible to the contemporary reader than they are in the pages of Aristotle. In addition, I planned to convey only those portions of Aristotle's doctrine which have a universality that transcends time and place, and so have relevance for men living in any historic society and culture. I had one other criterion of selection. I would report only those Aristotelian formulations which seemed to me to be true and coherent. After many readings of the *Ethics*, much remained that I could not assimilate to my purpose, because it was inconsistent with what I regarded as the controlling principles of Aristotle's doctrine, and much remained dark or obscure. Therefore, I would select only those points that I could expound clearly, defend as true, and put together into a consistent and coherent moral philosophy.

As this project developed in my mind and as the preparatory work for writing this book took the form of notes for lectures, I decided to keep my original intention a secret from the reader, mentioning it in a Postscript rather than in a Preface. I realized, of course, that for those readers who have studied Aristotle's *Ethics* and who have found it, as I have, a philosophical refine-

ment of common-sense wisdom, it would be a poorly kept secret.
But I also felt relatively sure that it would not be discovered
by casual readers of the *Ethics*, or even by many contemporary
philosophers whose interpretation and evaluation of that book
differ remarkably from my own. To preserve the secret, as much
as it could be preserved, I refrained from making references to
Aristotle's moral philosophy in the body of the book or in the
notes to its chapters. The attentive reader will have observed,
with some puzzlement perhaps, that—with one exception—all
the citations of, or quotations from, Aristotle are on logical or
meta-ethical points, not on matters germane to the substance of
moral philosophy.

Now that the book is written, my original plan for the Postscript is somewhat altered. I still think that the *Nichomachean
Ethics* is a unique book in the Western tradition of moral philosophy. As Aristotle is uniquely the philosopher of common
sense, so his moral philosophy is uniquely the ethics of common
sense. It is the only ethics that is both teleological and deontological, the only ethics that is sound, practical, and undogmatic,
offering what little normative wisdom there is for all men to
be guided by, but refraining from laying down rules of conduct
to cover the multifarious and contingent circumstances of human
action. In the history of Western moral thought, it is the only
book centrally concerned and concerned throughout with the
goodness of a whole human life, with the parts of this whole, and
with putting the parts together in the right order and proportion.
As far as I know, its only parallel is to be found outside of
Western culture in the moral teachings of Confucius, which
address themselves to the same problem and which offer a solution to it that also refines the wisdom of common sense—by
means of aphorisms rather than, as in Aristotle's case, by means
of analysis and argument. [1] But while I still hold this high regard for the *Nichomachean Ethics*, I now realize that it would be
misleading for me to claim that my book is nothing but Aristotle
in modern dress.

For one thing, I now realize that this book of mine contains
formulations, analytical distinctions, arguments, and elaborations
that cannot be found in the *Ethics*; in addition, the conceptions
and insights taken from Aristotle are not simply adopted without

modification, but adapted to fit together into a theoretical framework that is somewhat different from Aristotle's. If it appears immodest for me to claim some originality for what is set forth in these pages, it would be dishonest for me to pretend that I am merely translating into twentieth-century idiom the wisdom I have found in a book written almost 2,500 years ago. The most accurate description of what I have done, it seems to me, would be to say that certain things to be found in Aristotle's *Ethics* constitute my point of departure and control the general direction of my thought, but that I have gone further along the line of thinking about moral problems laid down by Aristotle— adding innovations to his theory, as well as extending and modifying it. Much of what is new or altered in my formulation of the ethics of common sense results from my effort to defend its wisdom against philosophical objections that were unknown to Aristotle, or to correct the misconceptions, misunderstandings, and ignorances that have dominated the scene in the last few hundred years.

However, even in dealing with the multifarious errors in modern and contemporary moral philosophy, I have been able to employ critical tools I have found in Aristotle. As an indirect confirmation of this, let me call attention to the fact that in criticizing such leading modern and contemporary moral philosophers as Kant, J. S. Mill, G. E. Moore, H. A. Pritchard, A. J. Ayer, and John Dewey, I have, usually without mentioning Aristotle's name or citing his work, pointed out misunderstandings of conceptions fundamental to Aristotelian doctrine or ignorance of distinctions and neglect of insights that, had they been learned from Aristotle, would have prevented these modern authors from making the mistakes they have made. They all certainly read the *Nichomachean Ethics* as students and most of them reconsidered it in the years of their own mature development; but the evidence is plain that for one reason or another, they read it very poorly, or perhaps I should say that their reading of Aristotle and their interpretation of his thought are as different from mine as if they and I were reading utterly different books. [2]

I know of few books that have been as variously interpreted as the *Nichomachean Ethics*. Many of the interpretations—in fact, most of them—make it out to be worth studying as a monument in the history of thought, or worth criticizing in order to point out errors we should avoid, but hardly a book that contains the one right approach to moral problems and more wisdom and truth in the solution of them than any book written since the fourth century B.C. [3] Among contemporary commentaries on Aristotle's *Ethics*, even the few interpretations that commend his approach or praise certain of his insights do not go all out in defense of his doctrine. [4] I know of only one book—Henry Veatch's *Rational Man*—that not only adopts Aristotle's approach without reservation, but also expounds and defends the wisdom and truth to be found in his doctrine, while at the same time acknowledging that Aristotle, like every other great philosopher, made mistakes that should not be perpetuated out of reverence for his authority. [5]

Scholars often argue for the correctness of their interpretation of a text; scholarly literature is full of controversy over the correct reading of this set of passages or that. Adjudicating such arguments or taking part in such controversies is not the business of a philosopher. Faced with the many divergent interpretations of the *Nichomachean Ethics*, I have no right or wish to claim that my reading of it has so perfectly grasped the meaning of every passage in that complicated text that I know with assurance precisely what Aristotle thought. For all I know, the meaning I attach to the words on this page or that may diverge from or even distort what Aristotle had in mind. I have already confessed that there is much in the book that remains dark or obscure to me, and that I have found many passages the apparent meaning of which I cannot easily reconcile with my interpretation of other passages that I have construed as expressing the controlling insights of the book.

What, then, can I claim for my reading of Aristotle's *Ethics?* Only this: (1) that it is an interpretation which sets forth a moral philosophy that is sound, practical, and undogmatic; (2) that it is an interpretation which, applying philosophical, not scholarly, criteria for judging what is morally true and wise, separates the wheat from the chaff and rejects what cannot be assimilated to a coherent ethical theory that is both teleological and deontological and that is based on the specific nature of man; and (3) that the ethical doctrine which emerges from this interpretation deserves to be called Aristotelian even if it does not represent the doctrine of Aristotle's *Ethics* in its entirety; or, in other words, that the moral wisdom and truths I have expounded as the ethics of common sense can be attributed to Aristotle more than to any other philosopher. [6]

Such support as can be given for the first two points in this threefold claim have already been given in the body of this book and in the notes appended to its chapters, especially the chapters of Parts Two and Three. It is the task of this Postscript to provide support for the third point. But how can that be done within the compass of a few pages, in view of the diverse interpretations of the *Nichomachean Ethics* and in view of the apparently conflicting passages in the book itself? It is a long and complicated book to deal with as a whole; furthermore, it presents more than the usual difficulties of rendering Greek into English; and, in addition, the close relation between Aristotle's *Ethics* and his *Politics* requires an examination of passages in the latter book that have a critical bearing on the interpretation of the former.

Some readers of these works, especially Aristotle's medieval commentators and their modern counterparts, have found the whole a seamless fabric of clear and coherent doctrine. I am unpersuaded by their efforts to make it appear so. Some readers, in modern times and especially in our own day, have gone to the opposite extreme—finding nothing but unresolvable difficulties or perplexities, irreconcilable strains of thought and inadequately expounded views. I cannot accept the picture they present, nor the estimate it implies. I myself have, from time to time, adopted a third alternative, which is probably as untenable. It is the old myth, for which there is certainly no clear or sufficient evidence, that these works originated in lectures that Aristotle gave to his students; that in the course of these lectures Aristotle was engaged in a systematic effort to explore for the first time the ethical and political dimensions of moral philosophy; that in the process of doing so, his own thought gradually developed and changed, with important insights and discoveries occurring at a later stage in the process, discoveries which called for the modification or even rejection of tentative formulations expressed at an earlier stage; that when he had finished giving his lectures, he had not yet reached the point where he was in possession of a clear-cut and coherent doctrine that he could expound systematically; that his lectures were either handed down to his students in manuscript, or taken down in extensive notes by them, compiled as treatises, and edited, but *not by Aristotle himself;* and that if Aristotle had re-read these compilations and then himself had written the books based on his lectures about ethics and politics, he would have produced two books in moral philosophy quite different from the ones we now have.

The difficulty with this myth, quite apart from any question about its factual authenticity, is that it might lead the person who adoped it to claim that he knew how Aristotle would have written the *Ethics* and the *Politics,* if he had carefully studied the notes based on his lectures and revised what he found there in order to present a clear and coherent doctrine, set forth demonstratively rather than dialectically and in the logical order of exposition rather than in the order of discovery. This would be tantamount to claiming that one had the inside track to all of Aristotle's thought, which is as impossible to support as the claim that one has the only correct interpretation of his works. What claim, then, can I make for the passages from the *Ethics* and *Politics* that I am going to quote in support of the proposition that the ethics of common sense expounded in this book is Aristotelian in tenor, even if it does not represent the whole of Aristotle's thought and may even run counter to certain aspects of it?

A letter William James wrote in 1900 to a graduate student at Harvard who had written a doctoral dissertation on his philosophy will help me to explain what I propose to do. "As a Ph.D. thesis," James told Miss S., "your essay is supreme, but why don't you go farther? You take utterances of mine written at different dates, for different audiences belonging to different universes of discourse, and string them together as the abstract elements of a total philosophy which you then show to be inwardly incoherent. This is splendid philology . . . [but] your use of the method only strengthens the impression I have got from reading criticisms of my 'pragmatic' account of 'truth,' that the whole Ph.D. industry of building an author's meaning out of separate texts leads nowhere, *unless you have first grasped his center of vision, by an act of imagination.* . . . . Not by proving their inward incoherence does one refute philosophies—every human being is incoherent—but only by superseding them by other philosophies more satisfactory. Your wonderful technical skill ought to serve you in good stead if you would exchange the philological kind of criticism for constructive work. I fear however that you won't—the iron may have bitten too deeply into your soul!!" The letter is signed: "Yours with mingled admiration and abhorrence, Wm. James." [7]

If Aristotle were alive today to read the commentaries that have been written about his philosophy, I could imagine him feeling about most of them what James felt about the efforts of Miss S. Therefore, I am going to try in this Postscript to follow James's excellent advice—by selecting those passages in Aristotle's *Ethics* and *Politics* that I regard as controlling any effort to get at the center of his vision. If, in the view of others, this is too much to claim, I am prepared to fall back on more modest claims and ones I think can be defended: first, that the passages I am going to cite must be given a controlling position in any interpretation of Aristotle's thought; and, second, that the insights expressed in these passages do in fact control the development of the moral philosophy I have expounded in this book, and justify my calling the ethics of common sense Aristotelian, even if it is not identical in content with Aristotle's *Ethics*.

I will proceed in the next five sections of this Postscript to quote and interpret what I have called the "controlling passages," and to indicate how other, apparently conflicting passages can, by interpretation, be reconciled with them. Then, in a final section, I will conclude with a few brief observations concerning the fate of Aristotle's *Ethics* in the history of moral philosophy in the West.

(2)

I have said that Aristotle's *Ethics* is both teleological and deontological. An ethical theory is teleological if it posits a single ultimate end as its first principle, and it is deontological if it makes the good which is this ultimate end the primary object of a categorical moral obligation that is universally binding on all men in the same way. For Aristotle, the single ultimate end is happiness conceived as the goodness of a human life as a whole. So conceived, happiness is the *totum bonum* (the whole of goods), not the *summum bonum* (the highest among the various partial goods that are components of happiness or parts of the whole). As the *totum bonum*, happiness or a whole good life is a normative, not a terminal, end—an end that takes a complete life to achieve, and therefore an end that is not achieved at any moment in the time of our lives. Therefore, happiness is neither experienceable nor enjoyable, for the satisfactions of desire that we experience and enjoy occur in passing moments of time. In contrast to happiness, all other goods—all of them less than the whole good and all of them parts of happiness— can be possessed and enjoyed during the course of our lives.

The passages in the *Nichomachean Ethics* (*NE*) that I am now about to cite reveal what, in my judgment, is the most distinctive feature of that book and what makes it unique among treatises in moral philosophy. It is the only ethical theory in which a good life as a temporal whole is the controlling or normative end of all action, and in which the goodness of particular types of activity or the goodness of the results they achieve is measured by their contribution to making a whole life good, each of these partial goods being a means to that end and all of them together being that end in the process of becoming. I will postpone until Section 3 the citation of the texts that give us Aristotle's enumeration of the partial goods or means to happiness and that indicate which among them is the highest good, and then, in Section 4, I will cite textual evidence to show that, in Aristotle's view, we are under a categorical moral obligation to make a really good life by choosing rightly —or virtuously—the activities or the results of action by which we can make our lives good as a whole.

"If we do not choose everything for the sake of something else (for at that rate the process would go on to infinity and our desires would be empty and vain), then there is some end of the things we do which we desire for its own sake—everything else being desired for the sake of this. Clearly, this must be the good and the chief good" (*NE*, I, 2, 1094ª18–22). Some goods may be merely means, some goods may be ends as well as means, but of the goods that are ends, only one is an end that is never a means, and it is, therefore, the ultimate or final end. "We call that which is in itself worthy of pursuit more final than that which is worthy of pursuit for the sake of something else; and that which is never desirable for the sake of something else is more final than the things that are desirable both in themselves and for the sake of something else. Therefore, we call final without qualification [i.e., the ultimate end, absolutely speaking] that which is desirable in itself and never for the sake of something else" (*NE*, I, 7, 1097^{a}30–35).

This, Aristotle declares, is happiness—the good "we always seek for its own sake and never for the sake of something else," whereas every other good, even those we desire for their own sakes, "we seek also for the sake of happiness, judging that by means of them we shall become happy" (*ibid.*, 1097^{a}37–1097^{b}6). Aristotle then points out that when we speak of happiness as the ultimate end, we must be careful not to speak of it as *a* good, but rather as *the* good. Although he himself has called it "the chief good," he makes clear that it is not to be thought of as the highest good, but as the whole of goods. Happiness is the chief good only in the sense that "it is the most desirable of all things without being counted as one good among others." His argument to support this point is unanswerable. If happiness were counted as one good among others, even though it were the highest or best of all such goods, "it would become more desirable by the addition of even the least of goods," in which case happiness by itself would not be the most desirable good, for the combination of happiness (as just one good) with any other additional good would be more desirable than happiness by itself, since "among goods the greater is always more desirable." Therefore, happiness as the ultimate end is not *a* good, but *the* good—that whole of goods to which nothing can be added and from which "nothing is lacking" (*ibid.*, 1097^{b}15–22).

The foregoing argument is repeated in Book X, where Aristotle says that "it is by an argument of this kind that Plato proves the good *not* to be pleasure; he argues that the life of pleasure is more desirable with wisdom than without it, and that if the combination of the two is better, then pleasure is not *the* good, for *the* good cannot become more desirable by the addition of anything to it" (*NE*, X, 2, 1172ª28–32). Aristotle then adds that no other partial good, any more than pleasure, can be *the* good if it is just one good among others, to which other goods can be added. Thus, as we shall see presently, the intellectual activity which, in Book X, Aristotle regards as the highest good (the *summum bonum*) does not constitute happiness (the *totum bonum*), for it, like pleasure, is only one good among others, and can be made more desirable by the addition of such other goods as wealth, health, and pleasure.

Happiness, Aristotle says again and again, is a good life as a whole; it consists in living well by choosing rightly among the various activities that can occupy our time and that can achieve certain results, each of which is only one good among others. However one describes the constituents of happiness, Aristotle insists that to any enumeration of its component parts, we must always "add 'in a complete life'; for one swallow does not make a summer, nor does one day; and so one day, or a short time, does not make a man happy" (*NE*, I, 7, 1098ª17–18; cf. X, 7, 1177ᵇ23–24). That is why children and youths cannot be called happy. If we ever attribute happiness to them in view of their promise or the good fortune that smiles on the beginning of their lives, it is "by reason of the hopes we have for them" not because they have achieved happiness, for that "requires a complete life, since many changes occur in life, and all manner of chances, and the most prosperous may fall into great misfortunes in old age" (*NE*, I, 9, 1100ª1–7). Aristotle confirms this in his discussion of Solon's observation that one can accurately judge the goodness of a human life only when it has been completed, but not while it is still in process (see *NE*, I, 10, 1100ª10–1100ᵇ10). Of a living man, we can never say *without qualification* that he is happy; only when a man's life is over can we say that it was a happy or a good life. While the individual is still engaged in trying to make a good life for himself, we can say only that the signs suggest that he is succeeding, that he is becoming happy, or that his life is becoming a good one. Happiness consists in living and acting well, under fortunate circumstances, "not for some chance period but throughout a complete life." At any moment in our lives, "the future remains obscure to us"; one's fortunes and one's character may change for better or for worse. As we shall see, good fortune and good character are essential conditions of happiness. So when we call a living man happy, our doing so is not only descriptive of his past but also predictive of his future: we are saying that he is one "in whom these conditions are *and are to be* fulfilled" (*NE*, I, 10, 1101ᵃ15–21; italics added).

(3)

Aristotle names a relatively small number of goods, each of which is a component of happiness—an element in the *totum bonum* that is a good life as a whole. A good life, he says, is impossible without a decent minimum of external goods, which include not only the means of subsistence but other forms of prosperity, some of which are conferred by good fortune (see *NE*, I, 8, 1099ᵃ31–1099ᵇ8; I, 10, 1101ᵃ16; VII, 13, 1153ᵇ18–24; X, 8, 1179ᵃ2–12). It is impossible without the goods of the body—health and vigor (see *NE*, VII, 13, 1153ᵇ17; X, 8, 1178ᵇ34–35). It is impossible without pleasure, not only the pleasures of sense, but the pleasures inherent in certain types of activity (see *NE*, VII, 13, 1153ᵇ13–15; VII, 14, 1154ᵃ1–22). It is impossible without friends or loved ones (see *NE*, IX, 8, 1169ᵇ3–22; IX, 11, 1171ᵃ34–1171ᵇ27). It is impossible without what Aristotle calls "the goods of soul"—the goods I have called the goods of self-improvement. These, as a class, stand highest among the partial goods that constitute the *totum bonum* (see *NE*, I, 8, 1098ᵇ14–16).

All the mistakes men make about happiness or the good life consist either in identifying it with one or another of the partial goods or in not correctly ordering these partial goods in relation to one another (see *NE*, I, 4; I, 5; I, 8; VII, 13, 1153ᵇ20–24; VII, 14, 1154ᵃ8–21; X, 3, 1174ᵃ1–14; X, 6, 1176ᵇ8–1177ᵃ12). The fact that each of these partial goods is something happiness depends on may explain but does not lessen the mistake of regarding any of them as the one thing in which happiness consists. The fact that each of these goods corresponds to a natural human need does not make them all coordinate or of equal value, for some of them, as Aristotle points out, serve as means to other ends as well as being means to happiness itself, and some, such as the goods of self-perfection, are not only means to happiness but good in themselves, as ends to be sought for their own sake.

In addition to naming the goods that are indispensable to happiness or a good life, Aristotle also names, with one exception, the basic types of activity by which these goods are obtained: wealth, by *work;* pleasure, by *play* or amusement; friendships and the goods of self-improvement, by *leisure.* The one exception is Aristotle's failure to name the various activities by which the bodily goods of health and vigor are obtained, for which I have employed the omnibus term *sleep.* Some of these activities, including the therapeutic form of play which Aristotle calls "relaxation," are mentioned in Book X of the *Ethics* (see Ch. 6 and 7) and are discussed again in the *Politics* (see Bk. VII, Ch. 14–15; Bk. VIII, Ch. 3, 5). Aristotle's ordering of these activities confirms his ordering of the goods with which they are associated. What he says about therapeutic play applies to all the activities I have grouped together under sleep; giving us health and bodily vigor, they are for the sake of work—either subsistence-work or leisure-work. Subsistence-work, in turn, is for the sake of leisure-work, and while a certain amount of play simply for the pleasure inherent in it is a necessary element in a good life, it should be engaged in with moderation in order to allow as much free time as possible for the self-cultivating pursuits of leisure.

Under the guidance of the controlling insight that happiness is *the* good (*totum bonum*), not the *highest* good (*summum bonum*), in which case it would be only one good among others, we can see that happiness does not consist in self-perfection, or the goods of self-improvement, even though these constitute the highest among partial goods. The same insight applies to leisure among the activities that occupy our time, and to that special form of leisure—speculative activity, contemplation, or thinking and knowing for the sake of thinking and knowing—which Aristotle prizes for its contribution to happiness.

Aristotle's views concerning the principal forms of leisure were somewhat conditioned and colored by the cultural circumstances of an aristocratic, agrarian, slave-holding society, but that need not prevent us from divesting his conception of the good life of its local trappings and universalizing its terms so that they apply not just to an elite living under certain historic conditions but to all men everywhere at all times. He says, for example, that men who have sufficient property and slaves to attend to chores, so that they do not have to work for a living or operate their estates, should "occupy themselves with philosophy or with politics" (*Politics*, I, 8, 1255^b37–38). This need not be read narrowly to signify the activity of the philosopher or the activity of the statesmen as Aristotle thought of these pursuits—activities which, in other places, he contrasts as the speculative or contemplative life, on the one hand, and as the political or active life, on the other (see *NE*, I, 5, 1095^b18; X, 7, 1177^b15–1178^a2; X, 8, 1178^a8–13; and cf. *Politics*, VII, 2, 1324^a 27–32; VII, 3, 1325^b15–23). The word "philosophy" can be broadly interpreted to stand for all the arts and sciences—for the whole range of creative intellectual work by which the individual himself learns and also, perhaps, makes some contribution to culture as a result of his learning. The word "politics" can be similarly extended to cover all the institutions of society and all public or quasi-public affairs, including those of business and other corporate enterprises, involving the individual in action as well as in thought, yet constituting genuine leisure for the individual only to the extent that his intellectual involvement results in learning or some other aspect of personal growth. Thus, broadly interpreted, philosophy and politics would appear to be the two principal forms of leisure, even though they may not exhaust every variety of leisure pursuit, among which must be included the activities concerned with love and friendship.

The man who is neither a philosopher nor a statesman in Aristotle's sense of these terms is not precluded from engagement in the pursuits of leisure. Considering the diversity of human aptitudes or talents and the wide range of individual abilities, it still remains the case that, for every man, leisure, in one form or another, is supreme among human activities, and the resulting goods of self-improvement constitute the most important ingredient in a good life. Aristotle's handling of the question whether speculative or political activity makes the greater contribution to happiness leaves the matter unresolved; there are passages, among those cited above, in which he favors the one, and passages in which he favors the other. However, a resolution is obtainable by altering the question somewhat. Considering an individual's talents and temperament, as well as the external circumstances of his life, what form of leisure-work will contribute most to his learning—to the growth of his mind and to the development of his personality? That, *for him*, is the highest form of leisure; *for someone else*, it may be something else; *for each man*, happiness is to be achieved to the highest possible degree by the fullest engagement in what is for him the highest form of leisure-work.

(4)

It is in one way easy to understand why modern philosophers, beginning with Kant, have regarded Aristotle's eudaimonistic ethics or ethics of happiness as the very opposite of a deontological ethics, or an ethics of categorical obligation. There can be no question that it gives primacy to the good rather than to the right. It proceeds mainly in terms of the desirable rather than in terms of the dutiful. It appears to lay down no moral laws: the pages of the *Nichomachean Ethics* are almost totally devoid of explicitly formulated rules of conduct, and of criteria for judging whether a particular action is right or wrong. Nevertheless, as I will now try to show, to dismiss Aristotle's doctrine, as Kant and others following him have done, as purely pragmatic or utilitarian, in the sense that it appeals only to what men do in fact consciously desire without considering what they ought to desire, represents a profound misreading of the book.

This misreading is remarkable because it fails to observe points that furnish the reader with controlling insights for interpreting the book as a whole. First of all, there is the fact so pervasive that it is very difficult to miss, namely, that Aristotle, in dealing with the diverse opinions men hold concerning happiness, directs his efforts toward discovering and formulating the one right conception of happiness. He is clearly denying that any version of the good life is as sound as any other, and just as clearly affirming that happiness, rightly conceived, is the same for all men precisely because, regardless of their individual differences, they are all human beings, the same in their specific nature. He rejects the opinion that happiness consists solely in a life of pleasure, a life of money-making, a life filled with external goods, a life devoted to the attainment of public honor or prestige or power over other men, and even a life that consists exclusively in being virtuous or in the pursuits of leisure (see *NE*, I, 4, 1095ª15–27; I, 5; I, 8, 1098ᵇ20–29, 1099ª32–1099ᵇ8; VII, 13, 1153ᵇ13–24; X, 3, 1174ª1–12; X, 6, 1176ᵇ27–1177ª11; X, 8, 1178ᵇ32–1179ª12; and cf. *Politics*, I, 9, 1257ᵇ35–1258ª7; VII, 1, 1324ª1–2; VII, 3, 1325ª20–33; VII, 13, 1332ª17–27). The reason in each case is the same. With the exception of arbitrary power over other men, each of the things mentioned is *a* good or is associated with the attainment of *a* good, but it is not *the* good, and therefore it is only a part of happiness, not the whole of it. Correctly conceived as the *totum bonum*, happiness consists in all the things that are really good for a man; none, not even the least of these, can be omitted if the individual is to achieve a good life, but they are not all of equal value, and so he must seek to relate and mix the ingredients of happiness in the right order and proportion. An ethics of happiness which insists upon seeking the one right end (happiness correctly conceived as the *totum bonum*) and seeking it in the right way (by correctly relating and proportioning the partial goods that enter into it) is clearly a moral philosophy that declares what a man *ought* to seek and how he *ought* to seek it.

This controlling insight is confirmed in a number of ways. It is confirmed by a statement in the *Politics*, in which Aristotle says that the successful pursuit of happiness depends upon two things: "one of them is the choice of the right end and aim of action, and the other the discovery of the actions which are means to it; for the means and the end may agree or disagree" (VII, 13, 1331ᵇ27–31). It is also confirmed by all the passages in the *Nichomachean Ethics*, in which Aristotle, considering the role of pleasure in the good life, distinguishes between good and bad pleasures, and between a right and wrong pursuit of them (see, for example, II, 3, 1104ᵇ8–12, 30–35; X, 5, 1175ᵇ22–35, 1176ª15–29). Commenting on the pleasures of sense, he points out that one can have too much of these goods. "The bad man is bad by reason of pursuing the excess, not by reason of pursuing the needed pleasures (for *all* men enjoy in some way or other both dainty foods and wines and sexual intercourse), *but not all men do so as they ought*" (*NE*, 1154ª16–18; italics added). Most of all, it is confirmed by Aristotle's use of the distinction between the real and the apparent good.

With regard to the desire for the good, Aristotle points out that "some think that it is for the real good; others, for the apparent good. Now those who say that the real good is the object of desire must admit in consequence that that which the man who does not choose aright seeks is not an object of desire . . . while those who say that the apparent good is the object of desire must claim that there is nothing which is naturally an object of desire, but only that which appears good to each man—and different things appear good to different individuals" (*NE*, III, 4, 1113ª15–23). Aristotle then goes on to suggest that the apparent good is that which men in fact consciously desire, whether they ought to or not, and the real good is that which they in fact naturally desire and ought consciously to desire. Hence the difficulty is resolved; both the real and the apparent good are objects of desire, but whereas the former is both the object of natural desire and that which men ought consciously to desire, the latter is only the object of conscious desire. "That which is really good is an object of desire for the good man [that is, the man who desires as he ought to desire], while any chance thing may be an object of desire [an apparent good] for the bad man" (*NE*, III, 4, 1113ª25–27). If real goods—the objects of natural desire—ought to be desired, and nothing but real goods ought to be desired, then the right conception of happiness—the good life that all men ought to seek and that is the same for all men because they are men—must be a conception of it as constituted by the sum of real goods. Aristotle's remark that "the end appears to each man in a form corresponding to his moral character" (*NE*, III, 5, 1114ª32–1114ᵇ1) clearly means that only the morally virtuous man—the man of right desire, the man who chooses aright—will be motivated by the right conception of happiness as the end to be pursued. The morally virtuous man is one whose will is aimed at the end that every man ought to seek, and whose actions in pursuit of that end are chosen as they ought to be chosen in relation and proportion to one another.

If any further confirmation were required to show that the *Nichomachean Ethics* is at once deontological and teleological —that it prescribes categorical oughts with respect to the ultimate end and the necessary means thereto—the *prima facie* evidence for it lies in the indispensability of virtue to happiness, the good life, or living well. It is so clear in Aristotle's mind that happiness can be rightly conceived and rightly pursued only by a person who has the habit of desiring and choosing aright (such good disposition of will, or habit of right desire and choice, being moral virtue), that he allows an elliptical definition of happiness, as "activity in accordance with virtue" or as "virtuous activity" (*NE*, I, 7, 1098^{a}27; I, 9, 1099^{b}26) to serve in place of the more exact and complete statement that happiness or the good life consists in possessing all the real goods that are the objects the morally virtuous man desires, as he ought, in the right order and proportion; for the morally virtuous man is one who aims at the end that he ought to seek and chooses the means to it in the way they ought to be chosen (see esp. *NE*, I, 10; I, 13, 1102^{a}5–6; X, 6, 1176^{b}37; and cf. *Politics*, VII, 2, 1324^{a}1–2; VII, 13, 1332^{a}8–25). Still another way of expanding the elliptical statement that happiness is activity in accordance with virtue or is virtuous activity is to say that the activities of a good life all aim at real goods, or at apparent goods only when they are innocuous, and these activities contribute to making a whole life really good because they and the goods they aim at have been sought and chosen virtuously, that is, in the right order and proportion.

Moral virtue is not itself a component part of happiness, except insofar as it is one aspect of self-perfection or self-improvement; its special relation to happiness consists in its being not the highest good, but rather the chief instrumental or operative means to achieving a good life. All the goods that are needed for a good life are either the goods of chance or the goods of choice. For some of the constituent elements of happiness, we depend wholly on the chance favors of fortune, including the good fortune of living in a just and benevolent society, but for those elements essential to a good life that depend wholly or even partly on our own free choices, moral virtue is the decisive factor (see *Politics*, VII, 2, 1323^{b}25–29; and cf. *NE*, I, 10, 1100^{b}23–32).

(5)

Since moral virtue plays so critical a role in Aristotle's theory of the good life, as the *sine qua non* of a man's effective pursuit of happiness, it is necessary to clarify two points that can be and usually are overlooked in the reading of the *Nichomachean Ethics*.

The first concerns Aristotle's use of the phrase "virtuous activity." It might be thought that virtuous activity is a special type of activity, as work, play, and leisure are distinct types of activity. But that is not the case. At the end of Book I, Aristotle, projecting an extended discussion of virtue that will occupy Books II–VI, points out that "some of the virtues are intellectual and others moral" (*NE*, I, 13, 1103^{a}5). Although the intellectual virtues can be inculcated by teaching as moral virtue cannot be, both consist in habits—in stable dispositions of mind or character (see *NE*, II, 1, 1103^{a}15–25). In the case of the intellectual virtues—take, for example, science or art—the virtue is a habit or disposition of the mind to act in a certain way. The scientist or the artist is a man whose mind can perform well certain operations that the man who is not a scientist or an artist either cannot perform at all or certainly cannot perform well. Excellence in a certain type of intellectual activity will be found in those men who possess the appropriate intellectual virtues—the good habits or dispositions of mind that give rise to such activities.

Moral virtue, in contrast, is a habit of willing and choosing, not a habit of acting in a certain specific way. It is, Aristotle writes, "a state of character concerned with choice" (*NE*, II, 6, 1106^{b}37). Specific activities of all sorts, intellectual and otherwise, are the things men choose to engage in or avoid in order to achieve the end that they seek. The habit of seeking a certain end and the habit of choosing and ordering activities in a certain way to gain that end is the habit of willing and choosing which is moral virtue. In one sense, of course, willing and choosing are actions, but they are not activities in the same sense in which working, playing, and leisuring are activities, nor in the sense in which scientific or artistic operations are specific forms of leisure activity. Thus, when the reference is to moral, not intellectual, virtue, the phrase "virtuous activity" must be treated as an elliptical expression that is short for "virtuously chosen activities," and this, like the phrase "activity in accordance with virtue," needs further expansion as follows: "activities directed to the right end and chosen in the right order and proportion."

The morally virtuous man is one who has a good character. This consists in a habit or disposition with respect to the end that he seeks and the means that he chooses; and the *goodness* of this habit of willing and choosing, which makes it a *virtue* rather than a vice, consists in its being a disposition to will the right end or the end that he ought to seek and to choose the means in the right way or in the way that he ought to choose them in order to achieve the end. Living as he ought by habit, the man of good character has no need of rules of conduct; moral virtue as good habit dispenses with rules.

This brings us to the second and more important point that requires clarification. Since an intellectual virtue is the habit of a certain specific type of intellectual activity, there can be a number of distinct intellectual virtues. But since moral virtue is a disposition to will the right end and to choose the means for achieving it in the right way, there cannot be a number of existentially distinct moral virtues, but only a plurality of analytically distinct aspects of one and the same existential state of good moral character.

The controlling text on this point is to be found in the last chapter of Book VI, though even there Aristotle himself uses the word "virtue" in the plural rather than the singular, and the passage is further complicated by an ambiguity in Aristotle's use of *phronesis* for two quite distinct qualities of mind: (a) moral wisdom, which consists in a correct understanding of the *ultimate end* to be sought and of the *means in general* for achieving it; and (b) prudence, which consists in the habit of reaching a sound judgment in *this particular case* about which is the better or best of alternative means for achieving the end. English translators usually render *phronesis* by "practical wisdom"; but wisdom *(sophia)*—whether speculative or practical—in Aristotle's understanding of it is always restricted to universal principles. In the practical or moral order, the principles with which wisdom is concerned are constituted by the *ultimate end* and the *means in general* (the means to happiness universally conceived). Deliberation about which is the better or the best of available means *in a particular case* does not come within the scope of moral or practical wisdom. It belongs to another habit of mind—the habit of prudence, which is a habit of proceeding in the right way to reach a decision about the means in a particular case, that is, by taking counsel, by weighing the alternatives, by deliberating carefully, and so on (see *NE*, VI, 7, 1141^{b}8–23; VI, 8, 1142^{a}20–31; VI, 9, 1142^{b}3–35). The only justification for calling prudence "practical wisdom" lies in the word "practical," not in the word "wisdom," for the word "practical" does refer to action; action always takes place in particular cases; and it is the particular case with which prudence is always concerned, as wisdom never is.

With these clarifications in analysis and vocabulary, let me now render the passage I regard as giving us the controlling insight for understanding Aristotle's theory of moral virtue, in itself, as a single habit of will and choice, and in its relation to moral wisdom, on the one hand, and to prudence on the other. Book VI ends with the statement: "It is clear, then, from what has been said that it is not possible to be good [morally virtuous] in the strict sense without being morally wise, nor prudent without being good [having moral virtue]. In this way we may refute the dialectical argument whereby it might be contended that the virtues [moral virtues] exist in separation from each other. . . . This is possible in the case of certain temperamental qualities [such as fearlessness, on the one hand, and mildness on the other], but not in the case of that attribute with respect to which a man is called without qualification morally good" (*NE* VI, 13, 1144^{b}30–1145^{a}2).

Aristotle's rejection of the view that the moral virtues can exist in separation from each other makes it impossible to hold

that there can be two existentially separate moral virtues, such
as fortitude or courage, on the one hand, and temperance on
the other, as there can be two existentially separate temperamental qualities, such as fearlessness and mildness. The plurality
of names used in the case of moral virtue (and there is a large
number of them in Books III and IV, of which fortitude and
temperance are the principal ones) must, therefore, be interpreted to signify a plurality of analytically distinct aspects of
one and the same good habit or state of good moral character,
not a plurality of existentially distinct moral habits, any one of
which can be possessed in the absence of others.

The reason for the existential unity of moral virtue should be
clear from what has been said earlier about a good moral character. It consists, as we have seen, in a habit of right desire,
which is to say a habit of desiring as one ought, a disposition
to will the right end and to choose the right means in the right
order and proportion. Since there is only one right end to be
sought and only one right order and proportion of the means
for achieving the end, there is only one habit of right desire and
that one habit is moral virtue, complete and entire. We can
read this insight back into the passage in Book I, where Aristotle,
having said that the good life consists of activity in accordance
with virtue, then adds: "and *if* there is more than one virtue,
then in accordance with *complete* virtue" (*NE*, I, 7, 1098ᵃ28;
cf. I, 10, 1101ᵃ15; italics added).

From what has been said, it should also be clear why it is
impossible for a man to be morally good without being morally
wise, since one could not have the habit of right desire without
having an understanding of the right end to be sought and
knowledge of the means in general for achieving it, together
with an understanding of how those means should be ordered
and proportioned. Such knowledge and understanding of the
end and the means constitute moral wisdom. But moral wisdom
can be possessed in two ways—*explicitly*, in the propositional
form typical of intellectual cognition, or *implicitly*, without
propositional or argumentative expression. The man of moral virtue or good moral character must certainly possess moral wisdom implicitly, but whether he must also possess it explicitly,
in the propositional and argumentative form appropriate to in-

tellectual cognition, is doubtful. This is not to deny that he would be better off if he did.

The reverse point that Aristotle makes at the end of Book VI is on one interpretation true and on another interpretation false. In the passage already cited, the usual translation has it that it is impossible to be "practically wise without moral virtue," as well as "morally good without practical wisdom." We have just seen that it is impossible to be morally good (have the habit of right desire) without having moral wisdom implicitly, though it remains questionable whether one must also have it explicitly. But the reverse relationship between moral virtue and "practical wisdom" holds only when "practical wisdom" is understood as referring to *prudence*, not when it is understood as referring to *moral wisdom*.

It is impossible to be prudent without being morally good; prudence as distinguished from mere cleverness or shrewdness consists in the habit of proceeding in the right way to reach a decision about the means in a particular case *only if* the choice is among means all directed to the right end. A thief or a murderer may exhibit that counterfeit of prudence which Aristotle calls cleverness or shrewdness, but it is not true prudence because the means with which it is concerned in the particular case are not means to the right end (see *NE*, VI, 12, 1144^a25–29; VI, 13, 1144^b1–16, 1145^a5–7). But while it is impossible to be prudent without being morally good, it is certainly possible to be morally wise—in a purely intellectual way—without being a man of good moral character or of moral virtue. Being able to recite the truths of moral philosophy or even being intellectually convinced of them does not necessarily carry with it that stable disposition of the will—that habit of right desire—which constitutes moral virtue or a man's good moral character. If only that were the case, then imparting moral wisdom to the young by the teaching of a sound moral philosophy would produce morally virtuous men, but we know moral virtue is not acquired in this way. Rather it is by discipline and training, by practice and habituation, that morally virtuous individuals are formed (see *NE*, X, 9, 1179^b19–1180^a4). Aristotle is careful not to give specific rules for the cultivation of moral virtue, just as he is careful not to rely on teaching moral philosophy to the young (see *NE*, I, 3, 1095ª2–11).

Among the many aspects of moral virtue discussed in Books II–IV, fortitude and temperance are the principal ones. Virtue, Aristotle says, is "concerned with pleasures and pains," for "it is on account of pleasures that we do the wrong things, and on account of pains that we abstain from doing the right ones" (*NE*, II, 3, 1104ᵇ10–11, 15; cf. IV, 1, 1121ª4–5). It is in these terms that he differentiates between temperance and fortitude as distinct aspects of moral virtue. Temperance consists in a disposition to give up immediate pleasures that are only apparent goods in order to achieve real goods that are often remote; fortitude consists in a disposition to suffer the pains or withstand the difficulties that are often attendant upon doing the things one ought to do for the sake of making one's whole life really good. Both are aspects of one and the same basic habit of choice—the disposition to prefer a good life in the long run (however hard it may be to work for that end) to a good and an easy time here and now (however pleasant that may be from moment to moment).

There is only one other principal aspect of moral virtue, and that is justice, which is treated in Book V. Here Aristotle distinguishes between justice in general, which is nothing but moral virtue as directed toward the good of other men, and the special forms of justice that are the qualities of human transactions, such as exchanges and distributions, or human laws and other acts of government. The latter, which in one place he refers to as a "part of virtue" (see Ch. 2) occupies his attention in the rest of Book V, but it need not concern us here for it is not an aspect of moral virtue except insofar as it is involved in a man's being generally just. "Justice in this sense is not a part of virtue, but virtue entire," yet it is complete virtue "not absolutely, but only in relation to our neighbor" (*NE*, V, 1, 1129ᵇ24–25, 1130ª10).

If, because they are merely distinct aspects of one and the same habit of right desire, a man cannot be temperate without having fortitude, or cannot be courageous without having temperance, then it is also true, for exactly the same reason, that a man cannot be generally just unless he is also temperate and courageous, and he cannot have temperance and fortitude without also being generally just in his dealings with his fellow-men and in relation to organized society as a whole. So the man who has a good moral character will not only be habitually disposed, in his making of choices, to act as he ought in the pursuit of his own happiness; he will also be habitually disposed to act as he ought in relation to the rights of other men and in relation to the good of the community as a whole—in Aristotle's language, both *fairly* in his transactions with other men, and *lawfully* in relation to the good of the community (see *NE*, V, 2, 1130^{b}7–1131^{a}9).

However, that aspect of moral virtue which is justice does not habitually incline a man to act in every way for the good of his fellow-men, but only to act in such a way as not to injure them by unfair treatment or the violation of their rights. Only the benevolence of love or perfect friendship impels a man to act positively for the happiness of another, as he would act for his own ultimate good. That is why "when men are friends they have no need of justice, while when they are just they need friendship as well" (*NE*, VIII, 1, 1155^{a}25–27).

(6)

One further point deserves brief comment, and that is the relation of the two branches of moral philosophy we have come to call ethics and politics. Aristotle himself used the term "politics" or "political science" for the branch of learning that is concerned with the ultimate human good, and because it is concerned with the ultimate end, he speaks of it as the "master discipline" or "architectonic science" (see *NE*, I, 2). Nevertheless, the book in which man's ultimate end and the means to it are given the most extended and detailed treatment is titled *Ethics*, whereas the book in which human happiness is treated only as a measure of the goodness of the state and its constitution is titled *Politics*. The purely verbal difficulty is resolved if we use the phrase "moral philosophy" to name the one architectonic discipline in the practical order or order of human action, and use "ethics" and "politics" to name related aspects of this one discipline, each of which has a certain primacy, but not in the same respect.

When Aristotle says that "the end is the same for the single man and for the state," he adds that "the end of the state . . . is something greater or more complete, whether to attain or to preserve" (*NE*, I, 2, 1094^{b}8–9; cf. *Politics*, VII, 2, 1324^{a}5–7). Now, if the end is the same for both, and that end is human happiness or the good life, then the only sense in which the end of the state is greater or more complete must reside in the fact that the state aims at the happiness of all its citizens, whereas the single individual aims only at his own or, at most, his own together with the happiness of his immediate friends whose lives are united with his own.

On the other hand, it is not merely for the sake of life, but for the sake of the good life, that the state comes into existence and continues in existence (see *Politics*, I, 2, 1252^{b}29–30; cf. III, 9, 1280^{a}21–32; III, 10, 1280^{b}39–40). And it is the good life for individual men (the *totum bonum hominis*), not the good of the community as such (the *bonum communitatis*), which is the ultimate end to be aimed at by all political arrangements. That is why Aristotle criticizes Plato for maintaining, in the *Republic*, that the ideal state is not concerned with the happiness of its guardian class or any other of its component groups. There is no meaning to the happiness of a society as a whole except in terms of the happiness of all, or most, or some of its human members (see *Politics*, II, 6, 1264^{b}16–24). Since, then, the ultimate end of the state is the happiness of its individual members, that aspect of moral philosophy (ethics) which deals with the pursuit of happiness *as such* has an obvious primacy, whereas that aspect of moral philosophy (politics) which deals with the external conditions that affect the pursuit of happiness has primacy only in relation to the problem of doing what can be done to make it possible for all men to engage in the pursuit of happiness.

Anyone who is concerned with thinking about the "best form of state," or the ideal conditions men should aim at in their social, economic, and political institutions and arrangements, must first determine "which is the most eligible life," that is, which

is the best life for man (*Politics*, VII, 1, 1232ª14–22). When that
is determined, as Aristotle has determined it in the *Ethics* (the
conclusions of which he summarizes in the *Politics*), the ideal
can be simply stated: "That form of government is best in
which every man, whoever he is, can act best and live happily"
(*Politics*, VII, 2, 1324ª24–25).

There is a sense in which the goals of the single individual
and of the organized community are not the same. The individual aims at his own happiness and, beyond that, only at the
happiness of his friends or loved ones. He does not aim at what
Mill called "the general happiness"; that is the objective of the
state or organized society, not the individual man. But since
moral virtue is the principal operative means in the individual's
making a good life for himself, the pursuit of his own happiness
and that of his friends involves him also in acting justly toward
other members of the community and for the good of the
community as a whole. Thus, it is only in the books concerned
with justice and with friendship (V and VIII–IX) that the
Nichomachean Ethics deals with the relation of the individual
to other men and to the community, but even when it does so,
the focus of attention always centers on the moral virtue or
good character of the individual as the factor indispensable to
his making a good life for himself.

However, there is another factor indispensable to the individual's making a good life for himself, and that consists of all
the things that he needs but does not have the power to obtain
wholly for himself, no matter how virtuous he is. These goods,
which can all be lumped together as wholly or partly goods of
fortune (goods of chance rather than of choice), include such
things as freedom from coercion and duress, political liberty, a
dignified and basically equal status in the community, equality of
educational opportunity, a healthful environment and medical
care, a decent share of the available economic goods, as much
free time as possible, recreational opportunities, and, last but not
least, a state of external and of civil peace. To provide the
conditions under which *all*—all, *not* some—of its human members can succeed in making good lives for themselves, if they
also have the moral virtue and moral wisdom requisite for success in that effort, the state, or organized community as a whole,

faces a complicated set of practical problems that are quite different from those of the individual man, though both aim at the same ultimate end.

Aristotle's *Politics* not only fails to provide us with satisfactory solutions to most of these social, economic, and political problems; it also advocates views that, if adopted, would prevent their being solved in a manner that would produce the good society—a society in which all men would have an equal opportunity, as far as external conditions were concerned, to engage effectively in the pursuit of happiness. Its chief contribution lies in its one controlling insight that the standard by which a society, in all its aspects, is to be judged as good or bad, better or worse, is the good life for the individual man. I do not mean to say that the *Politics* does not make a number of important contributions to the theory of the state and of government (such as its account of the origin and nature of the state, and its conceptions of constitutional government, of citizenship, and of political liberty), but it suffers much more from the limitations of the historic circumstances under which it was written than does the *Nichomachean Ethics*. It is relatively easy to universalize the truths to be found in the *Ethics* concerning the good life for man. I would like to think that this book of mine has done that with some measure of success. But to state the truths about the good society in an equally universal manner, one would have to repudiate much that is said in the *Politics*, transform in radical ways the sound conceptions it offers, and deal with many subjects it does not treat at all.

(7)

In the history of moral philosophy in the West, the *Nichomachean Ethics* has had a checkered career. The soundness of its approach to moral problems and the moral wisdom it offers for their solution were almost totally ignored by the leading schools of thought in the Hellenistic period. The Roman Stoics and Epicureans developed doctrines the flimsiness and fallacies of which would have been apparent to anyone who had read Aristotle's *Ethics* and had discovered its central and controlling insights. Cicero, who took pride in his effort to translate Greek thought into the Latin language, wrote two moral treatises—*De Officiis* and *De Finibus*—which show little or no evidence of his acquaintance with or understanding of the *Nichomachean Ethics*. In the later Middle Ages, when the works of Aristotle had been recovered and reintroduced into Western thought, Arabic, Jewish, and Christian commentators explicated the text passage by passage, usually erring in the direction of treating it with the same reverence for every sentence that governed their interpretation of Holy Writ. Nevertheless, in spite of this undue effort to make the text read as if it were a seamless whole from beginning to end, there existed for a brief period a better understanding of the book's pivotal conceptions and guiding principles than can be found in earlier centuries. Yet even this better understanding involved serious changes in emphasis that resulted from subordinating moral philosophy to moral theology in the writings of such devoted followers of Aristotle as Maimonides and Thomas Aquinas. I will return to this point presently.

From the seventeenth century on, the turn is for the worse again, with the *Nichomachean Ethics* either unread or misread by the leading moral philosophers of modern times—by Spinoza in the seventeenth century; by Hume and Kant, in the eighteenth century; by J. S. Mill and Henry Sidgwick, in the nineteenth century; and, in our own century, by John Dewey, G. E. Moore, H. A. Pritchard, and others among contemporary writers on ethics or meta-ethics. [8] Failure to refer to Aristotle's *Ethics* where it is plainly relevant to the problems with which these authors are concerned constitutes evidence either of their ignorance of the book or of their lack of sufficient understanding of it to perceive its relevance. Reference to it, accompanied by its dismissal as making little or no contribution to the solution of the problems with which they are concerned shows little or no understanding of its doctrine on their part. Explicit rejection of it as an erroneous or inadequate approach to moral philosophy, as in the case of Immanuel Kant or John Dewey, is based on their fundamental misapprehensions of Aristotle's theory, which I have taken pains to point out in the chapters of this book. [9] These misapprehensions not only convert their rejection of Aristotle's *Ethics* into an act of knocking down a straw man, but, in addition, they reappear as fundamental mistakes in their own doctrines—mistakes so crucial that they invalidate those doctrines at their core. I know of only one contemporary work in which the rejection of Aristotle's approach to moral problems is based on a criticism of it that shows an understanding rather than a misunderstanding of his theory, and that is Professor von Wright's *The Varieties of Goodness.* [10]

I am not saying that Aristotle's *Ethics* is above criticism, that its doctrine as expounded here is without errors or faults, or that it solves all moral problems perfectly. My only claim is that it is sounder in its approach to moral problems, advances more truth in their solution, and does so in a manner that is more practical and less dogmatic than any other ethical treatise in the tradition of Western thought. It is, in short, so substantial a contribution to man's thinking about good and evil, and right and wrong, in the conduct of human life that its shortcomings or faults deserve much better criticism than they have so far received. To be better, the criticism, of course, would have to be based on a better understanding of the *Nichomachean Ethics* than has been manifested in modern times and in contemporary discussion.

I mentioned earlier the changes in emphasis that resulted in the Middle Ages from subordinating moral philosophy to moral theology. Aquinas, for example, heavily stressed what Aristotle had to say about contemplation in Book X of the *Ethics* and, in addition, attached to contemplation a religious significance it could not have had for Aristotle; furthermore, in view of the Christian dogmas concerning the immortality of the soul and Divine rewards and punishments, Aquinas viewed man's terrestrial and temporal happiness, centering either exclusively or primarily in the activity of contemplating God, as nothing but an imperfect and unsatisfactory anticipation of the eternal happiness of heavenly rest in the beatific vision enjoyed by the souls of the blessed in the presence of God. [11] Looked at one way, this represents a transformation of Aristotle's doctrine, assimilating what truth there is in it to the dogmas of Christian moral theology; but looked at another way, it represents a rejection of Aristotle's position as false in its own terms, since for him the ultimate end—the *totum bonum*—is the temporal whole of a good life on earth, and since, as I have also shown, contemplation for Aristotle is not the contemplation of God but merely knowing for the sake of knowing, which may be the highest form of leisure activity in Aristotle's estimation but which, even so, is only one good among others, each of which is a part of happiness, and all of which contribute to the good life as a whole.

The rejection of the *Nichomachean Ethics* as false in its own terms, because it runs counter to the fundamental dogmas of orthodox, traditional Christianity, can also be based, as it has been by Jacques Maritain in our day, on the grounds that Aristotle proceeds on a hypothesis about human nature that is contrary to fact—the fact in this case being the revealed truth about man. The dogma of original sin and its consequences, which render man dependent on Divine grace for even the least measure of success in acting or living well, makes a sound and adequate moral philosophy inherently impossible. [12]

This criticism applies not only to Aristotle's *Ethics*, but to every other attempt on the part of philosophers to deal with the problems of human conduct, good and evil, right and wrong, on the purely secular and natural plane. Whether it is correct or not is hardly an arguable issue, for one side appeals to articles of faith the truth of which the other side does not acknowledge. Nevertheless, I would offer one reason for seriously questioning the view that a sound and adequate moral philosophy is impossible *as such* (that is, without the transformations and qualifications that a dogmatic moral theology would insist upon). My reason is couched in Aristotelian terms, and it is as follows.

The only standard we have for judging all of our social, economic, and political institutions and arrangements as just or unjust, as good or bad, as better or worse, derives from our conception of the good life for man on earth, and from our conviction that, given certain external conditions, it is possible for men to make good lives for themselves by their own efforts. It follows that those who take Maritain's view must also maintain that men of diverse religious faiths and men totally devoid of religious faith cannot find a common ground and make common cause against the social, economic, and political injustices that exist all over the world. If they take the opposite view, as Maritain himself does, [13] then there must be sufficient truth in moral philosophy to provide a rational basis for the efforts at social reform and improvement in which all men, regardless of their religious beliefs or disbeliefs, can join. Such common action for a better society presupposes that the measure of a good society consists in the degree to which it promotes the general welfare and serves the happiness of its people—this happiness being their earthly and temporal happiness, for there is no other ultimate end that the secular state can serve.

Notes

NOTES TO CHAPTER 8

1. (p. 71) See my discussion of the truth of common-sense opinions and the character of philosophical knowledge, both descriptive and normative (as *doxa* rather than *episteme*), in *The Conditions of Philosophy*, Ch. 2, esp. pp. 21–35; and with regard to the relation of common experience and common-sense opinion to philosophical knowledge, see *ibid.*, Ch. 6–8.

2. (p. 71) For expository, and to some extent critical, accounts of these contemporary positions, and of other schools of thought to be mentioned later in this chapter, see Mary Warnock, *Ethics Since 1900*; G. J. Warnock, *Contemporary Moral Philosophy*; George C. Kerner, *The Revolution in Ethical Theory*; William K. Frankena, "American Ethical Theory Since 1930," in *Philosophy*, ed. by R. Schlatter, and also Frankena's *Ethics*, Ch. 2, 3, and 6; A. C. Ewing, "Recent Developments in British Ethical Thought," in *British Philosophy in the Mid-Century*, ed. by C. A. Mace; W. Hudson, *Ethical Intuitionism*; Mary Warnock, *Existentialist Ethics*; Hazel E. Barnes, *An Existentialist Ethics*; Brand Blanshard, *Reason and Goodness*, Ch. V–X. See also the following articles in the *Encyclopedia of Philosophy:* "History of Ethics (20th Century)" by Kai Nielsen; "Problems of Ethics" by Kai Nielsen; "Ethical Relativism" by R. B. Brandt; "Ethical Naturalism" by Jonathan Harrison; "Emotive Theory of Ethics" by R. B. Brandt; "Deontological Ethics" by R. G. Olson; "Ethical Objectivism" by Jonathan Harrison; "Utilitarianism" by J. J. C. Smart; "Ethical Subjectivism" by Jonathan Harrison. For anthologies of contemporary contributions to moral philosophy and to meta-ethics, see *Theories of Ethics*, ed. by Philippa Foot; *Readings in Ethical Theory*, ed. by Wilfrid Sellars and John Hospers; *Contemporary Ethical Theory*, ed. by Joseph Margolis; and *Morality and the Language of Conduct*, ed. by Hector-Neri Castaneda and George Nakhnikian.

3. (p. 73) One objection will not be answered until Part Three, Chapter 18. This objection charges that the common-sense view fails to provide rules of conduct and criteria for judging particular acts as right or wrong. In Chapter 18, I will try to make clear that this omission, far from being a defect of the common-sense view, is one of its chief merits, for it enables it to avoid the

dogmatism that characterizes utilitarian as well as deontological theories of conduct.

4. (p. 74) See *The Conditions of Philosophy*, pp. 42–48, and fn. 20 on p. 66.

5. (p. 75) Professor Georg Henrik von Wright, in *The Varieties of Goodness*, p. 3, criticizes "the idea of a sharp separation of normative ethics and meta-ethics"; in his opinion, it rests "on an oversimplified and superficial view of the first and on an insufficient understanding of the nature of the second." He goes on to say: "Anyone who thinks that a sharp distinction can be maintained between meta-ethics and normative ethics is invited to consider the nature of such works as Aristotle's *Nichomachean Ethics*, Kant's *Grundlegung zur Metaphysik der Sitten*, or John Stuart Mill's *Utilitarianism*. Is their contents meta-ethics or normative ethics? Some, I think, would answer that the works mentioned contain elements of both types of ethics and perhaps deplore that their authors did not distinguish more sharply between the two. My own inclination would rather be to say that the difficulties in classification here show the artificiality of the distinction." Whichever answer is sounder, the point remains that long before the twentieth-century invention of "meta-ethics" as a separate discipline, the great moral philosophers of the past combined first-order discourse on what is good and right—or on what men should seek and do—with second-order analyses of such normative discourse.

NOTES TO CHAPTER 9

1. (p. 76) I have omitted references to "right" and "wrong" because, in my view, they add nothing to "ought" and "ought not." That which we ought to do is that which it is right for us to do, and wrong for us not to do; that which we ought not to do is that which it is wrong for us to do, and right for us not to do.

2. (p. 77) See *Principia Ethica*, pp. 9–10, where in his explanation of why he thinks the good is indefinable, Moore proposes the name "naturalistic fallacy" to cover any attempt to define the good "by reference to other properties belonging to all things which are good." He points out later (pp. 38–39) that exactly the same error of trying to define the good by reference to this or that property of all good things is the flaw in what he calls "Metaphysical Ethics" as well as in "Naturalistic Ethics"; and yet he admits, "I give it but one name, the naturalistic fallacy." Moore acknowledges that Sidgwick's *Methods of Ethics* had anticipated his contention that

the good is indefinable. "So far as I know," he writes, "there is only one ethical writer, Professor Henry Sidgwick, who has clearly recognized and stated this fact" (*ibid.*, p. 17). In his Preface, he also calls attention to somewhat similar views advanced by Franz Brentano in his *Origin of the Knowledge of Right and Wrong* (*ibid.*, pp. x–xi). But Moore appears to be completely ignorant of the fact that the leading moral philosophers from antiquity through the Middle Ages had asserted the indefinability of the good, and had offered an explanation of that fact which is not only more satisfactory than his, but also avoids the consequences drawn by him.

3. (p. 78) See *Principia Ethica*, Preface, pp. viii–x. Cf. E. F. Carritt, *The Theory of Morals*; W. D. Ross, *The Right and the Good*, and also his *Foundations of Ethics*; H. A. Pritchard, *Moral Obligation*, especially Ch. 1 and 5. For the views of earlier British moralists (Cudworth, Clarke, Reid, and Sidgwick) on the autonomy of ethics, see A. N. Prior, *Logic and the Basis of Ethics*, Ch. II–IV; and also Richard Price, *A Review of the Principal Questions in Morals*, ed. by D. Daiches Raphael.

4. (p. 80) See *Principia Ethica*, pp. viii–xi and 22–23, where Moore points out that propositions relating means to ends are causal propositions that can be supported or falsified by empirical evidence. If nothing could be regarded as good except as a means, then the only type of value statement employing the term *good* would be a causal proposition about the relation of means to ends —a proposition susceptible to empirical proof or disproof. Moore's rejection of the naturalistic position in ethics stems from his denial that all statements of value are propositions of this sort. Some propositions, the primary ones according to Moore, are propositions about things that are intrinsically good, good as ends and not as means, good "for their own sakes." Such propositions, he insists, are intuitively known, i.e., "incapable of proof" (*ibid.*, p. x). Their being so has, of course, some connection with the fact that the good is indefinable; but, as I pointed out in Note 2, *supra,* this fact was known long before Moore or Sidgwick recognized it and its recognition in no way depends on awareness of the "naturalistic fallacy." It is the other way around. Only those who first know that the good is indefinable, and understand why that is so, will be able to point out the error made by those who try to define it. As I see it, the so-called "naturalistic fallacy" is nothing but the error of trying to define the indefinable. Chapter 10 will, I hope, substantiate this.

5. (p. 81) See *The Conditions of Philosophy*, Ch. 11, esp. pp. 182–195, on the distinction of know-*how* from know-*that*. I pointed out that *is*-knowledge and *ought*-knowledge are both forms of know-*that*—the one descriptive know-*that*, the other normative know-

that. They stand together in sharp distinction from know-*how*. Understanding this is indispensable to understanding the difference between the problem of making a good life and the problem of making a work of art. The good life involves *ought*-knowledge; the work of art, know-*how*. A treatise in moral philosophy differs from a cook book and all other forms of the know-*how* book. "If you want to cook well," the cook book says, "here is how to do it." A book in moral philosophy would be like a cook book only were it proper for it to say: "If you want to make a good life for yourself, this is what you ought to do." The *ought* in this statement would then be a purely *pragmatic ought* and, like the *artistic* or *technical ought*, it would be a purely hypothetical *ought*, a piece of know-*how*. The knowledge constituting moral philosophy is know-*that*—not know-*how*—and therefore it must express itself in terms of categorical—not hypothetical—*oughts*. A categorical statement has no *ifs* and *thens* about it.

6. (p. 83) See *Human Nature and Conduct*, Ch. VI; and also *Reconstruction in Philosophy*, Ch. VII, esp. pp. 166, 177, 179, 183. When Dewey writes in *Reconstruction in Philosophy* that the end is not "a terminus or limit to be reached," and goes on to say that "growth itself is the only moral 'end,'" he fails to supplement his denial of terminal ends by developing a conception of an ultimate end that is purely normative. It must be added that, for Dewey, growth appears to function as that kind of end; and if Dewey had explicitly acknowledged it as an end that is not only normative but also ultimate (i.e., not a means to anything beyond itself), consistency would have led him to repudiate the reductionism of his naturalistic approach to normative questions and questions of value; for then he would have affirmed at least one good (growth) that was not good as a means, and so could not be converted into a matter of fact. However, in *Human Nature and Conduct*, he completely rejects the very notion of an ultimate end or an end in itself, an end that is not a means. "There is no such thing," he writes, "as the single all-important end"; "ends," he says, "are, in fact, literally endless, forever coming into existence as new activities occasion new consequences. 'Endless ends' is a way of saying that there are no ends—that is, no fixed self-enclosed finalities" (pp. 224–225, 229, 232).

7. (p. 83) It was pointed out in Chapter 5 (p. 41, *supra*) that "everything we do can be done for the sake of leading a good life as a whole. In this sense, no activity may be engaged in entirely for its own sake." Even play, which is an activity that we engage in for the pleasure intrinsic to it, is something that we also regard as contributing toward a good life as a whole. Play, together with the pleasure derived from it, is an indispensable part of a good life, and as such it functions as a means to that end. The only good

that never functions as a means to an end is the goodness of a whole life. There is no way of finishing the sentence: "I want a whole good life for the sake of . . ." But we can say, "I want the pleasures of play for the sake of a good life," or "I want the wealth to be earned by subsistence-work for the sake of a good life," or "I want the health and vigor that result from sleep for the sake of a good life." To understand this is to understand that a good life as a whole is an ultimate end. To understand, further, that a good life as a whole cannot be experienced or enjoyed at any moment or period of our life's time is to understand that it is not a terminal end; it is not an end that can be reached and held on to, because there is nothing more to seek—the moment of complete perfection that Mephistopheles had promised Faust. Finally, to understand that a good life as a whole, as an ultimate goal, is the standard or measure of judging the goodness of all the means we employ—the parts we put together to make the whole, the choices we make about the ordering of the parts—is to understand that this ultimate goal functions as a normative end. It is the norm that underlies all the normative judgments we make about the things we consider to be good as means.

NOTES TO CHAPTER 10

1. (p. 84) With regard to the misnaming of the fallacy and Moore's acknowledgment of that fact, see Chapter 9, Note 2, *supra*. Moore does have a relevant and cogent argument against the effort of the naturalist in ethics to reduce all statements of value to statements of fact and all ought-statements to is-statements, but this argument in no way employs or rests on what he mistakenly supposed was a logical fallacy on the part of the naturalists. In fact, his argument is first stated in the Preface to *Principia Ethica* before there is any mention of the so-called "naturalistic fallacy" (see Chapter 9, Note 4, *supra*). Moore there distinguishes between (a) ethical propositions that state primary oughts with regard to things regarded as good for their own sakes or as ultimate ends, and (b) ethical propositions that state secondary oughts with regard to actions that are good only as means to these ends. If that distinction is defensible, as I think I have shown it to be in Chapter 9, then ethics has relative autonomy; for the primary oughts are categorical, not hypothetical, and they do not rest on empirical evidence, but are self-evident or intuitively known. Since the secondary oughts do rest on empirical evidence, as Moore points out, ethics is only relatively, not absolutely, autonomous, and in making this point, he distinguishes himself from other philosophers whose position has come to be called "ethical intuitionism"; e.g., Carritt, Ross,

Pritchard (see Chapter 9, p. 78, and Note 3, *supra*). The basic point at issue between the naturalists and the intuitionists, moderate or extreme, is the autonomy of ethics, relative or absolute. See Prior, *Logic and the Basis of Ethics*, pp. 106–107. If the naturalists are in error, as I, in agreement with Moore, think they are, it is the error of denying any autonomy to ethics; but this is an error that arises from a substantive mistake about means and ends—ultimately from a failure to recognize the distinction between terminal and normative ends—and not from a logical mistake, certainly not from the mistake Moore incorrectly attributes to them, i.e., the mistake of trying to define the indefinable.

2. (p. 85) See especially C. D. Broad, "Certain Features in Moore's Ethical Doctrines," in *The Philosophy of G. E. Moore*, ed. by Paul A. Schilpp, pp. 41–68; C. L. Stevenson, "Moore's Argument Against Certain Forms of Naturalism," in *ibid.*, pp. 69–90; Abraham Edel, "The Logical Structure of Moore's Ethical Theory," in *ibid.*, pp. 135–178; G. E. Moore, "A Reply to My Critics," in *ibid.*, pp. 535–615; G. C. Field, "The Place of Definition in Ethics," in *Proceedings of the Aristotelian Society*, 1932; R. M. Hare, *The Language of Morals*, pp. 79–93; A. C. Ewing, *Ethics*, Ch. 6; P. H. Nowell-Smith, *Ethics*, pp. 32–34, 180–182; A. N. Prior, *Logic and the Basis of Ethics*, pp. 1–12, 24–25, 95–107; George Nakhnikian, "On the Naturalistic Fallacy," in *Morality and the Logic of Conduct*, ed. by Castenada and Nakhnikian, pp. 145–158; C. Lewy, "G. E. Moore on the Naturalistic Fallacy," in *Proceedings of the British Academy*, Vol. 1, 1964; David Rynin, "Non-Cognitive Synonymy and the Definability of 'Good,'" in *Logic and Language, Studies Dedicated to Rudolf Carnap*; W. K. Frankena, "The Naturalistic Fallacy," in *Theories of Ethics*, ed. by P. Foot, pp. 50–63; Bernard H. Baumrin, "Is There a Naturalistic Fallacy?," in *American Philosophical Quarterly*, Vol. 5, No. 2, April, 1968, pp. 79–89; Henry B. Veatch, *Rational Man*, pp. 188–197; A. C. Ewing, "Recent Developments in Ethics," in *British Philosophy in Mid-Century*, pp. 65–78. Cf. G. E. Moore, "The Conception of Intrinsic Value," in *Philosophical Studies*, pp. 253–275.

3. (p. 86) See W. K. Frankena, *op. cit.* (Note 2, *supra*), esp. pp. 57 ff.; H. B. Veatch, *op. cit.* (Note 2, *supra*), esp. pp. 193 ff.

4. (p. 86) The "open-question argument" is presented in *Principia Ethica*, Ch. 1, Sect. 13, pp. 15–17. Cf. Kai Nielsen, "History of Ethics," in *Encyclopedia of Philosophy*, Vol. 3, p. 101; "Problems of Ethics," in *ibid.*, p. 127.

5. (p. 86) See Chapter 9, Note 2, *supra*. That the good is indefinable was understood and affirmed by ancient and medieval philosophers who recognized that this concept and other terms with which it is convertible, such as being, transcend the categories that make

definition possible. As predicable of subjects in every category, such terms are not predicated univocally, but analogically, and analogical concepts are strictly indefinable. See Aristotle, *Nichomachean Ethics*, Bk. I, Ch. 6; Aquinas, *Summa Theologica*, Pt. I, Q. 5. Cf. H. von Wright, *The Varieties of Goodness*, pp. 12–13; and Note 7, *infra*.

6. (p. 87) The reason why Moore, in arguing against attempts to define good, proposes a definition of good in which the *definiens* is a single term (such as X), and not a complex of terms (X, Y), lies in his "point . . . that 'good' is a simple notion" (*Principia Ethica*, p. 7). But simple notions are *ipso facto* indefinable, and so if it be granted that good is a simple notion, it must be acknowledged that there can be no definition of it in any accepted sense of definition. The only thing that can be done to make the meaning of a simple term clear, without defining it, is to indicate other simple terms with which it is correlative or convertible. Thus, if X were such a term, then the statement "the good is X" would not be a definition of the good, but it might nevertheless throw light on the meaning of the good, by relating it to the meaning of X, especially if neither the term "good" nor the term "X" has a meaning independent of the meaning of the other. Moore fails to understand this because he mistakenly interprets a statement of the form "the good is X" as a statement of identity in meaning, making the terms "good" and "X" strictly synonymous. Were that the case, then the meaning of "X" could not possibly throw any light on the meaning of "good," as it can if its meaning is, on the one hand, not identical with the meaning of "good," and, on the other hand, not independent of the meaning of "good."

7. (p. 87) See Note 5, *supra*. On the analogical, as contradistinguished from both the univocal and the equivocal, see Aristotle, *Categories*, Ch. 1; *Physics*, Bk. VII, Ch. 4; *Metaphysics*, Bk. V, Ch. 6–7; and Aquinas, *Summa Theologica*, Pt. I, Q. 13, A.A. 5, 6, 10. Aristotle sometimes treats the analogical as a special type of equivocation, quite distinct from (1) the purely chance equivocation that is exemplified in the two totally unrelated meanings of the English word "pen" as the name for a writing instrument and for an enclosure for animals, and from (2) the intentional equivocation that is exemplified in the two related meanings of the English word "father" when it is used to signify a biological progenitor (in its primary sense) and when it is said in a derivative sense of a ruler (e.g., the Czar) in relation to his people. The word "sharp," Aristotle points out in *Physics*, Bk. VII, Ch. 4, is equivocal in a third way when it is said of a sharp cry, a sharp wine, and a sharp pencil. Here the three meanings of "sharp" are not unrelated, as in the case of "pen" in the first type of equivocation; nor is one meaning primary and the others derivative, as in the case of "father"

in the second type of equivocation. The meaning of "sharp" in all three uses is in part the same, and in part it is diversified by the three subjects of which it is predicated (a cry, a wine, and a pencil). When we consider this special type of equivocation and give it a special name (analogical ambivalence), we can properly interpret the statement that the analogical is intermediate between the univocal and the equivocal (i.e., equivocation of *both* type 1 *and* type 2). A name is applied *univocally* to two things when it is said of both in exactly the same sense, or with an identical meaning; it is applied *equivocally* to two things when it is said of both in senses that are not only different but clearly distinguishable; it is applied *analogically* to two things when it is said of both in different but not clearly distinguishable senses, because the meaning with which it is used in the two instances is *at once* both the same and different, and the difference comes from the diversification of that same meaning by the difference between the things to which it is applied. When Aristotle treats such terms as "being" or "good" as equivocal, he has in mind this special type of equivocation, which I have called "analogical ambivalence." And when he refers to things as being the same by analogy, in contradistinction to their being the same in genus or the same in species, he is referring to the way in which a sharp cry, a sharp wine, and a sharp pencil are alike in their respective sharpness. Such sameness, unlike sameness in species or sameness in genus, is strictly indefinable: it is impossible to abstract or to state what is common to the three meanings of "sharp" when it is applied to a cry, a wine, and a pencil, with a sameness of meaning that is diversified by each of the three things to which it is applied.

8. (p. 88) See Aristotle, *Posterior Analytics*, I, 2, 72ª6–19; I, 33, 88ᵇ30–89ª4; II, 19. See also my discussion of axioms or self-evident truths in *The Conditions of Philosophy*, pp. 25–26; 137–140.

9. (p. 88) See John Locke, *Essay Concerning Human Understanding*, Bk. IV, Ch. VII–VIII; Immanuel Kant, *Critique of Pure Reason*, Introduction, Sect. IV. Cf. David Hume, *Enquiry Concerning Human Understanding*, Sect. IV, Pt. I, Div. 20–21. Henry Veatch has recently written an excellent and penetrating critique of the modern distinction between analytic and synthetic propositions, with which I am in complete agreement. See *Two Logics,* esp. Ch. III, IV, and XII.

10. (p. 90) See *Principia Ethica*, pp. 66–67. Moore is correct in criticizing Mill for thinking that "desirable" means only "that which can be desired," as "visible" means only "that which can be seen." If that were the case, then Mill would be right in his contention that the *only* proof that anything is desirable consists in the fact of its being actually desired. See *Utilitarianism,* Ch. 2 and 4. But having

corrected Mill's error, Moore then falls into the opposite error. Using such words as "detestable" or "admirable" instead of "visible" as his models, he maintains that just as "admirable" means "ought to be admired" or "deserves to be admired" (whether in fact it is or is not), so "desirable" means "ought to be desired" or "deserves to be desired" (again whether in fact it is or not). While "admirable" and "desirable" do have this normative significance, that is certainly not their only meaning; they also mean "can be" and "is actually" admired or desired, and their having this factual significance no more excludes their normative significance than their having normative significance excludes their factual significance. When we ask, "Do you regard Smith as admirable?" we would not be surprised to have someone reply by saying, (a) "Yes, I think there is much about him that can be admired and, in fact, I know some who do admire him," or (b) "Yes, I think he deserves to be admired, even though I know no one who does in fact admire him as he ought to be admired," or (c) "He is in fact admired by others for certain traits that I do not regard as deserving of admiration, and I myself think that he ought to be admired for certain traits that are not in fact admired by most people." To the question whether something is desirable, similar answers can be meaningfully given; to wit, (a) that it can be desired, as evidenced by the fact that some actually do desire it; (b) that it ought to be desired, though no one in fact desires it. Since here we are considering a single object as the desirable rather than a person with the multiplicity of traits that may or may not be admirable, our third answer takes a slightly different form; to wit, (c) that (i) the object in question ought to be desired and also is in fact desired, or (ii) that the object in question is in fact desired but ought not be desired, or (iii) that the object in question ought to be desired but is not in fact desired.

The statement that the good is the desirable does not assert that the meaning of "good" is identical with the meaning of "desirable," as Moore supposes (see *op. cit.*, p. 67), or that the two words are strict synonyms (see *op. cit.*, p. 73). Desire is not identical with its objects; the beings that are objects of desire stand in a certain relation to other beings that desire them. The relationship is expressed by the words "aims at" and "satisfies," just as the relation between a whole and its parts is expressed by the words "greater than" and "less than." Hence, to call the good the desirable is to relate whatever is considered good to desire. Whatever it may be that desire aims at or that satisfies desire is in one or another sense good; to call it "desirable" is to say no more than that it is something which is thus related to desire. Depending on the mode of desire, as we shall see, it is desirable in one way or another, and good in one sense or another.

Moore's discussion of the good as the desirable occurs in the context of his effort to refute Mill's hedonism (see *Principia Ethica*, Ch. III). The effort miscarries because of Moore's failure to distinguish two quite distinct senses of the word "pleasure" and his failure to recognize and relate the two quite distinct senses of "desirable." The basic principle of hedonism that pleasure is the only good can be interpreted to mean (1) that pleasure is the only object that men do in fact desire for its own sake, or (2) that pleasure is the only object that men ought to desire for its own sake. Neither statement is a definition of the good. On the first interpretation, the principle of hedonism is so patently false as a matter of fact that it needs no refutation. On the second interpretation, the principle is neither indemonstrable and self-evident, nor is it capable of demonstration. Both of these points were obvious to the philosophers of antiquity (see Plato, *Philebus;* Aristotle, *Nichomachean Ethics*, Bk. VII, Ch. 3; Bk. X, Ch. 2–3), and they are obvious to the man of common sense. When pleasure is regarded as an object of desire, it is plainly false to say that pleasure is the only good—the only thing that is desirable in either of the two meanings of "desirable." But as the ancients knew, the word "pleasure" is not always used to signify an object of desire; it is sometimes used to signify the satisfaction of desire, as when we say that we are pleased or satisfied to have the thing we desired (whether the object desired or sought was pleasure or something else, such as wealth, or health, or knowledge). See my discussion of these two meanings of pleasure—(1) as object of desire and (2) as satisfaction of desire—in *A Dialectic of Morals*, pp. 34–36; and with regard to the same distinction, see William James, *Principles of Psychology*, Vol. II, pp. 549–559; Georg Henrik von Wright, *The Varieties of Goodness*, Ch. IV, esp. pp. 79–85. As von Wright points out, when pleasure is understood as satisfaction of desire, every object of desire is pleasant or pleasing (i.e., satisfying) when it is obtained, and so the good, which is the desirable, is also always the pleasant or pleasing when it is obtained and the desire for it is satisfied. In this sense of the word "pleasure" and *only in this sense*, there is a version of hedonism that is self-evidently true, as hedonism is neither true nor self-evident when the word "pleasure" signifies an object of desire. The truth of hedonism is expressed in the statement that pleasure (or satisfaction) accompanies the possession of every good that is desired.

In Chapters II and IV of *Utilitarianism*, which are the focus of Moore's attack, John Stuart Mill uses the word "pleasure" in both senses—as object of desire and as satisfaction of desire—and shifts from one meaning to the other without being aware of that fact, thus leaving his argument riddled by equivocation. Moore is also unaware of the equivocation, and so his criticism of Mill miscarries; it is widest of the mark in his mistaking the principle of hedonism for a definition of the good. The error of hedonism is a substantive error, not a logical error; it is the error of asserting that pleasure is the only object that either is or ought to be desired for its own sake. To assert this is not to define the good; on the contrary, it presupposes an understanding, *without definition*, of the good as the desirable—as that at which desire aims and as that which satisfies desire.

One question remains. On the conception of the good as the desirable, can nothing be called "good" except things that stand in relation to one or another mode of desire, either on the part of human beings or on the part of other living or even non-living things that, like men, have appetitive tendencies? The human good or the good for man relates to human desires; the good for anything else relates to its desires. But can it not be said that one thing is better than another—more perfect than another—without relation to the desires of man or the desires of any other terrestrial thing? This question can be answered affirmatively only by theologians who place all things in relation to God's creative will, love, or desire. It is in this sense that Augustine declares that although pearls may be, to men, more desirable than mice, a mouse is more perfect in its being than a pearl, i.e., better or more desirable in relation to the Divine will. It is in this theological—or, as it is sometimes called, metaphysical—sense of good that grades of being are correlative with grades of goodness or perfection. See *The City of God*, Bk. XI, Ch. 16, 22; and cf. Aquinas, *Summa Theologica*, Pt. I, QQ. 5–6.

11. (p. 91) See C. L. Stevenson, *Ethics and Language* and *Facts and Values;* and R. M. Hare, *Language of Morals* and *Freedom and Reason.*

12. (p. 91) See, for example, Plato's *Meno*, 77 a–d; and Aristotle, *Nichomachean Ethics*, Bk. III, Ch. 4–5, esp. 1113^a14–23, 114^a33–1114^b3. See also H. von Wright, *The Varieties of Goodness*, pp. 108–109; M. Grene, *A Portrait of Aristotle*, pp. 50–53, and my *A Dialectic of Morals*, pp. 75–80.

13. (p. 92) See *Ethics*, Pt. I, Appendix; but cf. *ibid.*, Pt. IV, Preface, and Propositions 19–36, *passim*, in which Spinoza takes a position opposed to that adopted by Hobbes in *Leviathan*, Pt. I, Ch. 6, and also at the end of Ch. 15.

14. (p. 92) See Montaigne's *Essays*, Book the First, Essay No. 40. The views advanced by the non-cognitivists and emotivists in recent years were anticipated not only by Hobbes and Montaigne three centuries ago but also by the Sophists of ancient Greece who, twenty-five hundred years ago, maintained that all values —right and wrong, good and bad—are dictates of convention and have no basis in the nature of things.

15. (p. 93) See Lewis Mumford, *Technics and Civilization*, pp. 378–400; John Maynard Keynes, *Essays in Persuasion*, pp. 365–366; John Kenneth Galbraith, *The Affluent Society*, Ch. XI; R. H. Tawney, *Equality*, 4th ed., pp. 82 ff. Cf. Adam Smith, *The Wealth of Nations*, Bk. III, Ch. I; Bk. V, Ch. II, Pt. II, Art. IV. This distinction between two modes of desire, noted by the economists but neglected by their contemporaries in philosophy, underlies the two meanings of "desirable" explicated in Note 10, *supra*. The desirable as that which deserves to be or ought to be consciously desired is the real good—the object of natural desire. The desirable as that which is in fact desired is the apparent good—the object of conscious desire. The statement that the good is the desirable thus covers both modes of desire and both modes of good, correlating the real good with natural desire and the apparent good with conscious desire. That at which natural desire aims and that which satisfies natural desire is really good, whether or not it also appears to be good because it is consciously desired. That at which conscious desire aims and that which satisfies conscious desire is apparently good, whether or not it is also really good, because it is naturally desired. Failure to grasp the full complexity of the truth that the good is the desirable not only vitiates Moore's treatment of the matter but also leads his more acute critics, such as Frankena and von Wright, into equally serious errors.

16. (p. 93) The opening statement in Aristotle's *Metaphysics*, that all men by nature desire to know, can be elucidated by saying that among the powers or properties of human nature is a cognitive faculty that makes man capable of developing organized bodies of knowledge. This capacity or power inherent in man's nature functions as a disposition to seek that which fulfills it, just as the hunger of an empty stomach functions as a disposition to seek food. All natural desires can be described as capacities or emptinesses that function as dispositions to seek that which fills them, as knowledge fills the mind or food fills the stomach. More abstractly and precisely stated, each natural desire is a definite potentiality that tends toward a certain actualization, and the object that satisfies such a desire is always one that produces the appropriate actualization. Cf. *A Dialectic of Morals*, pp. 80–81.

The distinction between a man's natural desires and his conscious desires—between the desires inherent in him at birth in the form of his innate capacities or potentialities, and the desires he himself forms in the light of his own experiences—will be misunderstood if it is supposed that the same objects cannot be both naturally and consciously desired. We often consciously want that which we naturally need. But this is not always the case, for we often do not want or are even averse to wanting what we need. When we do consciously desire or want that which we naturally desire or need, the object desired not only appears good to us but also is really good for us. This throws further light on the two meanings of the good as desirable—(1) as that which is in fact desired, whether it ought to be desired or not, and (2) as that which ought to be desired, whether it is in fact desired or not. The first meaning refers to that which appears to be good because it is consciously wanted, whether or not it is naturally needed and so is really good. The second meaning refers to that which is really good because it is naturally needed, whether or not it is consciously wanted and so appears to be good. Understanding this safeguards us from misinterpreting what is meant by "ought to be desired" as contrasted with what is meant by "is in fact desired." If what ought to be desired is that which is really good, then what ought to be desired is also in fact desired, in that mode of desire which is natural need; and "ought to be desired" means that we ought consciously to want that which we naturally need; that is, we ought to desire, in the mode of desire which is conscious want, what we already do in fact desire, in the mode of desire which is natural need. The critical significance of this last point will become clearer in subsequent pages, as will the conception of right desire as consciously wanting that which is naturally needed. Natural desires are neither right nor wrong; only conscious desires can be right or wrong according to whether that which is consciously wanted is an apparent good that is also a real good, or is something that only appears to be good and would, if obtained, prevent or impede the possession of some real good.

The following observations are added to reinforce the points made above: first, the object of a natural desire can *become* an object of conscious desire (something needed can *become* something wanted), but not conversely; second, objects of our conscious desires may include the objects of natural desire, but they may also include things that are not objects of natural desire (things that we want but do not need); third, all our wants are conscious desires, i.e., they are desires elicited by objects that we know or are aware of; but our needs may be either conscious or unconscious desires, i.e., they may be desires accompanied by an awareness of the objects desired or desires that are not accompanied by an awareness of the objects desired; and fourth, whether or not we are conscious of our needs, they are not formed in us or elicited by our knowledge or experience of the objects we naturally desire.

17.   (p. 94) See Notes 10 and 16, *supra*.

18.   (p. 95) I speak of a truth as intuitively known when it is the truth of a self-evident or indemonstrable proposition. The force of the word "intuitively" is mainly negative; it precludes reasoning or inference. A self-evident truth is immediately, not mediately

known—not known through the mediation of reasoning from other propositions that serve as its grounds or premises. It is in this sense that Aristotle refers to axioms or self-evident truths as "intuitive inductions"—indemonstrable propositions that can serve as premises in demonstrations. See Note 8, *supra*.

The self-evidence of an intuitively known proposition consists in our knowing it to be true from our understanding of its constituent terms. To someone who questions the self-evidence of the proposition, we cannot respond by any form of reasoning or demonstration, but only by calling his attention to the meaning of the terms in relation to one another. Thus, in the case of the proposition that the real good ought to be desired and that nothing but that which is really good ought to be desired, we can do no more than point out that the meaning of "ought to be desired" and the meaning of "real good" co-implicate each other. We cannot understand "ought to be desired" except by reference to our understanding of "real good," and we cannot understand "real good" without reference to our understanding of "ought to be desired." A more elaborate elucidation of what is involved here has already been given in Note 16, *supra*.

Another way of making this intuitive truth clear is by a kind of *reductio ad impossibile*. It is impossible to say that the apparent good *as such* ought to be desired, or even that the good ought to be desired. The apparent good *as such* is something that we do consciously desire, and so there is no ought about it. The good includes both the real and the apparent good, and since nothing but the real good ought to be desired, it is impossible to say that the good, without qualification, ought to be desired. Only when there is a question about whether the object we consciously desire or want is also something we naturally desire or need, can we meaningfully consider whether or not we ought consciously to desire that which we do consciously desire.

The normative force of "ought" applies only in the sphere of conscious desires. We cannot say we ought or ought not naturally to desire, as we can say we ought consciously to desire, this or that object; we cannot say that we ought to need a certain object, as we can say that we ought to want it. Only in the sphere of apparent goods that are the objects of conscious desire is it possible to desire amiss, because what is apparently good may or may not be really good; only if it is, ought we consciously to desire that which we do consciously desire; if it is not a real but an apparent good, then we cannot say that we ought to desire it but only that we do.

The truth of the proposition, "One ought consciously to desire that which is really good and nothing but that which is really good," does not depend on any empirically known facts. Even if there were in fact no natural needs and, consequently, we could point to no object that satisfies a natural need and, therefore, is a real good, it would still be true that nothing ought to be desired except that which is really good; and in this circumstance we would also have to say that as far as our knowledge of the facts goes, we know of nothing that ought to be desired. In other words, if the terms "natural need" and "real good" refer to null classes, then we cannot draw any ought-conclusions from the ought-principle that we ought to desire that which is really good and nothing but that which is really good; but this does not falsify the ought-principle itself, it only renders that principle logically infertile.

G. E. Moore, as we saw earlier, did not wish to be regarded as an intuitionist in ethics if being so regarded grouped him with those who held that *all* of the fundamental moral truths can be intuitively known, without any reference to empirically known facts. For him, only the primary ethical propositions are intuitively known; the truth of the secondary ones depends on empirical evidence, and so ethics is only relatively, not absolutely, autonomous. See Note 1, *supra*. In the view being expounded here, only two ethical propositions are intuitively known, and only one of these is, strictly speaking, a normative proposition—an ought-proposition. All other ought-propositions are conclusions, drawn from this single self-evident ought-principle conjoined with empirically established and empirically falsifiable is-propositions or statements of fact. The relative autonomy of ethics thus hangs by a single slender thread, i.e., the self-evident normative principle that we ought to seek that which is really good and nothing else; and this single thread is suspended from the intuitive truth that the good is the desirable, but only when that axiom itself is understood in terms of two modes of the good (the real and the apparent) as being correlative with two modes of desire (natural and conscious).

19.   (p. 95) The passage reads as follows:

I cannot forbear adding to these reasonings an observation, which may, perhaps, be found of some importance. In every system of morality which I have hitherto met with, I have always remarked, that the author proceeds for some time in the ordinary way of reasoning, and establishes the being of a God, or makes observations concerning human affairs; when of a sudden I am surprised to find, that instead of the usual copulations of propositions, *is* and *is not*, I meet with no proposition that is not connected with an *ought* or an *ought not*. This change is imperceptible; but is, however, of the last consequence. For as this *ought*, or *ought not*, expresses some new relation or affirmation, it is necessary that it should be observed and explained; and at the same time that a reason should be given, for what seems altogether inconceivable, how this new

relation can be a deduction from others, which are entirely different from it. But as authors do not commonly use this precaution,
I shall presume to recommend it to the readers; and am persuaded, that this small attention would subvert all the vulgar
systems of morality. . . . [*A Treatise of Human Nature*, Bk. III,
Pt. I, Sect. I.]

The discussion of this passage has been attended by what, in my
judgment, are futile efforts to show that an ought-conclusion can
be validly inferred from premises that are entirely is-statements.
See, for example, John R. Searle, "How to Derive 'Ought' from
'Is,'" in *Theories of Ethics*, ed. by P. Foot, pp. 101–114; Dorothy
Mitchell, "Must We Talk About 'Is' and 'Ought'?," in *Mind*, Vol.
LXXVII, No. 308 (October 1968), pp. 543–549; and cf. Prior, *op.
cit.*, pp. 32–35.

The most telling comment that has been made on the passage
is Frankena's observation that Hume probably failed to detect the
presence of an obvious enthymeme in the reasoning that he criti-
cized as fallacious. See "The Naturalistic Fallacy," in *Theories of
Ethics*, ed. by P. Foot, p. 54. Enthymemes occur in theoretical
reasoning when one particular is inferred from another without
making explicit the general proposition that is the major premise
of the inference; e.g., "Socrates is a man; therefore, Socrates is
mortal." Similarly, enthymemes occur in practical or normative
reasoning when an ought-statement is inferred from an is-statement
without making explicit the normative principle that is the major
premise of the inference; e.g., "John Doe is a murderer; therefore,
John Doe ought to be punished."

Unfortunately, in the context of pointing this out, Frankena offers
an example of reasoning which he himself misinterprets because of
his failure to recognize the distinction between the real and the
apparent good. The example is as follows: "(a) Pleasure is sought
by all men; (b) what is sought by all men is good (by definition);
(c) therefore, pleasure is good." The proposition (a) that pleasure
is sought or desired by all men is a factual proposition and probably true; it would certainly be true if "some men" were sub-
stituted for "all men"; the argument would be unaffected by the
substitution. The proposition (b) that whatever is sought or desired by all men (or by some men or even by one man) is good,
in some sense of good, is not a definition of the good, but the
axiomatic truth that whatever is desired (i.e., whatever is consciously desired or wanted and whatever is naturally desired or
needed) is good in some sense (apparently good or really good).
From propositions (a) and (b) in Frankena's example, not one
but two conclusions follow: (1) Pleasure appears to be good to all
men or to some men; (2) Pleasure is a real good for all men.
The first of these propositions is a statement of fact; to wit, who-

soever in fact desires pleasure deems it to be good. The second proposition leads to the normative conclusion that all men ought to desire pleasure. To make clear that this conclusion can be validly inferred, we need only make explicit the suppressed premise in the enthymeme; namely, whatever is really good ought to be desired. The reasoning then takes the following form: That which is really good, in that it satisfies a natural need, ought to be desired; pleasure does in fact respond to a natural need on the part of all men, and so it is a real good for all men; hence, all men ought to desire pleasure. When proposition (1) above is the conclusion, the reasoning takes the following form: Men (some or all) do in fact deem or call good that which they in fact consciously desire; they do in fact consciously desire pleasure; hence pleasure does in fact appear good to them. In this reasoning, all the propositions—both the premises and the conclusion—are is-statements; none is a statement of value or an ought-statement.

20. (p. 96) See Aristotle, *Nichomachean Ethics*, Bk. VI, Ch. 9, 1142ᵇ23–25; Bk. VII, Ch. 3, 1146ᵇ25–35; cf. Aquinas, *Summa Theologica*, Pt. I, Q. 86, A. 1, Reply 2; Pt. I–II, Q. 76, A. 1; Q. 77, A. 2, Reply 4. See also Takatura Ando, *Aristotle's Theory of Practical Cognition*, 2nd ed., Ch. V; and cf. Alexander Broadie, "The Practical Syllogism," in *Analysis*, Vol. 29, No. 1 (October 1968), pp. 26–28; G. E. M. Anscombe, "Thought and Action in Aristotle," in *Aristotle's Ethics*, ed. by J. J. Walsh and H. L. Shapiro; M. Mothersill, "Anscombe's Account of the Practical Syllogism," in *The Philosophical Review*, Vol. LXXI (1962), pp. 448–461.
It is possible to construct a piece of reasoning in which a factual conclusion *appears* to be validly inferred from two normative premises; e.g., only criminals ought to be punished by the state; John Doe ought to be punished; therefore, John Doe is a criminal. But this conceals what is really involved; for we could not know that John Doe ought to be punished, unless we independently knew, first, the factual truth that John Doe is a criminal, together with the normative principle that criminals—and only criminals—ought to be punished by the state. When the reasoning properly expresses what we must first know in the premises in order to know what can be inferred from such knowledge, it takes the form of a practical syllogism in which the major premise is a normative principle, the minor premise a statement of fact, and the conclusion an ought-statement.

21. (p. 96) See Note 18, *supra*.

22. (p. 96) Cf. G. E. Moore, *Principia Ethica*, pp. viii–x.

23. (p. 97) See my discussion of axioms or self-evident truths as the *only* philosophical propositions that are not empirically falsifiable opinions or *doxa*, in *The Conditions of Philosophy*, pp. 23–31.

The normative principle, that what is really good ought to be desired, is knowledge with the certitude of *nous;* and as such it is not falsifiable by experience; in contrast, all normative conclusions are *doxa;* they have only probable or relative truth and can be falsified by experience. Cf. Chapter 8, Note 1, *supra.*

NOTES TO CHAPTER 11

1. (p. 100) See Chapter 10, Note 7, *supra.*

2. (p. 100) The fact that we sometimes desire to continue in the possession of that which we already have does not alter the truth of the proposition that the thing desired is something not at the moment possessed; when we desire the continuance in the future of something we now possess, the object of such desire is something we do not now possess.

3. (p. 100) In this case, as we shall see, the thing consciously wanted but not needed may or may not be innocuous. It is innocuous only if wanting and getting it does not prevent us from wanting and getting that which we need. If wanting it conflicts with our wanting and getting something we naturally need, then our desire for it is a wrong, not a right, desire, and that means we ought not to desire that which we do consciously desire.

4. (p. 102) In *Mind,* Vol. XXI, No. 81 (1912) and reprinted (1949) as the first essay in a collection of Pritchard's writings entitled *Moral Obligations.* Cf. David Ross, *The Right and the Good;* and E. F. Carritt, *The Theory of Morals.*

5. (p. 103) See Chapter 9, *supra.*

6. (p. 103) See Chapter 9, *supra.* With regard to the question about the primacy of the good, see Brand Blanshard, *Reason and Goodness,* Ch. VI, esp. pp. 158–159. The primacy of the good *versus* the primacy of the right is not an academic question with which professional philosophers bemuse themselves. The way in which this issue is decided profoundly affects the approach one makes to moral problems. To affirm the primacy of the right means that what is right and wrong in our conduct, private or public, can be determined without reference to human desires. To affirm the primacy of the good means that what is desirable and what ought to be desired are the basic considerations underlying any determination of right and wrong in human conduct. The common-sense approach to moral problems is based on the conviction that the notion of the good or the desirable is primary, and that notions of right and wrong are secondary and derivative. This can be

summarized by saying that only when I know what is really good for me, can I know what it is right or wrong for me to do in my private life or in my conduct toward others. This fundamental thesis will become clearer when it is expanded in Chapter 14, *infra*.

7.   (p. 104) See Chapter 10, *supra*, and esp. Note 10.

8.   (p. 105) See *The Fundamental Principles of the Metaphysic of Morals*, in *Kant's Critique of Practical Reason and Other Works on the Theory of Ethics*, trans. by T. K. Abbott, 6th ed., pp. 9, 11–12, 35–36; *Critique of Pure Reason*, trans. by J. M. D. Meiklejohn, rev. ed., pp. 452–457; *Kant's Critique of Practical Reason*, trans. by T. K. Abbott, 6th ed., pp. 186–187, 206–207; *Kant's Critique of Teleological Judgment*, trans. by J. C. Meredith, pp. 93–94, 100, 116–118.

9.   (p. 105) See *Preface to the Metaphysical Elements of Ethics*, in *Kant's Critique of Practical Reason and Other Works on the Theory of Ethics*, trans. by T. K. Abbott, 6th ed., pp. 296–304; and *Lectures on Ethics*, trans. by L. Infield, pp. 117–126.

10.   (p. 106) We shall see that in the full development of the common-sense view, the obligation of the individual to make a good life for himself is not only a valid categorical ought, but also that it is the one primary obligation from which all other obligations and duties, whether to self or to others, can be derived. See Chapters 14 and 15, *infra*. The ethics of common sense will be seen to resemble the moral philosophy of Kant only in the formal respect that both attempt to combine the teleological consideration of ends that are good with the deontological formulation of categorical oughts; but on all major points of substance within that framework, the ethics of common sense and the moral philosophy of Kant are diametrically opposed. See Chapter 14, Note 2, *infra;* and also Chapter 18, *infra*.

11.   (p. 106) See the Kantian texts cited in Note 8, *supra*. Cf. John Locke, *Essay Concerning Human Understanding*, Bk. II, Ch. 21, Sect. 42 ff.; J. S. Mill, *Utilitarianism*, Ch. II and IV. For a twentieth-century conception of happiness in purely psychological terms, with no moral overtones, see Sigmund Freud, *Civilization and Its Discontents*.

12.   (p. 107) All these questions and many more are explored in a penetrating critical essay by John Wilson, "Happiness," in *Analysis*, Vol. 29, No. 1 (October 1968), pp. 13–21. Wilson's essay shows how this mixed concept—partly psychological and partly moral—is profoundly unsatisfactory from both points of view, raising as it does many more questions on both fronts than seem to be answerable.

13. (p. 109) An often quoted statement by Augustine has direct relevance here. Augustine said: "Happy is he who has all the things that he desires, *provided that he desire nothing amiss*" (italics added, *On the Trinity*, Bk. XIII, Ch. 5). To desire nothing amiss is to desire everything rightly. Happiness, thus conceived, consists in the satisfaction of right desires, the possession of the real goods that every man ought to desire; and in this meaning of the word, "happiness" becomes a synonym for "the good life"—the same for all men because all men have the same natural needs that determine the things that are really good for them. Cf. Aquinas, *Summa Theologica*, Part I-II, Q. 5, A. 8, Reply 3.

14. (p. 109) Only when a good life for each individual is correctly understood as consisting in the possession of all the things that are really good for every human being, because they correspond to the needs inherent in human nature, can we translate the proposition *that one ought to seek that and that alone which is really good* into the proposition *that one ought to seek a good life for one's self*. If the good life consisted, for each of us, in getting the things we consciously wanted whether we needed them or not, if, in other words, we acknowledged no distinction between real and apparent goods, or between right and wrong desires and if, in consequence, the good life for each man consisted simply in getting the things that he wanted, then it would be meaningless to say that he ought to make a good life for himself. He is under a moral obligation he can discharge or fail to discharge only if the life he strives to make involves the satisfaction of desires that can be either right or wrong. Only if he can choose between real and apparent goods, only if he is free to want or not to want the things he needs, can we meaningfully say that he ought to make a life that is really good because it consists in the possession of all real goods.

NOTES TO CHAPTER 12

1. (p. 111) In my judgment, the single most important contribution made by Kant to the formation of moral philosophy was his insistence that it should be able validly to formulate categorical obligations universally binding on all men in the same way. Any ethical doctrine or theory of human character and conduct that falls short of this may contain pragmatic or utilitarian wisdom; it may set forth reasonable and empirically sound recommendations about how men should act if they wish to achieve certain ends; it may even express generally agreed upon appreciations of the relative value of one end as against another, and cultivate attitudes of

respect for and devotion to ideals that are noble and honorable; but if its fundamental principles do not include categorical obligations universally binding on all men in the same way, then, however sound or wise it may be in other respects, it does not have the soundness or wisdom of moral philosophy. The ethics of common sense, as I am developing it here, meets Kant's requirement. See Chapter 14, Section 4, *infra*.

2. (p. 112) See Chapter 1, pp. 4–5, *supra*.

3. (p. 113) See *op. cit.*, Ch. V; and cf. Chapter 11, Note 12, *supra*. The source of the major differences between von Wright's conception of human welfare and the common-sense understanding of a really good life lies in his failure to relate the distinction between real and apparent goods, of which he is aware (see *loc. cit.*, pp. 108–109), to the distinction between conscious and natural desires—wants and needs. This, in turn, stems from his unexplained reluctance to employ the notion of human nature—a common or specific nature in which all members of the human species participate, just as the members of every other species of living organism share certain common traits or properties that are species-specific. As von Wright's Preface to *The Varieties of Goodness* frankly confesses, the doctrine of his book gradually emerged from his rejection of "the Kantian idea of duty and the Moorean idea of intrinsic value. . . . In this largely negative way," he continues, "I arrived at a *teleological* position, in which the notions of the beneficial and the harmful and the good of man set the conceptual frame for a moral 'point of view.'" He then points out that there are "two main variants of this position in ethics"—the teleological approach to moral questions in terms of the end as the ultimate principle and as the normative standard for judging everything else as means. One of these, he writes, "makes the notion of the good of man relative to a notion of the *nature* of man. The other makes it relative to the needs [in his sense, not mine] and wants of individual men. We could call the two variants the 'objectivist' and the 'subjectivist' variant respectively." In taking the second rather than the first, von Wright acknowledges that his position is "akin to that of some writers of the utilitarian position" (*loc. cit.*, pp. v–vi). That, unfortunately, is a correct alignment of his views; I say unfortunately because, in my judgment, it deprives his doctrine, for all its soundness and wisdom in other respects, of the kind of soundness and wisdom that characterize a moral philosophy that is able validly to formulate categorical obligations universally binding on all men in the same way. See Note 1, *supra*.

4. (p. 115) In contrast, in its purely psychological connotations, the word "happiness" signifies a condition that is morally indifferent,

in the sense that it is a condition equally attainable by bad men and by good. The man who wants what he ought not to want, and fails to want and get the things that he needs, can experience the contentment of having his desires satisfied just as frequently and just as readily as the man who wants the things that are really good for himself and wants nothing that would interfere with his getting them.

5. (p. 115) Using the word "happiness" in its purely ethical sense, and the word "happy" in its psychological and hedonic sense to signify either the experience of pleasures desired or the satisfaction experienced in the possession of desired things other than pleasure, it is possible to say "I want to be happy in order to achieve happiness, *i.e.*, a really good life." Pleasure is one of the real goods that is a component of the good life. In this sense, moments or periods of being happy are parts of a really good life, on the condition, of course, that the pleasures sought do not interfere with the possession of other real goods, or that the satisfactions experienced do not come from the possession of things that one ought not to want.

6. (p. 116) See Chapter 10, Note 10, *supra*.

7. (p. 116) Commenting on "the conception of the '*Summum Bonum*,'" Kant observes that "the conception of the *summum* itself contains an ambiguity which might occasion needless disputes, if we did not attend to it. The *summum* may mean either the supreme (*supremum*) or the perfect (*consummatum*)" (*Critique of Practical Reason*, trans. by T. K. Abbott, 6th ed., p. 206). In spite of this observation, Kant continually makes use of this highly ambiguous epithet. It seems to me mandatory to replace it by the phrase *totum bonum* when what is meant is not one good of supreme value as distinguished from other and inferior goods, but rather the whole or sum total of all real goods, however they may be ordered as inferior and superior from lowest to highest.

Kant's playing with the ambiguity of "*summum bonum*" is matched by his playing with the ambiguity of "happiness." He uses it, on the one hand, to signify the satisfaction of the individual's desires whatever they may be and, on the other hand, to signify only the satisfaction of virtuous desires on the part of the man whose attainment of happiness is deserved. All these ambiguities are multiplied in the following passage: "Happiness alone is, in the view of reason, far from being the complete good. Reason does not approve of it (however much inclination may desire it), except as united with desert. On the other hand, morality alone, and with it mere desert, is likewise far from being the complete good. To make it complete, he who conducts himself in a manner not unworthy of happiness must be able to hope for the possession of happiness. . . . Happiness, therefore, in exact proportion with the morality of rational beings (whereby they are made worthy of happiness), constitutes alone the supreme good of a world in which we absolutely must transport ourselves according to the commands of pure but practical reason" (*Critique of Pure Reason*, trans. by J. M. O. Meiklejohn, rev. ed., p. 457).

If Kant had used the term *happiness* as a purely ethical term, synonymous with a good life as the *totum bonum* (the sum total of the goods that all men ought to want and that morally virtuous men do want), he would have seen that happiness is *unattainable by men who, lacking virtue, are also unworthy of it,* and he might also have realized that virtuous men, who deserve happiness, can be prevented by misfortunes beyond their control from achieving it.

If we were to make this one correction in Kant's thought, and, together with all that it implies, were to follow it through relentlessly, we would erode most of what is distinctive about Kant's moral philosophy, including all its rationalistic purity and its formalistic trappings. The appeal to pure reason and the specious process of deducing specific duties from the categorical imperative would be replaced by a determination of particular obligations with respect to real goods that ought to be sought on the basis of the empirically known facts of human nature and human behavior. The development of moral philosophy in the last 150 years might have taken a radically different course if Kant had not misconceived happiness and had not ignored human nature as the source of our knowledge of what is ultimately good for man, which in turn is the basis of our categorical obligations with regard to the various means to this end.

8. (p. 117) In justice to J. S. Mill, it must be said that, although the term *happiness* as he uses it in *Utilitarianism* involves a mixture of psychological and quasi-ethical connotations, nevertheless, his conception of happiness as the ultimate end is a conception of it as *totum bonum,* not *summum bonum.* See Ch. IV, in which he speaks of the means to happiness as also being parts or ingredients of happiness, and refers to happiness as a concrete whole, constituted by all the things that a man may desire for himself, either as means to happiness or as parts of it.

9. (p. 117) Of the goods mentioned, only one, pleasure, is not an extrinsic result of activity, but an intrinsic accompaniment. I have used the word "play" as an omnibus term for any activity which is intrinsically pleasurable; other types of activity, such as sleep or leisure-work, which afford pleasure to the individual as he engages in them, thus have an aspect of play. But these other activities, even when they have an aspect of play and are intrinsically pleasurable, also produce extrinsic results, such as health

and vigor in the case of sleep, or one or another form of self-improvement in the case of leisure-work.

10. (p. 118) See Chapter 10, Note 16, *supra*.

11. (p. 118) See Chapter 15, pp. 163–164, *infra*. The reader can be apprised in advance of the important distinction more fully developed there, between two types of necessary means to happiness: (a) constitutive means, which are component parts of the *totum bonum*—the real goods, corresponding to natural needs, which all together make up the whole of goods; (b) instrumental or functional means, such as freedom and moral virtue, which are causal factors involved in the process of making a good life, and are indispensable to success in that venture. Cf. my discussion of this distinction in *A Dialectic of Morals*, pp. 48, 93–97.

12. (p. 118) To say that a life made good by the possession of all real goods leaves no natural desire unsatisfied does not imply the complete or perfect satisfaction of all natural desires. For example, it is unlikely that man's natural desire for knowledge can ever be fully satisfied in the course of this earthly life. It follows, therefore, that the achievement of the *totum bonum* is a matter of degree. All the real goods must be present in a good life, but they need not be present to the same degree.

13. (p. 119) In the context of his statement that a man achieves happiness through gaining all the things he desires, *provided that he desire nothing amiss*, Augustine adds a further observation relevant to the point that a man cannot be called happy in the course of his life, since happiness is the quality of a whole life that is good. A man, Augustine writes, can be called "almost happy who desires well, for good things make a man happy, and such a man already possesses some good—namely, a good will" (*On the Trinity*, Bk. XIII, Ch. 6). I would say that the man who has a virtuous or good will, one that is habitually disposed "to desire nothing amiss," possesses the principal operative or functional means for becoming happy. See Note 11, *supra*. I would not say that he is "almost happy," but rather that he is on the road toward making a good life for himself. His possession of a virtuous will increases the probability that he will succeed in his efforts, but it does not ensure his success, for other factors beyond his control may impede or defeat his pursuit of happiness. Cf. *A Dialectic of Morals*, pp. 61–63.

14. (p. 119) See *The Consolation of Philosophy*, Bk. III, Ch. 2. Cf. *A Dialectic of Morals*, pp. 51–58, 69.

15. (p. 120) See Chapter 10, Note 16, *supra*, concluding paragraphs; also Chapter 11, Note 3, *supra*.

16. (p. 120) On the specific nature of man, and the species-specific properties of human nature, which include potentialities or capacities and native dispositions that man shares with other animals, but which also involve certain powers that man alone possesses, such as the power of conceptual thought, see my examination and appraisal of the scientific evidence and of the relevant philosophical opinions in *The Difference of Man and the Difference It Makes*. Cf. *A Dialectic of Morals*, pp. 58-59, 67; and see also Chapter 17, p. 186, *infra*.

17. (p. 123) If the sociologists and anthropologists were correct about the impossibility of transcending the ethnocentric predicament, not only would they be unable to judge the value-systems of other societies and cultures without assuming the validity of their own, they would also be unable objectively to criticize their own society and culture. Yet they are often to be found among the most vocal and extreme critics of the social institutions, the *mores,* and the *value-system* of their native land. What objective criteria are available to them when they pass moral judgments on things at home which they think that the ethnocentric predicament deprives them of when they refrain from passing similar judgments on things abroad?

18. (p. 123) Unless there is a trans-cultural standard for judging social and cultural institutions—one based on that which is really good for man as man—not only is no objective comparison of societies and cultures possible, it is also impossible to give the notion of progress any objective meaning. See Charles Van Doren, *The Idea of Progress*, esp. Ch. 1 and 14.

NOTES TO CHAPTER 13

1. (p. 125) It does not take more than one crucial error in the beginning to produce an elaborate proliferation of errors in the final outcome. Elsewhere I have called attention to the widespread vitiating results, in the modern theory of knowledge, of two such initial failures—the failure to distinguish between *episteme* and *doxa*, and the even more serious failure to distinguish between the *quod* and the *quo* in the process of knowing—that which we know and that by which we know it. (See *The Conditions of Philosophy*, pp. 262-270.) The latter mistake also generates many of the serious errors that are made in the modern philosophy of mind, especially in the sphere of the vexatious mind-body problem. Only in the light of the distinction between the *quod* and *quo* of knowing, can the nature and function of intentionality be properly understood. See my treatment of these matters in *The*

Difference of Man and the Difference It Makes, Ch. 11–12, together with Notes 10, 11, 12 (to Ch. 11) and Notes 19 and 41 (to Ch. 12).

2. (p. 126) See *op. cit.,* p. 103. "If a sentence makes no statement at all," Ayer declares, "there is obviously no sense in asking whether what it says is true or false. And we have seen that sentences which simply express moral judgments do not say anything. They are pure expressions of feeling and as such do not come under the category of truth and falsehood. They are unverifiable for the same reasons as a cry of pain or a word of command is unverifiable—because they do not express genuine propositions" (*loc. cit.,* pp. 108–109).

   We need not be concerned with Ayer's criticism of utilitarianism (*ibid.,* p. 105), except to point out that in this connection he, too, proceeds in ignorance of the distinction between the real and the apparent good; nor need we be concerned with his discussion of ethical relativism and subjectivism, which reveals his adoption of a reductive naturalism in ethics (*ibid.,* pp. 110 ff.), because if he is wrong in his point of departure—his denial that moral judgments can, like descriptive statements, be true or false—then the views he develops in consequence of this denial are of little or no interest.

3. (p. 127) The effect of this negative statement applies not only to the common-sense view, but also to any variety of moral philosophy that claims for itself relative or absolute autonomy as a body of objective and valid knowledge, e.g., the position of Moore, on the one hand, and the position of the deontologists or intuitionists, such as Kant, Pritchard, and Ross, on the other. The only approach to moral questions not subject to Ayer's critical attack is, of course, that of reductive naturalism.

   I omit reference to utilitarianism here because its exponents themselves are never sufficiently clear on where they stand with regard to the autonomy of ethics as a discipline and as a body of knowledge. They must, in my judgment, ultimately choose between (a) continuing to ignore the distinction between the real and the apparent good and, in consequence, accepting reductive naturalism, or (b) adopting that distinction and, therefore, moving in the direction of the common-sense view of happiness and the good life. In the first alternative, Ayer's objection does not apply to them; in the second, the defense of the common-sense view against Ayer's objection will constitute a defense of them as well.

   For important recent contributions to the development of utilitarianism in diverse directions (none of which alters the judgment expressed above), see J. Narveson, *Morality and Utility;* D. Lyons, *Forms and Limits of Utilitarianism;* H. von Wright, *The Varieties of Goodness;* K. E. M. Baier, *The Moral Point of View;* R. B.

Brandt, *Ethical Theory;* S. E. Toulmin, *An Examination of the Place of Reason in Ethics;* J. O. Urmson, "The Interpretation of the Moral Philosophy of J. S. Mill," in *Theories of Ethics,* ed. by P. Foot, pp. 128–136; J. D. Mabbott, "Interpretations of Mill's 'Utilitarianism,'" in *ibid.,* pp. 137–143; J. Rawls, "Two Concepts of Rules," in *ibid.,* pp. 144–170; J. J. C. Smart, "Extreme and Restricted Utilitarianism," in *ibid.,* pp. 171–183; R. Brandt, "Toward a Creditable Form of Utilitarianism," in *Morality and the Language of Conduct,* ed. by H-N. Castaneda and G. Nakhnikian, pp. 107–144; and J. J. C. Smart, "Utilitarianism," in *Encyclopedia of Philosophy,* Vol. 8, pp. 206–212.

4. (p. 127) For the principal writings of Stevenson and Hare, see Chapter 10, Note 11, *supra.* For critical discussions of the non-cognitivist position in ethics and its *sequelae,* see B. Blanshard, *Reason and Goodness,* Ch. VIII–IX; W. Frankena, "American Ethical Theory Since 1930," in *Philosophy,* pp. 393–415; R. Brandt, "The Emotive Theory of Ethics," in *Philosophical Review,* Vol. 59 (July and October 1950), pp. 305–318, 535–540; P. R. Foot, "The Philosopher's Defense of Morality," in *Philosophy,* Vol. XXVII, 103 (October 1952), pp. 311–328. M. Warnock, *Ethics Since 1900,* Ch. 4–5; G. C. Kerner, *The Revolution in Ethical Theory,* Ch. II–IV; G. Warnock, *Contemporary Moral Philosophy,* Ch. III–IV; S. E. Toulmin, *An Examination of the Place of Reason in Ethics;* A. C. Ewing, *Second Thoughts in Moral Philosophy,* Ch. I–III.

5. (p. 128) See H. E. Barnes, *An Existentialist Ethics;* M. Warnock, *Existentialist Ethics;* F. A. Olafson, *Principles and Persons.* The denial of human nature as an ascertainable scientific fact amounts to saying that man, unlike every other species of living organism, does not have a set of genetically determined species-specific traits the possession of which, in one or another degree, constitutes membership in the species. However astounding this denial may be to the man of common sense, it is, nevertheless, a basic tenet, almost a fundamental creed, among certain social scientists and among contemporary moral philosophers, especially the utilitarians and the non-cognitivists. We saw that Professor von Wright's adoption of the subjectivistic and utilitarian variant of a teleological ethics stemmed, by his own confession, from his reluctance to appeal to the facts of a specific nature common to all men; hence he had nothing left to appeal to except the endlessly differing predilections, interests, or desires of individuals. See Chapter 12, Note 3, *supra.* There are a few striking exceptions. Economists such as R. H. Tawney and John Strachey do not hesitate to appeal to the common humanity of men as men, and all that that implies, in their arguments for equalitarianism and for social, economic, and political justice. See Tawney, *Equality,* esp. Ch. I–II;

and Strachey, *The Challenge to Democracy*, Encounter Pamphlet, No. 10, p. 41.

Henry Veatch puts his finger on the central weakness in moral philosophy since the eighteenth century when he says that "the trouble is that the very notion of human nature, and of nature generally, has apparently turned sour for most modern ethical thinkers, not just for the existentialists, but for the relativists, for those bewitched by the naturalistic fallacy, for just about everyone in fact" (*Rational Man*, p. 215). Even the naturalists, failing, as they do, to distinguish between natural and conscious desire, and between the real and apparent good, also fail to recognize how the facts of human nature fit into a moral philosophy that includes self-evident normative principles and so has relative autonomy as a body of knowledge.

6. (p. 129) See *supra*.

7. (p. 129) The sharp separation I am here insisting upon is between (a) the truth of axioms and (b) the merely verbal or tautological truth that belongs to analytical propositions. It is an improvement over the treatment of this matter in *The Conditions of Philosophy*, pp. 25–27, and esp. pp. 137–140. Cf. Henry Veatch, *Two Logics*.

8. (p. 130) Only descriptive propositions (is-statements and is-not-statements), it would appear, can be true by virtue of asserting that that which is, is, and that which is not, is not, or can be false by virtue of asserting that that which is, is not, or that which is not, is. See Plato, *The Sophist*, 240^b–241; and Aristotle, *Metaphysics*, Bk. IV, Ch. 7, 100^{b}26–290.

9. (p. 130) See *On Interpretation*, Ch. 4, 17^{a}1–8: "Every sentence has meaning . . . yet every sentence is not a proposition; only such are propositions as have in them either truth or falsity. Thus, a prayer is a sentence, but is neither true nor false. Let us therefore dismiss all other types of sentence but the proposition, for this concerns our present inquiry, whereas the investigation of the others belongs rather to the study of rhetoric or of poetry."

10. (p. 130) In the passage in *On Interpretation* just quoted (see Note 9, *supra*), Aristotle proceeds, in terms of grammatical distinctions, to separate declarative sentences, which assert something, from other types of sentences, such as the interrogative, the subjunctive, and the imperative, which do not assert anything, but merely ask a question, express a wish, or give a command. He then says that only declarative sentences express propositions—for only they make assertions, and nothing but an assertion can be either true or false. This would appear to be inconsistent with his effort elsewhere to explain how ought-statements can be

true, because, as was indicated a little earlier, every ought-statement can be expressed as a command, and a command—an imperative sentence—does not assert anything, and so cannot be true or false.

The apparent inconsistency is removed when we realize, first, that although all ought-statements can be expressed as commands, there are many commands that cannot be expressed as ought-statements and, second, that ought-statements are grammatically of the same type as is-statements; they are declarative sentences and make assertions. In short, the declarative mode of sentence is equally available to express two logically different types of propositions, each equally assertive: the descriptive proposition, which asserts that something is the case, and the normative proposition, which asserts that something ought to be desired or done.

11. (p. 131) See Note 8, *supra.*

12. (p. 131) Of those acts of the mind which are speculative, not practical or productive, Aristotle writes, the good and bad qualities are truth and falsity respectively (for this is proper to everything intellectual); whereas in the case of those intellectual acts that are practical (i.e., concerned with choice and directed toward action), "the good quality is truth in agreement with right desire" (*Nichomachean Ethics*, Bk. VI, Ch. 2, 1139^a30–31).

The best explication that I know of this too brief and cryptic statement of a remarkable insight is the one given by Aquinas in his *Commentary on the Nichomachean Ethics*, Bk. VI, Lect. ii, #1131. Aquinas writes: "If the truth of the practical intellect is determined by comparison with right desire and the rightness of desire is determined by being consonant with true reason, the argument is circular. Therefore, it must be said that desire is of the end as well as of the means. Now the end for man is determined by nature. The means, however, are not determined by nature but have to be found out by reason. Thus it is manifest that the rightness of desire with respect to the end is the measure of truth in practical reason. The truth of practical reason is accordingly determined by concordance with right desire [for the end]. And the truth of practical reason is itself, in turn, the basis for judging the rightness of desire for the means." Cf. *Summa Theologica*, Pt. I–II, Q. 57, A. 5, Reply 3. I am acquainted with only one contemporary commentary on this critical passage in Aristotle's *Ethics*, which is so fraught with consequences for meta-ethical discussion today. It occurs in Miss Anscombe's essay "Thought and Action in Aristotle"; as an interpretation of the text, it is as wide of the mark as it could possibly be. See *Aristotle's Ethics*, ed. by J. J. Walsh and H. L. Shapiro, pp. 68–69.

13. (p. 132) The self-evidence of the normative principle is unaffected by the degree of explicitness with which it is stated. It is

rooted in the recognition that the terms *really good* and *ought to be desired* are co-implicative. The meaning of each is involved in the meaning of the other, as the meanings of *whole* and *part* are co-implicative. When we understand that each real good that answers to a natural need is only a partial good, and not the whole or complete good, we further understand that the only good we ought to seek without qualification, is the *totum bonum* —the whole of real goods. We ought to seek any one of the partial goods only insofar as, being a part of the *totum bonum*, it contributes to a good life as a whole. It must not be sought for itself alone or in isolation from other real goods, but only as a part of the *totum bonum* and in relation to the other real goods that are parts of the *totum bonum*.

The normative principle prescribes the ultimate end to be sought; all other normative propositions are concerned with the means to this end—either the real goods that, as parts of the *totum bonum*, are constitutive means, or the instrumental goods that function as means of attaining one or another of the real goods. Since the normative principle both prescribes the ultimate end to be sought and also sets the standard of right desire, it follows that right desire is desire for the ultimate end, the *totum bonum*.

14. (p. 132) The circularity to be avoided was noted by Aquinas. See Note 12, *supra*.

15. (p. 136) See Chapter 8, Note 1, *supra*.

NOTES TO CHAPTER 14

1. (p. 138) See Chapter 11, Note 6, *supra*.

2. (p. 139) Cf. H. B. Veatch, *Rational Man*, pp. 182–185. There is one passage in Kant's writings that appears to agree with the thesis that the individual's moral obligation to himself takes precedence over his duties toward others and is, in a sense, their root. He writes: "No one has framed a proper concept of self-regarding duty. It has been treated as a detail and considered by way of an afterthought, as an appendix to moral philosophy, on the view that man should give thought to himself only after he has completely fulfilled his duty toward others. All moral philosophies err in this respect. . . . Far from ranking lowest in the scale of precedence, our duties toward ourselves are of primary importance and should have pride of place . . . the prior condition of our duty toward others is our duty to ourselves; we can fulfill the former only insofar as we first fulfill the latter" (*Lec-*

tures on Ethics, trans. by L. Infield, pp. 177–178). However, the appearance of agreement between the Kantian position and that of the common-sense view is completely dispelled by the following statements that occur within the context of the passage quoted above. "It was taken for granted that a man's duty towards himself consisted, as Wolff in his turn defined it, in promoting his own happiness. In that case, everything would depend on how an individual determined his own happiness. [Note here Kant's assumption of the relativity of the individual's happiness to his own individual wants, without any regard for the distinction between real and apparent goods. What Kant says in the very next sentence follows as a consequence of this mistaken conception of happiness.] This would, however, militate seriously against doing our duty towards others. In fact, the principle of self-regarding duties is a very different one, *which has no connexion with our well-being or earthly happiness*" (italics added).

Kant is correct in thinking that the individual's primary devotion to his own happiness, *if that were relative to his individual wants*, would militate against his doing his duty toward others. But that, as we have seen, is an incorrect—a psychological and non-moral—conception of happiness. When happiness is conceived, in moral terms, as identical with a whole life that is really good, Kant's insistence on the primacy of self-concern and his insight that the individual's duties toward others are subordinate to his primary obligation to himself, are more significantly and consistently carried out in the common-sense view, which makes happiness or the *totum bonum* the ultimate end and the primary object of obligation, than they are in Kantian ethics, which makes the individual's only duty to himself a duty to perfect his will by conforming it to the moral law. As I pointed out in an earlier note, the ethics of common sense resembles the ethics of Kant in certain purely formal respects, but they differ radically on all essential points of substance. See Chapter 11, Note 10, *supra*.

3. (p. 139) The critical impact of this chapter takes two directions. On the one hand, it is directed against such ethical doctrines as those of Kant and Mill, which either make right the primary notion, or the general happiness the primary objective. As Veatch says, it exposes "altruism as an ethical red herring" (see Note 2, *supra*). On the other hand, it is directed against such ethical doctrines as that of Epicurus in antiquity and that of Spinoza in modern times, which either totally neglect or insufficiently consider the individual's moral obligations toward others.

The ethics of the Roman Stoics (Seneca, Epictetus, and Marcus Aurelius) need not be considered, for it is self-refuting. If the individual cannot be injured, as the Stoics claim, by anything he suffers at the hands of fortune or of other men, then there are no grounds for saying, as the Stoics maintain, that the individual's only good lies in the goodness of his own will, a goodness the individual is said to possess when he does his duty toward society and acts rightly toward other men. If the individual cannot injure others, because no individual can be injured by another, how, then, can the virtuous man of good will, who does his duty and acts rightly, be distinguished from the vicious man who has injured himself alone by the badness of his own will? If one man cannot injure another, injustice is impossible, and if injustice is impossible, how can a man's will be good or bad, and his actions right or wrong, in relation to others? Conversely, if justice is possible, and if one man can injure another in various ways, but never by destroying the goodness of that other man's will, then the total good of each individual must include more than goodness of his own will, and that *totum bonum* must be the basis of determining what is right and wrong in the conduct of one individual toward another.

4. (p. 143) See Chapter 19, pp. 205–209, *infra*.

5. (p. 144) For a dialectical examination of diverse theories of justice and one which, in my judgment, reveals the superiority of the theory that grounds justice and injustice in natural rights, see Otto Bird, *The Idea of Justice*, esp. Ch. 6–7.

6. (p. 145) See Chapter 16, pp. 183–184, *infra*.

7. (p. 146) See Chapter 16, pp. 182–183, *infra*.

8. (p. 146) The importance of this point cannot be overemphasized. It would be impossible for organized society to do justice by securing, both positively and negatively, the fundamental right of all its members—the right to the pursuit of happiness—unless happiness were a common good, a *totum bonum* that is the same for all men. Let it be, as Kant and Mill conceive it, nothing but the satisfaction of conscious desires, whatever they may be, without regard to the distinction between real and apparent goods; the variety of goals that men would then pursue in the name of happiness, many of them bringing individuals into serious conflict with one another, could not constitute all together the common objective of a government's efforts to promote the general welfare. It would be under conflicting obligations that it could not discharge. Only if happiness is the same for all men, and involves them in the pursuit of real goods that are common goods, does the pursuit of happiness not bring individuals into conflict with one another, and make it possible for a government to secure, equally, for each and every one of them, their natural rights.

9. (p. 148) See M. G. Singer, *Generalization in Ethics*; and cf. J. Wilson, *Equality*, pp. 118–119; R. M. Hare, *Freedom and Reason*,

pp. 30–33, 118–119, and "Universalisability," in *Proceedings of the Aristotelian Society*, Vol. LV (1954–55), pp. 295–312; J. Rawls, "Two Concepts of Rules," in *Theories of Ethics*, ed. by P. Foot, pp. 144–170. For other writings by contemporary exponents of either act or rule utilitarianism, see Chapter 13, Note 3, *supra*.

10. (p. 149) See *op. cit.*, p. 39.

11. (p. 150) On the relation of the rule of equal treatment for all men to the sameness of human nature and its difference in kind from that of brutes, see *The Difference of Man and the Difference It Makes*, pp. 263–268. And on the equipollence of the equality rule and the generalization principle as subtended by one and the same premise concerning the sameness of human nature, see "The Idea of Equality," in *Great Ideas Today, 1968*, ed. by R. M. Hutchins and M. J. Adler, pp. 329–344.

12. (p. 151) See Chapter 12, Note 7, *supra;* and also this chapter, Note 8, *supra*. The fundamental flaw here lies in Kant's misconception of happiness as the satisfaction of individual wants or inclinations, which makes it impossible for him to avoid an ambiguous use of the term *happiness* when he speaks of the virtuous man being worthy of happiness, as the vicious man is not. This does not preclude the vicious man from achieving happiness, in his own terms; nor does it guarantee that the virtuous man who is worthy of happiness will attain it. In addition, Kant misconceives virtue as a good in itself, the only thing—a virtuous or good will—that is good without qualification. In this respect, his position resembles that of the ancient Stoics and is subject to the same difficulties. See Note 3, *supra*. Far from being good without qualification, moral virtue or a virtuous will is only an instrumental means to happiness, and its goodness is that of a means, not an end, and only that of an instrumental means, not a constitutive means—not a real good that is part of happiness, but a causal factor indispensable in the pursuit of it.

13. (p. 151) See, for example, John Dewey, *Human Nature and Conduct*, Pt. Three, Sect. VII; J. S. Mill, *Utilitarianism*, Ch. I; G. H. von Wright, *The Varieties of Goodness*, Ch. VIII–IX, *passim*.

14. (p. 151) It is certainly the case that a self-evident proposition is one that is incapable of proof or demonstration. But it may be wondered whether the deontologists, in regarding the duties mentioned as self-evident, have not made the error of supposing that a proposition difficult or impossible to prove must be self-evident.

15. (p. 153) *Utilitarianism*, Ch. III.

16. (p. 153) *Ibid.*, Ch. IV.

17. (p. 154) The two ends that Mill fails properly to relate to one

another can be properly related only when they are seen as, respectively, the ultimate end of the individual and the ultimate end of the state or political community. The ultimate end of the individual is only and always his own happiness (the *totum bonum commune hominis*). The ultimate end of the state or political community is the happiness of all its members—not the greatest good for the greatest number, but the general (or better, *common*) happiness that is the same for all men. Only the state can act for this end effectively and directly; the individual cannot. The individual, as we shall see in Chapter 16, is under the negative obligation not to interfere with or impair the pursuit of happiness by his fellowmen; his only positive obligation toward them calls for conduct that indirectly promotes their pursuit of happiness by directly serving the good of the political community itself (the *bonum commune communitatis*), which is prerequisite to the state's functioning as a means to the "general happiness"—the ultimate good of all its individual members. The happiness of the individual and the general happiness are both ends and both ultimate. This by itself creates no problem when their relationship is handled as Aristotle handled it. (See Postscript, pp. 259–260, *infra*.) But Mill made an insoluble problem of it for himself by treating both ends as ultimate ends for one and the same agent—the individual.

NOTES TO CHAPTER 15

1. (p. 161) Though the ethics of common sense is both teleological and deontological, it is primarily teleological because the *totum bonum* as ultimate end is its first principle and the object of the one basic moral obligation—the obligation to make a life that is really good as a whole. Every other good is a means to this end; every other moral obligation, either in regard to the goods one ought to seek for one's self or in regard to the rights of others, derives from the one basic moral obligation that relates to the ultimate normative end of all our actions. In order to be both teleological and deontological, and, more than that, in order properly to subordinate the deontological to the teleological, deriving categorical oughts from the consideration of end and means, an ethics must (a) affirm the primacy of the good and (b) distinguish between real and apparent goods. That is why the ethics of Kant and of Mill only *appear* to be both, but under careful scrutiny are not. While Kant appears to be concerned with ends as well as duties, he makes duties—or the right, not the good—primary. And while Mill appears to be concerned with duties as well as with end and means, his failure to recognize the distinction between real and apparent goods prevents him from making ends and means

objects of categorical obligation. See Chapter 18, Notes 1 and 2, *infra*.

2.   (p. 164) The instrumentality of moral virtue as an operative means to happiness or a good life should be clear to anyone who realizes that, in the course of living, we are required to choose from day to day, and from moment to moment, how we shall use our time, what activities we shall engage in, what order we shall engage in them, and to which we shall give preference in the economy of our limited time and energy. Moral virtue is simply a good habit of willing and choosing—a *habit* because it is an acquired and stable disposition to will and choose in a certain way, and a *good disposition* because it is a habitual inclination of the will toward the *totum bonum* as ultimate end, and a habitual tendency to choose between alternative courses of action or alternative goods according to whether they are or are not means to the ultimate end.

On the indispensability of a rightly directed will for a good life, see my discussion of the primary role of moral virtue as an instrumental means in *A Dialectic of Morals*, pp. 67–68, 97–102, 105–107. In commenting on Augustine's observation that happiness consists in having all our desires satisfied, provided that we desire nothing amiss, Aquinas points out that "desiring nothing amiss is needed for happiness, as a necessary disposition thereto" (*Summa Theologica*, Pt. I–II, Q. 3, A. 4, Reply 5). *Moral virtue is simply the habitual disposition to desire nothing amiss;* that is why it is necessary for a good life.

Prudence or sound judgment enters into the picture only with respect to such alternative means as are directed to the ultimate end. One may be better—more effective—than another, and it requires prudence to select the better of the several means that are morally sound, any of which a man of moral virtue would be inclined to choose because it is a means to the end his will is habitually inclined toward. While moral virtue and prudence are distinct—one being a habit of willing the end that ought to be sought and of choosing the appropriate means that ought to be employed, the other being a habit of deliberating about and deciding between morally acceptable means to the end—they are also existentially inseparable. Only a man of good moral character can also be prudent. Lacking moral virtue, the miser, the profligate, or the libertine may be clever or cunning in his calculations about the most effective means for achieving the apparent goods he wants and that he has made into ends, but such cleverness or cunning is only a counterfeit of prudence.

Furthermore, when different moral virtues are distinguished and given such names as temperance, fortitude, and justice, as has been traditionally done by those moral philosophers who have correctly understood moral virtue as consisting in a good habit of willing and choosing, the distinction is purely analytical—a distinction of aspects. It does not signify the existential separateness of diverse good habits. If it did, it would be possible for a man to be temperate without having fortitude, to have fortitude without being temperate, and to be just without either temperance or fortitude. But this cannot be the case if a good moral character or the possession of moral virtue consists in the habitual inclination of a man to the one ultimate end that he ought to seek. The unity of that end implies the unity of moral virtue, and requires us to deny an existential plurality of moral virtues. It is still useful to employ such terms as "temperance," "fortitude," and "justice," in order to distinguish diverse aspects of a good moral character, but whenever these terms are used for analytical purposes, it is necessary to safeguard their use against the serious error of converting them into the names of existentially distinct habits or dispositions, capable of existing separately, one without the others.

Although for the most part both Aristotle and Aquinas make this error, they do, nevertheless, in certain crucial passages, reveal some understanding of the unity of moral virtue, as well as of the existential inseparability of prudence from a good moral character. See Aristotle, *Nichomachean Ethics*, Bk. IV, Ch. 12; and Aquinas, *Summa Theologica*, Pt. I–II, Q. 61, A. 4. Cf. Jacques Maritain, *Art and Scholasticism*, pp. 15–17, 153–154; and John Dewey, *Human Nature and Conduct*, Ch. III.

3. (p. 165) For a dialectical analysis of the acquired freedom that is existentially inseparable from the possession of acquired moral virtue, see *The Idea of Freedom*, Vol. I, Ch. 6–7, 15–16; and Vol. II, Ch. 17. For a similar treatment of the circumstantial freedom that consists in freedom from coercion, duress, or the lack of enabling means, see *ibid.*, Vol. I, Ch. 12–14; Vol. II, Ch. 14; and for the special form of circumstantial freedom that is political liberty, see *ibid.*, Vol. I, Ch. 18; Vol. II, Ch. 6.

Man being by nature a political animal, having a natural capacity for participation in government, political liberty answers to a natural need and so is a real good and the basis of a natural right. To deprive a man of political liberty—the liberty of a citizen with suffrage, governed by his own consent and with a voice in government—is to deprive him of something he needs to make a good life for himself. Freedom from coercion, duress, or the lack of enabling means also corresponds to a natural need—the need that is implicit in man's capacity to choose this or that course of action, for when a man is prevented by circumstances from carrying out his choice, his natural tendency to execute his choice in overt action is frustrated or unfulfilled. Therefore, such freedom from coercion, duress, or the lack of enabling means is also a real good and the basis of a natural right.

While freedom of choice and the freedom that is acquired with moral virtue are both instrumental or operative means to happiness, they do not fulfill natural needs and so they are not constitutive means, or parts of a good life, as political liberty and freedom from coercion are. Either man's freedom of choice is an element in his specific constitution, or it does not exist at all. It cannot be acquired; it is not conferred upon him by outward circumstances. Whether one affirms or denies man's natural possession of freedom of choice, one cannot say that man has a natural right to such freedom. Similarly, one cannot say that man has a natural right to the freedom acquired with moral virtue. He needs such freedom just as he needs moral virtue—as an indispensable instrumental or operative means to making a good life—but his having it or not having it depends solely on how he uses his own freedom of choice, not upon any external circumstances or the actions of other men that might deprive him of it.

To sum up. Of the four forms of freedom, two—the circumstantial freedom of action and that special form of circumstantial freedom which is political liberty—are constitutive parts of the good life as well as instrumental means to becoming happy, and these two alone are involved in man's natural right to liberty. One of the remaining two—the acquired freedom of the virtuous man —is only an instrumental means to becoming happy, but not a constitutive part of the good life, except perhaps as one of the many ways in which, through leisure activities, a man improves himself—his character as well as his mind. In any case, this freedom is not involved in man's natural right to liberty. Finally, the fourth form of freedom—freedom of the will or of choice—either exists as a species-specific property of human nature, or it does not exist at all. If it does exist, and all men have this freedom as a native endowment, they cannot also claim it as a natural right. Nor can it be regarded as a good that answers to or fulfills a natural need. But can it be regarded as an instrumental means to happiness? If we understand a means to be something that we may or may not employ according to our choice, then freedom of choice cannot be a means. Nevertheless, it can be said that the moral problem of making a good life for one's self would not exist for us unless we had freedom of choice. This form of freedom is, therefore, even more fundamental than an indispensable instrumental means to happiness, for it is a condition prerequisite to there being any pursuit of happiness. See Chapter 17, Note 5, *infra*.

4.   (p. 165) See Note 2, *supra*. The relation between happiness and moral virtue is often imprecisely stated. It is sometimes said that happiness consists in being virtuous, which is plainly false. If a man had moral virtue and none of the real goods that constitute the *totum bonum*, his life would not be a happy one, or good as

a whole. While having some of the real goods that constitute the *totum bonum* may depend upon the exercise of moral virtue in the making of choices, this is certainly not true of all of them; some are wholly goods of chance or fortune, and some depend in part at least on chance or fortune.

It is also sometimes said that the happy life is the virtuous life. This is also plainly false. The happy life is a life made good by the possession, in the right order and proportion, of all the things that a man needs—all the things that are really good for him. Virtue enters into the picture as an instrumental means to a man's getting all the things that are really good for him, and perhaps also as one among many forms of self-improvement, which is the real good aimed at by the activities of leisure.

In addition, it is sometimes said that happiness consists in virtuous activity which, if not false, is a very misleading way of stating the truth. We have seen that the five basic types of activity are sleeping, playing, working, leisuring, and idling. The adjective "virtuous" does not designate a type of activity, in any way commensurate or coordinate with the five basic types mentioned above. Each of these five basic types of activity can be engaged in in such a way or to such an extent that the result is good or bad for the individual, and if the result is good because a good choice has been made among alternative courses of action for the sake of the good life as a whole, then we should say of the activity that it was virtuously chosen, not that it was a virtuous activity.

The truth concealed in the misleading statement that happiness consists in virtuous activity begins to appear in the statement that a good life consists of activities "in accordance with virtue," which is to say "chosen well, or virtuously, or as a man of good moral character would choose them." Even then the statement needs expansion to make it fully explicit and precise. Happiness, as the *totum bonum*, consists of, or is constituted by, the possession of all the real goods a man needs in the course of a whole life. In the definition of happiness, there need be no mention at all of moral virtue. Virtue becomes significant and relevant only when we turn from the constitution of happiness (the elements of a good life as achieved) to the pursuit of happiness (the process of making one's whole life good). It is only in the pursuit of happiness or in the process of making one's whole life good that moral virtue functions as an instrumental means. Hence it is precisely correct to say that the pursuit of happiness consists in choosing and acting in a manner that manifests a virtuous disposition, under favorable circumstances that confer a requisite minimum of the goods of fortune. If a man has moral virtue or a good moral character, he has one—*but only one*—of the things it takes to become happy, and while moral virtue is one of the principal means to becoming happy, it is by no means a principal part of being happy.

5. (p. 168) Cf. Plato, *Philebus*, 27^b–28^c.

6. (p. 169) To say that the activities of leisure make the greatest contribution to a good life as a whole is not to say that, of the five basic types of activity, leisure and leisure alone should be engaged in without limit. Every type of activity, even leisure-work must be limited in the amount of time devoted to it, in order to allow sufficient time for other types of activity, such as sleep and play, that are also indispensable to the making of a good life. Nevertheless, in terms of the order of the real goods that result from the various types of activity, the other indispensable types of activity should be subordinated to leisuring, not leisuring to them. Of the goods that result from different types of activity, the goods of self-improvement are the only ones that are unlimited goods—goods of which we cannot have too much. Self-improvement, in all its aspects, thus represents the *summum bonum*, the highest in the order of all the real goods that constitute the *totum bonum*, and leisuring is the highest type of human activity because it aims at and results in the highest type of good.

However, in one respect, play together with the pleasure intrinsic to it is more like the *totum bonum* than leisure together with the self-improvement that results from it. If a man at play forgets or ignores his life as a whole, he is for the moment engaged in an activity the pleasure of which satisfies him without reference to anything beyond itself. Just as a good life as a whole is not a means to anything beyond itself, so the pleasure of play is not a means to any other good *except a good life as a whole*. In contrast, the goodness of leisuring is always and only that of a means to a good life as a whole, and in the scale of goods that constitute the *totum bonum*, the goods of self-improvement resulting from leisure are more valuable—make a greater contribution—than the pleasure intrinsic to play.

NOTES TO CHAPTER 16

1. (p. 174) See Note 6, *infra*.

2. (p. 175) To underscore this point and to make it as clear as possible, let us for the moment adopt a hypothesis that I regard as contrafactual. Let us suppose that instinctual aggressiveness is built into human nature as a species-specific property and that every human being has a psycho-biological need for power or domination over other men, just as every human being has a need for food and shelter, or a need for the pleasures of the flesh that, in their myriad forms, are rooted in man's sexuality. If that were the case,

then just as wealth (including such consumables as food and shelter) and sensual pleasures are real goods satisfying natural needs, so, too, power or domination over other men, together, perhaps, with inflicting bodily injury or physical suffering on them, would be a real good answering to a natural human need. And if that were the case, then the things that satisfied instinctual aggressiveness would necessarily be part of the *totum bonum commune*—the ultimate good that is the same for all men.

These things being so, two consequences would inexorably follow: (1) *even under ideal conditions,* the pursuit of happiness by one man, if successful, would necessarily defeat the pursuit of happiness by other men, the individuals he dominated and abused in order to gratify his aggressiveness; and (2) no government could do justice by securing for all its human subjects their basic natural right to the pursuit of happiness, since this would now include an element that could be secured for some men only by allowing others to be deprived of it. In short, if aggressiveness were a species-specific instinctual drive in man, as it is in certain species of animals, or if it set up in man a natural need for power or domination over others as sexuality sets up in man a natural need for sensual pleasure, then the pursuit of happiness would be competitive, not cooperative; one man's success in making a good life for himself would, even under ideal conditions, entail the misery of others; the pursuit of happiness would not be the basic natural right that a government can attempt to secure; and no government could be just if political justice consists in a government's securing *all* the natural rights of *all* its human subjects. The same consequences would follow from the false supposition that each individual has a natural right not to a decent minimum of wealth, but to an unlimited amount of it, or a natural right, not to innocuous forms of pleasure, but to pleasures that are detrimental to the peace, health, or safety of the community.

Fortunately, the hypothesis proposed is contrafactual. The notion that man is instinctually aggressive was first promulgated by Sigmund Freud on the basis of what, by strict scientific criteria, must be regarded as insufficient and questionable evidence. It has more recently been re-introduced by Konrad Lorenz, among other ethologists, by the drawing of questionable parallels between human and animal behavior (see *On Aggression*); and such evidence of animal aggression as is supplied in the works of Lorenz and Tinbergen (see *A Study of Instinct*) has been uncritically interpreted as if it inevitably led to clear conclusions about human aggression by such popularizers of ethology as Robert Ardrey (see *The Territorial Imperative*).

See my brief discussion of Tinbergen, Lorenz, and Ardrey in *The Difference of Man and the Difference It Makes,* Note 6 on p. 319, Note 11 on p. 361, and Notes 15 and 18 on p. 362. For detailed and penetrating criticisms of Lorenz and Ardrey, and even more for the presentation of the scientific evidence and the lack of evidence that calls for the rejection of the hypothesis that man is instinctually aggressive, see *Man and Aggression,* ed. by M. F. Ashley Montagu, especially the following essays: "On the Hazards of Analogies" by S. A. Barnett; "Man Has No 'Killer' Instincts" by Geoffrey Gorer, "That Old-Time Aggression" by J. P. Scott; "Instinct and Aggression" by T. C. Scheirla; "The Human Beast" by Sir Solly Zuckerman, and "Taking Issue with Lorenz on the Ute" by John Beatty. Also see Theodore Lidz, *The Person,* pp. 31–33; and an excellent critical review of Anthony Storr's *Human Aggression* and J. H. N. Horsburgh's *Non-Violence and Aggression,* by Professor Edmund Leach of Cambridge, in *The New York Review of Books,* October 10, 1968, pp. 24–29, under the title "Ignoble Savages."

In *Education and Ecstasy,* by George B. Leonard, there is a striking passage on p. 128 that has a relevance which deserves remembering: "Anyone who thinks that man is 'naturally' aggressive should visit an infantry training school where the most ingenious, desperate measures are needed to turn young Americans into aggressive killers. . . . But the measures are never altogther successful. Even when killing is socially sanctioned and highly rewarded, even when it may save the soldiers' own lives, many GI's never fire their rifles. During the Korean war, studies show, only one out of four fired during battle." To which I would like to add the following passage from a recent book by Noam Chomsky: "One word of caution is necessary in referring to Lorenz, now that he has been discovered by Ardrey and Joseph Alsop and popularized as a prophet of doom. It seems to me that Lorenz's views on human aggression have been extended to near absurdity by some of his expositors. It is no doubt true that there are innate tendencies in the human psychic constitution that lead to aggressiveness *under specific social and cultural conditions.* [Italics added.] But there is little reason to suppose that these tendencies are so dominant as to leave us forever tottering on the brink of a Hobbesian war of all against all. Skepticism is certainly in order when a doctrine of man's 'inherent aggressiveness' comes to the surface in a society that glorifies competitiveness, in a civilization that has been distinguished by the brutality of the attack that it has mounted against less fortunate peoples" (*Language and Mind,* p. 82).

3. (p. 175) In Plato's and Aristotle's day, the state of technology was such that it may not have been possible for some few men to make good lives for themselves except by the use of slaves and under conditions that meant misery for many. What is true of ancient Greece is true, in varying degrees, of all historic civilization from the beginning down to the present day. Shall we con-

demn the privileged few as morally culpable, even though divesting themselves of advantages that made it possible for them to lead good lives would not have conferred upon all the rest the conditions they needed to make good lives for themselves? Yes, if they obtained their privileges by force or fraud, but not if they were simply blessed by good fortune and could not, under the conditions of their society, do anything about rectifying the misfortunes under which their fellow-men suffered. Men are morally responsible only for what is within their power to do or not to do; similarly, governments are morally accountable only within the limits of the possible.

4. (p. 177) See Chapter 15, Note 2, *supra*. The existential inseparability of justice from temperance and fortitude is to be understood in terms of the unity of moral virtue. A good moral character—a stable disposition to will the *totum bonum* as the end to be sought and to choose the appropriate means for achieving it—is one and the same whether it manifests itself under the aspect of justice (in relation to the good of others) or under the aspects of temperance and fortitude (in relation to one's own good).

Plato alone among the great moral philosophers raised and persistently explored the problem of how being just toward others serves the individual's own happiness, and as far as I know, he alone discovered the heart of the solution in the unity of moral virtue. See *Republic*, Bk. I–IV; and cf. *Apology*, 24^c–26^b, where Socrates looks at the problem in terms of the good of the community and its effect on the happiness of the individual. See also Plato's *Gorgias*, in which the same problem is approached through the consideration of the question of whether it is better to do injustice or to suffer it. Throughout this discussion, Plato strikes only one clearly false note and that is succinctly expressed in Socrates' remark at the end of his trial: "Wherefore, O judges, be of good cheer about death, and know of a certainty that no evil can happen to a good man, either in life or after death." That, as we have observed earlier, is the fundamental error of Stoicism (see Chapter 14, Note 3, *supra*). If no evil can befall a man through the force of external circumstances or through the actions of other men, then it is impossible for one man to injure another, and hence justice and injustice are meaningless terms. One could not then ask whether it is better to do or to suffer injustice. If that question is meaningful, as I think it is, and if the correct answer to it were the one that Plato tends to affirm (namely, that it is better to suffer injustice than to do it), the reason would have to lie in the fact that the individual's pursuit of happiness or his effort to make a good life for himself can be more seriously hampered or defeated by his lack of moral virtue (signified by his doing injustice to others) than by the injuries that can be inflicted upon him by other men. However, I am far from sure that Plato's answer is the correct one. Some forms of injustice suffered—being enslaved, for example—can defeat a man's effort to make a good life for himself as completely as the lack of moral virtue on his part.

5. (p. 178) See Note 3, *supra*.

6. (p. 180) "It is not reasonable to expect men to devote themselves to any other end than their own highest [more precisely, complete] good, and a superior society cannot be the highest good for those who must be annihilated as a condition of its realization. They will very naturally prefer to run the risk of securing their own welfare in a less perfect social organization. There is no duty constraining one section of the community—not simply to risk their lives, as in a just war—but to submit to be killed by the social authority, in order that the surviving citizens may have the benefit of a more efficient state" (John A. Ryan, *A Living Wage*, pp. 55-56).

The essential point here is the difference between risk and sacrifice. Under pathological social conditions, such as war or any other dire emergency, the individual may either volunteer to do things that involve serious threats to his pursuit of a good life for himself, or he may be required by the state to take such risks. But in no case can he be asked to lay down his life for his country, for that would involve a profound perversion in the order of goods —the subordination of the *totum bonum hominis*, which is the ultimate end, to one of its means, the *bonum communitatis*. Nevertheless, there seem to be circumstances in which the state does ask men to jeopardize their health and even their lives for the good of the community. If this demand is just—and let us concede that it sometimes may be—then it would *appear* that the good of the community *(bonum communitatis)* takes precedence over happiness *(totum bonum hominis)*, for if a man endangers his health and risks his life for the good of the community, he would seem to be forgoing the pursuit of happiness, which requires health and certainly life. It is only by considering dire emergencies that we can see how asking men to take certain risks can be justified, since the long-term consequences of their not taking risks may be even more detrimental to their achievement of happiness than putting themselves in temporary jeopardy.

During a serious epidemic, which endangers the state's well-being by threatening to decimate its population, all men, not only physicians and nurses, can be impressed into the service of public health, even at the risk of their own health, and perhaps life. When a community is similarly threatened by earthquake or flood, all of its members can be similarly expected to assume perilous risks. In times of peace, not only are officers charged with enforcing the law duty-bound to risk their lives in the apprehension of criminals, but so, in fact, is every citizen obligated to assist the police, if there be such need, or even, in the absence of police, to undertake the dangerous task of blocking the path of dangerous criminals. This case is misunderstood if it is supposed that the duty here lies between one individual and another, the one risking his health or life to protect the life or property of another. The obligation in justice is rather a civic duty to protect the peace and order of the community against the ravages of crime. The public peace of a community is as much menaced, though seldom as dramatically, by the spread of unchecked crime within its borders as by the advance of unchecked aggressors upon its territorial domains. Hence the duty of a citizen in time of peace is no different from his duty in time of war, though under the conditions of modern warfare, which efface the ancient distinction between soldiers and non-combatants, every member of the community is more likely to experience the precariousness of a front-line position in defense of the community's existence. The emergency of war differs from the emergency of crime in one other respect; not only is it usually a more intense emergency, having a more widespread impact on the whole population simultaneously, but it raises a question of justice which crime by definition does not. Absolutely speaking, no citizen can be justly required to take part in a purely predatory, or unjust, attack upon another community. The use of military force against outsiders is justified only in defense, just as the use of police power within the state is justified only by crime.

With all this understood, we must still ask, How can justice require us to risk our lives, or anything essential to happiness, such as health, even in those emergencies in which the state's survival or its peace is threatened? The answer turns on the fact that what is required is only a *risk*, and not an *absolute surrender*, of these essential goods. *The risk of life is not suicide.* Regardless of how dire the emergency may be, the state cannot ask a man to kill himself for its good. Nor can the state kill men who have not forfeited their lives by criminal attack upon the social welfare. Whether or not the capital punishment of criminals is justified by retributive justice, it is certainly true that apart from the sort of violence through which a man declares himself to be an enemy of the state, the state cannot kill men without committing the injustice of murder. Suppose a famine or a pestilence and suppose it would be obviously expedient, in the protection of the whole community, to kill a few—the aged or the infected. Is it not perfectly obvious that such expedients cannot be resorted to because they violate justice? And they violate justice because they wrongly place the good of the community before and above the inalienable rights of each individual to life, liberty, and the pursuit of happiness. Though it deprives men of less than life, the sterilization of the unfit is also judged to be contrary to justice, regardless of how strong a case can be made out, on clear factual grounds, for its expediency. Now, if the *bonum communitatis* were the *totum bonum*, if within the sphere of means and ends the *bonum communitatis* were the ultimate end, whatever was *truly expedient* as a means to it would be *naturally justified.*

These things not being so, we return to the important distinction between the *probability of risk* and the *certainty of sacrifice.* And the probability of risk is related to another probability—the *probability of threatening ruin* which confronts the state in dire civic emergencies. If it were possible to know with certitude that despite all efforts, the state was doomed to perish in this emergency, there would be no point to risking one's life, nor could that risk be justly required; just as, if it were possible to know with certitude that the act one was about to perform for the state's defense would lead to death, the act could not be obligated or rendered in justice for it would be murder (by the state which demanded it) or suicide (by the individual who, believing himself bound in justice, rendered it). To stay within the bounds of justice, we must stay within the domain of probabilities, in which there is a proportionality between the probable risk the individual undertakes and the probable threat the state faces. Within this domain we can understand why the state can ask, and why the individual can render, a service that *appears* to violate the order of real goods. The violation is only apparent because the risk the individual takes is balanced against another probability which threatens him. If the state were to perish, the individual himself might not survive the catastrophe, or at least its consequence would be a drastic impairment of the conditions he needed for continuing his pursuit of happiness. Therefore, he risks his life in the hope, not only of his own survival, but of the community's preservation and future prosperity, so that, the emergency surmounted, the danger past, peace and safety once more regained, the state will continue to play its normal role as a common good to be enjoyed and as a means to be used.

Within the sphere of probabilities, which permit men to cherish hope in the face of risks and threats, the individual does not *naturally* hope for the state's safety with no concern for his own fate, nor does he hope for his own survival with no thought of his community's endurance; rather he hopes that good fortune will attend his efforts in respect to both goods, and he hopes for both because either without the other would frustrate the intentions of his natural appetite. Moreover, the order of his hopes follows the order of his intentions; as both self-preservation and a benevolent society are means necessitated by happiness as the end, so does he hope for his own survival and the state's endurance as indispensable conditions prerequisite to the attainment of happiness. These two goods are not only means to the same end, but reciprocally means to each other, though not with the same stress under conditions of safety and peril; whereas under circumstances of peace and security society provides its members with aid in the struggle for subsistence, the reverse causality predominates in times of war and impending disaster, when men must help the state survive.

Because these two means to happiness (individual subsistence and society's endurance) are thus co-implicated in reciprocal causality, because the emergency situation involves two inseparable risks, not one, the individual is not free to disregard one threat and protect himself entirely against the other. His individual happiness is doubly threatened by the emergency; it is as much threatened by the probability that the community will not endure unless its members will assume risks proportionate to this danger, as it is threatened by the probability that he may perish if he undertakes to prevent disaster to the community. Clearly, then, it follows that when a man acts in such situations with the fortitude that justice commands, he is not exalting the good of the community above his individual happiness, and when the state justly exacts such conduct from its members, it is not preferring its own life to the life of its members, but rather regarding both as means to happiness and both as inseparably threatened.

Each member of the community enjoys the *bonum communitatis*, and profits by the state's ministry to his individual welfare. Each individual must, therefore, be prepared to pay a price, in effort and risk, for these benefits, because he cannot avoid such effort and risk without risking their total loss. But since, in a just community, all share equally in the *bonum communitatis* and all profit proportionately from its benefactions, the principle of justice requires a fair distribution of burdens to balance the distributive justice of properly shared goods. It is this principle which completes our resolution of the apparent conflict between the good of the community and the happiness of its members. If the burdens of effort and risk are justly distributed among the members of a community, each is called upon to do no more than the rest in the protection and support of goods they commonly enjoy and proportionately share. No man would then be sacrificing himself in any way for his fellows. Justice, be it remembered, never calls for sacrifice or generosity; it exacts only a just price; it asks only for what is due. Accordingly, if distributive justice prevails with respect to common goods and common burdens alike, then each man who acts justly in the performance of his civic duty in times of emergency cooperates with his fellows for the social welfare so that it in turn will continue to support the welfare of himself. Each acts with all for the good of all because upon that depends the good of each. And no risk of life can be too great so long as it is proportionate in its probability to the probability of disaster which threatens the state, and so long as one man's assumption of risk is not proportionately greater than another's.

If it were possible, in a complex modern society, for each man to think that everyone else was bearing proportionate burdens and risks—as that is almost certainly known by the members of a small frontier community—then justice would be sufficient; the just man would not hesitate to face the greatest risks for the community's welfare. But since in any large and complex society, the ideal of distributive justice is very imperfectly realized, and individuals are beset by doubts about the full cooperation of their fellow-men in a common cause, justice is not enough to impel men to take the risk which may turn out, in fact, to have been a sacrifice, because it exceeded the risks others have assumed. In such a situation, love is required. Only through love for one's fellow-man is anyone impelled, beyond mere justice, to take the chance of doing more than others. And it is certainly a question of whether ordinary human love is enough. See Note 8, *infra*.

7.   (p. 182) It is of the utmost importance to distinguish between the sacrifice of individual goods for the sake of the general welfare, which the state can justly require of its citizens, and the sacrifice of the individual's pursuit of happiness for the good of the community, which the state can never justly demand. Individual goods, by definition, are not common goods—not elements in the *totum bonum*. Hence sacrificing them, even when they are innocuous, does not interfere with the pursuit of happiness. Not being either real goods or common goods, individual goods cannot be claimed as a matter of natural right. Depriving the individual of them is, therefore, not an act of injustice.

Let us, for the moment, consider only such individual goods as are innocuous, and are not subject to the prohibition that they ought not to be sought by the individual for the sake of his own happiness. Such individual goods, being only apparent goods, are subordinate in the scale of values to real and common goods, the *bonum commune communitatis* as well as the *totum bonum commune hominis*. As subordinate, they should be sought or possessed only on condition that they remain innocuous, i.e., on condition that they do not interfere with or impede the attainment of any real good by the individual himself or by his fellow-men. (See Note 2, *supra*.) When the state justly calls for the sacrifice of individual goods on the part of its members, it does so either on the grounds that the good of the community itself is thereby served, or on the grounds that the sacrifice serves the general welfare. The state, as we shall see presently, has a double obligation in justice to its citizens, the *negative* obligation not to deprive them of the things to which they have a natural right, and the *positive* obligation to help them obtain the things they need for the pursuit of happiness. In discharging this positive obligation, the state promotes the general welfare, in which, under a just constitution and just laws, all citizens share equally. Therefore, we should be able to see that when the state requires its citizens to sacrifice individual goods either for the sake of the good of the community or in order to promote the general welfare, that sacrifice on the part of individuals is for their own ultimate good, since the *bonum communitatis* is a part of the *totum bonum hominis* and since the promotion of the general welfare is a means to that same end.

Failure to understand this has led men to the violent extremes of either individualism or totalitarianism, and the resultant controversy is made bitter by the fact that each extreme holds on to a half-truth which it cannot, and should not, surrender, but which it must not exaggerate into the whole truth at the expense of denying the complementary part. That, of course, is precisely what happens when the totalitarian, rightly demanding the sacrifice of individual goods for the good of the community and the general welfare, denies that individual happiness matters at all, and when the individualist, on his side, rightly affirms that the ultimate good is the happiness of the individual, but fails to understand happiness as a common good, and so regards any encroachment of the state on the propensities of the individual as an evil. The truth that man is not made for the state, but the state for man, means that man makes the state for his own ultimate good. He cannot, therefore, reasonably object to whatever is justly required by the state in order for it to serve effectively the purpose for which it was made.

8.   (p. 183) We have seen the sense in which justice is selfish or at least self-serving; moral virtue, whether in the aspect of justice or in the aspect of fortitude and temperance, is essentially an instrumental means to the individual's own ultimate good. To restrain one's self, in justice, from injuring one's neighbor is clearly different from the benevolent impulse to help one's friends or the persons one loves to attain the things they need in their pursuit of happiness. The saying that a friend in need is a friend indeed expresses everyone's realization that there are times when one is sorely bereft if one lacks friends, because only one's friends can be expected to make that extra, positive, and benevolent effort to come to one's aid in the emergencies that seriously threaten one's effort to make a good life for one's self.

But although love or friendship is benevolent, as justice is not, it too has a tincture of selfishness about it that requires us to describe it as self-interested benevolence. (See Robert Hazo, *The Idea of Love*, pp. 23–28, 43–50, 54, 56–60, 63–64, 97–100.) This is the meaning of the statement that the friend or loved one is one's *alter ego*—not simply *an other*, but *another self*. It is only the supernatural love that Christian theology conceives as *caritas*—

the Divine love that God instills in man whereby man loves both God and his neighbor—which is purely unselfish love, involving completely disinterested benevolence. When it is said, by contemporary Protestant theologians, that Christ is *the man for others* (see Bishop John Robinson, *Honest to God*, Ch. 4), what is being held up as a model to follow is the ideal of Christian love, which is concerned with the good of the other wholly for the sake of the other and without any thought of self. But what these contemporary theologians appear to overlook is that such purely disinterested benevolence is possible only for Christ as a supernatural person, and for other men who can imitate Christ only with the help of God's grace and through having the Divine gift of love. (See my criticism of the so-called "new" or "radical" theology as self-refuting in *The Difference in Man and the Difference It Makes*, pp. 282–285.) It is not attainable by man as a natural person or as a psycho-biological organism. On the purely natural plane, the plane of human needs and wants, love like justice serves the interests of the individual, though love goes beyond justice in attempting, benevolently, to promote the good of others with whom one identifies one's self.

9. (p. 184) See Note 6, *supra*. The familiar saying that politics is the art of the possible epigrammatically expresses the point that the application of moral criteria—especially the criteria of justice and injustice—to political or social action is limited by the consideration of what is feasible at a given time and under given circumstances. That limitation is removed only by *ideal conditions—* conditions under which doing complete justice is possible, and no injustice can be condoned on the grounds that it is unavoidable. It is certainly questionable whether ideal conditions, thus defined, will ever exist on earth, but there can be no question about the fact that ideal conditions have never existed at any time in man's history and do not exist anywhere at present.

NOTES TO CHAPTER 17

1. (p. 185) See *op. cit.*, Ch. 8–11. Since the publication of *The Difference of Man and the Difference It Makes*, its central theses—(a) that man and man alone has propositional speech, and (b) that his having propositional speech presupposes his having the power of conceptual thought—have been confirmed by the latest treatise of Professor Noam Chomsky (*Language and Mind*, 1968). This book represents a remarkable departure from Chomsky's earlier views, which led me to cite him, in *The Difference of Man and the Difference It Makes*, as an opponent of the position I undertook

to defend (see p. 229, Note 20 on pp. 336–337, and Note 9 on p. 353).

2. (p. 186) See *The Difference of Man and the Difference It Makes*, pp. 90, 131–133.

3. (p. 186) See *op. cit.*, pp. 115–118, 271–279. Cf. also the essays cited in Chapter 16, Note 2, *supra*, which not only deny the presence in human nature of aggression as an instinctual or inborn drive, but also deny the existence in man of any instinctive patterns of behavior.

4. (p. 187) See *The Idea of Freedom*, Vol. I, Ch. 20–24; Vol. II, Ch. 8–12, 19.

5. (p. 187) See *The Difference of Man and the Difference It Makes*, pp. 268–273, 288–290. Man's possession of a free will or of freedom of choice depends on whether the brain is only a necessary or the sufficient condition of conceptual thought, i.e., on whether or not man's thinking and willing require the operation of an immaterial or non-physical factor in addition to the action of his bodily organs, and especially his brain. This difficult philosophical issue, usually referred to as the mind-body problem, has not yet been resolved. Beyond establishing the two theses mentioned in Note 1 above, my main objective in *The Difference of Man and the Difference It Makes* was to project the possibility and likelihood of a resolution of this issue in the relatively near future by experiments performed with advanced generations of robots. See *op. cit.*, Ch. 12–15. While my own philosophical prejudices favor the proposition that the brain is only a necessary but not the sufficient condition of human thinking and willing, my mind remains open to the possibility that that proposition will be falsified by clearcut and decisive empirical evidence. If it is, then the moral philosophy expounded in this book—the teleological and deontological ethics of common sense—is, in my judgment, worthless, for unless man has freedom of choice (which must be ruled out if all his powers and operations can be adequately explained in physical terms), the pursuit of happiness is without meaning or reality; man has neither genuine moral problems nor any moral responsibility for solving them.

I made this point years ago in *A Dialectic of Morals* (see Ch. IV, esp. pp. 58–59); and I made it again in *The Difference of Man and the Difference It Makes* (see pp. 271–273 and cf. pp. 263–270). My writing of this book on the ethics of common sense indicates my belief, on the basis of all the scientific evidence and philosophical arguments with which I am acquainted, that the future will see the gradual and progressive confirmation of the proposition that the brain is only a necessary but not the sufficient condition of human thinking and willing, rather than its decisive falsification by experimental evidence.

NOTES TO CHAPTER 18

1. (p. 189) See Chapter 14 (pp. 152–154), and Note 16, *supra*, for a statement of the crucial errors of utilitarianism. They can be summed up as follows: (1) failure to distinguish between needs and wants and between real and apparent goods, (2) failure to distinguish between pleasure as object of desire and pleasure as satisfaction of desire, (3) failure to distinguish between the sum total of goods *(totum bonum)* and the highest in the scale of partial goods *(summum bonum)*, (4) failure to distinguish between happiness as an experienceable psychological state of complete satisfaction or contentment and happiness as identical with a whole life that is good, (5) failure to relate the two things it posits as ultimate ends —(a) the happiness of the individual, conceived differently by each individual according to his individual wants, and (b) the general happiness, or the greatest good of the greatest number. The last of these failures is the most serious for an ethics that tries to be teleological, as utilitarianism does, for there cannot be two ultimate ends for one and the same agent, and if there appear to be two ends, each of which has a certain finality, the apparent conflict between them must be resolved by the subordination of one to the other. This, as we have seen, utilitarianism fails to do. See Chapter 14, Note 17, *supra*. The combination of this failure with the failure to distinguish between real and apparent goods—the distinction underlying the difference between what ought to be desired by all men and what is in fact desired by some men and not by others —prevents utilitarianism from being both a deontological and teleological ethic, as well as rendering it defective even in its own terms as an ethics that tries to be teleological.

2. (p. 191) It may be objected that the ethics of Kant is not a purely deontological ethics; it may be claimed by Kantians that it is also teleological, for it treats of ends that are duties and is concerned with the problem of ultimate ends. See *Kant's Critique of Practical Reason*, pp. 295–299; and *Critique of Teleological Judgment*, pp. 591–595. I have already commented on these passages and have shown that they only give the appearance of combining the teleological with the deontological (see Chapter 11, Note 10; Chapter 12, Note 7; Chapter 14, Notes 2 and 12, *supra*). Two things plainly reveal that Kant's ethics is not teleological: (a) though he treats of ends, he never considers the means for achieving them, and to discuss ends without reference to means is empty talk; (b) his

rationalistic purity prevents him from dealing with means, for it is impossible to consider means in relation to ends without reference to empirical knowledge of matters of fact, and Kant excludes such considerations from moral philosophy as the product of pure practical reason. In consequence, his ethics cannot be either teleological or practical, and even in those passages in which Kant *appears* to be thinking teleologically, he fails to make the happiness that he acknowledges to be man's ultimate end the primary object of his moral obligation, and the source of all other derivative duties; in short, he fails to subordinate the right to the good, and the deontological formulation of categorical oughts to the teleological consideration of the *totum bonum commune* and the means of achieving it.

3. (p. 192) See Joseph Fletcher, *Situation Ethics, the New Morality,* esp. Ch. I, III, IV, V, VII; *Moral Responsibility, Situation Ethics at Work;* John Robinson, *Honest to God,* Ch. 6, on "The New Morality"; *The Situation Ethics Debate,* ed. by Harvey Cox, esp., Pt. IV, Ch. 3, 9, 10, 11, 14; *Norm and Context in Christian Ethics,* ed. by G. H. Outka and P. Ramsey, esp. essays by Frederick S. Carney, James M. Gustafson, Paul Ramsey in Part One, and by Joseph Fletcher, Basil Mitchell, and Ronald Evans in Part Four.

4. (p. 192) Fletcher's writings abound in such flashy falsehoods as "love is the only norm" or "love and justice are the same." The Institute for Philosophical Research has undertaken exhaustive critical studies of the major contributions to the discussion of both love and justice (see *The Idea of Justice* by Otto Bird; *The Idea of Love* by Robert Hazo), and on no recognizable conception of either love or justice can it be said that love and justice are the same. As for Fletcher's central thesis, that "nothing is prescribed except love" or that "love is the only norm," it is necessary to distinguish between human love (i.e., the kind of love of which man is capable as a psycho-biological organism) and Divine love (i.e., the kind of love of which man is capable only when he is imbued with it by God's grace). See Chapter 16, Note 8, *supra.*

Augustine's statement, *dilige et quod vis fac,* which Fletcher quotes in support of his own position, may be true in moral theology, but it is false in moral philosophy. On the theological plane, and in the context of dogmas concerning God as a supernatural being, original sin, and Divine grace as the gift to man of the supernatural virtues of faith, hope, and charity, it is true to say that the saints who, through God's grace, imitate Christ and obey his two precepts of charity, need no other norms or prescriptions in order to act rightly. They and they alone, loving with Divine love, can do as they please; or, in Fletcher's rendition of Augustine's maxim, what they will, they should do. On the philosophical plane, in the context of our knowledge of man as a natural and finite being, with all the limitations and defects of an animal that is also rational, it is false to say that no other guidance is needed for human conduct than the prescription that men should love their fellow-men. For one thing, human love, even when it reaches the highest degree of benevolence of which man is naturally capable, remains self-interested; for another, it extends only to a few among one's fellow-men, never to all with whom one is associated in the communal life of a populous society.

The most serious error that Fletcher and his followers commit lies in their failure to recognize that ethics is not primarily or exclusively concerned with how men should behave toward their fellow-men, either through love or justice; it is primarily concerned with the problem of what the individual ought to do in order to make a good life for himself. Self-love may be relevant to this problem, but fraternal love and justice toward others are not. "Situation ethics," like the rigid deontological ethics that its exponents criticize, makes the mistake of giving the right primacy over the good, or worse, of being concerned exclusively with the right—with duties toward others. It is therefore inadequate and unsound as moral philosophy. If this criticism is met by the defense that it is not offered as moral philosophy, but as a "Christian ethics," or as a form of moral theology, then its exponents must be asked whether they subscribe to the theological dogmas concerning the existence of a supernatural being and concerning the supernatural, as contrasted with the secular, plane of human life, without which the basic tenets of "situation ethics" are either meaningless or false. Since the exponents of "situation ethics" are also exponents of the so-called "new" or "radical" theology that denies the existence of a supernatural being and any distinction between the secular and religious dimensions of human life, they undermine their own position. Nor can they claim that Christ and those who may try to follow in his footsteps have a spirituality that somehow transcends nature, for, as I have pointed out elsewhere, there can be no transcendence of nature unless there is, apart from nature, a transcendent divine being whose creative act produces in man a psycho-biological organism that also has a spirituality which cannot be explained in terms of purely natural causes. In short, there is no middle ground between what Bishop Robinson regards as the error of supernaturalism and what he regards as the error of naturalism, and in the absence of such a middle ground, the "new theology" either ceases to be *new* or ceases to be a *theology*. See *The Difference of Man and the Difference It Makes*, pp. 282–285, 292.

5. (p. 194) Moral philosophy, comprising such wisdom as can be formulated about the ultimate end to be sought and about the means that all men ought to adopt and employ to achieve it, con-

sists of a relatively small number of true normative propositions. It is a slender body of wisdom, inadequate by itself for the solution of the infinitely varied and concretely complicated practical problems that confront individuals in the course of their daily lives. Such moral wisdom affords a plan of living that each individual must supplement for himself. Without it, he would have no assured guidance at all, even though the guidance it affords does not suffice at every turn in the road. One does not demand of even the best road map that it should dispense with the need for being attentive to the terrain, to road signs, to the varying condition of the road mile after mile; even the best road map often requires us to ask questions on the way and make further inquiries, nor does it relieve us of the responsibility of paying attention to other drivers, of circumspectly operating the vehicle we are driving, or of taking into account the innumerable other circumstances that can affect our reaching the destination we have in mind.

In addition to providing us with indispensable though inadequate guidance in the form of a plan of life, moral philosophy also provides us with the indispensable principles that underlie political, social, and economic morality. Unless we know what a good life is and how it can be attained, we cannot know what a good society is and the shape that its institutions should take in order progressively to realize the ideal of a healthy community and one that is just in its economic and political arrangements.

6. (p. 195) "It is the mark of an educated man," Aristotle writes, "to look for precision in each class of things just so far as the nature of the subject admits; it is evidently equally foolish to accept probable reasoning from a mathematician and to demand from a rhetorician scientific proofs" (*Nichomachean Ethics*, Bk. I, Ch. 3, 1094^{b}23–29). "The whole account of matters of conduct must be given in outline and not precisely . . . the accounts we demand must be in accordance with the subject-matter; matters concerned with conduct and questions of what is good have no fixity, any more than matters of health. The general account being of this nature, the account of particular cases is yet more lacking in exactness; for they do not fall under any art or precept but the agents themselves must in each case consider what is appropriate to the occasion, as happens also in the art of medicine or of navigation" (*ibid.*, Bk. II, Ch. 2, 1104^{a}1–9). These passages must be interpreted in the light of what was said, in Note 5, *supra*, about the inadequacy of such moral wisdom as we can attain. See also Aquinas, *Summa Theologica*, Pt. I–II, Q. 94, A. 4: "The practical reason . . . is busied with contingent matters about which human actions are concerned; and consequently, although there is a necessity in the general principles, the more we descend to matters of

detail, the more frequently we encounter defects. . . . In matters of action, truth or practical rectitude is not the same for all of us in matters of detail, but only as to the common principles; and where there is the same rectitude in matters of detail, it is not equally known to all."

7. (p. 195) In the sphere of practical thought—thought concerned with action—this intermediate level of general principles is sometimes called the "practically practical," in contrast to the highest level, the level of universal principles, which is called the "speculatively practical." The latter is called "speculatively practical" in order to indicate that it is at this highest level, and only at this level, that practical thought has the universality and a measure of the certitude that can be achieved in speculative as opposed to practical thought, whereas at the intermediate or practically practical level, our thinking has only a general, but not a universal, applicability, and is subject to the inexactitude and uncertainty appropriate to practical but not to speculative formulations. Therefore, to say of this intermediate level of general policies that it is "more fully practical" than the highest level of universal principles is to say, on the one hand, that it has none of the characteristics that belong to or are aimed at by speculative thought and, on the other hand, that it is more proximate to the particular cases in which decisions must be made and action taken. It thus mediates between the highest level—the level of universal principles—and the lowest level, the level in which prudence must be exercised in reaching decisions in particular cases.

8. (p. 196) The three levels of practical thought can also be differentiated by reference to end and means. The highest level of universal principles is concerned with the ultimate end to be sought by all men and with the means to be adopted and employed by all in striving to achieve the end. It is on this level, and on this level alone, that we have such wisdom as moral philosophy can afford concerning the *totum bonum commune hominis,* and the various partial real goods, including the *bonum commune communitatis,* that are constitutive means to the end, as well as instrumental means, such as moral virtue, prudence, and freedom, which are indispensable to the effective pursuit of happiness. It is on this level also that we can place the various partial goods— both the constitutive and the instrumental means to happiness— in some order as operating in relation to one another, and discern which among them is the highest good or *summum bonum,* and which the primary instrumental means. Moral philosophy stops at this level. To go beyond it, the individual must, at the intermediate level, consider means available to him under the special circumstances of his own life and in relation to the temperamental characteristics that make him a certain type of man. Finally, at

the lowest level, the level of prudent decisions, the individual must apply to action in this particular case the universal principles concerning end and means that have been made applicable to his own temperament and circumstances by such general policies as he can formulate. It is at this lowest level that the individual makes decisions and choices with respect to the means available here and now, and puts those decisions and choices into practice by taking this or that course of action as a means to the ultimate end that, rightly or wrongly, wisely or foolishly, he has set for himself.

The logic of these three levels of practical thought can be described in the following way. At the highest level of moral principles, only the one first principle concerning the ultimate end to be sought is an axiomatic or self-evident normative proposition. All other normative propositions at this level are conclusions of reasoning, in the light of the facts about human nature and human behavior, concerning the means that ought to be employed by all men in order to achieve the end that all men ought to seek. The fact that, logically, they are reasoned conclusions rather than self-evident axioms does not prevent them from being regarded as moral principles because of their universality. They can, perhaps, be called "secondary principles" to distinguish them from the one normative proposition concerning the end that is a principle both logically and morally. At the intermediate level, general policies are formulated not as conclusions of reasoning, but rather by a process of determination that tends to particularize the universal principles and make them applicable in different ways to different types of men and different types of circumstances. And at the lowest level, the applicable policies are applied to cases by the consideration of what is unique about each case. This final step in the process of applying universal principles to particular cases is called "casuistry."

The three levels can be distinguished in still another way. I have refrained from reference to "the natural law," "the moral law," or "the natural moral law" because of all the confusions and misinterpretations that have attended the use of these phrases. Nevertheless, in the context of the analysis that has so far been developed, it should be possible to use them with clarity and precision. When it is used in connection with human voluntary conduct, the word "law" signifies a command or prohibition that men are free either to obey or disobey. Laws that proclaim commands or prohibitions universally applicable to all men differ only grammatically, not morally, from normative propositions that state categorical obligations universally binding on all men. The first principle of moral philosophy can be expressed either as a categorical ought (one ought to seek a really good life as a whole), or it can be expressed as an injunction or command to seek what is really good and nothing less than everything that is really good. When it is expressed in the latter way, it is traditionally referred to as the first principle of the moral law. The secondary principles of moral philosophy thus become the secondary principles of the moral law when instead of being expressed as categorical oughts with respect to the means to be employed in achieving the *totum bonum*, they are expressed as injunctions or commands. The same transformation holds for those categorical ought-nots that prohibit us from injuring others or the community, and the categorical ought that commands us to act for the good of the community.

The exposition of the principles of moral philosophy is thus an exposition of the principles of the moral law. The content of moral wisdom is the same in both, only differently expressed. When the word "natural" is used in this connection, as in the phrase "natural law" or as in the phrase "natural moral law," its meaning is one with which we have already become familiar in our understanding of natural rights as those rights which have their foundation in the natural needs of man and, therefore, in the things that are really good for man. This is the positive meaning of "natural"; its negative meaning in both cases is also the same: moral laws and moral rights are natural in the sense that they do not owe their existence to political institution or enactment, as the positive laws of the state and positive legal rights do.

Some but not all the rules of positive law are determinations of the principles of moral law, particularizing them and making them applicable to the special, contingent circumstances of a certain type of society under certain historic circumstances. When we pass from the principles of moral law to the rules of positive law, we are passing from the highest level of practical thought (the level of universal principles) to the intermediate level of practical thought (the level of determinate and particularized general policies). When a court applies a rule of positive law to a case under adjudication, we are at the third level of practical thought (the level of casuistry and singular decisions). And since general rules are always defective by reason of not being able to foresee the whole range of contingent circumstances that are involved in particular cases, casuistry—and what is sometimes called "equity"—often calls for making an exception of this particular case which, even though it may fall under the letter of the law, lies outside the sphere of things covered by the intention or spirit of the law.

This last way of distinguishing the levels of practical thought indicates the parallelism between the principles of moral philosophy and the principles of the natural moral law. Cf. John Deely, "Evolution and Ethics."

9.   (p. 196) In traditional expositions of the moral law, "Thou shalt not commit adultery" is placed on a par with "Thou shalt not kill." This treatment of the matter seems to me questionable. That

murder and enslavement do irreparable injury to another man cannot be questioned, but while there may be circumstances in which adultery injures a spouse or the society of the family, the injury may not be irreparable, and so the wrong done is not on a par with the wrong done by murder or enslavement. It may impede the injured party's effort to make a good life, but it does not totally remove the possibility of his or her succeeding in that effort. And there may even be cases in which the circumstances are such that adultery, like simple fornication, results in no injury at all.

Because sexual morality is a matter of such general interest, it may be useful to say a word more. Let me preface what I am about to say by the observation that in my judgment, as in the judgment of leading liberal Catholic theologians, contraception is not a violation of the natural moral law. The official position of the Vatican rests on the factually false proposition that human sexuality is intended by nature to serve only one end—procreation. If that were so, any form of birth control, whether by mechanical or pharmacological devices or by resorting to the "free period" in the female menstrual cycle, would be against the moral law. But human sexuality serves at least two purposes; one is procreation, the other is the mutual pleasure and even, perhaps, the fulfillment of erotic love on the part of those who are thus united, whether married or not. The fact that the human female has no estrous cycle like that which governs coupling in most other species of sexual animals, restricting it to the brief period favorable to procreation, is by itself sufficient evidence for the proposition that human sexuality serves other purposes, and this is confirmed by the wide variety of forms human sexuality takes, only some of which are effective for procreation, and none of which can properly be called perverse or unnatural. Those terms would be applicable only if procreation were the sole purpose that human sexual activity was intended by nature to serve.

Aquinas, expressing a view that the Catholic Church still officially adheres to, says that "the emission of the semen ought to be so directed that both the proper generation may ensue and the education of the offspring be secured" or, in other words, copulation should occur only within the bonds of matrimony, so that the possible offspring can be adequately cared for by the family, and it should never occur without the intention of producing offspring. If this formulation of the moral law with regard to sexual conduct is incorrect, as I have argued that it is, then the correct view of simple fornication is the one that Aquinas states in the following manner: "Given a woman free from a husband, and under no control of father or any other person, if any one approaches her with her consent, he does her no wrong, because she is pleased so to act, and has the disposal of her own person; nor does he do any wrong to another, for she is under no one's control; therefore there appears to be no sin. Nor does it seem to be a sufficient answer to say that she wrongs God, for God is not offended by us except by what we do against our own good; but it does not appear that this conduct is against man's good; hence no wrong seems to be done to God thereby. In like manner also it does not appear to be a sufficient answer, that wrong is thereby done one's neighbor, who is scandalized; for sometimes a neighbor is scandalized by what is not a sin" (*Summa Contra Gentiles,* Bk. III, Ch. 122). The only "sufficient answer" according to Aquinas is the one based on the moral law that sexual congress should be entered into only for the purpose of generating offspring and only under conditions (i.e., matrimony) which provide care for the possible offspring. If we reject this, then, according to Aquinas' own reasoning, there is nothing morally wrong in simple fornication.

10. (p. 198) The point made about a habit of lying as bad for the individual leads us to a similar observation about sexual behavior. We have seen that simple fornication is not morally wrong, and also that no sexual acts which yield mutual pleasure to consenting individuals can be condemned as perverse or unnatural (Note 9, *supra*). But this must not be interpreted to mean that sexual behavior is subject to no moral restrictions whatsoever. On the contrary, it is subject to the same kind of moral restrictions that are applicable to other forms of playful activity, indulged in for the sake of the pleasure that attends them. The intemperance that manifests itself in the disposition to prefer the pleasures of the moment to a good life as a whole, or that consists in habitual overindulgence in sensual pleasures, can defeat an individual's pursuit of happiness. While sexual pleasure is a good thing, it is, like many other real goods of that category, a good of which one can want too much, and getting too much of it can interfere with getting other real goods that one needs, or getting them to the fullest degree in which they are good for us.

There is currently much talk about the sexual revolution—the shift from prohibitive restrictions to almost unlimited permissiveness. This shift is on solid moral grounds, as far as social prohibitions, coercively imposed by the community, are concerned. The community has no grounds whatsoever for prohibiting or censuring simple fornication, or other forms of sexual behavior that were once regarded as perverse or unnatural. But while the community should be permissive rather than prohibitive, the individual should not be self-indulgently permissive to the extreme at which he becomes a sexual addict. The vicious character of the libertine operates against success in the pursuit of happiness to the same extent and in the same way that the vicious character of the drug addict does, or the alcoholic, the glutton, the money-grubber, or anyone else who has the *bad habit* of seeking a real good to a degree or in a manner that is not good for him or, as in the case of a power-hungry man, the *bad habit* of seeking what is only an apparent good to the displacement or disorder of real goods in his life.

To the question, How much sexual indulgence is compatible with moral virtue?, there is no general answer. It will differ from individual to individual, from one set of external circumstances to another, and for one and the same individual, the answer will differ at different times in his life. To the question, Is this act of fornication good or bad?, there is again no general answer. Rules cannot be formulated to govern such matters. But good habits do govern them. The man of moral virtue or of good moral character, being one who habitually aims at what is really his own ultimate good, will judge the particular act, not as an isolated singular which, as such, he cannot possibly estimate for its effect on his whole life, but rather as one in a series of acts which, if allowed to occur without limit, would gradually undermine his character and transform him into a vicious man—one who tends habitually away from rather than toward his own ultimate good. In short, it is never a single act of fornication that is to be morally condemned, but rather the habitual fornicator who is disposed to seek sexual pleasure on all occasions and without limit, thus displacing other real goods in the economy of his time and energies.

11. (p. 199) The ethics of common sense, unlike either the deontological ethics of Kant or the utilitarianism of John Stuart Mill and some of his followers, is not an ethics that lays down rules of conduct by which a wide variety of particular acts can be judged good or bad, right or wrong; instead it is an ethics that judges particular acts mainly by reference to the moral quality of the habit or disposition that they manifest. Given a man of good moral character, one who is disposed to seek everything that is really good for himself and to choose whatever means serve this end, any act he performs in accordance with his character tends to be a good act. Such a man can act badly only by acting out of character or against his character, and if by repetition of such acts, his habit or disposition itself is changed, he can become a man of bad moral character and thereby fail to achieve what is really good for himself.

NOTES TO CHAPTER 19

1. (p. 207) In the eighteenth century, those men who had what Locke called "estates" had some grasp on the economic goods needed for the pursuit of happiness. Let us refer to them as "men of property," where property means not just some supply of

consumable goods, but sources of income. Only men who had substantial property in this sense really had access to the whole range of economic goods for themselves and their families, such things as educational facilities, adequate medical care, and ample free time for the liberal pursuits of leisure, over and above a decent supply of the means of subsistence. Men of limited estates, owners and operators of small farms or small businesses, were often unable to do much more than provide for their daily needs by toil which consumed a large part of their time. Nevertheless, in the eighteenth-century view, the men of property had, in varying degrees, the economic independence requisite for political liberty and access to the economic conditions requisite for the pursuit of happiness.

It was in these terms that eighteenth-century statesmen defended a property qualification for suffrage. It was also in these terms that we can understand what Jefferson might have had in mind when he revised Locke's "life, liberty, and estates" to read "life, liberty, and the pursuit of happiness." If those who had estates were secured in their possession, the protection of their property rights by government was equivalent to abetting their pursuit of happiness insofar as that involved something more than the preservation of their lives and liberties, and perhaps also the preservation of peace, at home and abroad. In addition, the protection of property rights (in the sense of "estates") was certainly one of the principal things contemplated in the eighteenth century by those who called for the establishment of justice. Hence, if justice were done, domestic tranquillity preserved, the common defense maintained, and the blessings of liberty conferred, little if anything more was needed to promote the general welfare in the sense in which Madison identified it with the happiness of the people, i.e., of the enfranchised citizens of the republic who were fortunate enough to be in an economic position that facilitated their pursuit of happiness or even made it possible.

What about those less fortunate, the men with insufficient property or no estates at all and little or no opportunity for access to them? Both Adams and Jefferson proposed the widest possible diffusion of the ownership of property (thinking mainly, of course, in terms of land) as the only way to realize their ideal of the republic as a free society. It is not clear how far either Adams or Jefferson intended his recommendations to go, but we know they wished for a large middle class of small property owners. In their view, the safety and prosperity of the republic as a free society depended on a citizenry thus constituted in the main. Even though it was not possible for them to see it through to its logical conclusion, their view contains, in germ, the ideal of a politically and economically classless society, i.e., one in which the ever-growing middle class pushes out the upper and lower fringes and becomes the only class. This is just another way of describing our twentieth-century approximation of the mass society in which all men are enfranchised citizens and men of property, *or* men who have the economic equivalents of property.

Within the framework of the pre-industrial and far from afflu-ent economy of the eighteenth century, the widest possible diffu-sion of the ownership of income-producing property would necessarily have fallen far short of the universalism implicit in the ideal. Until technological advances increased the power of capital instruments to produce a volume of wealth fully commensurate with the basic economic needs of the whole population, and these capital instruments were able to produce that wealth while diminishing the consumption of individual time spent in toil, our society was simply not wealthy enough to conceive of its government's hav-ing, in justice, the obligation to promote the general welfare through the widest possible diffusion of the economic goods needed for the pursuit of happiness.

Under the conditions of affluence already attained or within reach, the widest possible diffusion no longer need fall short of the whole population. It is now practicable, as it never was before, for justice to be done by securing to every man his natural rights, especially the right to political liberty and the right to the pursuit of happiness, insofar as both these rights involve the economic welfare of individuals or families. Any reconstruction of the Con-stitution in accordance with present realities must, therefore, take the greatly enlarged view of the obligations of government which results from seeing how far it is now practicable to do justice by treating *all* men as equally endowed with natural rights and equally entitled to their protection.

Insofar as this enlarged view concerns the general welfare clause in the Preamble, and the empowerment of Congress to provide for the general welfare in a revised version of Article I, Section 8, it calls on us to solve the problem of how the widest possible dif-fusion of economic goods should be accomplished. That we should try to solve it in a way which would make the promotion of the general welfare consistent with the preservation of our fundamental liberties need not be argued here; nor need it be argued that a just distribution of wealth among individuals or families should be based on the contribution they make to its production. But this leaves quite open the question of whether the widest possible dif-fusion of economic goods can or should be accomplished (a) through private property in the means of production, with the traditional rights of possessory private property fully restored, or (b) through what I have been calling "the economic equivalents of such property." Let us consider these alternatives.

The first (a) consists in the widest possible diffusion of private ownership of income-producing property instead of the widest possible diffusion of the economic equivalents of such property. It calls for a twentieth-century realization of the ideal proposed by Adams and Jefferson in the eighteenth. That ideal, as we have seen, envisaged a nation of property-owning citizens, whose economic independence, derived from property, would match and reinforce their political liberty as citizens.

The other course (b) is one we have in fact been taking for the last forty years or a little more. It involves the widest possible diffusion of economic goods through the economic equivalents of income-producing property. When I speak of "the economic equivalents of income-producing property," I have two situations in mind. (1) The situation of a wage-earning family in the United States, one that owns no share of capital at all and has no private property except in consumable goods, and one in which the wage-earners are unionized. *In the total absence of income-producing property*, such a family can have a decent supply of the means of subsistence and the comforts and conveniences of life; it can have living and working conditions conducive to health; it can have adequate medical care; it can have access to the pleasures of sense; it can have access to formal educational facilities and to other opportunities for learning; and it can have all these things with enough time free from toil to take advantage of them, *though it may not have them with enough economic independence to exercise a politically independent voice in public affairs.* In other words, without any income-producing property, it can have almost all the economic goods that were enjoyed by an eighteenth-century family with an estate large enough to supply these goods. Therein it has a reasonably firm hold on the economic conditions requisite for citizenship, for engagement in the liberal activities of leisure, and for an effective pursuit of happiness. (2) The situation of a family whose income is partly derived from wages and partly from the dividends of the profits earned by capital, or even a family whose income is entirely derived from the latter source. Such families might also conceivably have all the economic goods that were enjoyed by an eighteenth-century family with an estate large enough to supply these goods, but they would still have it *in the absence of possessory property in the eighteenth-century sense;* under the form that corporate or collective capitalism has taken in this century, their ownership of shares in corporate equities does not carry with it the full parcel of rights which belonged to eighteenth-century proprietors. These rights have been in large part eroded or attenuated. Therefore, such families can also be described as having the economic equivalents of property, excepting, of course, some of the rights possessed by 18th-century proprietors. Lacking these, they may also, to a considerable degree, lack the economic independence and power which such rights conferred upon their ancestors, and in this respect, they may not be as well off as unionized wage-earners who derive some economic independence from the power of the union to which they belong.

Both ways of solving the problem of promoting the general economic welfare can be called "socialistic," if that term is understood to refer to the end aimed at, and not to the means of achieving it. The end is the welfare state—a society in which all individuals or families enjoy a decent supply of economic goods. Any set of economic arrangements that tries to diffuse economic welfare to all is socialistic in its aim. On the side of the means, however, what is traditionally called "socialism" proposes the creation of the welfare state through the state's ownership of the means of production and the widest possible diffusion of the economic equivalents of property. Those who reject the socialism of means, i.e., communism, may attempt to achieve the welfare state through what has come to be called the "mixed economy," in which private ownership of capital is combined with a wide diffusion of the economic equivalents of property, or they can, more radically, adopt the private-property solution to the problem, which proposes the widest possible diffusion of the ownership of capital, together with a reduction in the government's distribution of the economic equivalents of property. This is the solution Mr. Kelso and I have called "the capitalist revolution." We favor it because it achieves the objectives of socialism by measures that preserve political liberty and reduce the concentration of economic power in the central government and in the giant corporations. See L. O. Kelso and M. J. Adler, *The Capitalist Manifesto; The New Capitalists;* L. O. Kelso and P. Hetter, *Two-Factor Theory: The Economics of Reality.* This last book originally had the striking title: *How to Turn Eighty Million Workers into Capitalists on Borrowed Money.*

The most important thing to note about the substitution for property of its economic equivalents is that the economic power which the eighteenth-century proprietor possessed is not among the substitutable equivalents. Adams, following Harrington, made much of the fact that power follows property, and that as property is diffused, so is power. But when, in the twentieth century, we try to diffuse the economic equivalents of property instead of property itself, we cannot also diffuse economic power. On the contrary, we must concentrate economic power in the hands of those agencies which are engaged in diffusing the economic equivalents of property. Consequently, while the communist solution to the problem of promoting the general welfare through diffusing the economic equivalents of property (i.e., all except the economic independence of the individual) may succeed to whatever extent the affluence of the economy makes it practicable to see that every family has at least a minimum supply of the economic goods needed for the pursuit of happiness, it does so in a manner that would appear to be inconsistent with the preservation of liberty.

2. (p. 208) In the opening pages of this book, I called attention to the relationship of ethics and politics as the two faces of moral philosophy and pointed out that, in different respects, each is the architectonic discipline: *ethics,* with respect to the ultimate end to be sought by the individual and to be served by society; *politics,* with respect to the means by which all men can be provided with at least the external conditions of making good lives for themselves. We now see that the efforts of society are limited to measures that directly affect the individual's possession of political, economic, and social goods, though the conditions controlled by society may also contribute indirectly to the individual's enjoyment of the goods of the body, the goods of the mind, and the goods of personal relationships. Since ethics is concerned with the ultimate end and with all the means of achieving it, both constitutive and instrumental, whereas politics is concerned only with such means as are not wholly within the power of the individual to obtain for himself, ethics, strictly speaking, is the dominant discipline and politics is subordinate to it.

3. (p. 208) As political democracy abolishes the distinction between a ruling class and a subject class, so economic democracy abolishes the distinction between the *haves* and the *have-nots* with respect to the economic goods that are needed for the pursuit of happiness. The meaning of economic equality thus parallels the meaning of political equality. When, in the pages that follow, I refer to democracy and socialism as the twin characteristics of the technologically advanced societies, what I have in mind is the combination of political and economic democracy—moving toward the completely classless society in which an equality of conditions, both political and economic, is achieved without the loss of political liberty and without the diminution of individual freedom of action. Also, for it to be achieved with the maximization rather than the minimization of economic independence on the part of individuals and families, the widest possible diffusion of private property must be the principal means of promoting the general welfare and creating economic equality. See Note 1, *supra.*

4. (p. 208) Even though the establishment of our Constitution was preceded by the declaration that all men are by nature equal and are equally endowed by nature with certain inalienable rights, and even though the Preamble to the Constitution calls for the establishment of justice, those who drafted our Constitution in the eighteenth century did not and could not think of political and economic democracy as something practicable. For some of them, it was not even desirable; their image of "the people" did not embrace the whole population, but only men like themselves or of their own class. For others in the eighteenth century, as Lincoln later remarked, the propositions about human equality and equal rights in the

Declaration of Independence were at best a pledge to the future, in the faith that future conditions might make politically and economically practicable what no prudent statesman would have attempted to institute under eighteenth-century conditions. The industrial and technological revolutions have at last made our society affluent enough to make economic democracy practicable, and over the last hundred years, as more and more men have come to share in the economic conditions prerequisite for active citizenship, we have progressively extended the suffrage to more and more. Where the eighteenth century was compelled by circumstances to think of the few, or considerably less than all, as participants in political life and in the pursuit of happiness, we in the twentieth century can and, for the most part, do think practically in terms of human equality and equal rights. When we say that all men should be free politically, or that government should promote the general welfare so that all men can effectively engage in the pursuit of happiness, we mean *all* men, *not* some. *Nothing could be more revolutionary.*

5. (p. 211) Thucydides, *The Peloponnesian War*, Bk. II, Ch. VI, pp. 37–41.

NOTES TO CHAPTER 20

1. (p. 214) In the recently published fourth annual report of The Program on Technology and Society, Dr. E. G. Mesthene summarizes the findings of his group by pointing out that technology, far from crushing and dehumanizing human beings, creates a society of such complex diversity and richness that its members have a greater range of personal choice, wider experience, and a more highly developed sense of personal worth than ever before. Speaking of American society today, he writes: "This is probably the first age in history in which such high proportions of people have felt like individuals." Cf. John G. Burke, "Technology and Values," in *Great Ideas Today, 1969.*

2. (p. 215) Precisely because the twentieth century is the first century in which technological advances have made it possible to have world wars, global in their scope, it is also the first century in which world peace through world government has become a practicable objective. When I wrote *How to Think About War and Peace* in 1943, I allowed the maximum of five hundred years for the establishment of world government (see *op. cit.*, Pt. Three). But that was before Hiroshima, and it was also before the emergence of a détente between the United States and the Soviet Union. There

is good reason to hope for increasing cooperation between these two major powers in the cause of world peace. See Andrei D. Sakharov, *Progress, Coexistence and Intellectual Freedom.* I would now predict that world peace through world government, either through world conquest or world federation, will come about in a great deal less than 500 years—within the next century, perhaps, or at most the next two.

3. (p. 216) See Will and Ariel Durant, *The Lessons of History,* esp. Ch. VIII–XI, XIII.

4. (p. 216) See Arnold Toynbee, *Civilization on Trial,* esp. Ch. 2, 5, 7, 8.

5. (p. 216) See Alexis de Tocqueville, *Democracy in America,* ed. by P. Bradley, Vol. I, pp. 3–16; Vol. II, pp. 331–334. See also Tocqueville's letter to Eugene Stoffels, of February 21, 1835, in *The Annals of America,* ed. by M. J. Adler and C. Van Doren, Vol. 6, pp. 205–206.

6. (p. 216) Plutarch tells us that someone once asked Plato in what respects he considered himself blessed by good fortune. His answer was: "That I was born a Greek rather than a barbarian, and in the time of Socrates rather than at some earlier time." Plato might have added that these were blessings only for a man who knew how to make use of such good fortune to achieve a really good life for himself. Other Athenians shared the blessings Plato was grateful for, and many—perhaps most—of them did not use them as he did. Why? Because making a good life for one's self is the hardest, not the easiest, thing for a man to do. As Spinoza said, whatever is excellent or noble is as difficult as it is rare.

The number of men who can count it a blessing to be born in the twentieth century rather than at some earlier time is a larger percentage of those now alive than would be the case in any preceding century. In the next chapter I will attempt to show that that percentage is even greater for those now alive in the United States than it is for those in any other country of the world. If those as yet unborn in this century could choose the place of their birth, their choice would be the United States, if it was based solely on the calculation of the probability that they would be blessed by a fair modicum of the external conditions required for a good human life.

NOTES TO CHAPTER 21

1. (p. 218) Cf. Will and Ariel Durant, *op. cit.,* pp. 55, 60, 69–73.

2. (p. 219) See J.-J. Servan-Schreiber, *The American Challenge,* esp.

Pt. One, Five, and Six. Cf. Herman Kahn and Anthony Wiener, *The Year 2000.* One set of figures, more than any other, symbolizes the superiority of the United States in providing a larger percentage of its population with the external conditions of a good human life. From 1950 to 1968, the number of those in colleges and universities increased in the United States from 2,600,000 to 7,000,000. In the same period of time, the increase in all of Western Europe was only from 739,000 to 1,700,000, and in all of Latin America, it was much less—from 380,000 to 888,000. Consider also, as another basis of comparison between the United States and other countries, the following statement by a member of the Writers' Union in Prague, just before the Russian occupation of Czechoslovakia: "Ideally, we want enlightened communism. By that we mean a Communist system that provides constitutional rights, free speech and a free press, a secret ballot and elections in which the voter has a real choice to make, a responsible parliament and a genuine opposition, a passport for everybody, higher living standards, and, gradually, a chance for us to become the masters of our own destiny." While many dissident Americans would complain that they do not have all these things to the fullest degree or complain of their unavailability for everyone in the United States today, they would also have to admit, if their eyes could be opened to statistically supported comparisons, that more individuals enjoy these conditions in the United States, and to a greater degree, than anywhere else in the world.

3. (p. 220) See Chapter 19, Note 4, Chapter 20, Note 2, *supra.*

4. (p. 220) See Russell Davenport, *U.S.A., The Permanent Revolution.* A significant excerpt from this book is included in *The Annals of America,* Vol. 17, pp. 89–95.

5. (p. 220) See J. H. Plumb, "When Does a Riot Become a Revolution?" in *Horizon,* Fall 1968, pp. 46–47. Professor Plumb writes: "America is, in a sense, entering a political phase curiously akin to that of Europe in the nineteenth century, a world of savage conflict and possible revolutionary turmoil. Which way will riot develop? Will it be molded by revolutionary leaders into a revolutionary movement, dedicated to social change, and if need be to civil war? Or will the riots fade away, as they did in Britain, by the creation of true, not false, social hope and by full, not spurious, political participation? . . . The hope must be real. If time and time again it proves illusory, then the looting will stop, the rioters will become disciplined, ferocious, dedicated, willing to die by the tens of thousands so that they can kindle an unquestionable spark of hope in the hearts of their own people. They will start fighting not for the present but for the future."

6. (p. 220) In a Commencement Address at Cornell University in

June, 1968 (an abbreviated version of which was published in *The Washington Post* for June 9), John W. Gardner imagines a twenty-third-century scholar who, with retrospective insight, points out that "twentieth century institutions were caught in a savage crossfire between uncritical lovers and unloving critics. On the one side, those who loved their institutions tended to smother them in an embrace of death, loving their rigidities more than their promise, shielding them from life-giving criticism. On the other side, there arose a breed of critics without love, skilled in demolition but untutored in the arts by which human institutions are nurtured and strengthened and made to flourish. . . . Where human institutions are concerned, love without criticism brings stagnation and criticism without love brings destruction. . . . The swifter the pace of change, the more lovingly men have to care for and criticize their institutions to keep them intact through the turbulent passages. In short, men must be discriminating appraisers of their society, knowing coolly and precisely what it is about society that thwarts or limits them and therefore needs modification. And so they must be discriminating protectors of their institutions, preserving those features that nourish and strengthen them and make them more free. *To fit themselves for such tasks, they must be sufficiently serious to study their institutions, sufficiently expert in the art of modifying them*" (italics added).

Patriotism is love of one's country and its institutions, but the only kind of patriotism that can be recommended is the kind Gardner has described—the patriotism of "critical lovers." Patriotism thus conceived is neither blind to faults, as parental love usually is, nor is it given to an over-estimation of virtues, as romantic love usually is. It is like mature, conjugal love—the love for a spouse which, while fully cognizant of all defects, would still wish to have no other. That is, perhaps, the reason why it is futile to expect the young of this or any other generation to be patriots in the true sense, rather than "uncritical lovers" or "unloving critics," as most of them are.

7. (p. 222) See Chapter 20, Note 6, *supra*.

NOTES TO CHAPTER 22

1. (p. 224) See H. Marcuse, *One-Dimensional Man*, and *Negations;* J. K. Galbraith, *The New Industrial State*.

2. (p. 225) In a speech to the students of the Free University of Berlin in the summer of 1968, Marcuse drew wild ovations for approving the sexual rebellion of youth. While the so-called "sexual revolution" is soundly motivated, the moral problem of the indi-

vidual with respect to sexual indulgence remains unchanged. See Chapter 18, Note 10, *supra*. While advocating complete permissiveness on the part of society with regard to sexual behavior, Marcuse gives no evidence of understanding the moral conflict between a good time, usually enjoyed on the level of sense-experience, and a good life, which involves the subordination of sensual pleasures and the pleasures of play to the achievements of leisure-work. His philosophical commentary on Freud in *Eros and Civilization* reveals his commitment to the pleasure principle. In Part II of *Eros and Civilization*, entitled "Beyond the Reality Principle," Marcuse tends to go in a direction opposite to the one that Freud took in *Beyond the Pleasure Principle*.

3. (p. 225) *The Affluent Society*, p. 270. "To have argued simply," Galbraith writes, "that our present preoccupation with production of goods does not best aid the pursuit of happiness would have got nowhere. The concepts to which one would have been committed would have been far too vague. Any direct onslaught on the identification of economic goods with happiness would have had another drawback. Scholarly discourse, like bullfighting and the classical ballet, has its rules and they must be respected. In this arena nothing counts so heavily against a man as to be found attacking the values of the public at large and seeking to substitute his own." Nevertheless, Galbraith cannot totally refrain from considering the good life, even though he has ruled it out of the discussion. Released from our preoccupation with the production of consumable goods, "we become free for the first time to survey our opportunities. These," Galbraith observes, "at least have a plausible relation to happiness. But it will remain with the reader, and ultimately one hopes with the democratic process, to reconcile these opportunities with *his own sense of what makes life better*" (*ibid.*, pp. 270-271; italics added). In a review in *The New Yorker* of Galbraith's *The New Industrial State*, Naomi Bliven writes: "One can scarcely be less than grateful to an economist who begins by telling us about factories and concludes by asking us, 'What is the chief end of man?'" Unfortunately, Galbraith appears to think that each man can decide that for himself, and that moral philosophy cannot possibly have anything significant, precise, or valid to say on the subject.

4. (p. 226) See C. Jencks and D. Reisman, *The Academic Revolution;* and cf. Jacques Barzun, *The American University*, esp. Ch. 3, 7-8; *Learning and the Professor*, ed. by O. Milton and E. J. Shoben, Jr.; Noam Chomsky, "The Function of the University in a Time of Crisis," in *The Great Ideas Today, 1969*, ed. by R. M. Hutchins and M. J. Adler, pp. 41-61; *Confrontation: The Student Rebellion and the Universities*, ed. by Daniel Bell and Irving Kristol; Joseph J. Schwab, *College Curriculum and Student Protest*.

5. (p. 227) In a brief essay entitled "The Case for the Rebellious Students and Their Counterrevolution," in *Harper's Magazine*, August 1968, pp. 9–12, John Fisher points out that the undergraduate can expect and will get "scant nourishment" if he seeks light on basic moral and social problems. "The questions he asks— What is the good life? The nature of justice? The remedy for the evils of society?—are a bore and an embarrassment to his professors. After all, none of them professes to have the answers to such large and unscholarly questions; each professes his own narrow specialty—econometrics, say, or minor British poets of the 18th century. The students who expect 'a visible relationship between knowledge and action, between the questions asked in the classroom and the lives they live outside of it' get instead 'pedantry and alienated erudition' (Jencks and Reisman). Is it any wonder that they are 'completely turned off' and convinced that 'all systematic and disciplined intellectual effort is a waste of time'? The tragedy is compounded because they are often 'the best students in the best universities'—a Jencks and Reisman conclusion which I can confirm from my own conversations with dozens of them." Instead, in some cases, they "turn for guidance to *gurus* such as Paul Goodman and Herbert Marcuse who do profess to have answers to the Big Questions. (The answers may be wrong, as in the case of Marcuse, or ridiculously oversimplified, as with Goodman; but in the absence of anything better they find many buyers.) In other cases, they simply drop out—both from the university and from society—turning to drugs, hedonism, and the pathetic private world of the hippies."

Cf. an essay by Irving Kristol, entitled "The Strange Death of Liberal Education," in *Fortune*, May 1968, reprinted in *The Annals of America*, Vol. 18, pp. 677–679. Kristol writes: "Over the past year, there has been born a student-faculty movement toward the founding of off-campus anti-universities, where the prevailing academic conventions are ignored and where students can study (or play at studying) whatever and however they wish. This is a kind of *reductio ad absurdum* of the campus revolt. But it is also, in a perverse way, witness to the tendency of our higher educational institutions to impoverish the intellectual experience and to leave discussion of 'the most important things'—touching on the meaning of the good life and the good society—to amateur enthusiasts or cynical popularity seekers."

6. (p. 227) See three reports by Stephen Spender on the student rebellions in Paris, Prague, and Berlin, published in *The New York Review of Books* (July 11, August 22, and September 12, 1968). One passage in the essay "Paris in the Spring" reveals extraordinary misunderstandings on the part of the young about the nature of subsistence-work, play or sport, and leisure-work, and the relation

of these activities to "leading a life of better value" (*loc. cit.,* July 18, 1968, p. 20).

7. (p. 228) See *Democracy and the Student Left,* which contains George F. Kennan's address at Swarthmore College, "Rebels Without a Program," subsequently published in the *New York Times Sunday Magazine,* together with letters from students at a wide range of campuses and letters from the older generation, to all of which Mr. Kennan replies in Part IV of the book. Commenting on the prevalent student view of the crisis in Vietnam, which, as an experienced and seasoned diplomat, he regards as a "dangerously over-simplified view of a complex situation," Kennan asks: "Where, one wonders, have the teachers been while a view so lacking in balance and historical perspective was being formed?" That question, most appropriately addressed to the teachers of history and international politics, can be repeated many times over and addressed to the teachers of philosophy, the teachers of literature, the teachers of economics, who have failed the students as signally on other matters currently producing confusion.

8. (p. 229) The superiority of schooling in the past for the few who were given the kind of discipline in the liberal arts no longer available in our best colleges and universities may explain why of the few, whose privileged circumstances afforded them the opportunity to make good lives for themselves, a larger percentage made reasonable efforts to take advantage of that opportunity than is the case today when that opportunity is open to a much larger number, larger both absolutely and relative to the size of the population.

NOTES TO CHAPTER 23

1. (p. 230) See Chapter 22, Notes 5, 6, and 7, *supra.*

2. (p. 231) There is much talk by and about the young which describes them as "alienated." Alienation, strictly speaking, consists in dehumanization or depersonalization through the loss of essential freedoms. The chattel slave represents the archetypical case of an alienated human being. In the United States and in the countries of Western Europe, the young, far from being alienated by technology, are emancipated by it. Far from having too little freedom, they often have too much of it, and far from suffering the restriction of their individual propensities, they wallow in unrestrained, individualistic self-expression and self-indulgence. If they are alienated in any sense at all, it has come about through the disorder in their scale of values, which has given idiosyncratic,

individual, and merely apparent goods (*bonum individuale*) priority over common and real goods (*bonum commune*). In consequence, they tend to glorify individuality to the detriment of personality, and deprived as a result of the self-esteem a human being should derive from his sense of the dignity that belongs to the human person *as such*, the young are *self*-alienated. They are immediately responsible for their own dehumanization and depersonalization though, of course, the ultimate responsibility lies with their permissive parents and their unphilosophical or anti-philosophical teachers, who have failed to provide them with moral guidance in the form of an intelligible plan of life and a reasoned and reasonable scale of values.

3. (p. 232) See "The Challenge of Facts," in *The Annals of America,* ed. by M. J. Adler and C. Van Doren, Vol. 10, pp. 546–547. "The power of the human race today over the conditions of prosperous and happy living," Sumner wrote at the end of the last century, "is sufficient to banish poverty and misery, if it were not for folly and vice." How much truer that is today than it was then!

4. (p. 233) See Will and Ariel Durant, *op. cit.,* Ch. VI, on "Morals and History."

NOTES TO POSTSCRIPT

1. (p. 236) At the Aspen Institute of Humanistic Studies in the summer of 1967, the eminent Confucian scholar Dr. Wing-sit Chan and I conducted a joint seminar devoted to a comparison of the Confucian and Aristotelian conceptions of the good life for man. The major points in the doctrines of Confucius and of Aristotle were respectively summarized by Dr. Chan and by me, and the members of the seminar were asked to discuss the similarities and differences they noted. It was generally agreed that the outstanding difference between the two philosophers was in their intellectual style and method; on the side of substance, it seemed equally clear to all present that the fundamental notions and insights were either the same or closely parallel.

2. (p. 237) In the chapters of this book, and especially in the notes, I have indicated the basic differences between my own views and those of Kant, J. S. Mill, and John Dewey. Since my views, expounded as the ethics of common sense, also represent my understanding of the pivotal and controlling insights in the *Nichomachean Ethics* of Aristotle, it seems to me a reasonable inference that Kant, Mill, and Dewey settled for an understanding of that book quite different from my own. With regard to Kant, see

Chapter 11, Note 10; Chapter 12, Note 7; Chapter 14, Notes 2, 3, and 8; Chapter 15, Note 1; and Chapter 18, Notes 2 and 11. With regard to J. S. Mill, see Chapter 12, Note 8; Chapter 13, Note 5; Chapter 14, Notes 3, 8, and 12; Chapter 18, Notes 1 and 11. With regard to Dewey, see Chapter 9, Note 6. An examination of these critical comments on Kant, Mill, and Dewey will, I think, reveal what I mean by the chasm between their reading of Aristotle's *Ethics* and mine.

Kant, Mill, and Dewey did not write what professed to be commentaries or interpretations of the *Nichomachean Ethics;* their attack on it was oblique. That, however, is not the case with H. A. Pritchard and G. E. Moore. We have essays from them about it which, in my judgment, are egregious misreadings—almost non-readings—of the book. See "The Nature of Moral Philosophy," in Moore's *Philosophical Studies*, pp. 310–339; and "The Meaning of 'ΑΓΑΘΟΝ in the *Ethics* of Aristotle," in Pritchard's *Moral Obligation*, pp. 40–53. The latter was subjected to a penetrating critical dissection by J. L. Austin in a posthumously published essay: " 'ΑΓΑΘΟΝ and ΕΥΔΑΙΜΟΝΙΑ in the *Ethics* of Aristotle" (in *Aristotle, A Collection of Critical Essays*, ed. by J. M. E. Moravcsik, pp. 261–296).

3. (p. 238) See, for example, Whitney J. Oates, *Aristotle and the Problem of Value*, esp. Ch. VII; R.-A. Gauthier, *La morale d'Aristote;* H. H. Joachim, *Aristotle, The Nichomachean Ethics, A Commentary*, ed. by D. A. Rees; Frederick Siegler, "Reason, Happiness, and Goodness," in *Aristotle's Ethics*, ed. by J. J. Walsh and H. L. Shapiro, pp. 30–46; G. E. M. Anscombe, "Thought and Action in Aristotle," in *ibid.*, pp. 56–69. J. Donald Monan, *Moral Knowledge and its Methodology in Aristotle;* W.F.R. Hardie, *Aristotle's Ethical Theory*.

4. (p. 238) See, for example, Stuart Hampshire, "Fallacies in Moral Philosophy," in *Contemporary Ethical Theory*, ed. by J. Margolis, pp. 158–159; W. F. R. Hardie, "The Final Good in Aristotle's *Ethics*," in *Aristotle, A Collection of Critical Essays*, ed. by J. M. E. Moravcsik, pp. 297–322; and Georg Henrik von Wright, *The Varieties of Goodness*.

5. (p. 238) See, for example, Veatch's rejection of Aristotle's overemphasis on contemplation or knowing for the sake of knowing: *op. cit.*, pp. 58–69. My one serious criticism of Veatch's interpretation of Aristotle is his identification of human happiness with human perfection—the perfection of the individual man as a man—rather than with the goodness of his life as a whole. See *ibid.*, pp. 69–71.

Even though they are not exclusively concerned with Aristotle's *Nichomachean Ethics*, two other books should be cited here as exceptions to the contemporary misinterpretation of its doctrine.

One is by F.J.E. Woodbridge: *Aristotle's Vision of Nature* (see Lecture IV); the other is by J.H. Randall, *Aristotle* (see Ch. 12).

6. (p. 239) In view of all the conflicting interpretations to which the book has been subject, I certainly cannot claim that mine is the right interpretation of its message. However, I think I can defend the statement that mine is an interpretation that produces a sound and practical moral philosophy, and one that has a great deal of wisdom.

7. (p. 241) *The Letters of William James,* ed. by his son Henry James, in two volumes: Vol. II, pp. 352–356.

8. (p. 262) See Note 2, *supra.*

9. (p. 262) See Note 2, *supra.*

10. (p. 263) Professor von Wright tells us his reason for turning away from Aristotle's teleological ethics in the direction of Mill's utilitarianism. Having adopted a *teleological* position, he then distinguishes "between two main variants of this position in ethics. The one makes the notion of the good relative to the *nature* of man. The other makes it relative to the needs and wants of individual men. We could call the two variants the 'objectivist' and the 'subjectivist' variant respectively. I think it is right to say that Aristotle favored the first. Here my position differs from his and is, I think, more akin to that of some writers of the utilitarian tradition" (*op. cit.,* p. vi).

11. (p. 263) See *Summa Theologica,* Pt. I–II, QQ. 1–5.

12. (p. 264) See Jacques Maritain, "Reflections on Moral Philosophy," in *Science and Humanism,* pp. 137–220; and *Moral Philosophy,* Ch. 3, 5.

13. (p. 265) See Jacques Maritain, *Scholasticism and Politics,* pp. 194–248; *Ransoming the Time,* pp. 126–140; *The Range of Reason,* pp. 172–184.

References

ADLER, MORTIMER J.: *A Dialectic of Morals*, Frederick A. Ungar Publishing Co., New York, 1941.

————. *How to Think About War and Peace*, Simon and Schuster, New York, 1944.

————. *The Idea of Freedom*, Volumes I and II, Doubleday & Company, Garden City, N.Y., 1958 and 1961.

————. "The Future of Democracy," in *Humanistic Education and Western Civilization*, Essays for Robert M. Hutchins, ed. by Arthur A. Cohen, pp. 30–43.

————. *The Conditions of Philosophy*, Atheneum, New York, 1965.

————. *The Difference of Man and the Difference It Makes*, Holt, Rinehart and Winston, New York, 1967.

ADLER, M. J., and CHARLES VAN DOREN (eds.): *The Annals of America*, 20 vols., Encyclopaedia Britannica, Inc., Chicago, 1968.

ANDO, TAKATURA: *Aristotle's Theory of Pure Cognition*, 2nd ed., Martinus Nijhoff, The Hague, 1965.

ANSCOMBE, G. E. M.: "Thought and Action in Aristotle," in *Aristotle's Ethics*, ed. by J. J. Walsh and H. L. Shapiro, pp. 56–69.

AQUINAS, THOMAS: *Commentary on Nichomachean Ethics; Summa Theologica; Summa Contra Gentiles*.

ARDREY, ROBERT: *The Territorial Imperative*, Atheneum, New York, 1966.

ARISTOTLE: *Categories; Metaphysics; Nichomachean Ethics; Physics; Politics; Posterior Analytics*.

AUGUSTINE: *The City of God; The Happy Life; On the Trinity*.

AURELIUS, MARCUS: *Meditations*.

AYER, ALFRED J.: *Language, Truth and Logic*, 2nd ed., rev., Victor Gollancz, Ltd., London, 1946.

BAIER, K. E. M.: *The Moral Point of View*, Cornell University Press, Ithaca, N. Y., 1958.

BARNES, HAZEL E.: *An Existentialist Ethics*, Alfred A. Knopf, New York, 1967.

BARNETT, S. A.: "On the Hazards of Analogies," in *Man and Aggression*, ed. by M. F. Ashley Montagu, pp. 18–26.

BARZUN, JACQUES: *The American University*, Harper & Row, New York, 1968.

BAUMRIN, BERNARD H. M.: "Is There a Naturalistic Fallacy?" in *American Philosophical Quarterly*, Vol. 5, No. 2 (Apr. 1968), pp. 79–89.

BEATTY, JOHN: "Taking Issue with Lorenz on the Ute," in *Man and Aggression*, ed. by M. F. Ashley Montagu, pp. 111–115.

BELL, DANIEL, and IRVING KRISTOL (eds.): *Confrontation: The Student Rebellion and the Universities*, Basic Books, New York, 1969.

BERGSON, HENRI: *The Two Sources of Morality and Religion*, Henry Holt and Company, New York, 1935.

BIRD, OTTO: *The Idea of Justice*, Frederick A. Praeger, New York, 1966.

BLANSHARD, BRAND: *Reason and Goodness*, Humanities Press, New York, 1961.

BRADLEY, F. H.: *Ethical Studies*, Clarendon Press, Oxford, 1927.

BRANDT, R. B.: "The Emotive Theory of Ethics," in *Philosophical Review*, Vol. 59 (July and Oct. 1950), pp. 305–318, 535–540.

———. *Ethical Theory*, Prentice-Hall, Inc., Englewood Cliffs, N.J., 1959.

———. "Emotive Theory of Ethics," in *Encyclopedia of Philosophy*, ed. by Paul Edwards, Vol. 2, pp. 493–496.

———. "Ethical Relativism," in *Encyclopedia of Philosophy*, ed. by Paul Edwards, Vol. 3, pp. 75–78.

———. "Toward a Creditable Form of Utilitarianism," in *Morality and the Language of Conduct*, ed. by H-N. Castaneda and G. Nakhnikian, pp. 107–144.

BRENTANO, FRANZ: *The Origin of the Knowledge of Right and Wrong*, Archibald Constable and Co., Ltd., London, 1902.

BROAD, C. D.: *Five Types of Ethical Theory*, Harcourt, Brace and Company, New York, 1930.

———. "Certain Features in Moore's Ethical Doctrines," in *The Philosophy of G. E. Moore*, ed. by Paul A. Schilpp, pp. 41–68.

BROADIE, ALEXANDER: "The Practical Syllogism," in *Analysis*, Vol. 29, No. 1 (Oct. 1968), pp. 26–28.

BURKE, JOHN G.: "Technology and Values," in *Great Ideas Today, 1969*, ed. by R. M. Hutchins and M. J. Adler, pp. 191–235.

CARRITT, E. F.: *The Theory of Morals*, Oxford University Press, London, 1928.

CASTANEDA, HECTOR-NERI, and GEORGE NAKHNIKIAN (eds.): *Morality and the Language of Conduct*, Wayne State University Press, Detroit, 1965.

CAWS, PETER: *Science and the Theory of Values*, Random House, New York, 1967.

CHENU, M. D.: *The Theology of Work*, Henry Regnery Company, Chicago, 1963.

CHOMSKY, NOAM: *Language and Mind*, Harcourt, Brace & World, Inc., New York, 1968.

———. "The Function of a University in a Time of Crisis," in *Great Ideas Today, 1969*, ed. by R. M. Hutchins and M. J. Adler, pp. 41–61.

COHEN, ARTHUR A. (ed.): *Humanistic Education and Western Civilization*, Essays for Robert M. Hutchins; Holt, Rinehart and Winston, New York, 1964.

COX, HARVEY (ed.): *The Situation Ethics Debate*, Critical Back Talk About Situation Ethics and a Sharp Reply from Joseph Fletcher; Westminster Press, Philadelphia, 1968.

DAVENPORT, RUSSELL: *U.S.A., The Permanent Revolution*, Prentice-Hall, New York, 1951.

DEELY, JOHN N.: "Evolution and Ethics," in *Proceedings of the American Catholic Philosophical Association*, Vol. XLIII (1969).

DEWEY, JOHN: *Reconstruction in Philosophy*, Henry Holt and Co., New York, 1920.

———. *Human Nature and Conduct*, Henry Holt and Co., New York, 1922.

DURANT, WILL, and ARIEL DURANT: *The Lessons of History*, Simon and Schuster, New York, 1968.

EDEL, ABRAHAM: "The Logical Structure of Moore's Ethical Theory," in *The Philosophy of G. E. Moore*, ed. by Paul A. Schilpp, pp. 135–178.

EDWARDS, PAUL (ed.): *The Encyclopedia of Philosophy*, 8 vols., Macmillan Co., and Free Press, New York, 1967.

EPICTETUS: *Discourses*.

EPICURUS: *Letters*.

EWING, A. C.: *Ethics*, Macmillan, New York, 1953.

———. "Recent Developments in British Ethical Thought," in *British Philosophy in the Mid-Century*, ed. by C. A. Mace.

———. *Second Thoughts in Moral Philosophy*, Routledge and Kegan Paul, Ltd., London, 1959.

FIELD, G. C.: "The Place of Definition in Ethics," in *Proceedings of the Aristotelian Society*, Vol. 32 (1931–32), pp. 79–94.

FINDLAY, J. N.: *Values and Intentions*, George Allen and Unwin, London, 1961.

FISHER, JOHN: "The Case for the Rebellious Students and Their Counterrevolution," in *Harper's Magazine*, Vol. 237, No. 1419 (Aug. 1968), pp. 9–12.

FLETCHER, JOSEPH: *Situation Ethics, the New Morality*, Westminster Press, Philadelphia, 1966.

———. *Moral Responsibility, Situation Ethics at Work*, Westminster Press, Philadelphia, 1967.

FLEW, ANTONY: "Ends and Means," in *Encyclopedia of Philosophy*, ed. by Paul Edwards, Vol. 2, pp. 508–511.

FOOT, PHILIPPA: "The Philosopher's Defense of Morality," in *Philosophy*, Vol. XXVII, 103 (Oct. 1952), pp. 311–328.

————. *Theories of Ethics*, Oxford University Press, New York, 1967.

FRANKENA, WILLIAM K.: "Ethical Theory," in *Philosophy*, ed. by R. Schlatter, pp. 347–463.

————. "The Naturalistic Fallacy," in *Theories of Ethics*, ed. by Philippa Foot, pp. 50–63.

————. *Ethics*, Prentice-Hall, Inc., Englewood Cliffs, N.J., 1963.

FREUD, SIGMUND: *Beyond the Pleasure Principle*, trans. by Joan Riviere, Hogarth Press, London, 1922.

————. *The Ego and the Id*, trans. by Joan Riviere, Hogarth Press, London, 1927.

————. *Civilization and Its Discontents*, trans. by Joan Riviere, Hogarth Press, London, 1930.

GALBRAITH, JOHN KENNETH. *The Affluent Society*, Houghton Mifflin Co., Boston, 1958.

————. *The New Industrial State*, Houghton Mifflin Co., Boston, 1967.

GAUTHIER, R. A.: *La morale d'Aristote*, Presses Universitaires de France, Paris, 1958.

GORER, GEOFFREY: "Man Has No 'Killer' Instincts," in *Man and Aggression*, ed. by M. F. Ashley Montagu, pp. 27–36.

GRAZIA, SEBASTIAN DE: *Of Time, Work and Leisure*, Twentieth Century Fund, New York, 1962.

Great Ideas Today, 1968, 1969, ed. by R. M. Hutchins and M. J. Adler, Encyclopaedia Britannica, Inc., Chicago, 1968, 1969.

GRENE, M.: *A Portrait of Aristotle*, Chicago, 1963.

GRIFFITHS, A. P.: "Ultimate Moral Principles: Their Justification," in *Encyclopedia of Philosophy*, ed. by Paul Edwards, Vol. 8, pp. 177–182.

HAMPSHIRE, STUART: "Fallacies in Moral Philosophy," in *Contemporary Ethical Theory*, ed. by J. Margolis, pp. 158–159.

HARDIE, W. F. R.: "The Final Good in Aristotle's *Ethics*," in *Aristotle, A Collection of Critical Essays*, ed. by J. M. E. Moravcsik, pp. 297–322.

————. *Aristotle's Ethical Theory*, Oxford University Press, New York, 1969.

HARE, R. M.: *The Language of Morals*, Clarendon Press, Oxford, 1952.

————. "Universalisability," in *Proceedings of the Aristotelian Society*, Vol. LV (1954–55), Harrison and Sons, Ltd., 1955, pp. 295–312.

————. *Freedom and Reason*, Oxford University Press, New York, 1965.

HARRISON, JONATHAN: "Ethical Naturalism," in *Encyclopedia of Philosophy*, ed. by Paul Edwards, Vol. 3, pp. 69–71.

————. "Ethical Objectivism," in *Encyclopedia of Philosophy*, ed. by Paul Edwards, Vol. 3, pp. 71–75.

————. "Ethical Subjectivism," in *Encyclopedia of Philosophy*, ed. by Paul Edwards, Vol. 3, pp. 78–81.

HAWKINS, D. J. B.: *Man and Morals*, Sheed and Ward, New York, 1960.

HAZO, ROBERT: *The Idea of Love*, Frederick A. Praeger, New York, 1967.

HOBBES, THOMAS: *Leviathan*.

HUDSON, W.: *Ethical Intuitionism*, St. Martin's Press, New York, 1967.

HUME, DAVID: *A Treatise of Human Nature; Enquiry Concerning Human Understanding*.

HUTCHINS, R. M., and M. J. ADLER (eds.): *Great Ideas Today*, Encyclopaedia Britannica, Inc., Chicago, 1961–1969.

JAMES, WILLIAM: *Principles of Psychology*, Henry Holt and Company, New York, 1891.

————. *The Letters of William James*, 2 vols., ed. by (his son) Henry James, Atlantic Monthly Press, Boston, 1920.

JENCKS, C., and DAVID REISMAN: *The Academic Revolution*, Doubleday & Co., Inc., New York, 1968.

JOACHIM, H. H.: *Aristotle, The Nichomachean Ethics, A Commentary*, ed. by D. A. Rees, Clarendon Press, Oxford, 1951.

JOHNSON, OLIVER: *Moral Knowledge*, Martinus Nijhoff, The Hague, 1966.

KAHN, HERMAN, and ANTHONY WEINER: *The Year 2000*, Macmillan Company, New York, 1967.

KANT, IMMANUEL: *Critique of Teleological Judgement*, trans. by J. C. Meredith, Clarendon Press, Oxford, 1928.

————. *Lectures on Ethics*, trans. by Louis Infield, Methuen, London, 1930.

————. *Critique of Pure Reason*, trans. by J. M. D. Meiklejohn, rev. ed., Wiley Book Co., New York, 1943.

————. *Critique of Practical Reason and Other Works on the Theory of Ethics*, trans. by T. K. Abbott, 6th ed., Longmans, Green and Co., 1948.

————. *Fundamental Principles of the Metaphysic of Morals*, in *Critique of Practical Reason*, trans. by T. K. Abbott.

————. *Preface to the Metaphysical Elements of Ethics*, in *Critique of Practical Reason*, trans. by T. K. Abbott.

KELSO, L. O., and M. J. ADLER: *The Capitalist Manifesto*, Random House, New York, 1958.

————. *The New Capitalists*, Random House, New York, 1961.

KELSO, L. O., and P. HETTER: *Two-Factor Theory: The Economics of Reality*, Random House, New York, 1968.

KENNAN, GEORGE F.: *Democracy and the Student Left*, Little, Brown and Co., Boston, 1968.

KERNER, GEORGE C.: *The Revolution in Ethical Theory*, Oxford University Press, New York, 1966.

KEYNES, JOHN MAYNARD: *Essays in Persuasion*, Macmillan Co., London, 1931; Harcourt Brace and Co., New York, 1932.

KRISTOL, IRVING: "The Strange Death of Liberal Education," in *Fortune*, Vol. 77, No. 5 (May 1968), pp. 253–256.

LEACH, EDMUND: "Ignoble Savages," review of *Human Aggression* by Anthony Storr and *Non-Violence and Aggression* by H. J. Horsburgh, in *New York Review of Books*, Oct. 10, 1968, pp. 24–29.

LEHMAN, PAUL: *Ethics in a Christian Context*, Harper & Row, New York, 1963.

LEONARD, GEORGE B.: *Education and Ecstasy*, Delacorte Press, New York, 1969.

LEWY, C.: "G. E. Moore on the Naturalistic Fallacy," in *Proceedings of the British Academy*, Vol. L, Oxford University Press, London, 1964.

LIDZ, THEODORE: *The Person*, Basic Books, New York, 1968.

LOCKE, JOHN: *Essay Concerning Human Understanding*.

Logic and Language, Studies Dedicated to Rudolph Carnap, D. Reidel Publishing Co., Dordrecht, 1962.

LORENZ, KONRAD: *On Aggression*, Harcourt, Brace & World, Inc., New York, 1963.

LYONS, D.: *Forms and Limits of Utilitarianism*, Clarendon Press, Oxford, 1965.

MABBOTT, J. D.: "Interpretation of Mill's 'Utilitarianism,' " in *Theories of Ethics*, ed. by P. Foot, pp. 137–143.

MACE, C. A. (ed.): *British Philosophy in the Mid-Century*, George Allen and Unwin, Ltd., London, 1957.

MACLAGAN, W. G.: *The Theological Frontiers of Ethics*, George Allen and Unwin, Ltd., London, 1961.

MARCUSE, HERBERT: *Eros and Civilization*, Beacon Press, Boston, 1955.

———. *One-Dimensional Man*, Beacon Press, Boston, 1964.

———. *Negations*, Beacon Press, Boston, 1968.

MARGOLIS, JOSEPH: *Contemporary Ethical Theory*, Random House, New York, 1966.

MARITAIN, JACQUES: "Reflections on Moral Philosophy," in *Science and Humanism*, Charles Scribner's Sons, New York, 1940.

———. *Ransoming the Time*, Charles Scribner's Sons, New York, 1941.

———. *Scholasticism and Politics*, Macmillan Company, New York, 1941.

———. *The Rights of Man and Natural Law*, Charles Scribner's Sons, New York, 1943.

———. *The Range of Reason*, Charles Scribner's Sons, New York, 1952.

———. *Art and Scholasticism*, Charles Scribner's Sons, New York, 1962.

———. *Moral Philosophy*, Charles Scribner's Sons, New York, 1964.

MILL, JOHN STUART: *Utilitarianism*.

MILTON, O., and E. J. SHOBEN, JR. (eds.): *Learning and the Professor*, Ohio University Press, Athens, 1968.

MITCHELL, DOROTHY: "Must We Talk About 'Is' and 'Ought'?" in *Mind*, Vol. LXXVII, No. 308 (Oct. 1968), pp. 543–549.

MONAN, J. DONALD: *Moral Knowledge and Its Methodology in Aristotle*, Oxford University Press, New York, 1969.

MONRO, D. H.: *Empiricism and Ethics*, Cambridge University Press, Cambridge, 1967.

MONTAGU, M. F. ASHLEY (ed.): *Man and Aggression*, Oxford University Press, New York, 1968.

MONTAIGNE: *Essays*.

MOORE, G. E.: *Principia Ethica*, Cambridge University Press, Cambridge, 1903.

———. "The Conception of Intrinsic Value," in his *Philosophical Studies*, pp. 253–275, Routledge and Kegan Paul, Ltd., London, 1922.

———. "The Nature of Moral Philosophy," in *ibid.*, pp. 310–339.

———. "A Reply to My Critics," in *The Philosophy of G. E. Moore*, ed. by Paul A. Schilpp, pp. 535–615.

MORAVCSIK, J. M. E. (ed.): *Aristotle, A Collection of Critical Essays*, Anchor Books, Garden City, N. Y., 1967.

MOTHERSILL, M.: "Anscombe's Account of the Practical Syllogism," in *Philosophical Review*, LXXI (1962), pp. 448–461.

MUELDER, WALTER G.: *Moral Law in a Christian Social Ethics*, John Knox Press, Richmond, 1966.

MUMFORD, LEWIS: *Technics and Civilization*, Harcourt, Brace and Co., New York, 1934.

NAKHNIKIAN, GEORGE: "On the Naturalistic Fallacy," in *Morality and the Language of Conduct*, ed. by H–N. Castenada and G. Nakhnikian, pp. 145–158.

NARVESON, J.: *Morality and Utility*, Johns Hopkins Press, Baltimore, 1967.

NIELSEN, KAI: "History of Ethics (Twentieth-century)," in *Encyclopedia of Philosophy*, ed. by Paul Edwards, Vol. 3, pp. 100–117.

———. "Problems of Ethics," in *Encyclopedia of Philosophy*, ed. by Paul Edwards, Vol. 3, pp. 117–134.

NOWELL-SMITH, P. H.: *Ethics*, Penguin Books, Ltd., Baltimore, 1954.

OATES, WHITNEY J.: *Aristotle and the Problem of Value*, Princeton University Press, Princeton, 1963.

OLAFSON, FREDERICK A.: *Principles and Persons*, Johns Hopkins Press, Baltimore, 1967.

OLSON, R. G.: "Deontological Ethics," in *Encyclopedia of Philosophy*, ed. by Paul Edwards, Vol. 2, p. 343.

————. "The Good," in *Encyclopedia of Philosophy*, ed. by Paul Edwards, Vol. 3, pp. 367–370.

————. "Teleological Ethics," in *Encyclopedia of Philosophy*, ed. by Paul Edwards, Vol. 8, p. 88.

OUTKA, G. H., and P. RAMSEY (eds.): *Norm and Context in Christian Ethics*, Charles Scribner's Sons, New York, 1968.

PIEPER, JOSEPH: *Leisure the Basis of Culture*, Pantheon Books, Inc., New York, 1952.

————. *Fortitude and Temperance*, Pantheon Books, Inc., New York, 1954.

————. *Justice*, Pantheon Books, Inc., New York, 1955.

PLATO: *Republic; Apology; Gorgias; Philebus; Meno.*

PLUMB, J. H.: "When Does a Riot Become a Revolution?" in *Horizon*, Vol. X, No. 4 (Autumn 1968), pp. 46–47.

PRICE, RICHARD: *A Review of the Principal Questions in Morals*, ed. by D. Daiches Raphael, Oxford University Press, Oxford, 1948.

PRIOR, A. N.: *Logic and the Basis of Ethics*, Clarendon Press, Oxford, 1949.

PRITCHARD, H. A.: *Moral Obligation*, Clarendon Press, Oxford, 1949.

RANDALL, J. H., *Aristotle*, Columbia University Press, New York, 1960.

RAPHAEL, D. DAICHES (ed.): *A Review of the Principal Questions in Morals*, by Richard Price, Oxford University Press, Oxford, 1948.

RAWLS, J.: "Two Concepts of Rules," in *Theories of Ethics*, ed. by P. Foot, pp. 144–170.

ROBINSON, JOHN: *Honest to God*, Westminster Press, Philadelphia, 1963.

ROSS, W. D.: *The Right and the Good*, Clarendon Press, Oxford, 1930.

————. *The Foundations of Ethics*, Clarendon Press, Oxford, 1939.

RYAN, JOHN A.: *A Living Wage*, Macmillan Co., New York, 1906.

RYNIN, DAVID: "Non-Cognitive Synonomy and the Definability of 'Good,'" in *Logic and Language, Studies Dedicated to Rudolph Carnap*, pp. 234–241.

SAKHAROV, ANDRE D.: *Progress, Coexistence and Intellectual Freedom*, W. W. Norton & Co., Inc., New York, 1968.

SCHEIRLA, T. C.: "Instinct and Aggression," in *Man and Aggression*, ed. by M. F. Ashley Montagu, pp. 59–64.

SCHILPP, PAUL A. (ed.): *The Philosophy of G. E. Moore*, Tudor Publishing Co., New York, 1952.

SCHLATTER, R. (ed.): *Philosophy*, Prentice-Hall, Inc., Englewood Cliffs, N.J., 1964.

SCHLICK, MORITZ: *Problems of Ethics*, Prentice-Hall, New York, 1939.

SCHWAB, JOSEPH J.: *College Curriculum and Student Protest*, University of Chicago Press, Chicago, 1969.

SCOTT, J. P.: "That Old-Time Aggression," in *Man and Aggression*, ed. by M. F. Ashley Montagu, pp. 51–58.

SEARLE, JOHN R.: "How to Derive 'Ought' from 'Is,' " in *Theories of Ethics*, ed. by P. Foot, 101–114.

SELLARS, WILFRID, and JOHN HOSPERS (eds.): *Readings in Ethical Theory*, Appleton-Century-Crofts, New York, 1952.

SERVAN-SCHREIBER, J.-J.: *The American Challenge*, Atheneum, New York, 1968.

SIDGWICK, HENRY: *The Method of Ethics*, 7th ed., rev. by E. E. Constance Jones, University of Chicago Press, Chicago, 1962.

SIEGLER, FREDERICK: "Reason, Happiness, and Goodness," in *Aristotle's Ethics*, ed. by J. J. Walsh and H. L. Shapiro, pp. 30–46.

SIMON, YVES R.: *The Tradition of Natural Law*, Fordham University Press, New York, 1965.

SINGER, M. G.: *Generalization in Ethics*, Alfred A. Knopf, New York, 1961.

SMART, J. J. C.: "Utilitarianism," in *Encyclopedia of Philosophy*, ed. by Paul Edwards, Vol. 8, pp. 206–212.

———. "Extreme and Restricted Utilitarianism," in *Theories of Ethics*, ed. by P. Foot, pp. 171–183.

SMITH, ADAM: *The Wealth of Nations*.

SPENDER, STEPHEN: "Paris in the Spring," "The Young in Berlin," and "The Young in Prague," in *New York Review of Books*, July 11, Aug. 22, and Sept. 12, 1968.

SPINOZA: *Ethics*.

STEVENSON, C. L.: *Ethics and Language*, Yale University Press, New Haven, 1944.

———. "Moore's Argument Against Certain Forms of Naturalism," in *The Philosophy of G. E. Moore*, ed. by Paul A. Schilpp, pp. 69–90.

———. *Facts and Values*, Yale University Press, New Haven, 1963.

STRACHEY, JOHN: *The Challenge to Democracy*, Encounter Pamphlet No. 10, p. 41.

TAWNEY, R. H.: *Equality*, 4th ed., Unwin Books, New York, 1964.

THORPE, W. H.: *Science, Man and Morals*, Methuen and Co., Ltd., London, 1965.

THUCYDIDES: *The Peloponnesian War.*

TILLICH, PAUL: *Morality and Beyond,* Harper & Row, New York, 1963.

Times Literary Supplement, No. 3, 447 (Mar. 21, 1968), p. 287: "Rule Over Act, D. H. Hodgson's *Consequences of Utilitarianism.*"

TINBERGEN, N.: *A Study of Instinct,* Clarendon Press, Oxford, 1951.

TOCQUEVILLE, ALEXIS DE: *Democracy in America,* 2 vols., ed. by P. Bradley, Alfred A. Knopf, New York, 1945.

TOULMIN, S. E.: *An Examination of the Place of Reason in Ethics,* Cambridge University Press, Cambridge, 1950.

TOYNBEE, ARNOLD: *Civilization on Trial,* Oxford University Press, New York, 1948.

URMSON, J. O.: "The Interpretation of the Moral Philosophy of J. S. Mill," in *Theories of Ethics,* ed. by P. Foot, pp. 128–136.

VAN DOREN, CHARLES: *The Idea of Progress,* Frederick A. Praeger, New York, 1967.

VEATCH, HENRY B.: *Rational Man,* University of Indiana Press, Bloomington, 1962.

———. *Two Logics, the Conflict Between Classical and Neo-Analytic Philosophy,* Northwestern University Press, Evanston, Ill., 1969.

WADDINGTON, C. H.: *The Ethical Animal,* University of Chicago Press, Chicago, 1960.

WALSH, J. J., and H. L. SHAPIRO (eds.): *Aristotle's Ethics,* Wadsworth Publishing Co., Inc., Belmont, 1967.

WARNOCK, G. J.: *Contemporary Moral Philosophy,* St. Martin's Press, New York, 1967.

WARNOCK, MARY: *Ethics Since 1900,* Oxford University Press, New York, 1960.

———. *Existential Ethics,* St. Martin's Press, New York, 1967.

WEISS, PAUL, and JONATHAN WEISS: *Right and Wrong,* Basic Books, Inc., New York, 1967.

WILSON, JOHN: *Equality,* Hutchinson and Co., London, 1966.

———. "Happiness," in *Analysis,* Vol. 29, No. 1 (Oct. 1968), pp. 13–21.

WOODBRIDGE, F. J. E.: *Aristotle's Vision of Nature,* Columbia University Press, New York, 1965.

WRIGHT, GEORG HENRIK VON: *Norm and Action,* Humanities Press, New York, 1963.

———. *The Varieties of Goodness,* Humanities Press, New York, 1963.

ZUCKERMAN, SIR SOLLY: "The Human Beast," in *Man and Aggression,* ed. by M. F. Ashley Montagu, pp. 91–95.

Index

Index of Proper Names